introducing

Designs for Making a First Impression
Die Gestalten Verlag

Foreword

by Boris Brumnjak and Mika Mischler

In an age where jobs for life have most certainly become a thing of the past, the pressures of competition as well as the scope offered by a huge range of new design and printing tools have spawned a more flexible, spontaneous and – most of all – faster moving design scene and language. To sell your style and creativity, it has become vital to set yourself apart, to stick out from the rest of this vibrant, heterogeneous scene. In all matters large and small, self-promotion has become the key and starting point.

At some point in their career, all designers thus find themselves in the predicament of having to translate their own style and approach, their essence, so to say, into a coherent CI. As this demands a fair amount of self-reflection, discipline and methodology, many prefer to shirk the issue and ask a colleague to provide them with a brand new look instead. Nevertheless, over the last few years, many designers have become a lot more willing to experiment and jump at the opportunity to exploit any unused printing space for small-scale experimentation – and business cards or self-promotional giveaways are perfectly suited to the task. A business card often constitutes a direct link, a connecting element that changes hands and owners through personal contact, immediately connecting the card's style with its designer. An active and tangible process, it makes the card's overall appearance, material and format extremely important: to ensure that it will not be discarded at the first opportunity, it should ideally be something the recipient would love to have himself. Yet, in this age of increased self-promotion, a plain card is often not enough. As a very reduced, personal means, it only reveals a small facet of the designer's style and personality, while clients have come to expect an entire range of coherent self-promotional measures, from stationery to website, that either convey an overall design language or hint at the range and variety of styles and techniques on offer.

In this, designers have come to employ very different means to the same end: whether provocative, subtle, oblique, playful, reduced, straightforward, intricate or plain weird – some develop a timeless CI and stick with it more or less for life, others love to reinvent themselves anew every few weeks or month.

In a comprehensive overview of contemporary self-promotional measures, Introducing pursues the question of how designers approach this tricky task and presents the specific instruments and design solutions they employ to leave a good first impression. Clearly structured for easy access and to aid comparability, the book examines how individual designers and agencies choose to portray themselves.

As the corner stone and starting point of any CI, the business card is given centre stage, often accompanied by a range of further identity-conveying, self-promotional measures from straightforward stationery and extravagant acquisition tools or giveaways to self-indulgent, playful exercises. To convey an accurate impression of their style, surface characteristics and overall appearance, all business cards are printed in their original size. Stationery ranges, on the other hand, are reduced to 50% to present a comprehensive overview, yet retain sense of scale.

Content

Introducing

by Justus Oehler

Pentagram

Justus Oehler
Geschäftsführer

Pentagram Design Limited
Leibnizstrasse 60
D-10629 Berlin
Tel +49 (0)30 27 87 61 0
Fax +49 (0)30 27 87 61 10
oehler@pentagram.de

"Please allow me to introduce myself, I'm a man of wealth and taste…". Well, I am not the devil nor am I wealthy, but I do believe in good taste. I am a partner of Pentagram, an international design consultancy. And usually when I introduce myself to a prospective client, they would have already visited our website and looked at our beautifully designed little black booklets which contain samples of our work. Or – better still – they would have received a copy of our latest book Profiles. In it they would have had the chance to read about what Pentagram is all about, our ideas, beliefs and our individual viewpoints. Our promotional publications work well for us. They open doors. People like them, so they keep telling us. They like them because every single one looks like it wants to be kept and treasured, and nothing like the usual A4-size brochure which most of our competitors hand out.

In our publications, we present Pentagram in a straight-forward and unpretentious way. We say that we are all about good design and ideas. Because that's what we enjoy most. And we show examples of our work from small individual design projects to fully-blown corporate design projects. This is our way of demonstrating that we understand and handle all kinds of projects, whatever their size or nature. And that we have extensive experience, without having been pigeon-holed. But we deliberately don't go into a lot of detail on how we approach projects, and we don't elaborate on the processes. And, most importantly, we don't fill our publications with the standard agency-speak and with those words which most clients expect to read, the "Brand"-words. In short, we don't sound much like our competitors. Altogether we put the emphasis on ideas, craft, intuition and on the practical side of design, on coming up with solutions as opposed to selling recipes and theories.

So when I am invited by prospective clients to introduce myself and Pentagram I can imagine that some of them don't know who and what to expect. A clever, smooth talking business man in a suit and tie, or an arty designer? The trick is to be a combination of the two. To be both designer and business person in one. Why? Because business people are run mainly by the left-hand side of their brain, whilst designers are dominated by the right-hand side of the brain. Two separate worlds, which don't usually meet very often. But when business needs design, these two worlds need to come together, communicate and get along with each other. You and your clients need to become a team. This can only work if the client feels that you speak the same "language", and that you understand him and his business. But at the same time he or she needs to feel that you are the right person to come up with a solution for his design problem.

Let me give you an example. Two years ago one of the major Italian Internet service providers (let's call them "T") had decided to change their visual identity. They had grown from a local to a pan-European company in a very short time and felt they had outgrown their original corporate design. I was invited to do a credentials presentation at their offices in Milan. They had seen our books and booklets and had selected Pentagram to be one of three agencies on their shortlist.

Of course I was a little bit nervous – as I usually am when I "hunt for work", especially when I need to compete against other agencies – but I was also confident because I had worked on a large Italian corporate project before which had given me some valuable insight into that culture.

When someone came to fetch me from the waiting area at their offices the first question they asked me was "Did you come alone?" Meaning "Where's the rest of the team? Or did you actually come on your own?" The question came as no surprise because I know that most other agencies would send teams of two or three, mostly to impress. Quantity rather than quality… Anyway, as I was led to the meeting room, I was asked another question which I had heard before in similar situations: "Did you bring your own projector or do you need us to set one up for you?" When I answered that I didn't need a projector because I had nothing to project, the reaction was a mix of disbelief and amusement. They were probably thinking something like: "He's on his own, he's unshaven, he didn't bring a presentation – let's hope he's not a waste of time…"

When you are in a room with two or more representatives of the company that you want to win over as a client, and when you're on your own, without a colleague to share the pressure with and who would help you by simply nodding in support every now and then, then it is completely up to you to run the show. You have to perform.

So I told them about Pentagram, our structure, our work, our processes and about relevant projects. And I did this the way I always do, which is the only way I know: passionately and honestly. And since I always speak from my own experience, I knew exactly what I was talking about. I explained the benefits of good design and intelligent solutions, and how design needs to strike the right chords with people subconsciously.

After I had finished they asked me to have a quick word with their CEO. He only had ten minutes for me, but that's more time than most CEOs care to spend. He went straight to the point and asked me what I thought of "T"s original logotype, which he had commissioned and signed off personally when he started the company. I replied that I felt it was no longer appropriate for his company, not well enough crafted and that it looked dated. He then wanted to know what I would do to improve the design and so I explained the process we would go through and I also told him what I thought needed to be done to improve the logotype visually.

Introducing

by Justus Oehler

I could have been more subtle, I agree, but I enjoy the power of honesty – or bluntness, as many would call it –, and it didn't feel as if he minded. Then we shook hands and I was off to the airport.
Two weeks later they called me to let me know that they had chosen Pentagram for the project. Great news! I immediately asked what had led them to this decision. Why had they picked us instead of one of the other agencies? They said two things had made the difference.
Firstly they had liked the way I had presented because I'd been passionate and because they felt that I truly believed in what I was doing.
Secondly their CEO had picked me because apparently I was the only one of the three who was willing to discuss the design of the "T" logotype.

You can imagine that I was pleased and flattered. But I was also amazed about what I'd heard. If these people felt that I was passionate – and I do agree that I am – then how on earth did the others present their case? How can you even talk about design if you're not passionate about it? Unless it's just a business to you like any other business, of course…
In my view too many design and brand agencies send business people and theoreticians out to meet their clients and to present the company's work. These people sell design like they would sell an insurance policy or a new vacuum cleaner. They argue with logic and facts and with analytical data. They talk about brands, the value of brands, markets and market forces. But they don't talk about the intuitive and emotional aspects of design let alone the actual act of creation, because all that is incomprehensible to them and they simply don't know enough about it.

The point I am trying to make is perfectly obvious. To most designers design is a way of life, a true passion. We can't switch design on and off, we're always "on design". And that's what makes us good at it: To those designers who are also eloquent, open minded, humorous, diplomatic, good performers and who have an understanding for business, presenting and selling design should come easy. There is no need to sound like a salesman or a "suit". There are clients who feel insecure when talking to designers, that's certainly true, and they are the ones who prefer to deal with business-like consultants. But you'd be surprised how many clients out there actually enjoy and respect dealing directly with designers. And they are the clients who I usually get on best with.

If you are a designer, and you want to introduce yourself to a prospective client in person, don't try and sound like a business- or salesman. Be yourself.
If you manage to capture their imagination – the way I did with "T" in Italy –, if you manage to convince them of your abilities, make them believe in you and trust you, but above all if they respect you for how you are, then you might win something that's more important than the actual project: you might win their heart. And let me tell you, there's nothing better than a client who is also your friend.
Now, to "close the circle" let me come back to our Pentagram publications. Pentagram has always had long-term relationships with friends and clients who like what we do and how we do it. For them especially we produce a series of A5-sized booklets called "Pentagram Papers". Here we publish examples of curious, entertaining, stimulating, provocative and occasionally controversial points of view that have come to our attention, or in some cases are actually originated by us.

For me the beauty of this series is the extreme variety of themes. Pentagram Paper No 23 for example deals with the meaning and history of cigar papers, whereas No 28 is about the history of money. No 31 features a collection of old Japanese Kimono pattern books, and No 32 is all about home- and hand-made objects discovered and photographed in Cuba. There were Pentagram papers on crop circles, on the visual identity of the Suffragettes and on Australian letter boxes. Some of these are out of print and have since become collectors' items. Pentagram will continue to publish this series because we keep seeing and hearing things which we enjoy, and this is our way of sharing them with others.

Profile

Lance Knobel on *John McConnell*
Janet Abrams on *Lisa Strausfeld*
Emily King on *Angus Hyland*
Karrie Jacobs on *Paula Scher*
Deyan Sudjic on *Daniel Weil*
Kurt Andersen on *Michael Bierut*
Jeremy Myerson on *Lorenzo Apicella*
Kurt Weidemann on *Justus Oehler*
Mike Hicks on *Lowell Williams*
Lorraine Wild on *Abbott Miller*
Alain de Botton on *John Rushworth*
John Hockenberry on *Woody Pirtle*
Bruce Sterling on *Robert Brunner*
Stephen Bayley on *David Hillman*
Owen Edwards on *Kit Hinrichs*
Louis Begley on *James Biber*
Robert Draper on *DJ Stout*
Paul Goldberger on *Michael Gericke*
Rose George on *Fernando Gutiérrez*

PHAIDON

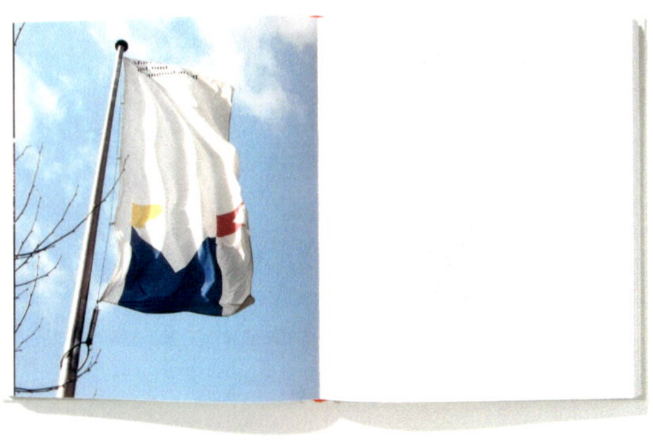

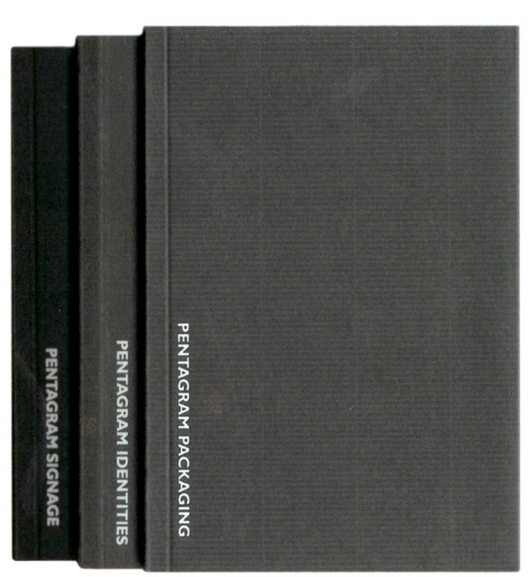

1–2   Pentagram Design, 215 x 250 mm, offset printing, 2004
3   Pentagram Design, A6, offset printing

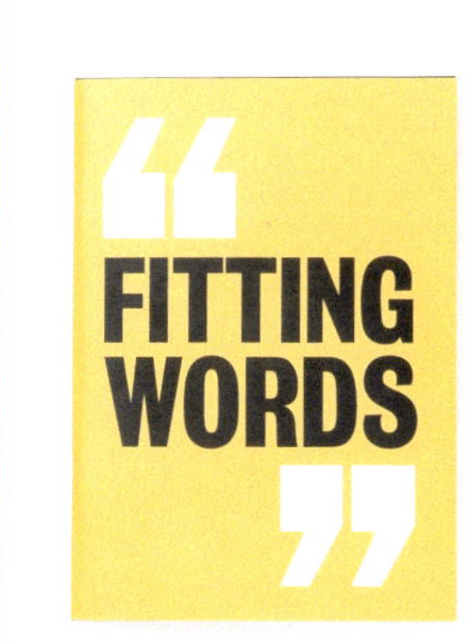

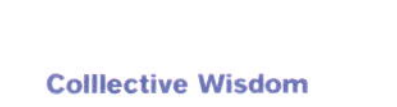

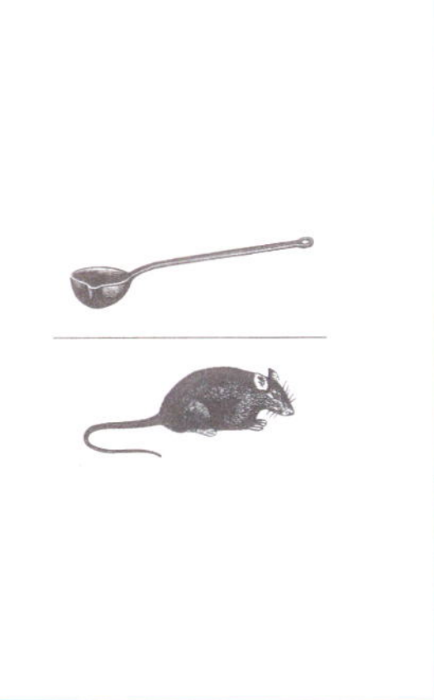

Why do you
say that?

'You made a right
cock-up of that'

'Scandal-monger
got given the
cold shoulder'

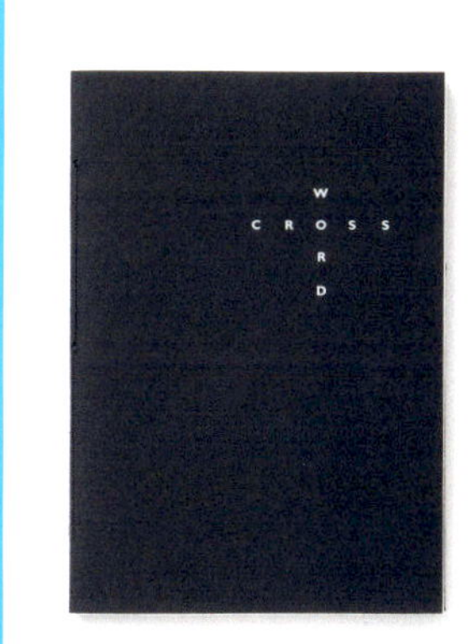

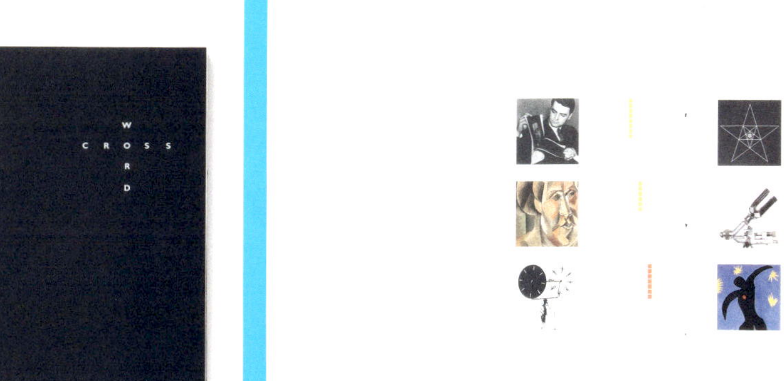

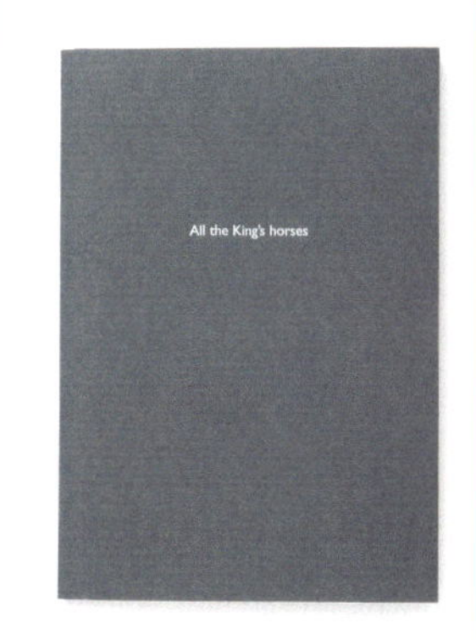

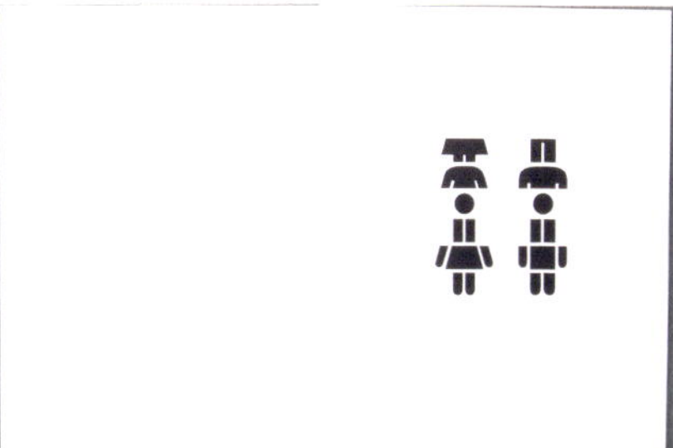

Pretty in Ink

Harmen Liemburg

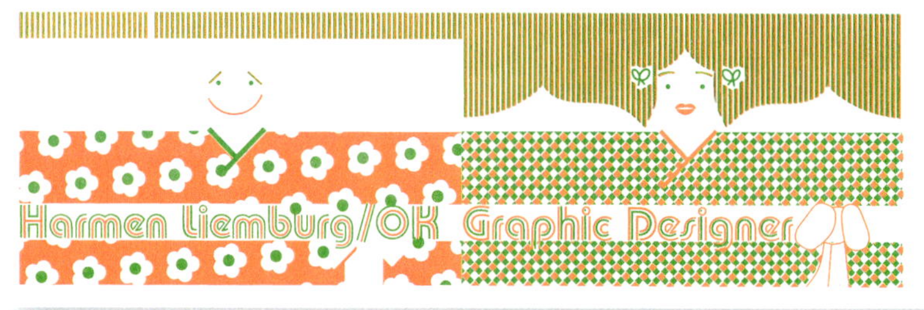

Intro: My mailshots are not only aimed at attracting new assignments, they also serve as a means of exchange and communication with kindred spirits. All invitations for projects and shows, announcements, greetings etc. that have been sent or given away to friends, colleagues, clients and other since 1998 have been initiated by myself. The value of these prints for me is not simply the "hard information". The time and energy involved is equally important and making them is an aim in itself. Silkscreen printing gives me complete freedom in the design and the way they are published.

Good Taste: The moment I started at the Gerrit Rietveld Academy in Amsterdam, I came into contact with a group of designers and artists who published their own magazines, made their exhibitions, or organized obscure parties in old warehouses for which they distributed their own flyers. One of these meeting places was the artist-run exhibition space W139, which invited different designers to design their invitations and, as they weren't paying them, allowed them to experiment in anyway they wanted. The work made for W139 by the former offset printer Bas Oudt is now legendary. Overprinting, reversal, black on black, opaque white on slowly discolouring newsprint… Drawing on his knowledge of inks, paper, and printing presses, Bas pushed his designs to the edge of the technically impossible. I wanted to do that too!

At that time there was also the publication TYP/Typografisch Papier, established in 1986 by the designer Max Kisman. TYP's design or appearance was subordinate to the content. Its look was sober, simple and un-designed and it was produced by the most simple of means, such as photocopying. With a limit of 500 copies per edition, each number assumed a different form: a newspaper, box, CD, or website. The magazine served an important purpose as a platform and was supported by a large group of creative minds, alongside the regular editors. TYP occupied a special and often provocative position in the graphic design and typography debates around "good taste".

In an environment where designers thought themselves to be so important, and self-mockery was seldom found, the ironic, wanton tone of TYP appealed to me greatly. It soon became clear that as a graphic designer you didn't have to wait for work to come to you. You could also issue yourself with assignments, couldn't you?

Publish Yourself: I recognized the drive to make work oneself, using the most simple and cheap means, in the demos Richard Niessen published for his band the How to Plays. After one meeting it became clear that we had many interests in common and we began to work together. One of the first projects we did together (with the designers Thomas Buxó and Yolanda Huntelaar) was the magazine Sec. The first number (No. 0) – a pile of colour copies stapled together – was made spontaneously by a group of young photographers who had an affinity for each other's work. Once we found a printer who was prepared to sponsor the lithography and printing it all got serious. We had to think about editing, design, distribution. The Sec. formula was very loose in the beginning: a platform for photographic experiments that were submitted from the Netherlands and abroad. A couple of numbers later and this formula was exhausted. We began to ask people to send in copy based on a particular theme or brief. Besides photography, we also published work by illustrators, stylists and designers. One of the high points was Sec. 08 in which an exhibition at the Netherlands Photo Institute Rotterdam corresponded one to one with the publication. Considering the response, Sec. might have been able to go grow into a professional magazine, but as an unpaid hobby it simply became too time-consuming for all involved. A few years after the publication of the final number, Sec. 10 in 2001, requests are still coming in for back issues…

Organize It Yourself: Other media besides print were explored. In order to be able to observe how different personalities working in a range of media develop their ideas, Richard and I conceived a project that was carried out for an audience by a collection of writers, musicians and designers. We called it JACK, alluding to the famous audio plug used to connect equipment. JACK sought out the links between different disciplines and thence the creative process. JACK's aim was to stimulate discussions around attitude, method, and result through a mix of entertainment and serious conversation. Richard and I became an all-round production team for JACK. Fundraising, production, logistics, publicity, etc. – we did it all ourselves. More so than with Sec. we now had a reason to invite people who we were interested in taking part in a JACK evening either as participants or presenters. There also automatically arose a reason for a stream of products in which we could display our own creations: flyers, instructions sheets, posters. Most of the work we printed, mailed and fly-posted in night-time sessions around Amsterdam ourselves. The highpoint of the series was JACK 04 "PopKit". For an audience of 600 at Amsterdam's famous temple of music, Paradiso, 60 different artists performed their versions of the PopKit CD we had given them. In the footlights on stage it became apparent how complicated it was to wheedle out of our guests what it was we were looking for.
The emphasis shifted strongly towards entertainment. Considering the interest shown by the Amsterdam art audience, this was not a problem, and JACK had clearly identified a need.

Like It Yourself: My first encounter with the visual culture of Japan was in the 1990s at the symposium "Japan-Holland" in The Hague on graphic design in both countries. As a newcomer to the field I knew a bit about the Dutch designers, but I had never heard of designers like Koichi Sato, Makoto Saito and Mitsui Katsui. Their work, particularly their posters, are characterized by a high level of abstraction. In contrast to what I was taught at art school, this work did not communicate a single, clear message in a few seconds. It was intended to offer a poetic moment of mental repose, to travellers at a busy station, for instance.
The designers presented themselves as being highly independent of the client and the brief. It didn't matter whether they were announcing an exhibition or launching a product. I saw a super-aesthetic cosmos of flowing colours and light in which traditional elements were mixed with hyper-modern computer technology. It blew me away. I wanted to work like that too.

Pretty in Ink

Harmen Liemburg

My interest in Japan simmered away for years until in 2001 I went to the exhibition Surimono at the Rijksmuseum Printroom. According to the catalogue, surimono is Japanese for something that is printed. The woodcut prints consist of an image accompanied by a poem and were made to be given away among a small circle of people. Not mass-produced items like the more famous ukiyo-e of geishas and actors, but small, colourful artworks with a spiritual and intimate character. Friends gave each other surimono on special occasions. New year was one occasion, but in the Japan of 1800 there were numerous others. They depict an abundance of subjects, from still lifes to landscapes, from courtesans to classical tales. By embossing, overprinting in transparent inks and using special metallic pigments, some of these prints have a delicate sensibility that only comes into its own in certain light... I had found the roots of my own fascination in printmaking!

Print It Yourself: In my search for my own medium, I came across silkscreen printing at the Rietveld Academy. I saw a final year student printing a large edition of posters and I thought it was fantastic! I immediately understood its qualities.

A cheap, fast, strong process that enables you to produce and publish editions of prints independently. Being able to control the kind of paper, the number of layers, and the compositions of the inks opens up a realm of possibilities for expression. From the delicate and subtle to the saturated and powerful, and all that lies between. It is, moreover, a flexible process which allows you to make changes right up to the last minute. I am extremely lucky that after art school I was able to make a deal with my silkscreen teacher, Kees Maas, who has since given me a free reign at Interbellum, his print workshop and publishing house. Compared with other printers, Interbellum is far from perfect. We work on old equipment, sometimes literally held together by string. Printing with water-based inks also has its limitations. Nonetheless, this has never prevented us from pushing it to the limits. I have always loved the imprecision you can find in everyday mass-produced objects like sweet papers and fruit boxes. Small mistakes and irregularities make the work livelier and more dynamic. In fits and starts I have learnt to anticipate these imperfections and integrate them in my design process. The perfection of the vector line, which in any case becomes less tight during printing, increasingly makes way for a warmer and more organic signature. I still get a huge kick out of seeing another edition of cards or posters has been printed and is ready to go out

Hail Snail Mail: Following the skilled processes of printing, cutting, perhaps folding, and packing, printed articles pass through yet more hands and machines. While the post offices in many countries are being privatized, and the "consumer" is being approached in ever more commercial ways, sending strange, deviant forms by post is still relatively cheap. Mechanical disfigurements such as creases and tears, plus all the stamps and stickers and barcodes that are added en route, all enrich the work. E-mail and websites simply can't compete. What could be nicer than opening your letter box to find that someone has taken the time to make something special for you?

Links
www.typ.nl
www.interbellum.nl
www.tm-online.nl
www.harmenliemburg.nl

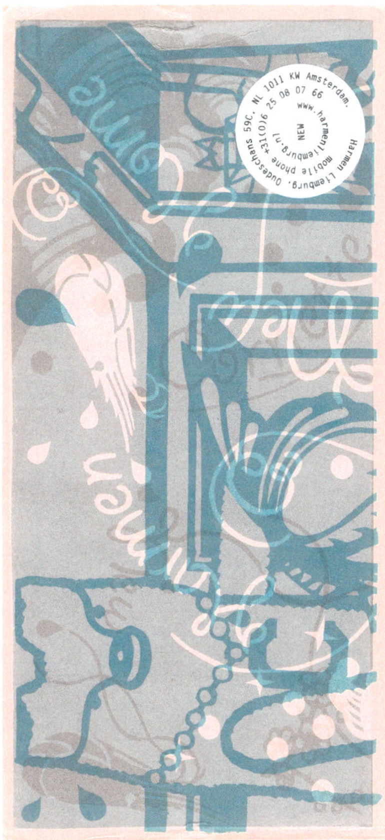
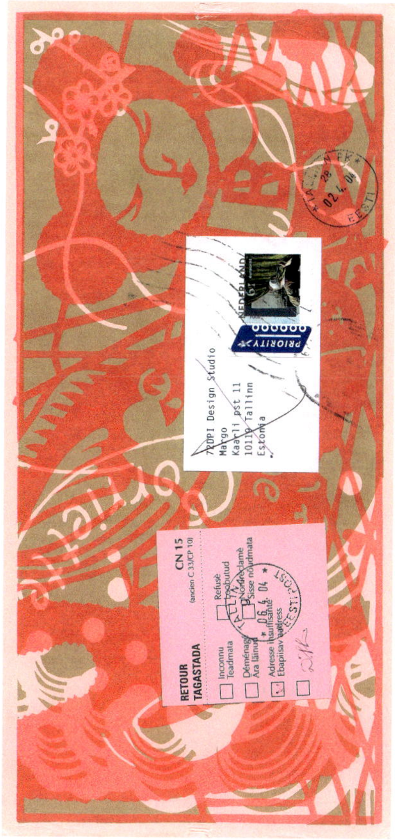
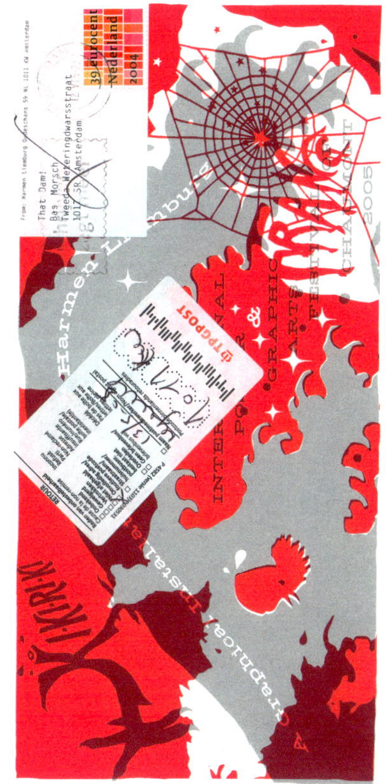
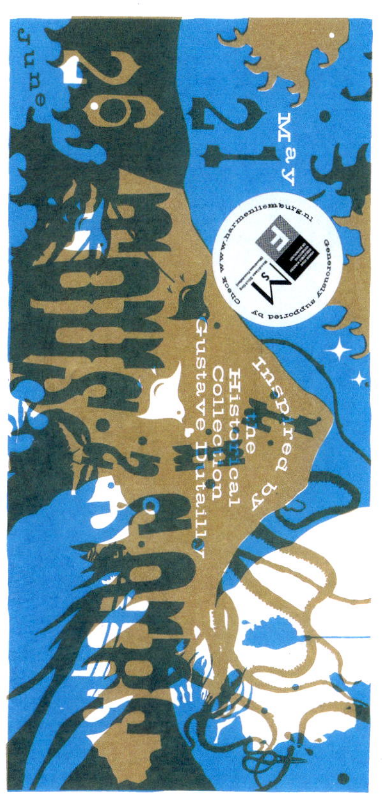

1   Harmen Liemburg, Corriette New Home,
    silk-screen printing, 2004
2   Harmen Liemburg, Ki ki ri ki Tous les Soirs,
    Invitation card, silk-screen printing, 2005

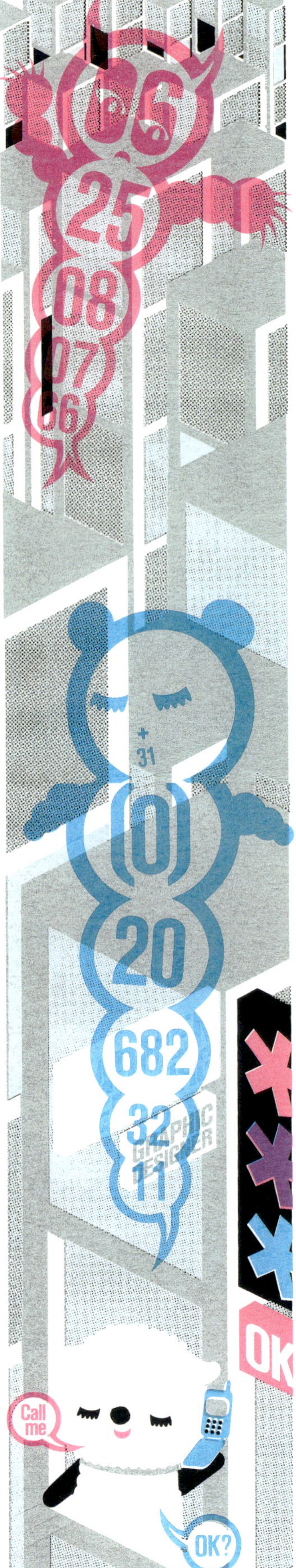

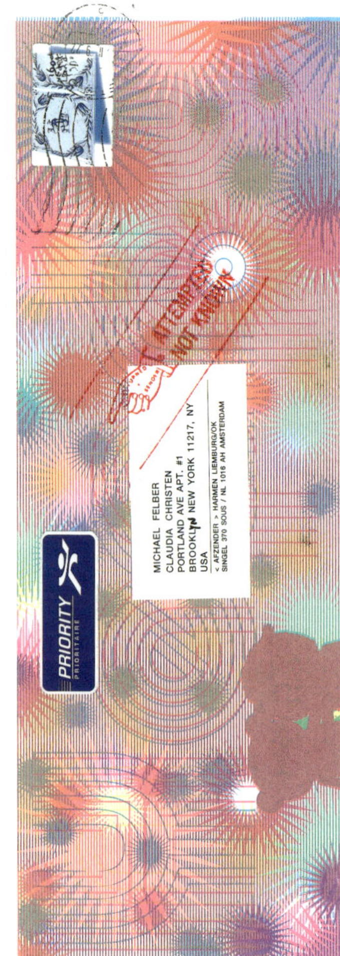

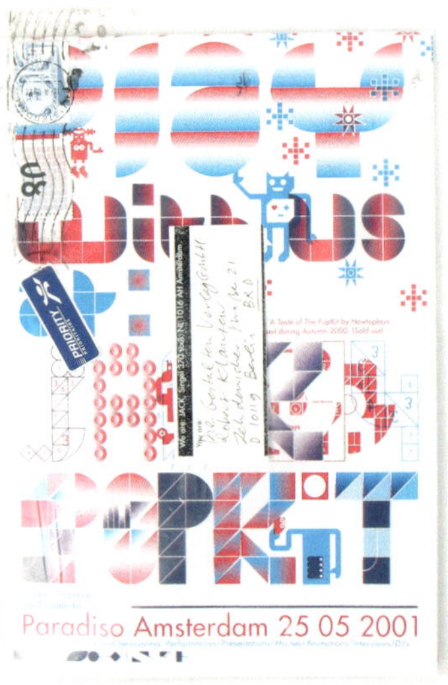

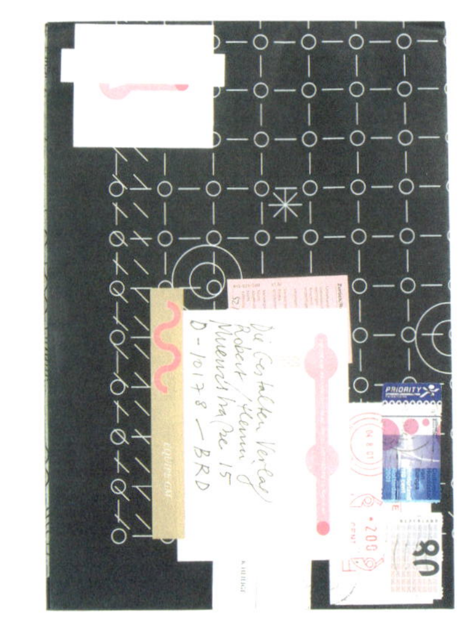

1   Harmen Liemburg, Call Me, Okay?, Business card, silk-screen printing 2000
2   Harmen Liemburg, Happy New Year, Season's Greetings, silk-screen printing, 2000
3   Harmen Liemburg and Richard Niessen, Play with us, Jack 04 invitationposter folded, 2001
4   Harmen Liemburg and Richard Niessen, Harmen New Home, poster, folded, silk-screen printing, 2001

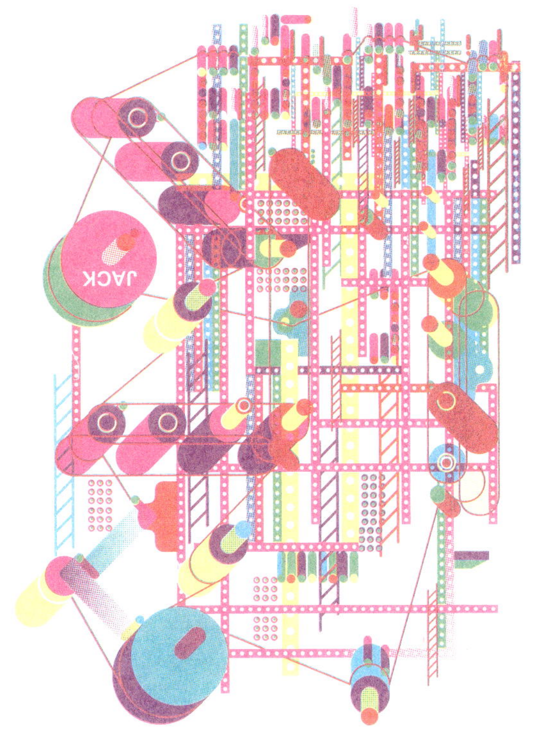

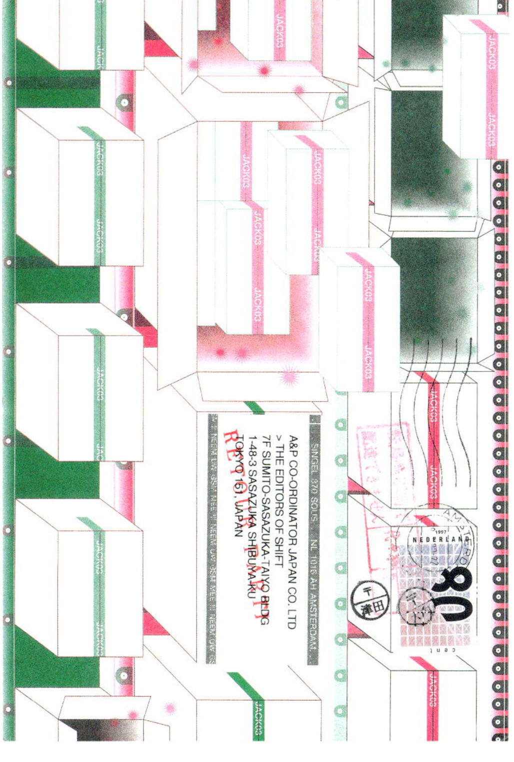

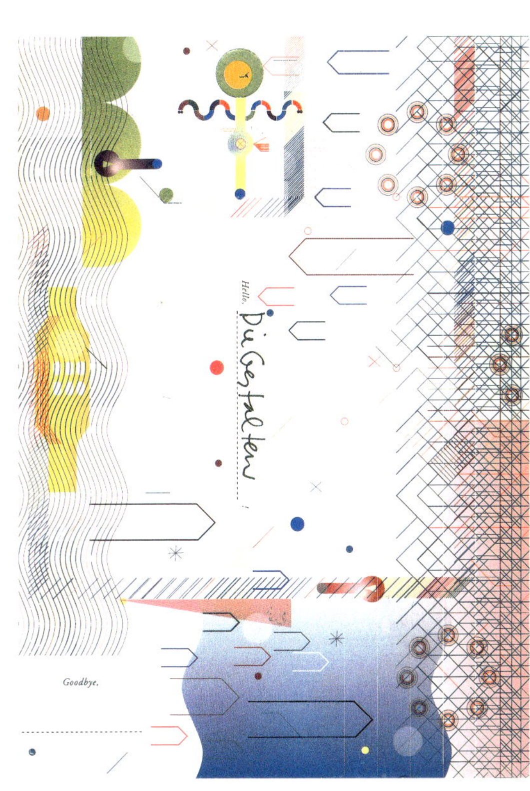

1 Harmen Liemburg and Richard Niessen, JACK, Correspondence card, silk-screen printing, 2000
2 Harmen Liemburg and Richard Niessen, JACK 03, Flyer/Invitation card, offset printing, 2000
3 Harmen Liemburg and Richard Niessen, Hello... , Correspondence card, offset printing, 2000

Biz Cards

Ina Fliegen

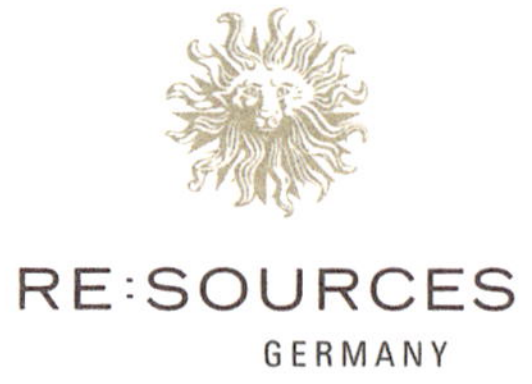

My name is Ina Fliegen, and I am Human Resources Director at the Shared Service Center for the French PUBLICIS Groupe S.A. agencies. This is the fourth largest agency network in the world. It deals with a large number of important international accounts. I'm also a doctor of psychology, and have spent my entire career in personnel management (with various agencies, insurance companies, exhibition construction firm, business consultancies).

We're going to take a look at business cards. What part do they play in our private and professional lives? When and where do they turn up? What are they trying to do? How are they perceived?

Let's take the moment a card changes hands – we'll call it "the handover" – without bothering about whether it's done person-to-person or by post.

Two ways of looking at this handover – psychological theory and working practice – can help us to understand it better: social psychological theory looks at the social context for intentional behaviours, and the branch of social psychology called "Social Cognition" concentrates on how the self is seen in the context of other people. The communication psychology sub-field examines concrete tranches of behaviour when trying to communicate.

Context presents the classic communication situation when looking at handing over and using business cards: a sender (say someone applying for an art director post) sends a "message" (it could be an application with letter, CV, photograph and a visiting card) couched in a certain code that the recipient is generally supposed to understand (German or English language, pictures, pictograms, signs, typography, formal language) via a certain medium (e-mail on the internet, pdf file with specimens of work scanned in) to a recipient (the head of personnel).

Perceptual psychology examines reactions to stimuli. You have been given a Biz Card. What strikes you first? What material is the card made of, does it feel good, what does it smell like? Is it elaborately and professionally produced, or does it look home-made? Does it flash any additional "gimmicks"? Does it seem like an invitation to get stuck in? How much does it appear to matter amongst all the other stuff? These are the stimuli. Then come the socio-psychological considerations when you can see people in action: how generous or stingy is the owner when handing cards out to other people? What's his body language like when handing the card over?

There are two main responses, depending who the recipients are – or feel themselves to be – and their predetermined attitudes. There can be a so-called "primacy effect" when you remember a card, a first and lasting impression, or a "recency effect" – what sticks in your mind after the incident is over. So if you are designing a card, you need to look at the beginning and the end of the handover process, and the visually eye-catching aspects, the anchors.

So much for the theory.

I know about the theory and practice of the handover from my personal and professional life, and I'm going to try to bring them together intellectually here.

A practical example. Take an everyday location predestined to distil the essence of self-representation and effect: the recruitment section of a human resources department in an international agency network. Now let's look at Biz Cards in this context. The working process here is built around a flood of documents sent in on spec or by request. Umpteen e-mails, website contacts, postal items containing written documents and business cards, visits or telephone calls are handled every day – many opportunities for the business card as a special case and its handover.

Theory tells us that it matters where in his loop I catch the recipient at the handover point. In fact what the sender intends to communicate often fails to come over a hundred per cent for the recipient – content and intentions are confused, misunderstood, misinterpreted, assumed, implied. This can apply both the quantity and also the content of what has been said or written. Actually this is quite normal, but still disappointing and annoying for the sender.

As soon as the message has been sent off, the sender loses control of the result. Recipients really do decide for themselves what they find pleasing, striking, serious or good. Applications and business cards can end up in the bin however interested the applicant is, or he might receive a politely sympathetic letter. The best result might be landing up in the fish tank: the house applicants database.

Representing yourself with a business card – unlike a CV – does give you equality of opportunity. Here all that counts is creativity, not the track record, in other words the list of great achievements, pitches acquired, accounts handled, branded articles promoted in the time you have spent in the well-known agencies. Here students are effectively on the same footing as creative directors in post or their own university professors. But the resources available for production do make a difference – like money, for example.

Under what circumstances are business cards used, i.e. when do people give out little cards or creative nuggets of self-representation, intended to impress and jog memories?

Business cards tend to matter in applications if there is personal contact: if you are invited for interview, or in the privileged position of not having to apply anonymously in writing, so you can gain access and find work informally through contacts. Anyone responsible for personnel is aware who the really creative people are; if not, they will at least know a good headhunter who will know who the really creative people are.

For the ordinary mortal applicant without boosted vitamin B the classical three – CV, letter of application and samples of work – are still more effective if you are looking for meaningful, fulfilling and gainful employment. Enclosing a business card can't do any harm here!

Business cards are a lot more common when hunting for commissions; they often change hands right at the beginning or end of a conversation. They invite, seal and create intimacy – and sometimes even trust.

Business cards are often left lying around at trade shows and congresses. They are exchanged formally at presentations and pitches. Exchanging them is seen as a standard part of a normal client meeting. They change hands at industry events, in advertising in huge quantities at Effie, ADC or in Cannes.

Generally the handover is a reciprocal process, meaning that you receive a card in return. That's why agency employees spend their first few weeks apologizing: "Sorry, I've still not got a card!"

Cards seem to change hands even more frequently in a semi-private or completely private context. Here they are presented personally; both or all the people involved in the conversation will not necessarily come out with a card. A young designer might give away a card actually intended for business purposes in the bar, angling for a date, a contemporary form of peacockery. If cards are exchanged at friends' parties it is usually about what use people can be to each other ("mail me your details / the information / contact x / fact y / the price of z"). Here the work-life balance seems to be maintained, private and professional interests chime. And among your proud relatives a card can help to prove that you've really made it. On business trips by train or plane the cards underpin tender contacts, extending or formalizing the acquaintanceship.

Biz Cards

Ina Fliegen

Freedom is not unlimited when designing a business card, as many people cannot or do not want to present themselves as private individuals. Large networks allow their agencies and employees only minimal creative scope within a defined Corporate Identity and fixed design standards. Here creativity would presumably only be counter-productive, unless the network's strategy explicitly stresses individuality. Many people also carry different cards for different functions or for different firms and free-lance networks they belong to.

It is not unusual within the usual agency mergers and take-overs for the company details on the card to have become ancient history; the company no longer exists.

It is exciting to see what intentions lie behind the handover, though of course the individual is not aware of all these intentions.

Does the hander-out of business card intend the gesture to make money, an impression, to make himself look absolutely wonderful or alternatively, understated? Does he simply want to pass on his contact data to this man or woman? Make a justifiable contact? Gain a commission? Emanate trust or even a certain creative independence and personal freedom?

Paul Watzlawick says: "One cannot not communicate". This may be banal, but it is true, and it is worth taking a closer look at communication. Like all communicative situations, the handover takes place on two planes, objective and relational, not necessarily in parallel. The important sparks, the subliminal stimuli are not usually present on the so-called objective level. They are matters for the gut or the heart, and not always accessible on the surface.

Communication theorists like Schulz von Thun concretize the objective and relational planes? by considering four possible aspects of a sent message:

The relational plane level? says something about how the relationship between the two communicating partners is perceived. In other words, whether they are acting with equal weight, and reciprocally, or whether a kind of inferiority/superiority power relationship is perceived. The relational plane? is neglected in the handover situation: the card is an item for one-way communication, prepared for a wide range of recipients. Sometimes the resonance of an implicit interlocutor is built in. There can be a sense of empathy with the anonymous recipient, while another time it will be the above-mentioned one way communication.

Statements relevant to the relationship are more likely to be found in the handover gesture than on the card itself.

On the plane level of self-presentation, the sender is giving out signals about how he sees and presents himself in the world. Is he a creative bird with bright plumage in a grey world, or a grey, purist mouse in an world of predatory strutters and show-offs? What identity does he convey over and above this, and what image does he create for himself in this way? Self-representation plays a major role in business cards.

The appeal plane level refers to the implicit or explicit demands the message conveys. Is the intention here to trigger admiration, purchase, sympathy, respect or something like that, or are there other sub-aims? Sometime a kind of direct appeal can arise from a "mail to xyz@abc" or "visit our website www.bla.com", but usually the appeal is in the background with a business card, accessible only in the handover situation.

The plane level of content simply conveys date data, info-bits, pure software. So possibly name, address, telephone number, mobile number, website and email address, and perhaps home details and sometimes a hand-written addition – for example a personal mobile number – almost always a charming touch.

The two most expressive sides of a business card are self-representation and content. Information could be lost if mere peacockery or the will to impress gain the upper hand, or an attack on the relational plane? distracts objective attention.

In the ideal case, message, channel and intention fit together overwhelmingly. It can be anything between unfortunate and embarrassing if self-presentation outweighs everything else and is counter-productive in terms of intentions. Wanting-to-look-different-at-all-costs might make the matter look less serious, for example. Single-channel communication is more difficult than twin-channel communication: interpretations of the way back fall away, and recipient's reactions have to be anticipated mentally.

Creation, and this includes designing business cards, is generally a more personality-related discipline than project management, for example, acting as an assistant or writing reports. The creator often feels that he is being denigrated himself if his work is condemned. Most people will tend to be reticent about criticizing a business card because they have a sense of this.

Then there is the excitement of what happens after business cards change hands. Only a minute number of people now have a handsome Rolodex on their desk to take the cards on a roundabout ride. A lot of CEOs get their PAs to record the cards meticulously in the sales database, and the personnel boss feeds his applicants database. Other industrious people store the card information in their PDA (usually known as "the Palm"). Special programs scan and organize data in address lists and storage media almost automatically nowadays.

My personal empire empiricism shows that business cards have a long life, even if their content is no longer accurate. Once things have found their way into the little card-box they don't come out again that easily. I still have business cards from my first job in the training department of a health insurance company in my "Fossil" clock tin, and that is over ten years ago … I suspect that this box would not relate very well to the current state of my address file, accumulated over the same period. Old hat, somehow, somehow or other nice. But throw it away – I can't imagine doing that.

So all in all, this is a highly subjective matter. Creativity and beauty lie in the eye of the beholder here as well.

I wish you all luck with your creative-psychological exploration and design judgements.

Typography

Interview:

Spin

London-based design bureau Spin was formed in 1992 by Tony Brook and Patricia Finegan. Bold in type and attitude, Spin offer simplicity with a twist for clients from all sectors and sizes (Nike to Channel 4).

How can a company or designer distil their own style and convey it to the outside world?

With great difficulty and a lot of pain. A lot of effort goes into creating the right impression, but in the end, it is all about the quality of what you deliver and you can't really fake that. Design companies evolve, often quite quickly, and this development can mean that a fairly neutral approach has the best chance of surviving. Ultimately though, I do not think you can really distil your approach, you can only hint at it.

Which means do you consider appropriate and effective?

It depends really. 99% of photographers' cards, photo library and paper company promotions are atrocious, which is strange because they are targeting designers. A piece based around your own projects should work as an introduction to potential clients. This is better than a cold call and you have a much more productive conversation if they like your work – and if they don't, you don't waste their time or yours.

So, which approach did you take?

Our identity (if you could call it that) is
direct and legible. Our stationery is printed
on an extremely utilitarian uncoated stock.
The pre-cut holes in the letterhead and the
matt Pantone warm black of the type rein-
force our unfussy, down to earth approach.
The white foil-blocked mark on the business cards adds a little texture and quality.
For our book, we wanted something small
and understated that would show our work
and not end up in the bin. Hand-bound
in Holland using "cold glue" to allow the
pages to lie flat when opened, the French
folding lends it a delicate spongy feel.
Internal projects, on the other hand, give
us an opportunity to play and explore.
When we have time, we like to make things
like T-Shirts, posters etc. - these are just
used to say hello to existing or new clients.
Quite often, we make things (short films,
interactive projects and the like) that aren't
made for any other reason than that we had
an idea and got excited by it. In the end, all
roads lead to our website (spin.co.uk) and
then hopefully to us.

So how do these more playful elements fit
in with your overall strategy?

We do not really have anything as grand
as a strategy as far as promoting ourselves
goes. Doing things outside of commissioned projects occasionally seems like
a good thing to do for the soul and the
company.
Accessibility is an issue sometimes. It is
important that your identity doesn't get in
the way of what you have to say, so we just
kept it simple.

As part of the "spin are tourist" series, all
staff are sent out to different locations
every year. The resulting "tourist maps"
seem to have a very unusual folding technique…

To be honest, they were a pain in the arse
to fold. It's very complicated to do, we
could not get anyone to do it for us, so we
had to do it ourselves. Serves us right…

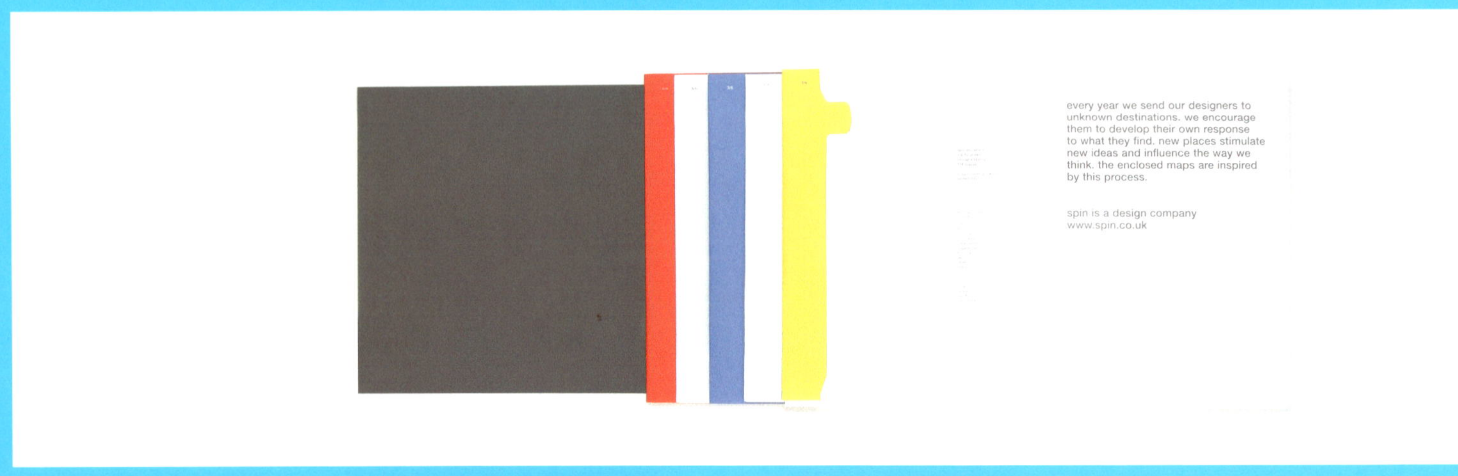

Every once in a while, Spin's staff enjoy a spontaneous mini-sabbatical – in small groups, they head out to selected locations in order to experience the local flavour and devise a creative response to it. On their return, these impressions and experiences are summed up in a beautiful set of colour-coded "tourist maps".
Tagged "Spin are Tourists" and "Because how do you know unless you go there?", the resulting, intricately folded posters transform this visual quest and cultural exchange into a refreshingly ambitious travelogue and giveaway.

1–3 Spin, poster set, unfolded 595 x 420 mm, offset printing, 2001

spin

spin

Spin   with compliments

12 Canterbury Court
Kennington Park
1–3 Brixton Road
London SW9 6DE

Tel/Fax
+44 (0)20 7793 9555
+44 (0)20 7793 9666

post@spin.co.uk
spin.co.uk

Spin   with compliments

12 Canterbury Court
Kennington Park
1–3 Brixton Road
London SW9 6DE

Tel/Fax
+44 (0)20 7793 9555
+44 (0)20 7793 9666

post@spin.co.uk
spin.co.uk

spin

1–4   Spin, offset printing, 2003
5   Spin, offset printing and embossing, 2003

MIGHT

Cahan & Associates
171 Second Street, Fifth Floor
San Francisco, California 94105
415.621.0915 ph 415.621.7642 fx
gwendolynr@cahanassociates.com
Gwendolyn Rogers, Account Director

FLARE

Cahan & Associates
171 Second Street, Fifth Floor
San Francisco, California 94105
415.621.0915 ph 415.621.7642 fx
info@cahanassociates.com

CAPER

Cahan & Associates
171 Second Street, Fifth Floor
San Francisco, California 94105
415.621.0915 ph 415.621.7642 fx
ninah@cahanassociates.com
Nina Howell, Account Director

PITCHER

Cahan & Associates
171 Second Street, Fifth Floor
San Francisco, California 94105
415.621.0915 ph 415.621.7642 fx
lucyr@cahanassociates.com
Lucy Regan, Director of Business Development

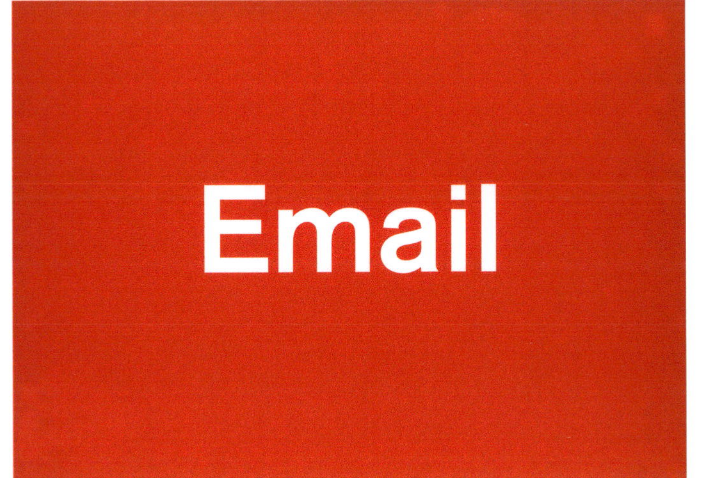

 Daniel Eatock, A6, 2004

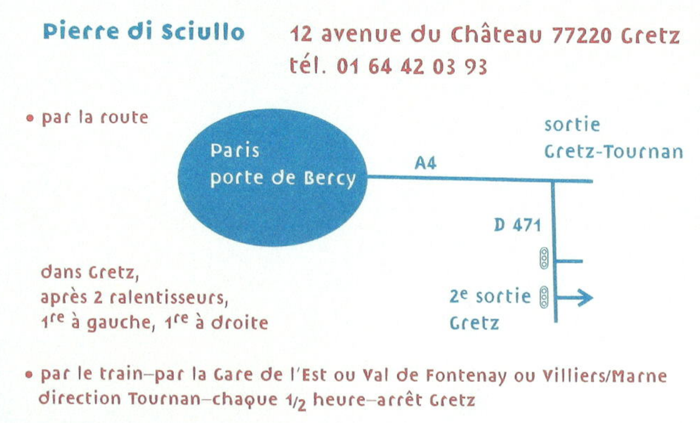

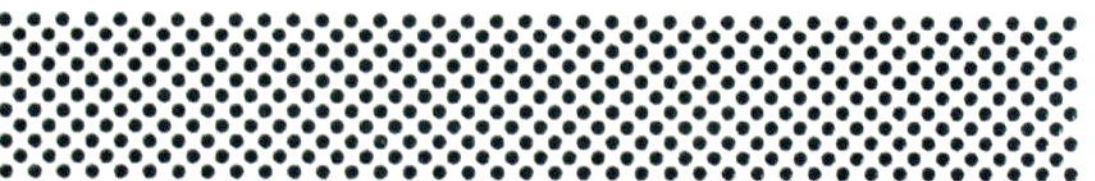

1   Daniel Eatock, paper, offset printing
2   Pierre di Sciullo, paper, offset printing, 2002
3-4 The Remingtons / Balland & Vögeli, chromocard one-side coated 300 g,
     offset printing, 2005
5   Norm, (printed in Tehran, Iran), offset printing, 2001
6   Pentagram Design Slimited
7   Norm, (printed in Chinatown, NYC), puffprint, 2004

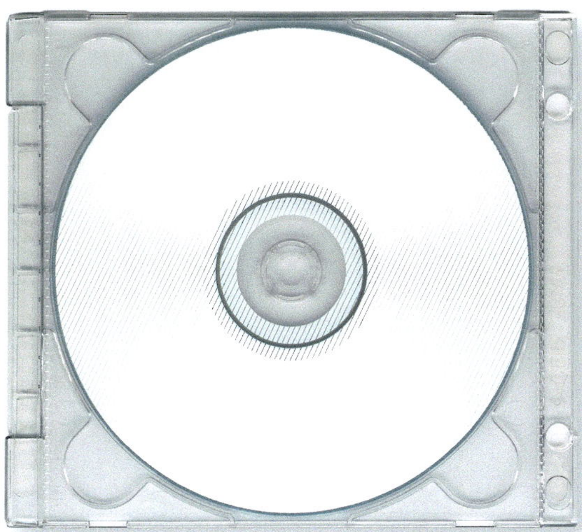

1   Kummer & Herrman, transparant clip with sleeve, silk-screen printing on CD, 2005
2–3   Kummer & Herrman, Silken 90 g, offset printing, 2005
4   Kummer & Herrman, Silken 300 g, offset printing, 2005
5   Kummer & Herrman, Butek Copy 80 g, offset printing, 2005

代表取締役
立沢トオル Toru Tachizawa Bold Inc.

有限会社ボールド
153-0063 東京都目黒区目黒 2-11-8 マリーンビルヂング 4 階
telephone+81(3)5496-7601 facsimile+81(3)5496-5836
tachizawa@boldstyle.com http://www.boldstyle.com

1

Bold Inc. 4F 2-11-8 Meguro Meguro-ku Tokyo, Japan

2

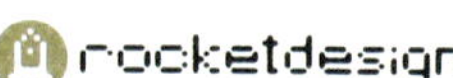

Graphic designer.
SHINGO KIKUCHI · 菊池 信悟

〒 060-0002 札幌市中央区北2条西14丁目1-1-104

090·5071·9927   shin@rocketdesign.org

TEL+FAX 011·271·1227

http://rocketdesign.org/

3

4

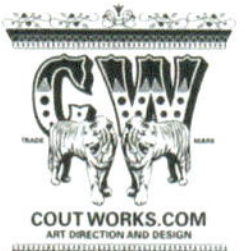

グラフィックデザイナー
森 住 和 雅

コウトワークス
〒 107-0052 東京都港区赤坂4-1-30 AKABISHI-2 4F
Tel.03-3560-5226 Fax.03-3560-5134
e-mail:k-morizumi@coutworks.com
http://www.coutworks.com

5

黒田　潔
Kiyoshi Kuroda

sasaki-bldg 2F-A

1-1-13 taishidou setagaya-ku

tokyo JAPAN 154-0004

tel 813-5779-7375

fax 813-5779-7374

e-mail: info@kiyoshikuroda.jp

hp: www.kiyoshikuroda.jp

6

1–2　Bold Inc. / Bonzaipaint, Toru Tachizawa, paper, offset printing and silk-screen printing, 2004
3–4　Rocketdesign, Shingo Kikuchi, paper, offset printing, 2005
5–6　Coutworks, Daisuke Sato, paper, offset printing, 2004,

CUSTOM CARD

Please write or draw a personal message for the card's recipient in the space below.

To

From

BIRTHDAY CARD

Before giving card, tick box or specify which birthday is being celebrated.

- [ ] Eighteenth
- [ ] Fiftieth
- [ ] Twenty-first
- [ ] Hundredth
- [ ] Fortieth
- [ ] Other*

*Please specify

THIS WAY UP

OCCASION CARD

Before giving card, tick the box relevant to the occasion being celebrated.

- [ ] Birthday
- [ ] New Year
- [ ] Valentine
- [ ] Anniversary
- [ ] Mother's Day
- [ ] Good luck
- [ ] Easter
- [ ] Congratulations
- [ ] Father's Day
- [ ] Well done
- [ ] Christmas
- [ ] Other*

*Please specify

A MESSAGE OF NO MORE THAN FIFTY WORDS SHOULD BE HAND-WRITTEN INSIDE THIS CARD

LATE CARD

Write an excuse or apology in no more than fifty words to explain why this card is late.

I promise that I will try harder next time to make sure your card arrives on time!

Signed

Date

Hans Peter Dubacher
3 Neustadtstrasse
6003 Luzern
041 211 16 30 T
041 211 16 31 F
hpdubacher@tic.ch E

Hans Peter Dubacher
3 Neustadtstrasse
6003 Luzern
041 211 16 30 T
041 211 16 31 F
hpdubacher@tic.ch E

TYPOSITION.

Peter Reichard	T 069. 260 178 65	reichard@typosition.de
Waldstraße 10a	F 069. 260 178 63	www.typosition.de
63065 Offenbach	M 0173. 316 72 49	www.spatium-magazin.de

REALA / GREV TUREGATAN 60, SE-114 38 STOCKHOLM, SWEDEN
(TELEPHONE) +46 8 545 885 85 (FAX) +46 8 545 885 86
--

Jonas Williamsson, +46 70 324 02 26 (cell)

mailto:jonas@reala.se / http://www.reala.se

Angela Gilroy
angie@daltonmaag.com

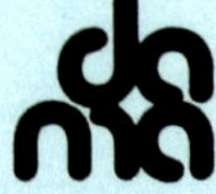

Dalton Maag
Unit M2
245a Coldharbour Lane
London SW9 8RR
UK
Ph +44 (0)20 7924 0633
Fx +44 (0)20 7738 6410
www.daltonmaag.com

1–2   Hans Peter Dubacher, Conqueror CX 22 diamant, digital print, 2003
3   Typosition / Peter Reichard, lake paper E-motion, offset printing and stamping ("Bölling" embossing), 2004
4   Reala, paper, offset printing, 2001
5–6   Mode / Ian Styles and Phil Costin, paper Fedrigoni, offset printing 1c and foil block, 2001

1–5   Feurer Network AG / Richard Feurer, diverse paper, offset printing and stamping, 2001

Fellow Designers
Paul Kühlhorn
Tel 08-33 22 00
Fax 08-31 24 10
Hälsingegatan 12
113 23 Stockholm
paul@fellowdesigners.com
www.fellowdesigners.com

Fellow Designers
Eva Liljefors
Tel 08-33 22 00
Fax 08-31 24 10
Hälsingegatan 12
113 23 Stockholm
eva@fellowdesigners.com
www.fellowdesigners.com

Fellow Designers
Paul Kühlhorn
Tel 08-33 22 00
Fax 08-31 24 10
Hälsingegatan 12
113 23 Stockholm
paul@fellowdesigners.com
www.fellowdesigners.com

Fellow Designers
Eva Liljefors
Tel 08-33 22 00
Fax 08-31 24 10
Hälsingegatan 12
113 23 Stockholm
eva@fellowdesigners.com
www.fellowdesigners.com

Fellow Designers
Paul Kühlhorn
Tel 08-33 22 00
Fax 08-31 24 10
Hälsingegatan 12
113 23 Stockholm
paul@fellowdesigners.com
www.fellowdesigners.com

Fellow Designers
Eva Liljefors
Tel 08-33 22 00
Fax 08-31 24 10
Hälsingegatan 12
113 23 Stockholm
eva@fellowdesigners.com
www.fellowdesigners.com

1–6   Fellow Designers / Paul Kühlhorn and Eva Liljefors,
       ivory board (ivory-white), silk-screen printing, 1999

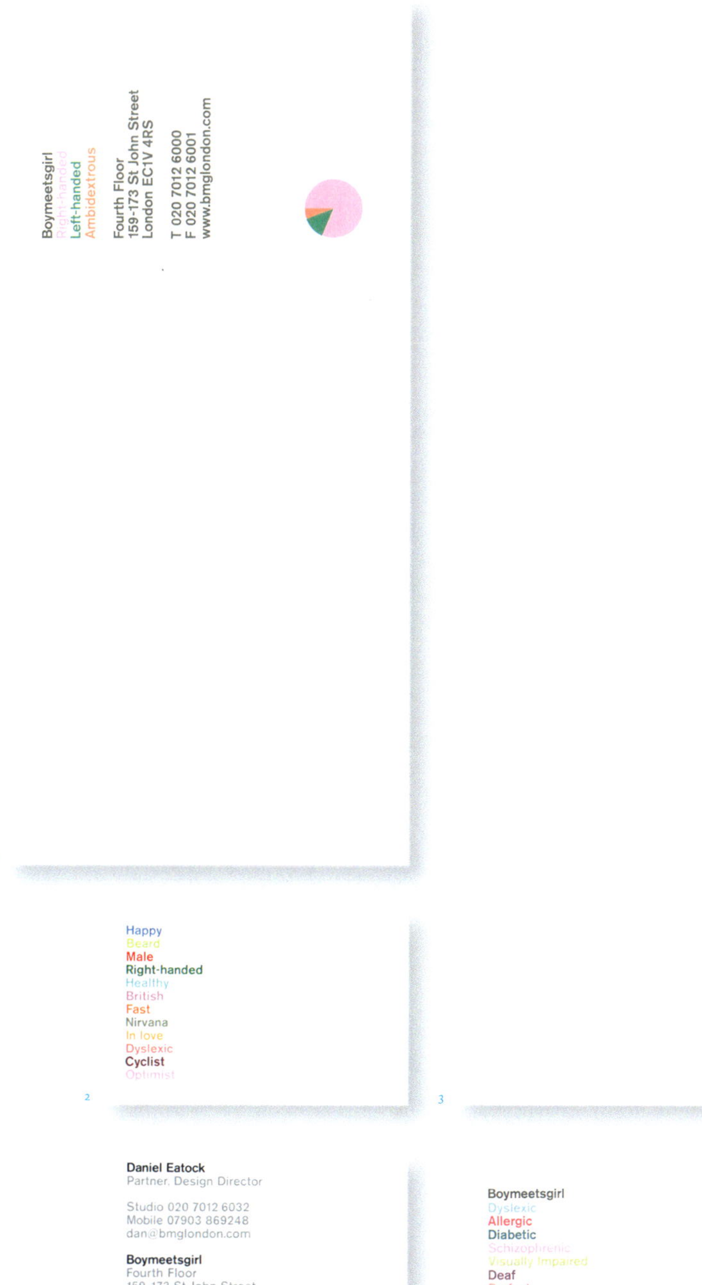

2

3

4

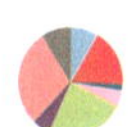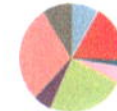

5

To highlight the huge diversity of its 85 staff, creative company Boymeetsgirl came up with a fun way to represent their assembled individuality. Asking each employee to complete a detailed questionnaire on a selection of attributes, the resulting insights into eating habits, state of mind and general characteristics – sometimes intimate, always tongue-in-cheek – were translated into a total of 35 colourful pie charts to adorn the company's official cards and stationery.

As each variant reveals a different aspect of their collective personality, any written contact with Boymeetsgirl should improve a client's understanding of what makes them tick.

1–5   Daniel Eatock, offset printing, 2005

1–6   Lollek und Bollek / Lollek und C. Wiehl, JAC 170 g, offset printing and embossing, 2003

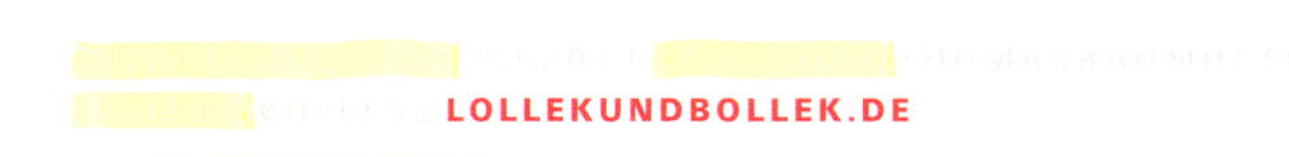

MARTA GLINDELIC
UL. JANA SKRZETUSKIEGO 100 31
310-114 KRAKOW
POLSKA

12.07.05 LIEBE MAMMA,

WIE GEHT ES DIR? WIE GEHT ES PAPA UND WAS FRISST GERADE ANTONOW?
HIER SCHEINT GERADE DIE SONNE UND ICH WAR MIT BOLLEK AN DER FRISCHEN
LUFT MINIGOLF SPIELEN. ES IST UNENTSCHIEDEN AUSGEGANGEN, ABER ICH
GLAUBE, BOLLEK HAT MICH GEWINNEN LASSEN, WEIL ER DOCH WEISS, WIE
UNGERN ICH VERLIERE. AUF DEM MINIGOLFPLATZ GAB ES AUCH EIS UND BOLLEK
UND ICH HABEN EIN RIESENEIS GEKAUFT. VANILLE UND SCHOKOLADE UND ERDBEER.
HMMMMH! LECKER!

IN DER STADT IST ES JETZT GANZ SCHÖN HEKTISCH WEIL JETZT IST JA SCHON
FAST BALD SOMMERFERIEN. ABER DA DRAUSSEN AUF DEM MINIGOLFPLATZ FÜHLEN
WIR UNS FAST WIE IN RACIBORZ. NUR PARKEN HIER GRÖSSERE AUTOS.

ACH, MANUSCHKA [...]

GRÜSST, KÜSST UND KOSSEN,

LOLLEK

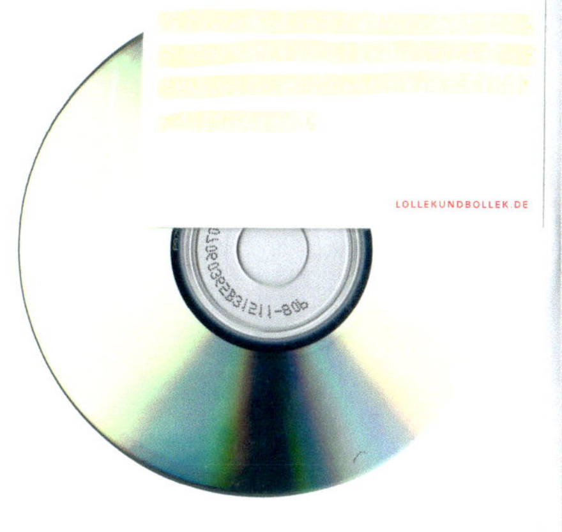

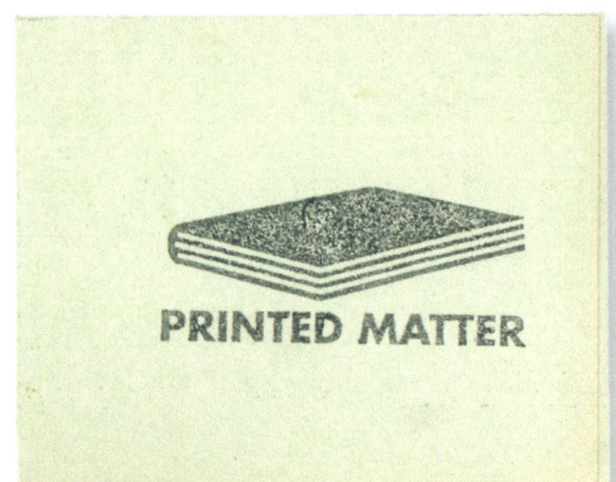

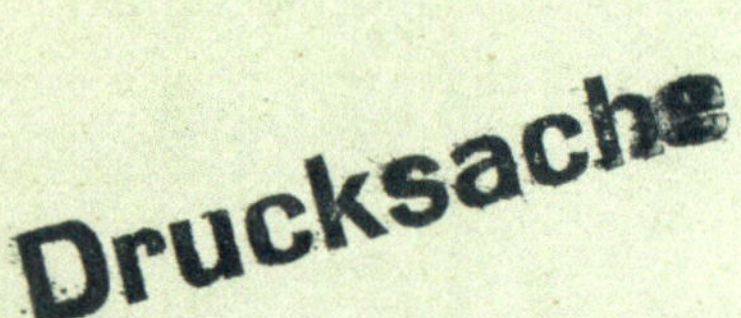

1–3   Alexander Meyer, paper, stamp, 2000
4   Alex Rich, offset printing
5   Carsten Nicolai, offset printing

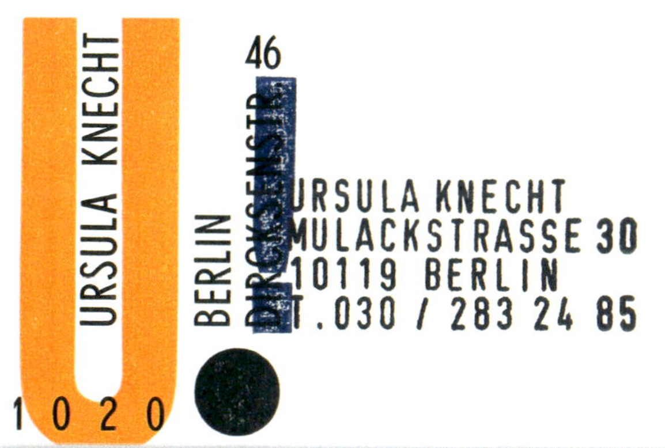

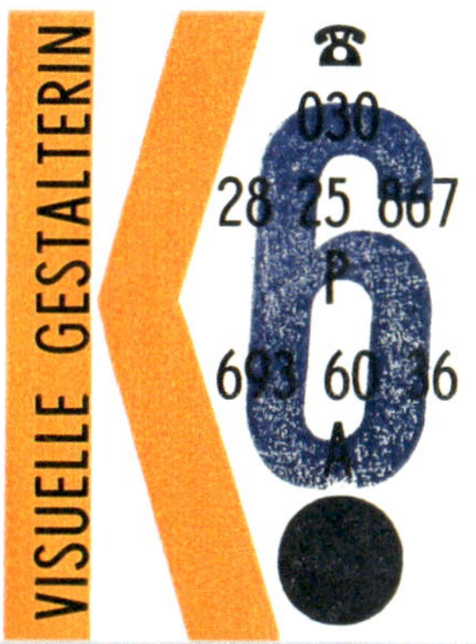

Design: Edward Fella

646.7582

775   Bates
Birmingham, Michigan   48009

w/   Office: Skidmore Sahratian Inc.

2100   Big Beaver
Troy, Michigan   48084

643.6000

ELEKTROSMOG

ઇन्टरनेशनल

Hindermann & Welser
Pfingstweiestrasse 6 ZurichCH-8005
Switzeland
(1 Stock Links)
Tele :   41 1 2732327
Fax   : + 41 1 2732317
E-maij : + info@esmog.org

Gerard A. Unger

Diseñador de Tipos

Marie Luise Emmermann
0176 - 20 10 72 44
emm.a@gmx.de

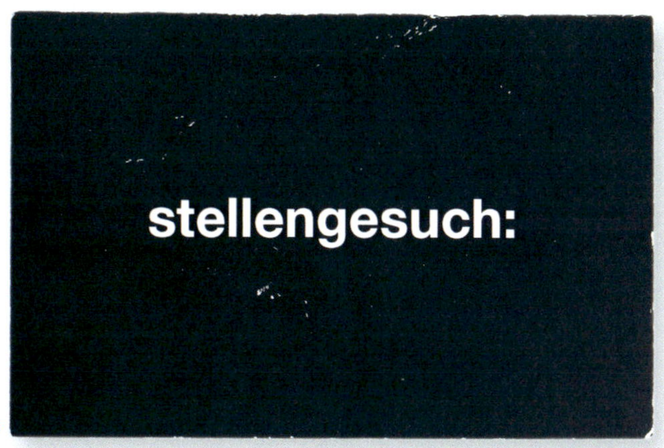

1–2   Ursula Knecht, paper, lead composition, 1997
3   Ed Fella, offset printing, 1977
4   Elektrosmog, (printed in India, Anil Printing), letterpress, 2002
5   Gerard Unger, local craftsman, unfortunately unknown, cardboard, letterpress, 1903
6–7   Marie Luise Emmermann, laser print, 2003

Fax Free

Copy it. Fill it. Fax it. The ultimate ready-to-use faxpad!

3rd edition!

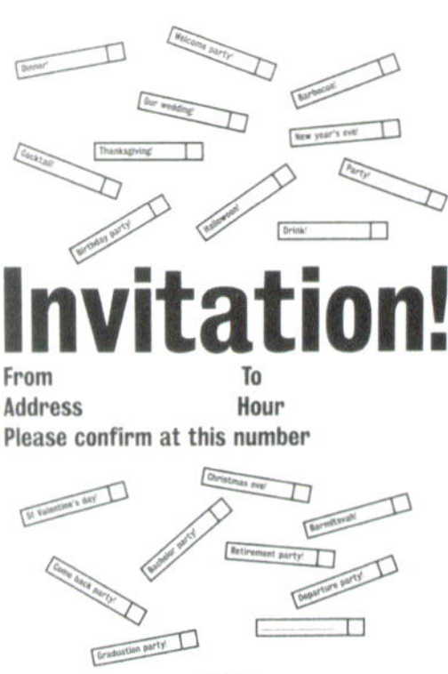

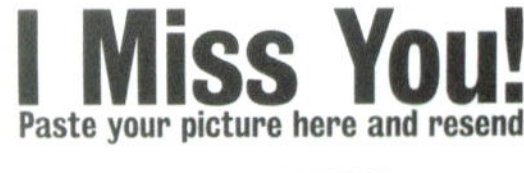

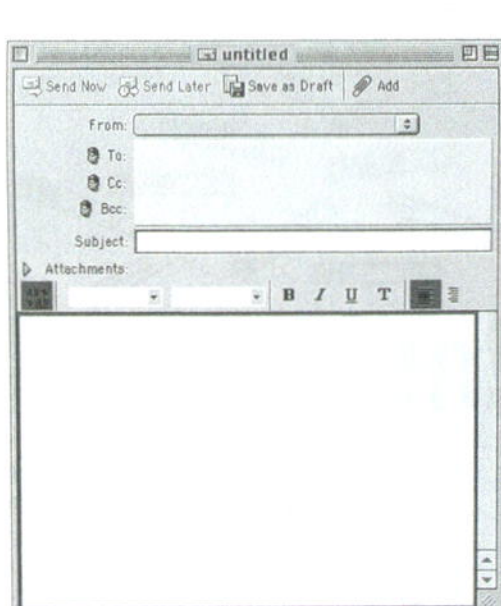

Anthony Burrill, 50 x 75 mm, poster paper, woodblock, 2004

1–2   Mode / Phil Costin, Ian Styles, Darrell Gibbons, letterhead, Tervakoski Tercoat plus 60 g, offset printing, 2003
3   Mode / Phil Costin, Ian Styles, business card folding twice, Modo M-real Datacopy Salmon, 160 g, offset printing plus metallic foil, 2005
4   Mode / Phil Costin, Ian Styles, Darrell Gibbons, envelope, portrait with tear-off security strip, 115 g offset printing, 2003

BaseBRU Rue de la Clé 5, 1000 Brussels, Belgium. Telephone +32 2 2190082 Facsimile +32 2 2293160. Email basebru@basedesign.com

Date   Subject

BaseBRU message

Base Design © All rights reserved

Project Name   Date

BasePROJECT

Base Design © All rights reserved

Project Name   Date

BasePROJECT

Base

Juliette Cavenaile Production Director / Partner

Base

BaseBRU
Rue de la Clé 5, 1000 Brussels / Belgium
T +32 2 219 0082 / F +32 2 229 3160
www.basedesign.com
juliette@basedesign.com

Other Bases

BaseNYC	T +1 212 625 9293	New York / USA
BasePARIS	T +33 1 4274 6360	Paris / France
BaseBCN	T +34 93 390 8750	Barcelona / Spain
BaseMAD	T +34 91 539 9708	Madrid / Spain

BaseBRU Rue de la Clé 5, 1000 Brussels, Belgium. Telephone +32 2 2190082 Facsimile +32 2 2293160. Email basebru@basedesign.com

With compliments

Base

1   Base, adhesive paper, offset printing, 1999
2–3   Base, Strathmore Writing ultimate white 90 g, offset printing, 1999
4–5   Base, Strathmore Writing ultimate white 298 g, offset printing, 1999
6   Base, Strathmore Writing ultimate white 298 g, offset printing, 1999

MICHAEL C. PLACE/
BUILD/TEL: +44 (0)7816
100 391/FAC: +44 (0)207
371 7920/EMAIL: MICHAEL
@DESIGNBYBUILD.COM/
WEBSITE: WWW.DESIGNBY
BUILD.COM

(PLEASE SEE OVER FOR
INFORMATION)

Boris Brumnjak
Visuelle Gestaltung
++49 30

Prisdorferstraße 14 b
D–13581 Berlin
366 37 02
Fax 36 71 04 61
brumnjak@gmx.de

moiré MARC KAPPELER
SCHÖNEGGSTRASSE 5
CH – 8004 ZÜRICH
MOBILE + 41 79 247 36 60
T/F +41 1 240 57 34
http://www.moire.ch
marc@moire.ch

moiré MARKUS REICHENBACH
SCHÖNEGGSTRASSE 5
CH – 8004 ZÜRICH
MOBILE + 41 78 736 61 44
T/F +41 1 240 57 34
http://www.moire.ch
markus@moire.ch

Bernadette Kremser – Graphic Designer (Design Austria)
Zentagasse 45/8, 1050 Wien, Austria
+43(0)699/11059348, bernadette.kremser@gmx.at

see you, b.

1–2   Build / Michael C. Place, offset printing, 2003
3–4   Boris Brumnjak, paper, silk-screen printing, 2000
5–6   Moiré / Bianca Brunner, Marc Kappeler, Markus Reichenbach, paper one side coated, offset printing, 2004
7   Bernadette Kremser, lakepaper extra 250 g, offset printing, 2004

AdfontesRegular abcdefghijklmnopqrstuvwxyz
ABCDEFGHIJKLMNOPQRSTUVWXYZ (0123456789)
[fiflß],;.!?&©@ß{áäâàåçéëèóöôﬆﬀÖÑ}←€£¢$→

AdfontesCaps ABCDEFGHIJKLMNOPQRSTUVWXYZ
ABCDEFGHIJKLMNOPQRSTUVWXYZ (0123456789)
[fiflß],;.!?&©@ß{ÁÄÂÀÅÇÉËÈÓÖÔﬆﬀÖÑ}←€£¢$→

AdfontesDingbats

Graphic Design David Clavadetscher
Lucerne, Switzerland +41 [0]78-736 85 75
david@clavadetscher.org

Image Bank / Busaba / RAC / The Photographers' Gallery / BIG Magazine
Tate Modern / Fi Group / Syn Production / Rachel Whiteread / Hugo Boss
Marc Quinn / John Pawson / Ikepod / 4th Floor / D&AD / Norico.com
Hakkasan / Mill + Mill Film / Selfridges / Jenny Saville / Speirs + Major
Own Home / NMEC / Accenture / Digital Channel Partners / Circus
IDEA Japan / The Serpentine Gallery / Booth-Clibborn Editions
Gagosian Gallery / VData / Telewest / VRX Technologies / Inscape
Liverpool Victoria / Schroders / Environment Agency / Samas Roneo
Abbey National / Jane & Louise Wilson / White Cube Gallery / Paul & Joe

North   +44 (0)20 7357 0071

ABCDEFGHIJKLMNOPQR
STUVWXYZ+äbcdefghijklm-
nopqrſstüvwxyzʒ&0123456789
ch ck ﬆ ﬀ ﬁ ﬅ ﬄ ﬃ ﬁ ﬅ ﬅ ﬄ ﬂ ſt ʒ tʒ
Ignaz Textura 2004

Type and Graphic Design Schrift- und Grafikdesign

daniel_j_reynolds
@hotmail.com

Type Nerd
Geisberg Straße 3 | 65193 Wiesbaden | Germany
+49(0)611/58 02 873 MOBILE +49(0)174/57 56 710

Name Daniel Eatock **Company** Foundation 33 **Vocation** Multi-Disciplinary Design

Address 33 Temple Street London E2 6QQ England
Telephone +44 [0]20 77399903 **Facsimile** +44 [0]20 77398989
Internet www.foundation33.com **Electronic Mail** danieleatock@foundation33.com

Current Employment Senior Lecturer in Graphic Design University of Brighton Previous Employment Graphic Designer Walker Art Center Minneapolis USA October 1998 – December 1999 Education Graphic Design Masters Degree Royal College of Art 1996 – 1998 / Communication Design Degree Ravensbourne College of Design & Communication 1993 – 1996 Awards American Center of Design 100 show award for Walker Art Center Intern Poster 1999 / American Center of Design 100 show award for Allan Wexler Exhibition Catalogue 1999 / American Center of Design 100 show award for AIGA Insights Lecture Poster 1999 / International Design Magazine Award top 40 designers under thirty January/February 2000 / Creative Futures Summer 1998 / Energy Efficiency Award first prize Royal College of Art Spring 1997 Articles/Reviews Andrew Blauvelt Towards a complex simplicity Eye Magazine Issue 35 Spring 2000 / David Brown Walk This Way International Design Magazine January/February 2000 / Work also published in the following magazines Emigre Summer 2000 / Interior View Summer 2000 / *Surface Spring 2000 / Creative Review Summer 99 & Summer 98 / Design Week Summer 98 / Blueprint Summer 98 / & the book Subtraction: Aspects of Essential Design 2000 Exhibitions/Shows 100% Design Earls Court London October 2000 / Black > Blank Village Fête Victoria & Albert Museum curated by Claire Catterall July 2000 / Salone Satellite Milan April 2000 / Creative Futures July 1998 / Ten Idea Objects Hockney Gallery Royal College of Art March 1998 / Black Board Coffee Bar Royal College of Art May 1998 / 24 hour sensory deprivation Red Room Royal College of Art October 1997 Conferences Professional practice applied & self initiated graphic design, University of Brighton Design Department January 2000 / Professional practice Conceptual graphic design from Royal College of Art, University of Brighton Design Department September 1998 Consultancy Work ADC LTSN / Save the Children / Travel Counsellors / Atlanta Art Gallery & City Gallery Chastain / Maguffin Interests Alphabetising / Believing / Conceptualising / Designing / Eliminating / Finding / Giving / Helping / Innovating / Joining / Kerning / Listening / Making / Numbering / Organising / Publishing / Questioning / Racing / Simplifying / Thinking / Uncovering / Verifying / Watching / Xeroxing / Yawning / Zigzagging Motto Say YES to fun & function & NO to seductive imagery & colour! Pocket Size Curriculum Vitae & Contact Card Second Update September 2000 Copyright Daniel Eatock 2000

1–2   David Clavadetscher, natural paper, uncoated paper extra white, 200 g, offset printing, 2002
3   North Design, paper, offset printing
4–5   TypeOff / Dan Reynolds, paper, offset printing
6   Daniel Eatock , paper, offset printing

1–2   Mode / Phil Costin, Ian Styles, Richie Clarke,
credentials / proposal 170 x 238 mm french folded, Challenger
Lite 100 g, offset printing, perforation, plus metallic blue foil, 2005

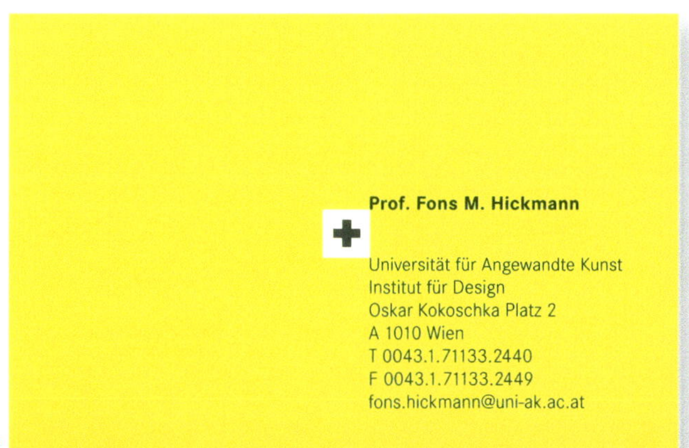

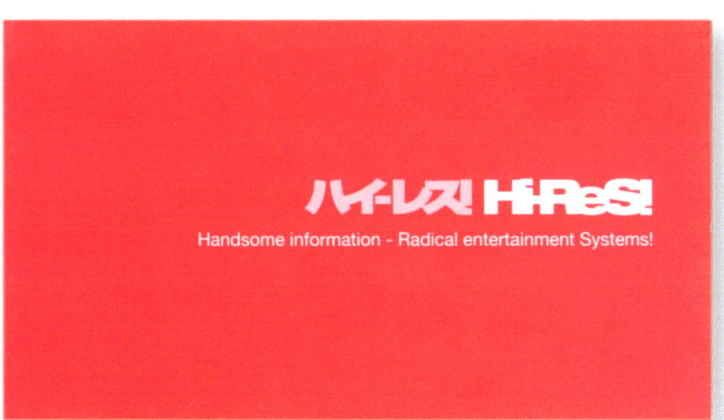

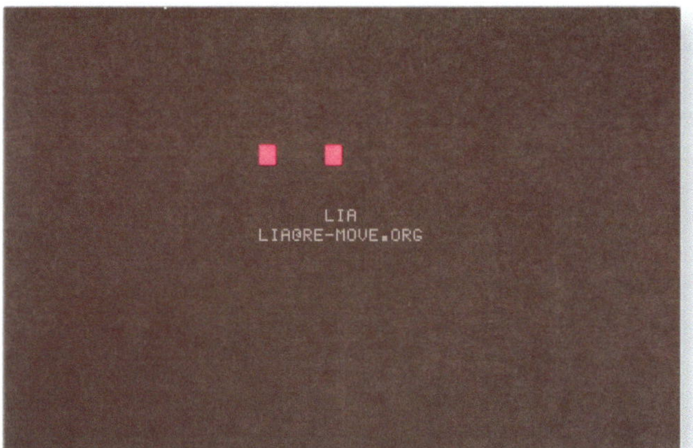

1–2 Fons Hickmann m23
3–4 Hi-Res!, offset printing
5–6 Farrow Design, Parilux mat 300 g, special mix yellow, double hit and black, offset printing, 2000
7–8 Lia with Miguel Carvalhais, paper, offset printing, 2003

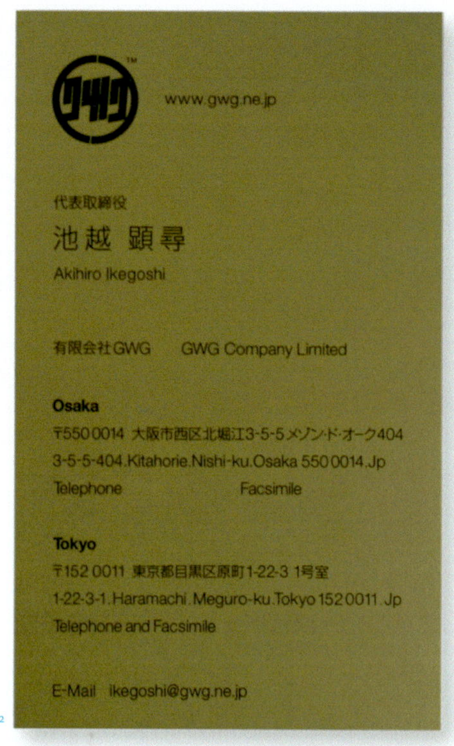

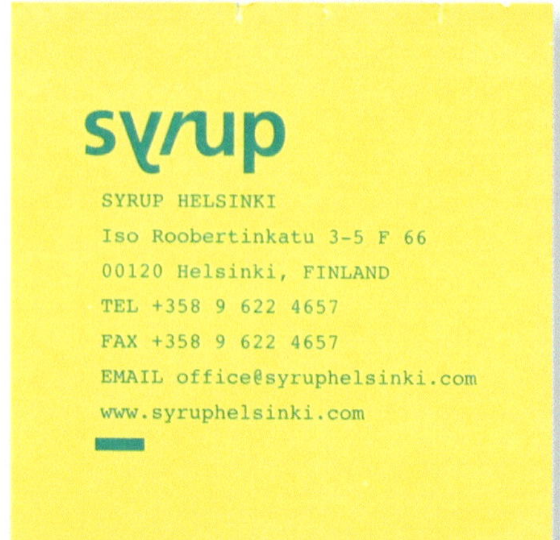

1   123Buero / Timo Gaesser, cardboard and adhesive paper, offset printing, 2004 / 2002
2   GWG CO. LTD / Akihiro Ikegoshi, paper, silk-screen printing, 2003
3   Syrup Helsinki, Munken Lynx, offset printing, 2004
4–5 Thonik, uncoated paper, offset printing, 2000
6   Underware, Tiny Underware ephemera showing the Sauna typeface, offset printing, 2000
7   Underware, self promotion stickers, showing the lightest weight of the typeface Sauna,
    offset printing, 2003

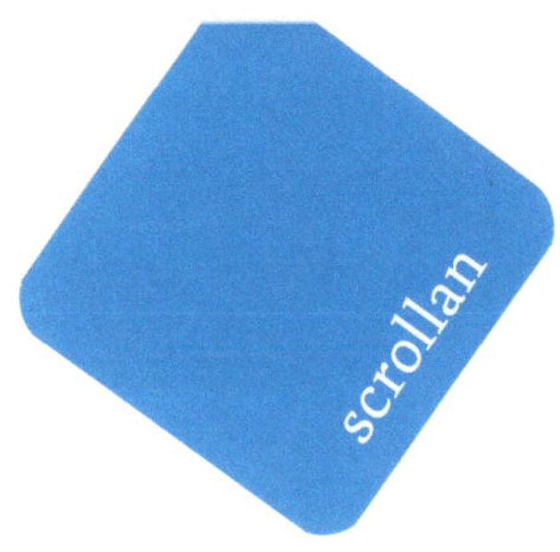

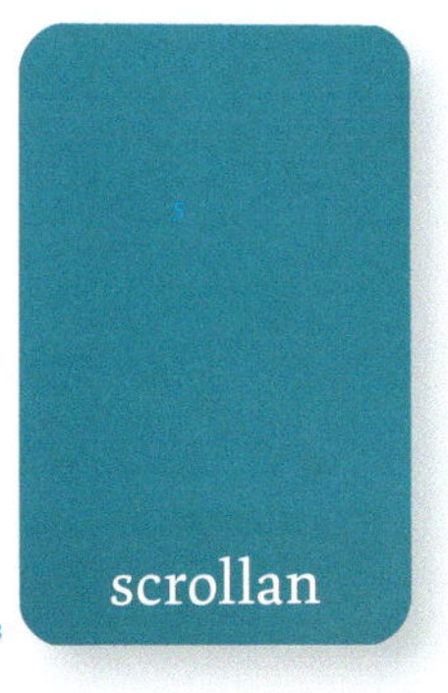

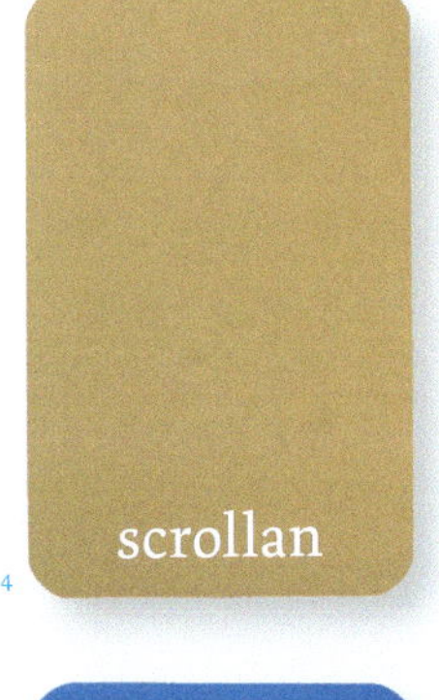

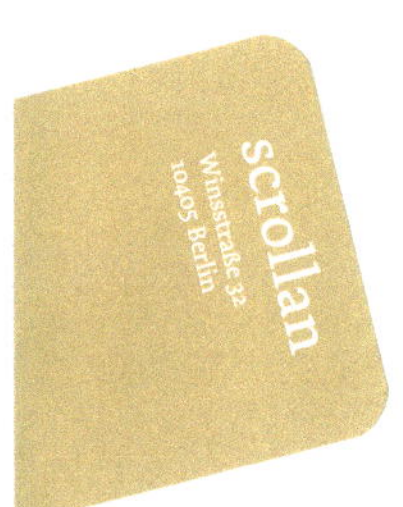

1–7   Scrollan / Peter Bünnagel, Barbara Kotte, Michael Weies, sticker, offset printing, 2003

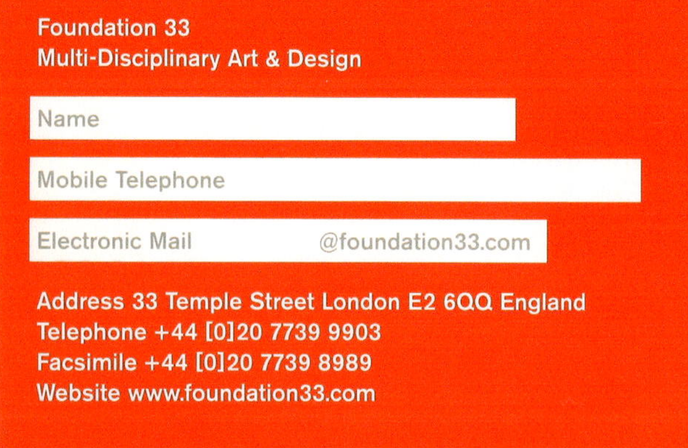

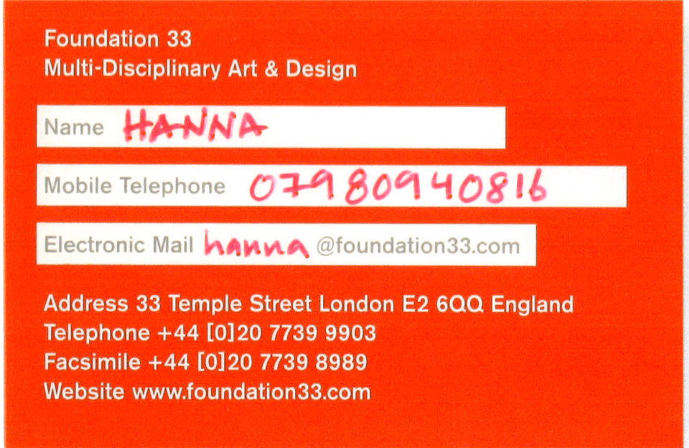

1–3   Daniel Eatock, offset printing
4–7   Codesign / Leonardo Sonnoli, offset printing

The Workstation 15 Paternoster Row
Sheffield S1 2BX United Kingdom.
E: vicki@thedesignersrepublic.com
URL: www.thedesignersrepublic.com
P: +44 [0] 114 275 4982
M: +44 [0] 7946 034 298.
F: +44 [0] 114 275 9127.

TDR is a division of Pho-Ku Corp.
1-6 3F Daikanyama-cho Shibuya-ku
Tokyo 150-0034 Japan.
〒150-0034 東京都渋谷区代官山町 1-6 3F
F: +81 3 3496 0747

The Workstation 15 Paternoster Row
Sheffield S1 2BX United Kingdom.
E: dr@thedesignersrepublic.com
URL: www.thedesignersrepublic.com
P: +44 [0] 114 275 4982
F: +44 [0] 114 275 9127.
ISDN: +44 [0] 114 276 6339.

TDR is a division of Pho-Ku Corp.
1-6 3F Daikanyama-cho Shibuya-ku
Tokyo 150-0034 Japan.
〒150-0034 東京都渋谷区代官山町 1-6 3F
F: +81 3 3496 0747

The Workstation 15 Paternoster Row
Sheffield S1 2BX United Kingdom.
E: abby@thedesignersrepublic.com
URL: www.thedesignersrepublic.com
P: +44 [0] 114 275 4982
F: +44 [0] 114 275 9127.
ISDN: +44 [0] 114 276 6339.

TDR is a division of Pho-Ku Corp.
1-6 3F Daikanyama-cho Shibuya-ku
Tokyo 150-0034 Japan.
〒150-0034 東京都渋谷区代官山町 1-6 3F
F: +81 3 3496 0747

The Workstation 15 Paternoster Row
Sheffield S1 2BX United Kingdom.
E: vicki@thedesignersrepublic.com
URL: www.thedesignersrepublic.com
P: +44 [0] 114 275 4982
M: +44 [0] 7946 034 298.
F: +44 [0] 114 275 9127.

TDR is a division of Pho-Ku Corp.
1-6 3F Daikanyama-cho Shibuya-ku
Tokyo 150-0034 Japan.
〒150-0034 東京都渋谷区代官山町 1-6 3F
F: +81 3 3496 0747

The Workstation 15 Paternoster Row
Sheffield S1 2BX United Kingdom.
E: dr@thedesignersrepublic.com
URL: www.thedesignersrepublic.com
P: +44 [0] 114 275 4982
F: +44 [0] 114 275 9127.
ISDN: +44 [0] 114 276 6339.

TDR is a division of Pho-Ku Corp.
1-6 3F Daikanyama-cho Shibuya-ku
Tokyo 150-0034 Japan.
〒150-0034 東京都渋谷区代官山町 1-6 3F
F: +81 3 3496 0747

The Workstation 15 Paternoster Row
Sheffield S1 2BX United Kingdom.
E: nick@thedesignersrepublic.com
URL: www.thedesignersrepublic.com
P: +44 [0] 114 275 4982
M: +44 [0] 7775 681 807.
F: +44 [0] 114 275 9127.

TDR is a division of Pho-Ku Corp.
1-6 3F Daikanyama-cho Shibuya-ku
Tokyo 150-0034 Japan.
〒150-0034 東京都渋谷区代官山町 1-6 3F
F: +81 3 3496 0747

Ian Anderson's Business card.
The Designers Republic.
85 X 55MM.
PMS 8403.
miTDR.

1–7 The Designers Republic, offset printing, 2001

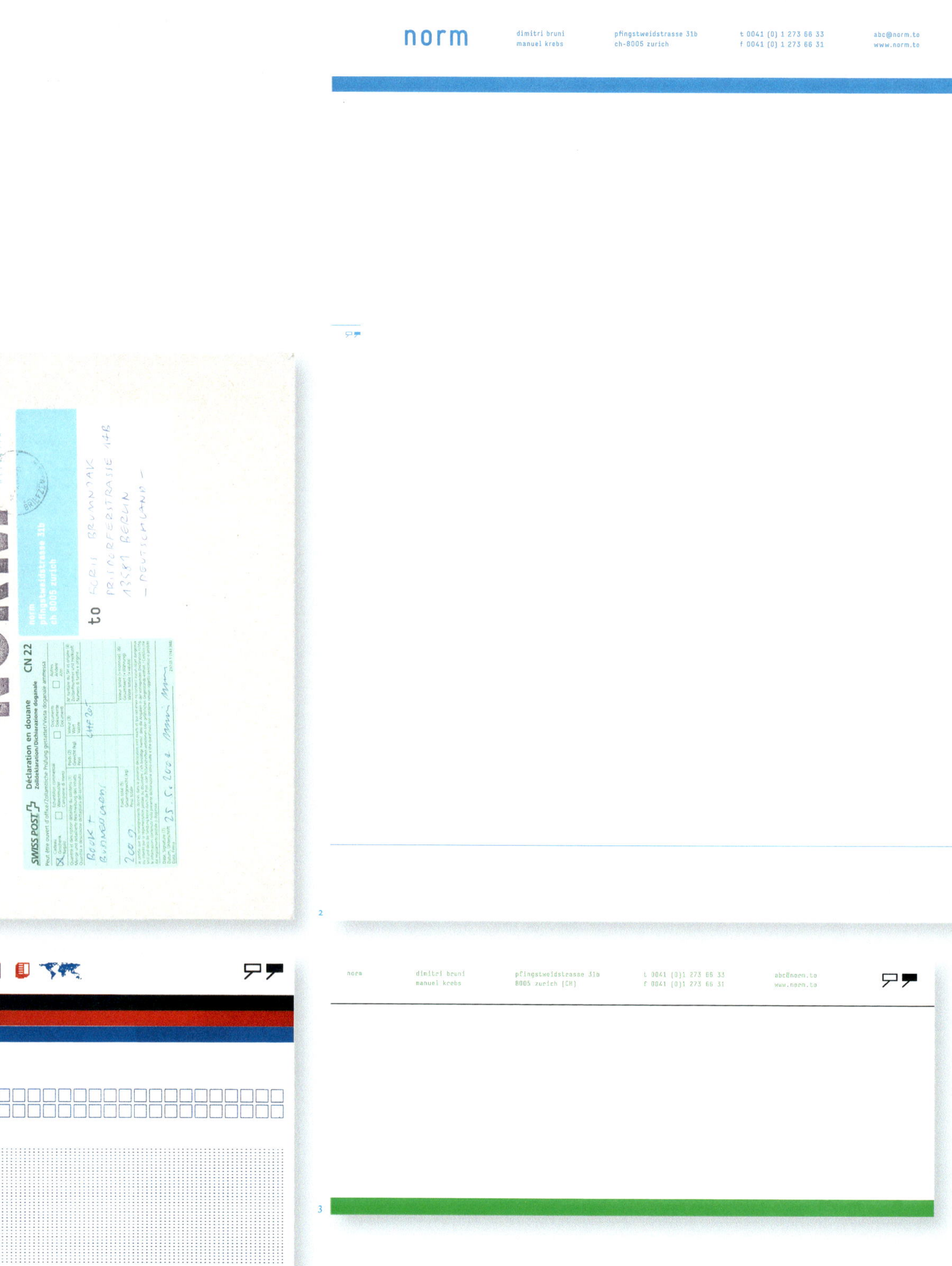

1   Norm, 2005
2   Norm, Z-offset 100 g, offset printing, 2004
3   Norm, Cyclus offset 200 g, offset printing, 2003
4   Norm, Swissboard 250 g, offset printing, 2003

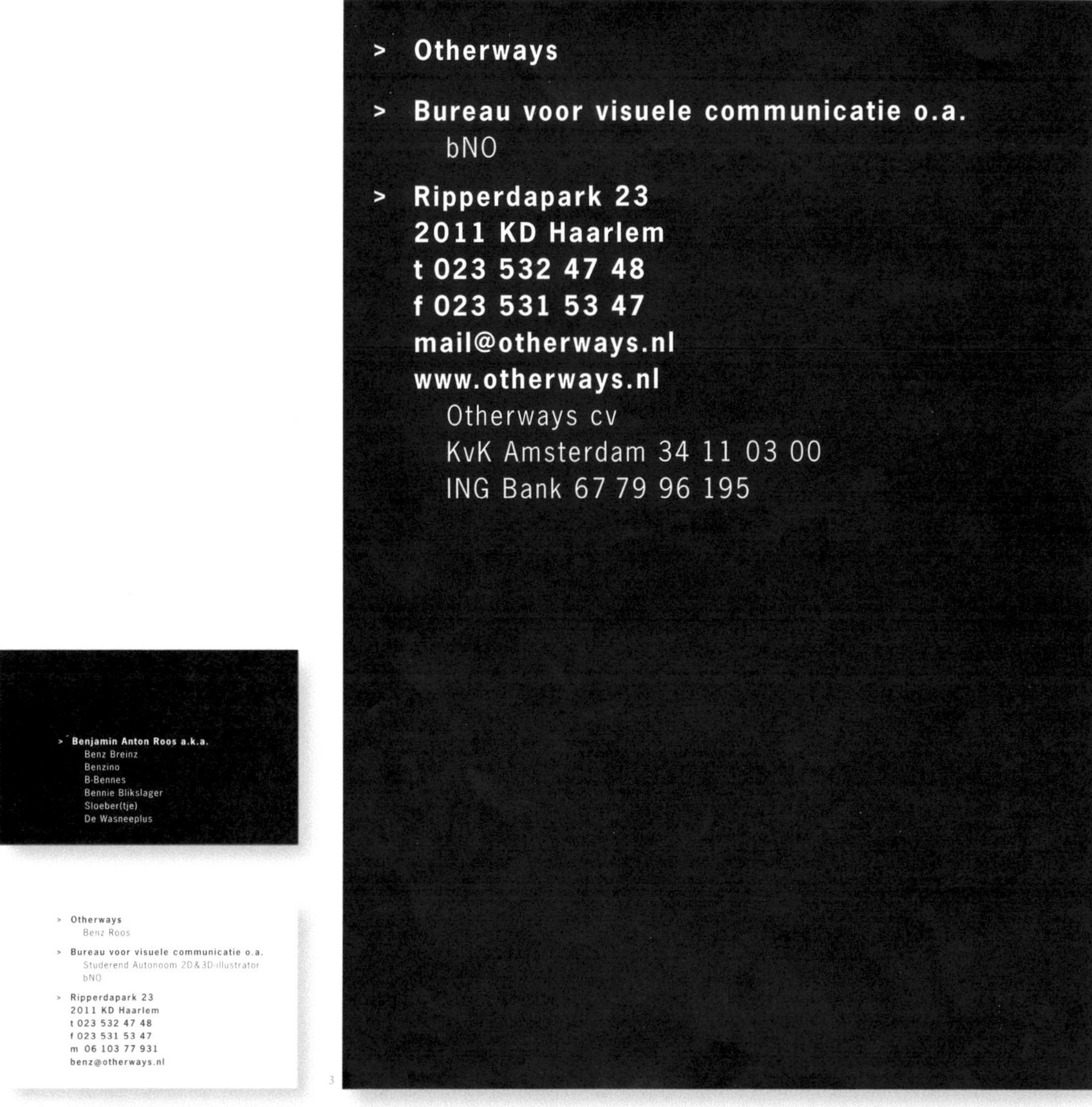

1–5   Otherways / Donald Roos, offset printing, 2002

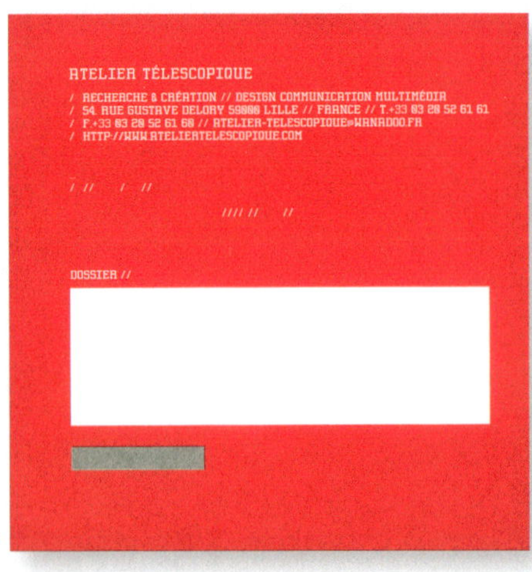

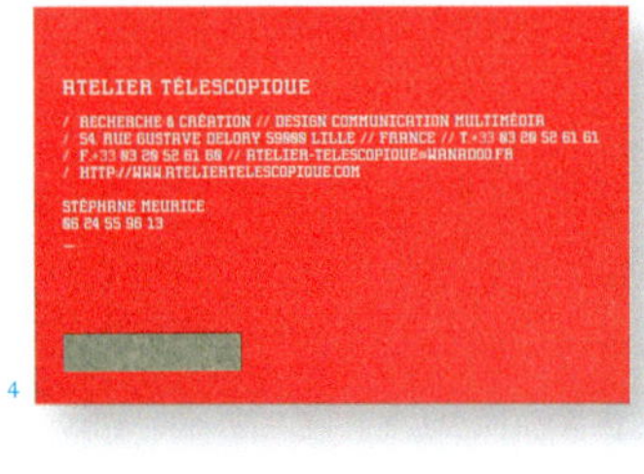

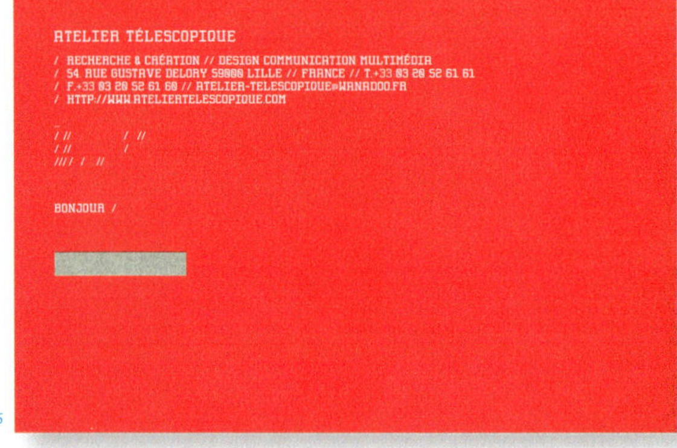

1–2   Atelier Télescopique, paper and plastic pocket, offset printing, 2004
3–6   Atelier Télescopique, Iridescent paper, offset printing, 2004

1   Neeser & Müller, Munken pure tac (adhesive label), offset printing, 2003
2–3 Neeser & Müller, Munken pure 80 g, offset printing, 2003
4–5 Neeser & Müller, Munken pure 300 g, offset printing, 2003
6   Neeser & Müller, Munken pure, offset printing, 2003

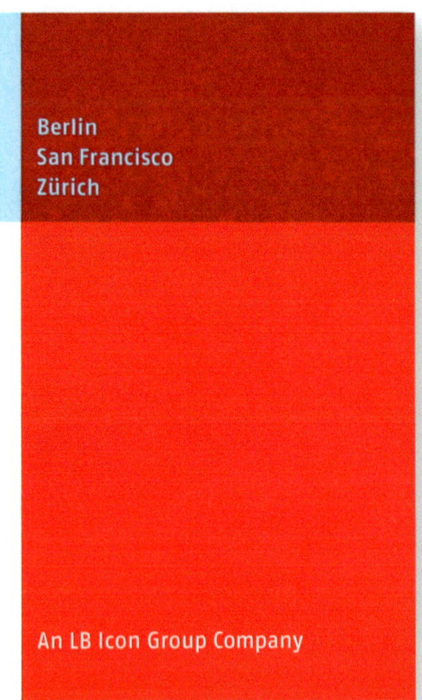

MetaDesign
Visible Strategies

Stefan E. Bischof
Corporate Communication
Assistant to the
Executive Board

MetaDesign AG
Leibnizstraße 65
10629 Berlin
seb@metadesign.de
+49·30·59 00 54·319
Mobil +49·173·217 22 81
Fax +49·30·59 00 54·111
www.metadesign.de

TelDesign

Emmapark 12 – 14
2595 ET Den Haag
Telefoon (070) 385 63 05
Fax (070) 383 63 11
www.teldesign.nl

TelDesign

Emmapark 12 – 14
2595 ET Den Haag
Telefoon (070) 385 63 05
Fax (070) 383 63 11
www.teldesign.nl

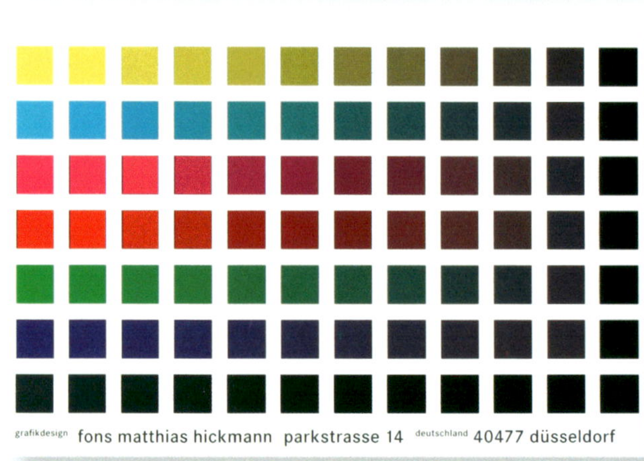

1–2   MetaDesign, paper, offset printing, 2005
3–5   TelDesign, paper, offset printing, 2004
6   Fons Hickmann m23 / Fons Hickmann

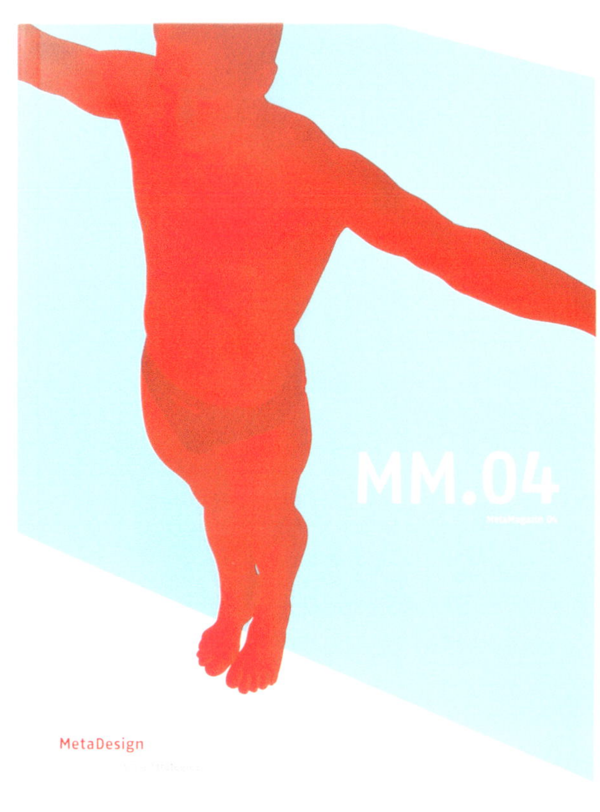

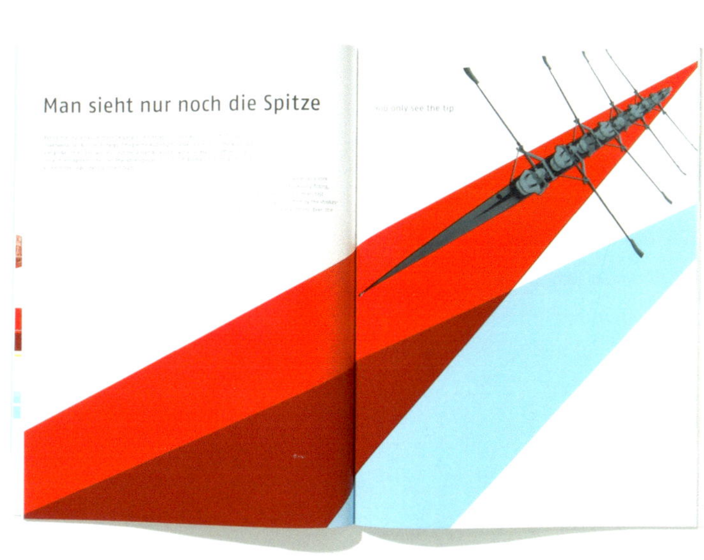

1–2   MetaDesign, 210 x 280 mm, paper, offset printing, 2005
3   MetaDesign, press kit 240 x 310 mm, paper, offset printing, 2005

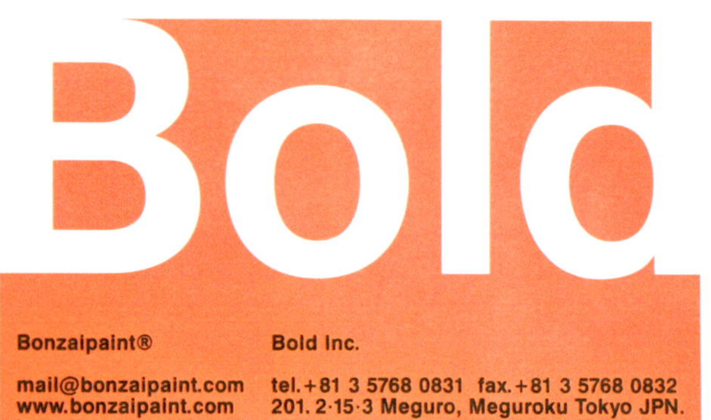

1–2   Manuel Rickert, Arjowiggins Impressions 240 g, offset printing, 2005
3–4   010 Publishers / Thonik, paper, offset printing, 2002
5–6   Bold Inc./ Bonzaipaint, Toru Tachizawa, paper, offset printing, 2000
7   Intro / Mat Cook, paper, offset printing, 2004

N KIA 076 402 78 19 S ALBANESE@GMX.CH W RSTKAESE S LAT
NO IA 076 402 78 19 S. LBANESE@GMX.CH WU STKAESE SA AT
NOK A 076 402 78 19 S.A BANESE@GMX.CH WUR TKAESE SAL T
NOKI 076 402 78 19 S.AL ANESE@GMX.CH WURS KAESE SALA
NOK A 076 402 78 19 S.ALB NESE@GMX.CH WURST AESE SAL T
NO IA 076 402 78 19 S.ALBA ESE@GMX.CH WURSTK ESE SA AT
N KIA 076 402 78 19 S.ALBAN SE@GMX.CH WURSTKA SE S LAT
 OKIA 076 402 78 19 S.ALBANE E@GMX.CH WURSTKAE E ALAT
N KIA 076 402 78 19 S.ALBANES @GMX.CH WURSTKAES   S LAT
NO IA 076 402 78 19 S.ALBANESE GMX.CH WURSTKAE E SA AT
NOK A 076 402 78 19 S.ALBANESE@ MX.CH WURSTKA SE SAL T
NOKI 076 402 78 19 S.ALBANESE@G X.CH WURSTK ESE SALA
NOK A 076 402 78 19 S.ALBANESE@GM .CH WURST AESE SAL T
NO IA 076 402 78 19 S.ALBANESE@GMX CH WURS KAESE SA AT
N KIA 076 402 78 19 S.ALBANESE@GMX. H WUR TKAESE S LAT
 OKIA 076 402 78 19 S.ALBANESE@GMX.C   WU STKAESE   ALAT
N KIA 076 402 78 19 S.ALBANESE@GMX. H W RSTKAESE S LAT
NO IA 076 402 78 19 S.ALBANESE@GMX CH   URSTKAESE SA AT
NOK A 076 402 78 19 S.ALBANESE@GM .CH W RSTKAESE SAL T
NOKI 076 402 78 19 S.ALBANESE@G X.CH WU STKAESE SALA
NOK A 076 402 78 19 S.ALBANESE@ MX.CH WUR TKAESE SAL T
NO IA 076 402 78 19 S.ALBANESE GMX.CH WURS KAESE SA AT

S SSSSSSSSSSS SSSSSSSSSSS SSSSSSSSSSS SSSSSSSSSSS S
AA AAAAAAAAAA AAAAAAAAAA AAAAAAAAAA AAAAAAAAAA
BBB BBBBBBBBBBB BBBBBBBBBBB BBBBBBBBBBB BBBBBBBBBBB
IIII IIIIIIIIIII IIIIIIIIIII IIIIIIIIIII IIIIIIIIII
NNNNN NNNNNNNNNN NNNNNNNNNN NNNNNNNNNN NNNNNNNNNN
AAAAAA AAAAAAAAAAA AAAAAAAAAAA AAAAAAAAAAA AAAAAAAAA

AAAAAAA AAAAAAAAAAA AAAAAAAAAAA AAAAAAAAAAA AAAAAAAA
LLLLLLLL LLLLLLLLLLL LLLLLLLLLLL LLLLLLLLLLL LLLLLLL
BBBBBBBB BBBBBBBBBBB BBBBBBBBBBB BBBBBBBBBBB BBBBBB
AAAAAAAAAA AAAAAAAAAAA AAAAAAAAAAA AAAAAAAAAAA AAAAA
NNNNNNNNNN NNNNNNNNNNN NNNNNNNNNNN NNNNNNNNNNN NNNN
EEEEEEEEEEE EEEEEEEEEEE EEEEEEEEEEE EEEEEEEEEEE EEE
 SSSSSSSSSS SSSSSSSSSSS SSSSSSSSSSS SSSSSSSSSSS SS
E EEEEEEEEEEE EEEEEEEEEEE EEEEEEEEEEE EEEEEEEEEEE E

GG GGGGGGGGGG GGGGGGGGGGG GGGGGGGGGGG GGGGGGGGGGG
RRR RRRRRRRRRR RRRRRRRRRRR RRRRRRRRRRR RRRRRRRRRRR
AAAA AAAAAAAAAAA AAAAAAAAAAA AAAAAAAAAAA AAAAAAAAAAA
FFFFF FFFFFFFFFFF FFFFFFFFFFF FFFFFFFFFFF FFFFFFFFFF
IIIIII IIIIIIIIIII IIIIIIIIIII IIIIIIIIIII IIIIIIII
KKKKKK KKKKKKKKKKK KKKKKKKKKKK KKKKKKKKKKK KKKKKKKK

Peter Chadwick
Art Director

07970 004 670
peter@zipdesign.co.uk

Unit 2A Queens Studio
121 Salusbury Road London NW6 6RG
T 020 7372 4474 F 020 7372 4484
ISDN 020 7328 2816
www.zipdesign.co.uk

hello studio

-

Irin Schneider

Linienstraße 52, 10119 Berlin
Tel. +49 (0)30 440 471 03, mobil +49 (0)178 925 7270
www.hellostudio.de, irin@hellostudio.de

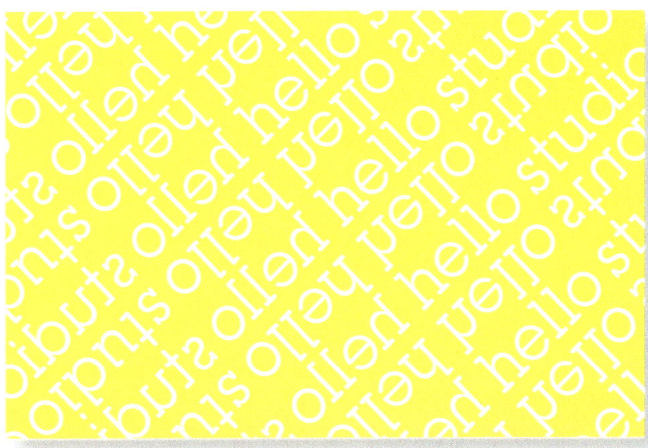

this is a magazine
www.thisisamagazine.com

andy simionato
co-editor/graphicart/illustration

tel.   +39.02433628
cel.   +39.3337933034
e.   andy@thisisamagazine.com
studio. viale coni zugna, 4 milano 20144 Italy

1–2 Sabina Albanese Grafik, paper one-sid coated, offset printing, 2004
3–4 Zip Design, Peter Chadwick, white ivory board 355 g, 2003
5–6 Hello Studio / Irin Schneider, chromo cardboard 270 g, offset printing, 2004
7–8 This is a Magazine, offset printing

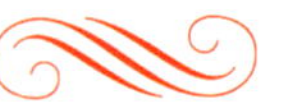

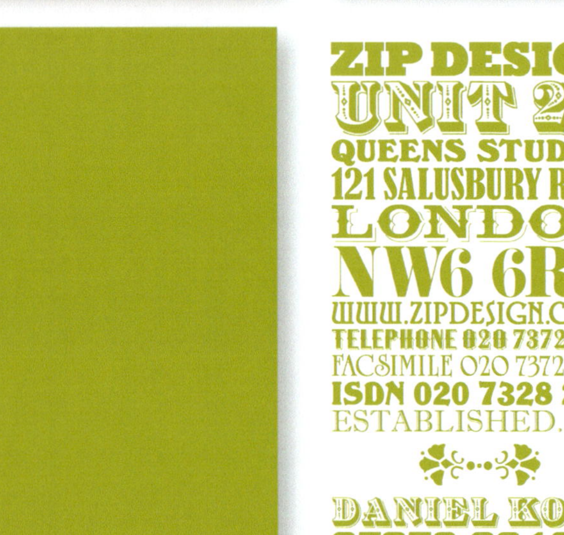

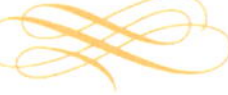

1–8   Zip Design / Peter Chadwick and Hannah Woodcock,
       white ivory board 355 g, 1 / 1 c with overall wash on reverse, 2004

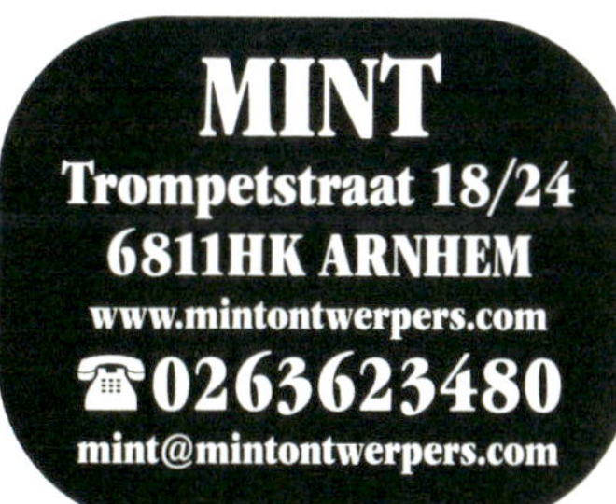

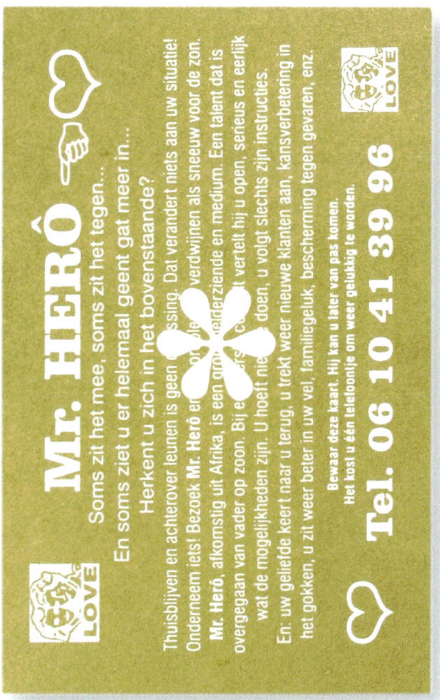

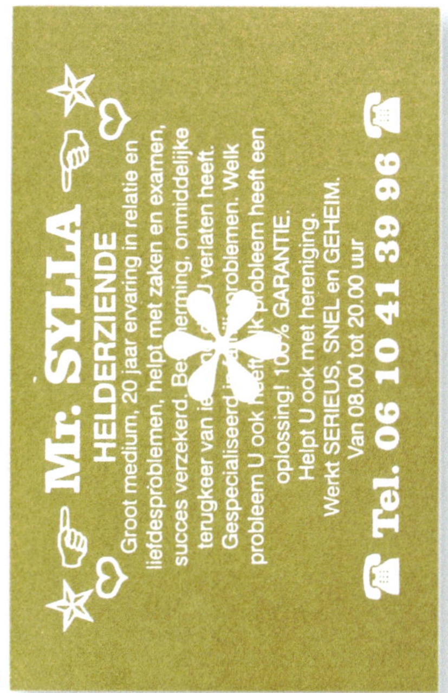

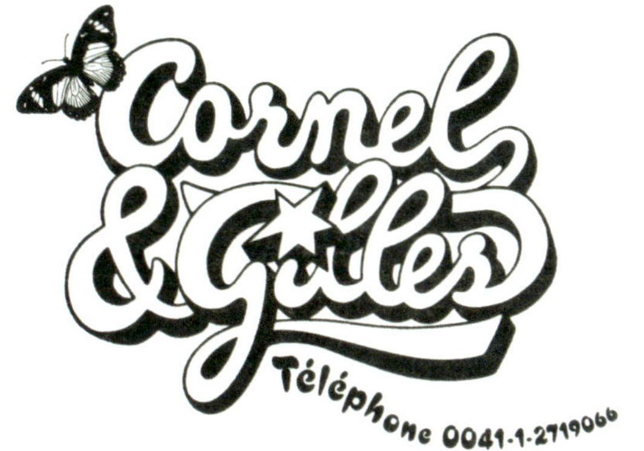

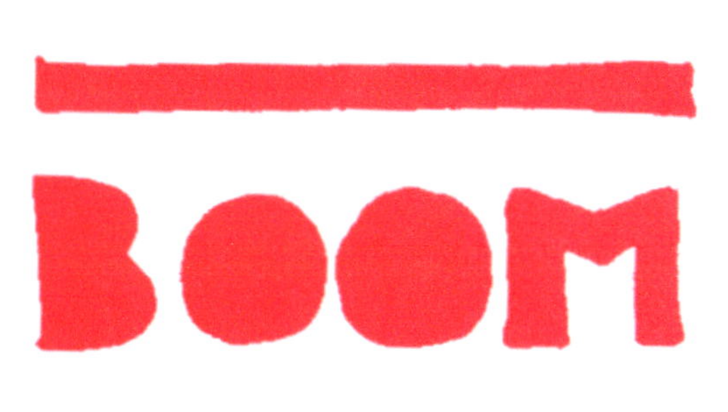

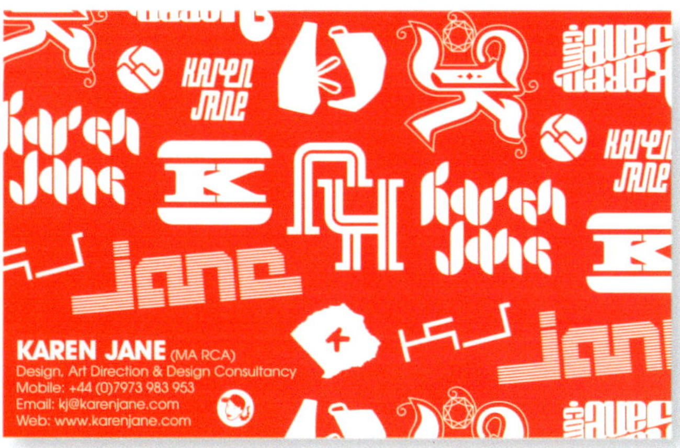

1–3   Mint, paper, offset printing, 2002
4   Gilles Gavillet and Cornel Windlin, original design by Domenic Geissbühler, Invercote G, 170 g, postcard cardboard, letterpress with printing block, 1999
5   Irma Boom, offset printing
6   Karen Jane, cardboard and mat laminate, offset printing, 2005
7   Norm, Invercote G 240 g, offset printing, 2004

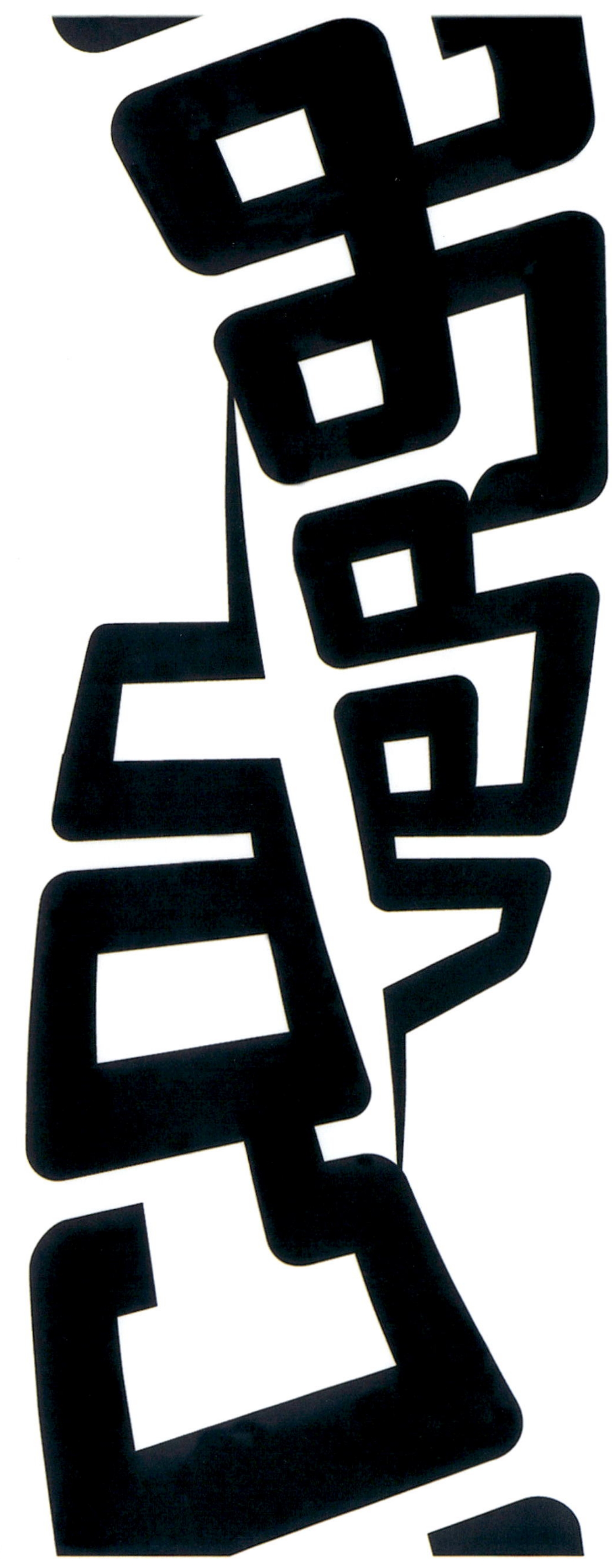

karenjane
www.karenjane.com
all work © karenjane 2005

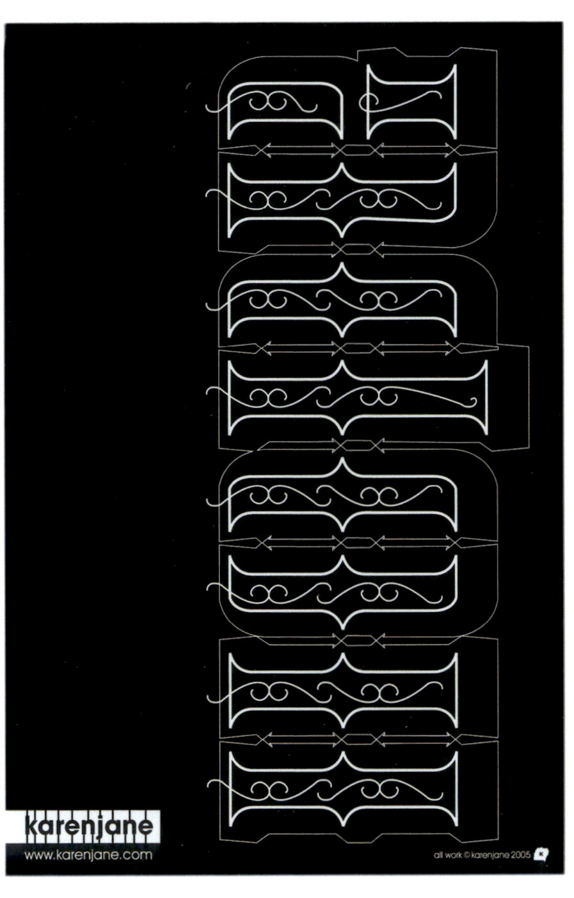
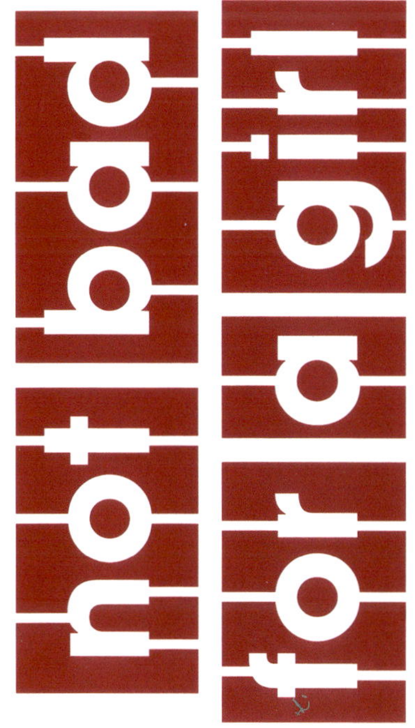

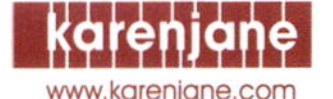
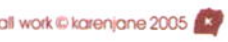
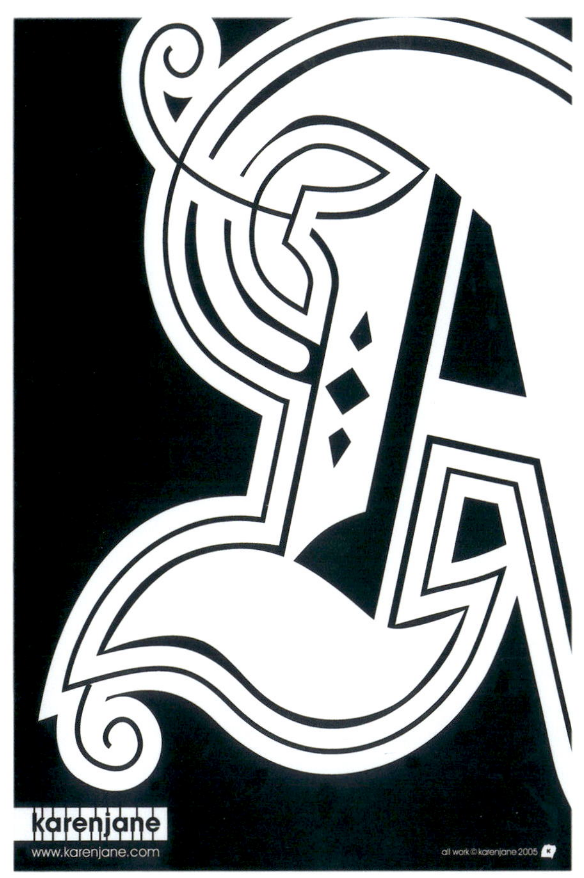
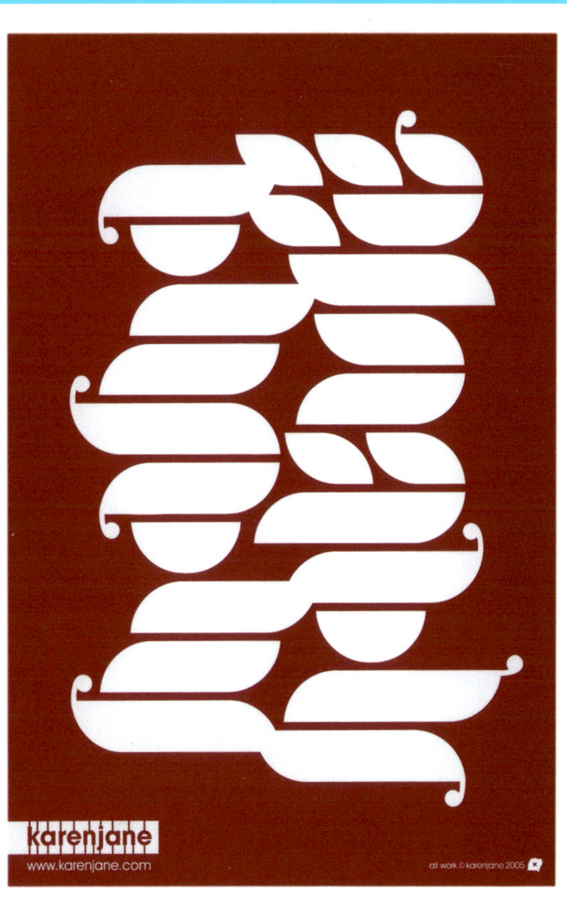

1–4   Karen Jane, 150 x 100 mm, photo paper, photo print, 2005

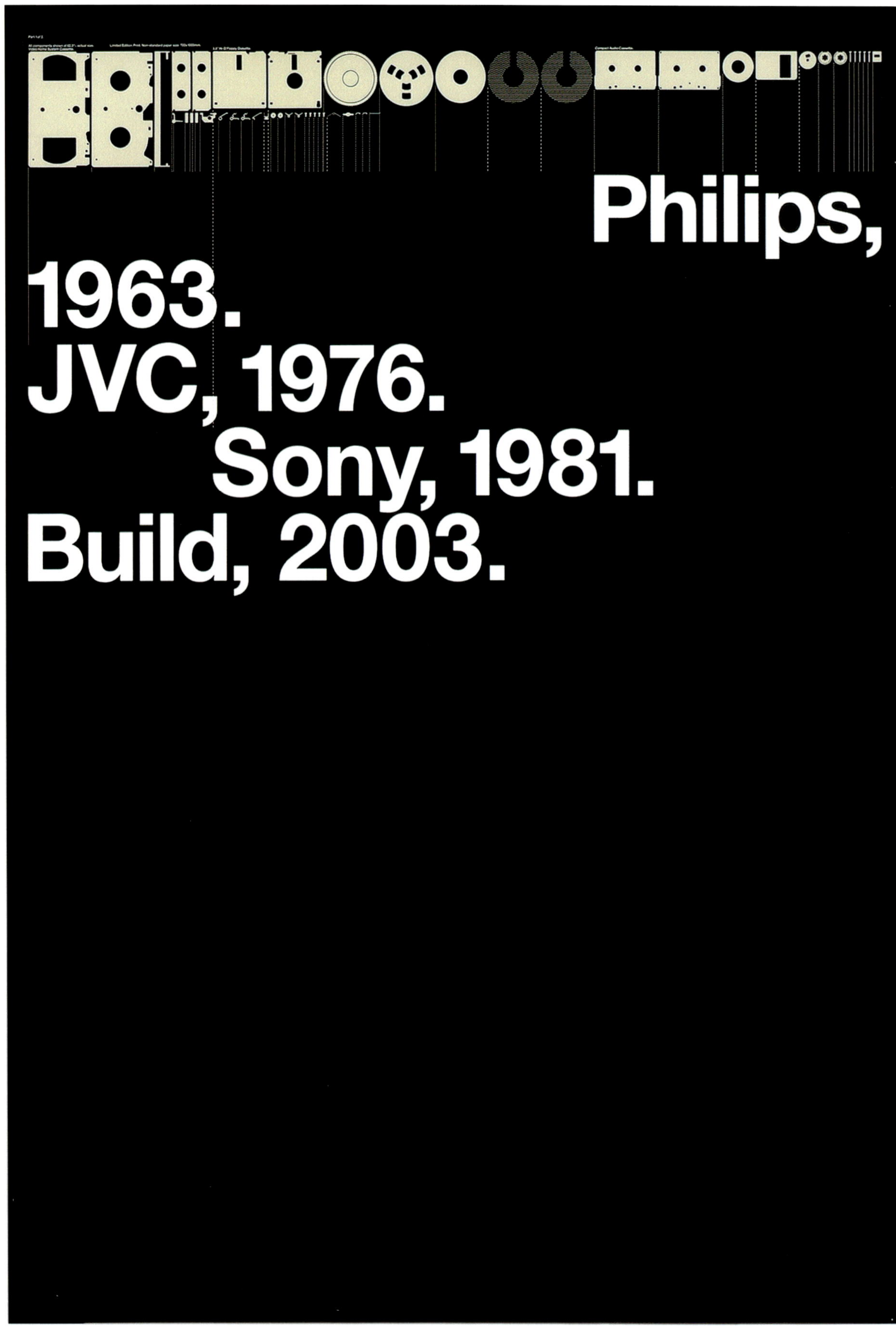

Philips,
1963.
JVC, 1976.
Sony, 1981.
Build, 2003.

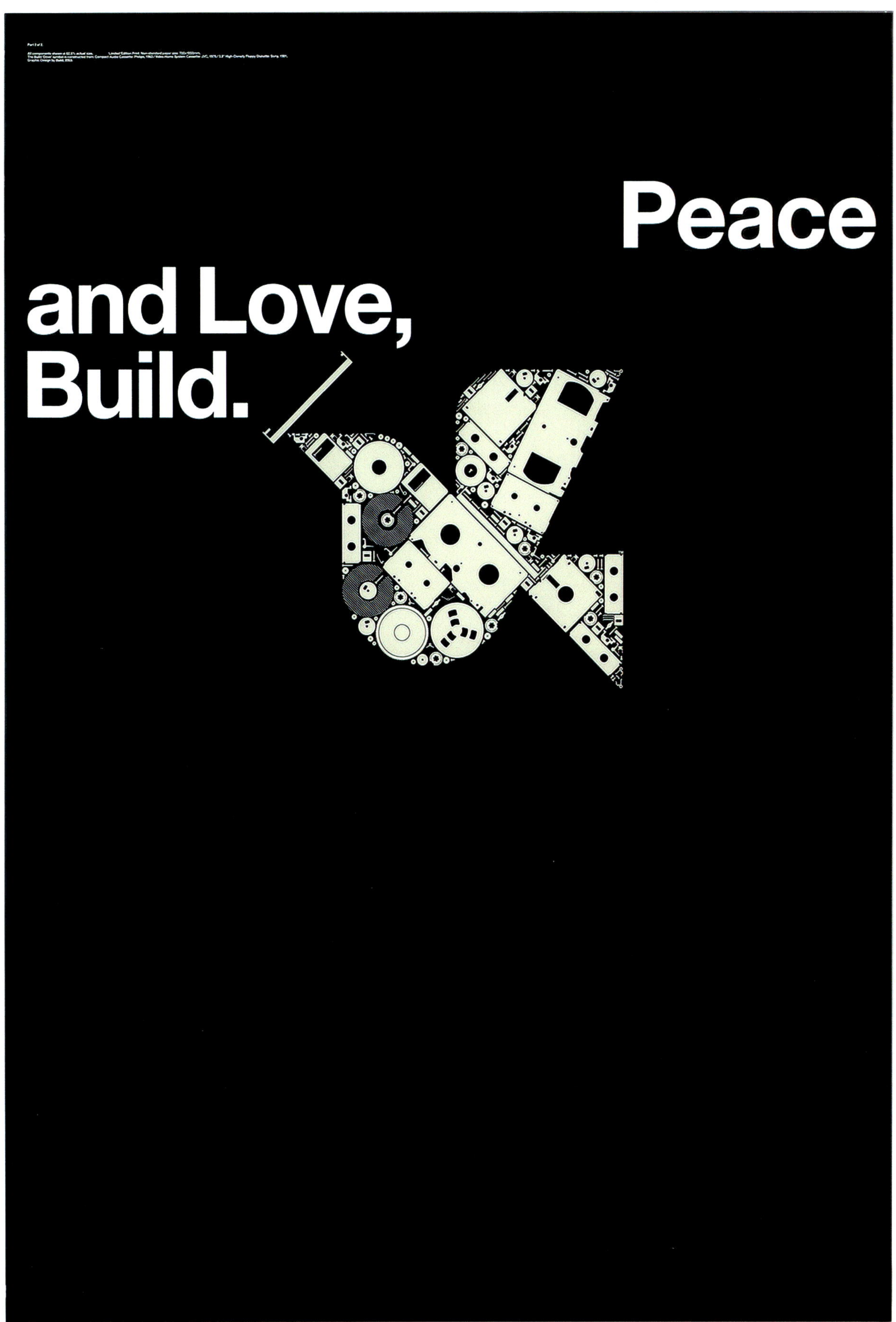

Build / Michael C. Place, offset printing, 2003

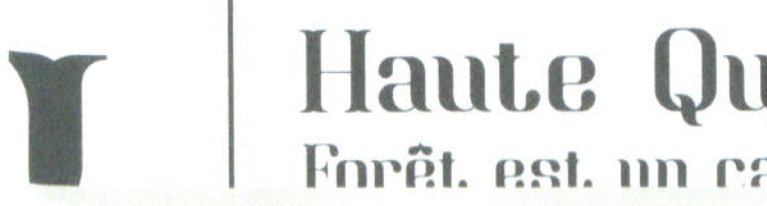

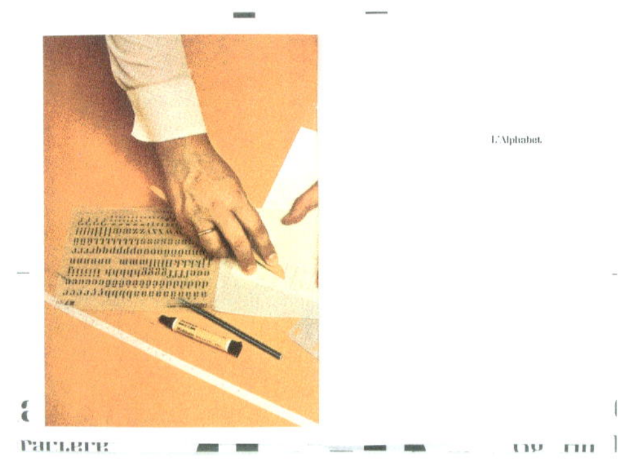

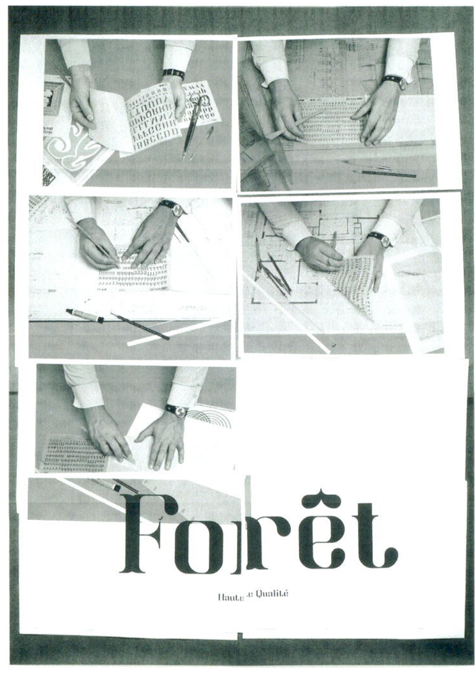

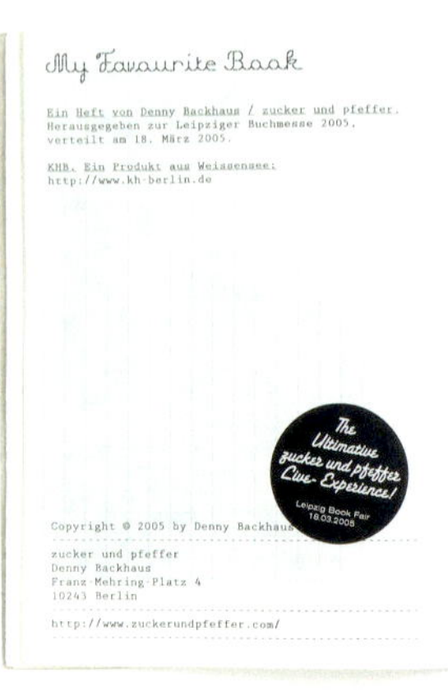

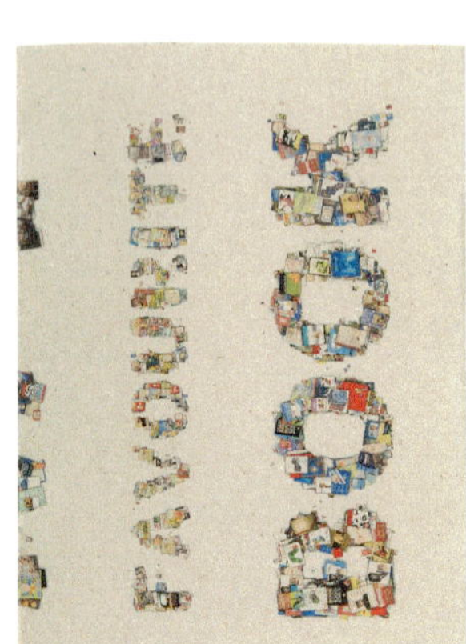

Besides covering all his outgoing communications in a range of 120 different "Zucker & Pfeffer" stickers (amounting to an impressive 64.000 possible permutations), Zucker und Pfeffer's Denny Backhaus loves to explore ever new means of self-promotion.

While his new font and sample book Forêt (available in a limited edition of 10) comes with a personalised button and wrapped in a matching A1 poster, another project, "My Favourite Book", could be seen as a prime example of self-promotion gone wrong – and right in the end. Containing nothing but a list of his friends' favourite books, this quickly compiled volume met with next to no interest at the Leipzig book fair, yet later became a coveted collector's item amongst like-minded designers.

1   Denny Backhaus, Forêt Specimen, cover (folded poster), 154 × 218 mm
    plotter paper 80 g, A0 plotter, 2005
2   Denny Backhaus, Forêt specimen, 154 × 218 mm, Munken Pure 170 g,
    glossy roll offset paper 60 g, laser print, 2005
3   Denny Backhaus, My Favourite Book, 108 × 148 mm, rough sketch paper 120 g,
    at least 15 years old paper 60 g from squared school note book, laser print, 2005
4   Denny Backhaus, Forêt Typeface Poster, 594 × 841 mm, plotter paper 80 g,
    A0 plotter, 2005

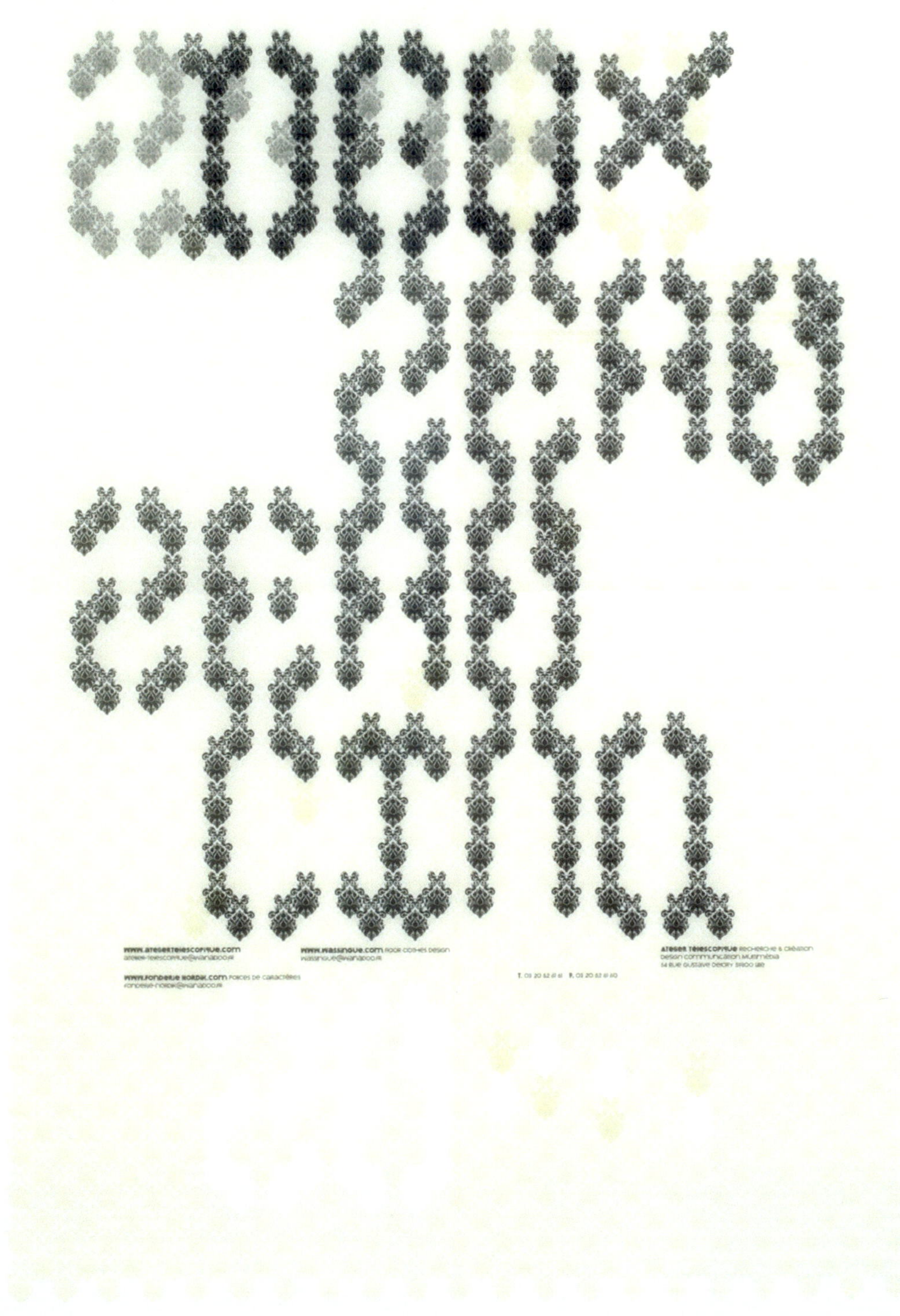

 Atelier Télescopique, 600 x 420 mm, OnionSkin paper, offset printing, 2005

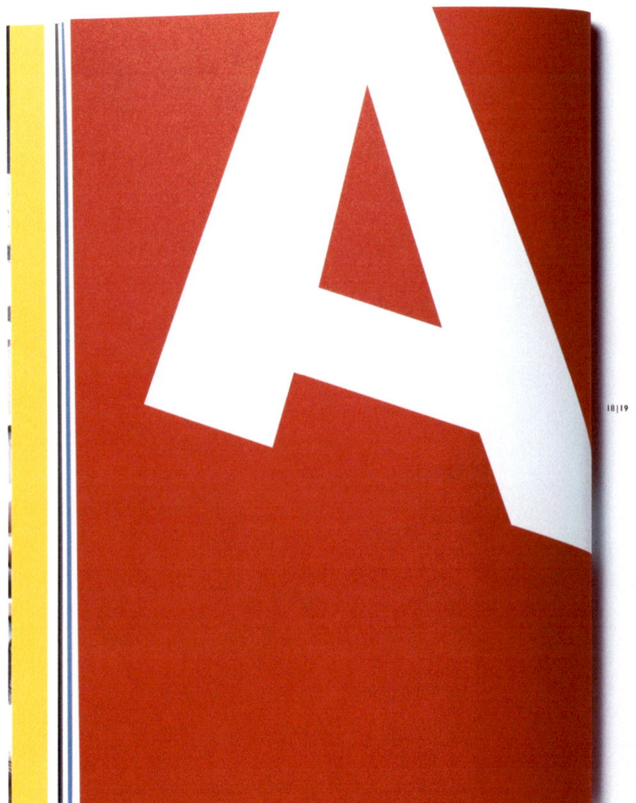

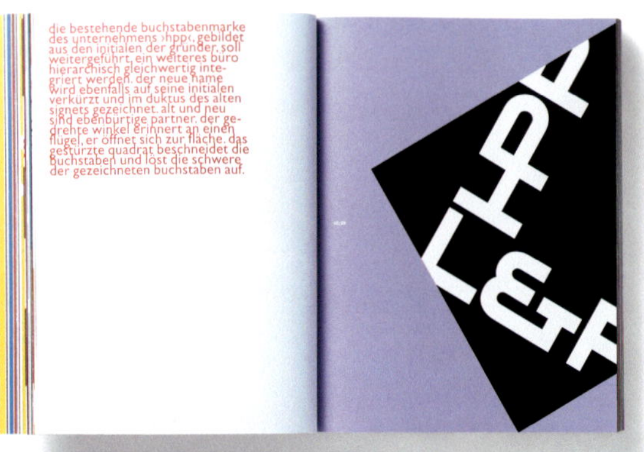

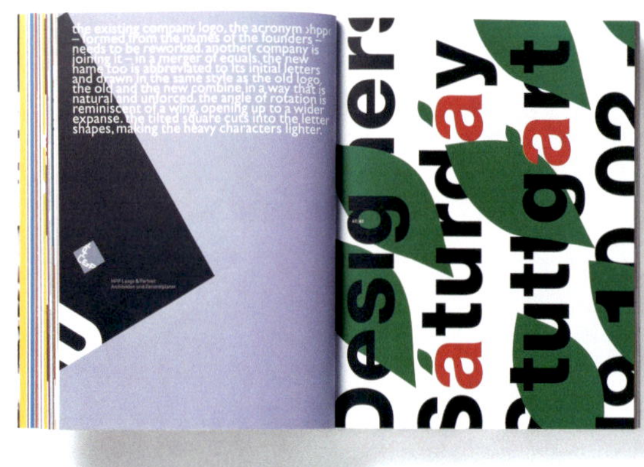

To highlight the wealth of his studio's work, designer Andreas Uebele, of Büro Uebele Visuelle Kommunikation, decided to take the decisive step from straightforward portfolio to fully-fledged design book. His most recent example worthy of any coffee table (Weg Zeichen/My Type of Place) features excellent essays by internal and external experts. Juxtaposing words with great chunks of his inimitable graphic style, "Weg Zeichen" not only signposts the extensive projects and commissions realised by Uebele and his team.

1–3 Büro Uebele visuelle kommunikation / Andreas Uebele, photography: Dirk Altenkirch, Lothar Bertrams, Claudio Hils, Werner Huthmacher, Andreas Keller, Andreas Körner, Christian Richters, Bernhard Widmann, 185 x 240 mm, Samat Römerturm 180/280/150 g, offset printing, 2003

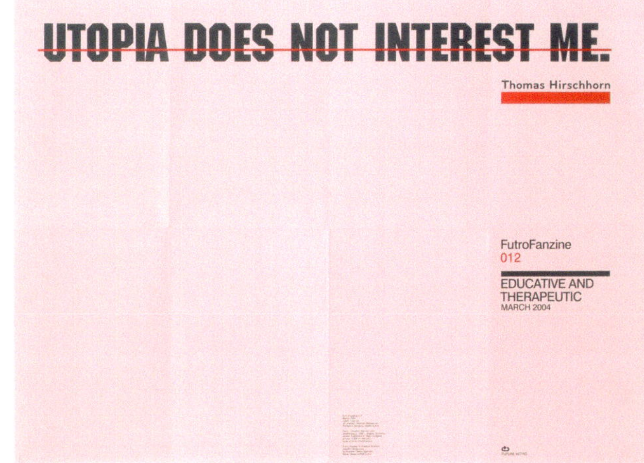

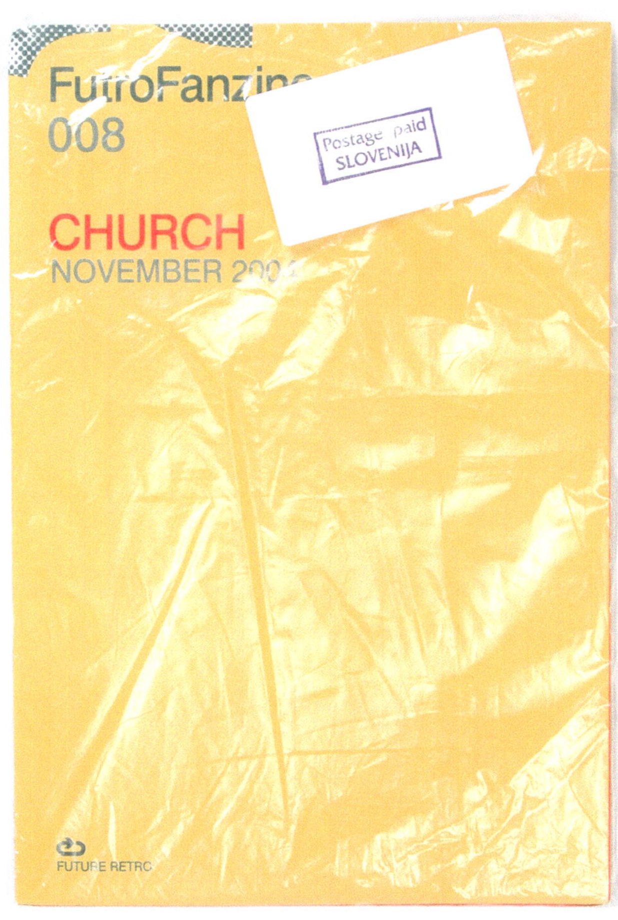

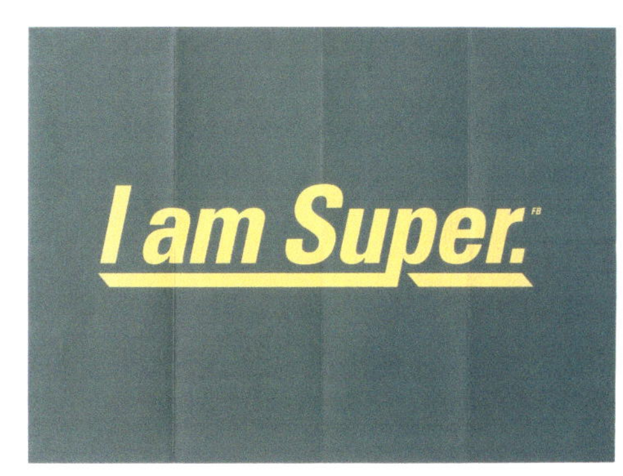

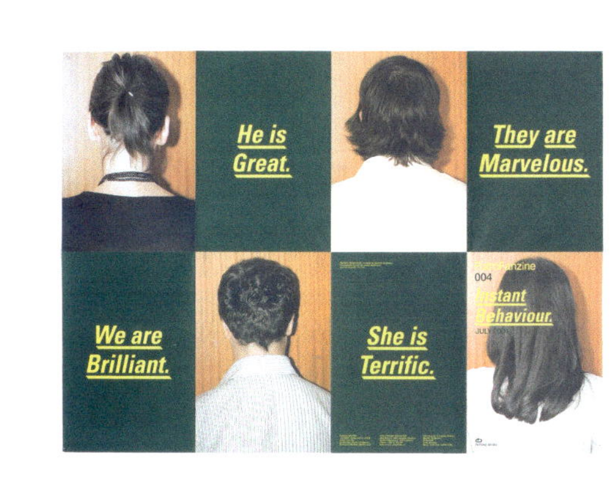

1–5 Futro / Slavimir Stojanovic, Educative And Therapeutic Editor: Ivan Ilic,
460 x 640 mm, Tauro paper 150 g, offset printing, 2004/2005

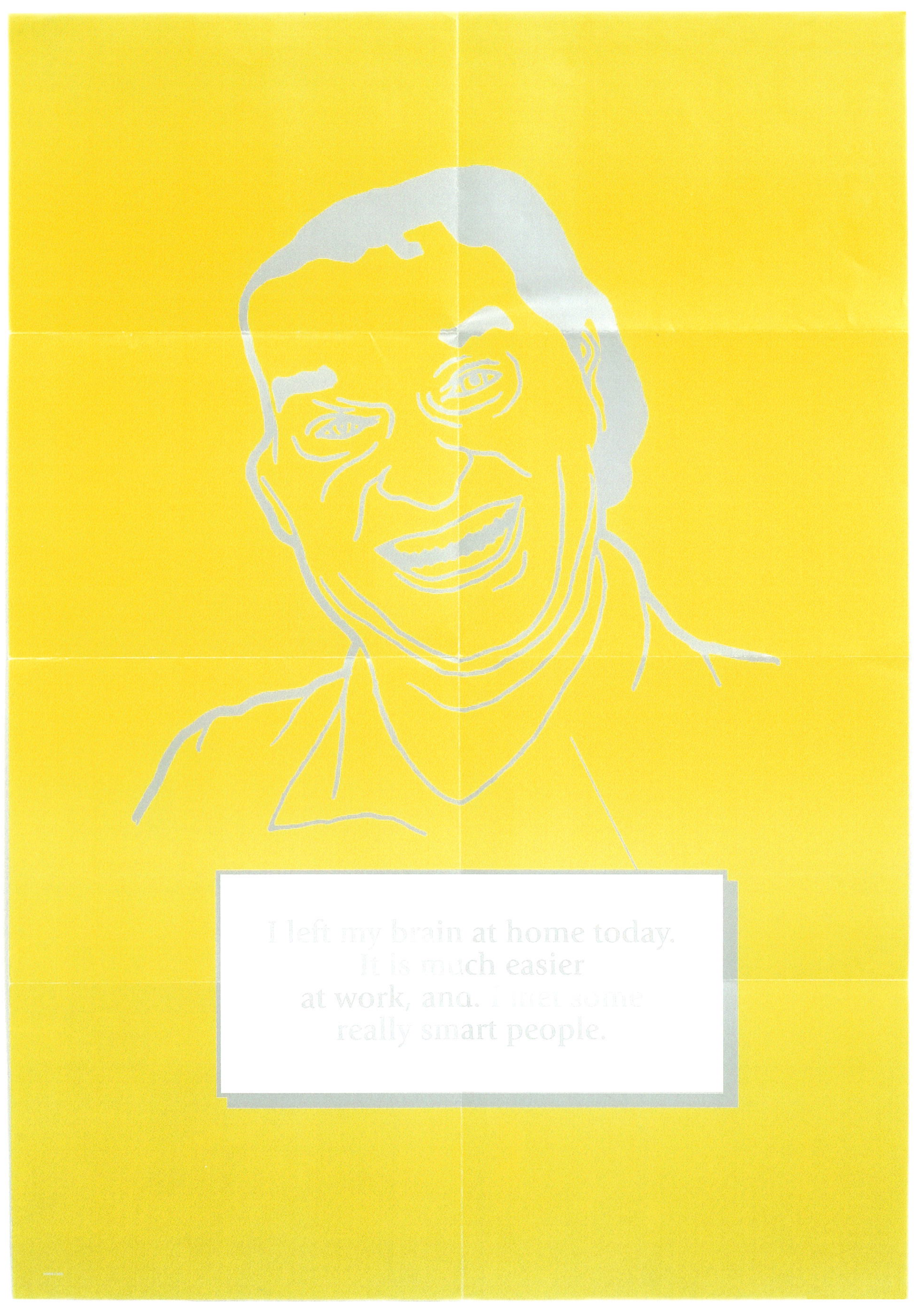

Futro / Slavimir Stojanovic, Stories Editor: Ivan Ilic Stories & Illustrations: Slavimir Stojanovic,
460 x 640 mm, Garda-mat paper 150 g, offset printing, 2004/2005

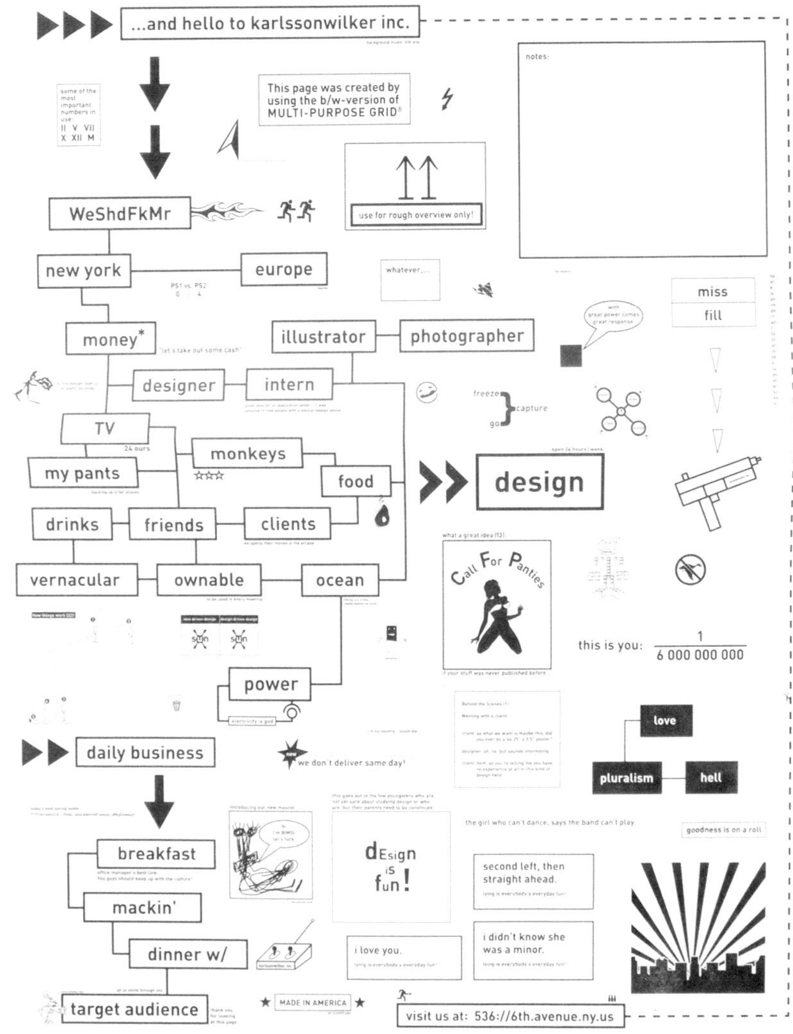

Karlssonwilker Inc., two former Sagmeister acolytes who rattled the design scene with their semi-autobiographical "Tellmewhy: The First 24 Months of a New York Design Company", take a decidedly oblique view on self-promotion. "Welcome to Colour", their latest, slimline giveaway, immediately contradicts its own claim by adopting a monochrome approach. "Well, neither of us can handle more than two colours at the most. In addition, we like the simplicity of b/w, it's all you need to say something anyway – colour is often just used to cover up a lack of variety of thoughts.'
Originally created for the studio's opening announcement, this newspaper-style publication does not feature any tangible work examples, but instead chooses to highlight karlssonwilker's artful sense of humour and playful abstraction.

Karlssonwilker Inc. / Jan Wilker & Hjalti Karlsson, 297 x 420 mm, newsprint, 2003

Interview:
The Remingtons

Swiss designers Ludovic Balland and Jonas Vögeli aka The Remingtons love to contrast the intricacy of their work (for a. o. Weltwoche, Mini Cooper, Museum für Gestaltung Zürich and Warner Music) with ultra-simple and almost naïve promotional measures. Introducing a little something of themselves into anything from calling cards to catalogues, any self-promotional material thus becomes a straightforward introduction to the duo.

What is your general take on self-representation?

Anything that evokes and provokes memories tends to be effective. To us, any method of self-promotion only becomes meaningful when it serves an alibi function! Representation of the self is the prime motivation behind taking a picture or looking at it. Good examples are images that become meaningful evidence, and this happens when you are at the right place, at the right time, with the right person.

To an outsider, you seem to have taken the idea of self-promotion a decisive step further – you literally use your own image to convey an image. How did you arrive at this idea?

It all started with a visit to Berlin – we simply wanted to preserve some memories and the camera was our constant travelling companion. Those pictures were the result of a spontaneous idea and situation and later found their way into our promotional campaigns.
Our set of perforated business cards, for example, shows us on our travels, in front of the office or in the car, while our promotional booklet features a collection of pictures of us with our clients. In future, we plan to sneak in as extras in a number of different situations.

Many of these images look like happy-
go-lucky, spontaneous tourist snapshots
– both of you always in view and looking
straight at the camera. Why this obsession
with showing your faces? Is this a matter
of vanity or exalted self-importance?

On the contrary, we consider all of these
images evidence of actual (hi)stories and
situations we have experienced. They are
all about capturing an anecdote, not in the
least about ourselves.
All pictures are posed and carry some very
fond memories of specific clients and
places.

In addition, the "naivety" of the portrayal
is emphasised by a photographic style
and colouring reminiscent of postcards
from the 50s to 70s. How do you convince
potential clients to agree to your style? Do
you use your promotional materials as a
means to provoke or filter out the "right",
open-minded clients?

B/W images are cheaper to print than
coloured ones! To convince means to sell
– everyone has their own strategy! And
naturally, the overall concept is meant to
challenge conventions.
The reactions we get from potential clients
are usually great. Once people have seen
our business cards, they expect a real experience when they finally meet us!

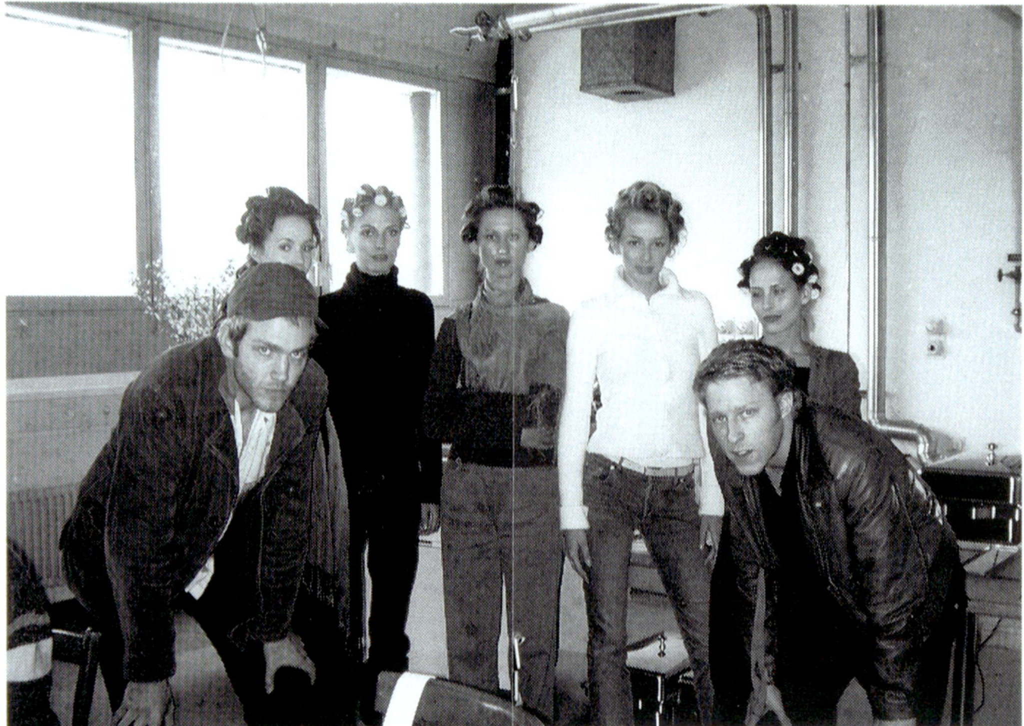

02.05.2003
Quer Fashion-Lounge in Zürich.

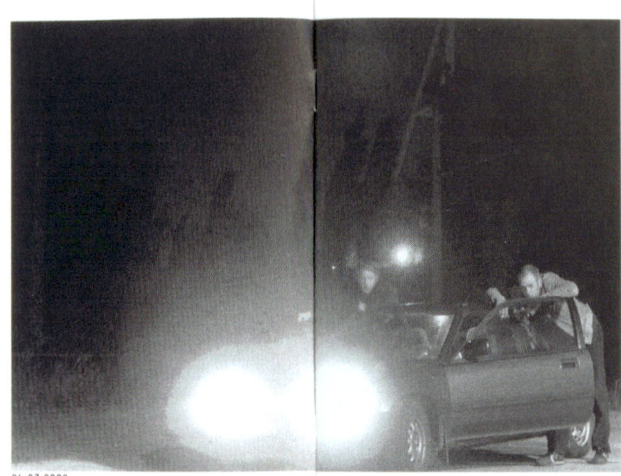

24.07.2002
Berlin, um Mitternacht beim Mauer-Park.

N° 1 – 12.10.03
CHF : 5.00

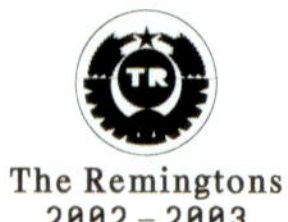

The Remingtons
2002 – 2003

1–3   The Remingtons / Balland and Vögeli,
        80 x 142 mm, Alpanova Paper , silk-screen printing, 2004

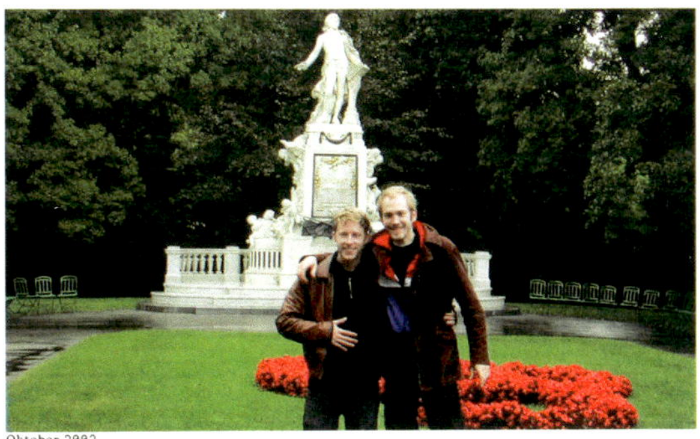

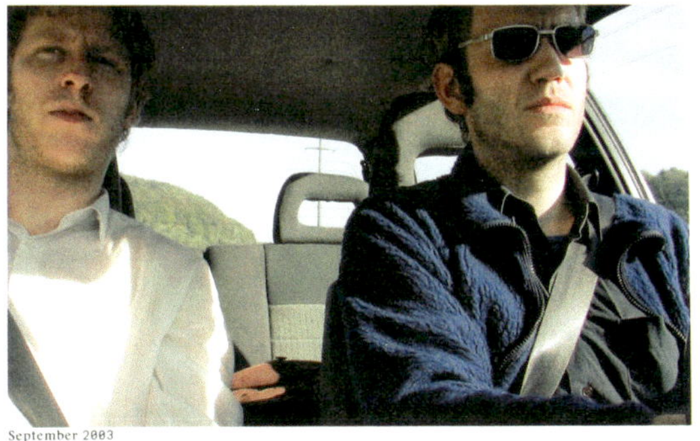

The Remingtons

Ludovic Balland & Jonas Vögeli
Hafenstrasse 25
CH-4019 Basel
T : +41 61 631 34 45   F : +41 61 631 34 46
contact@theremingtons.ch

The Remingtons

Ludovic Balland & Jonas Vögeli
Hafenstrasse 25
CH-4019 Basel
T : +41 61 631 34 45   F : +41 61 631 34 46
contact@theremingtons.ch

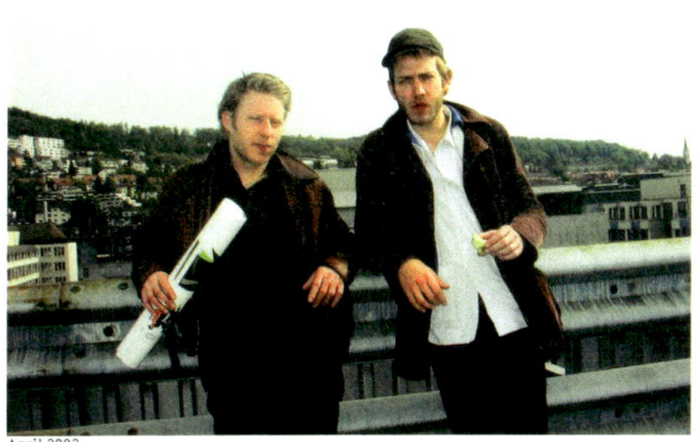

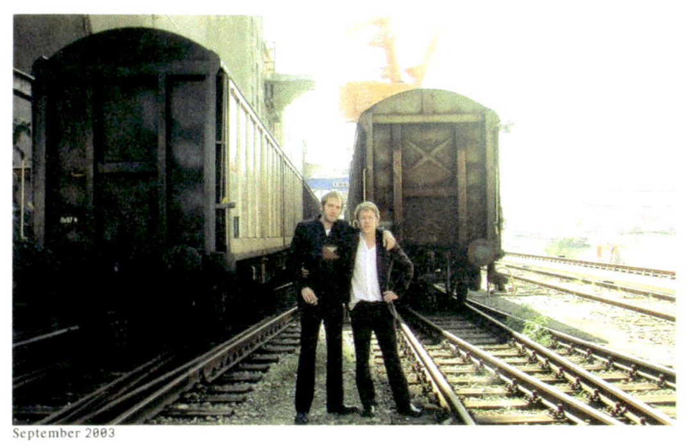

   1–4   The Remingtons / Balland and Vögeli, chromo cardboard, offset printing, 2004

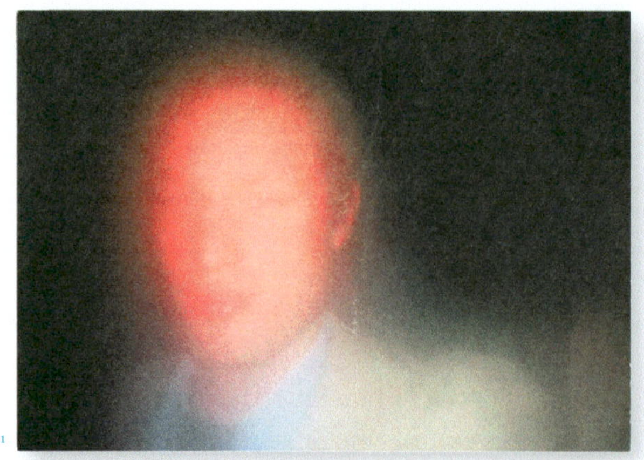

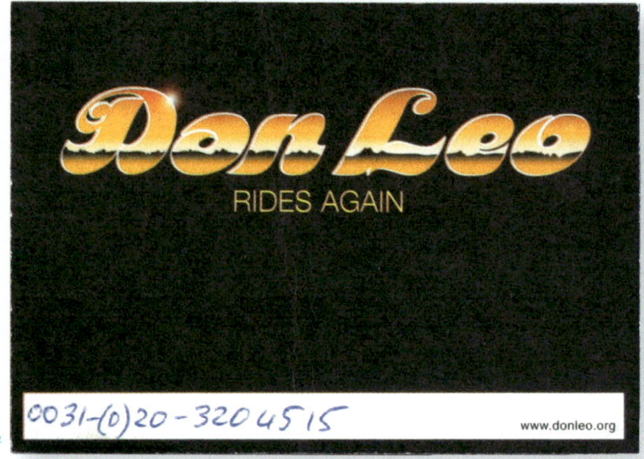

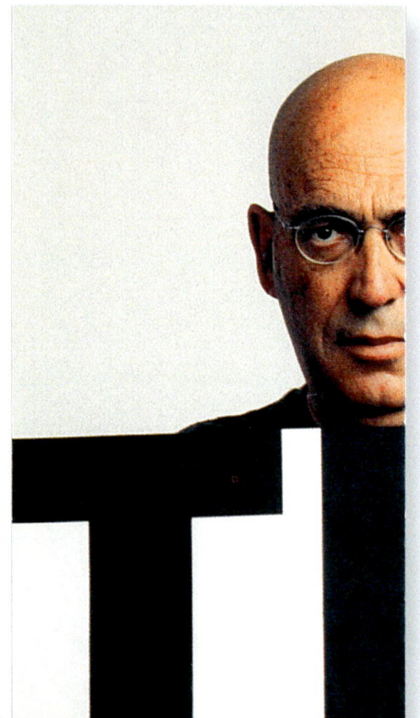

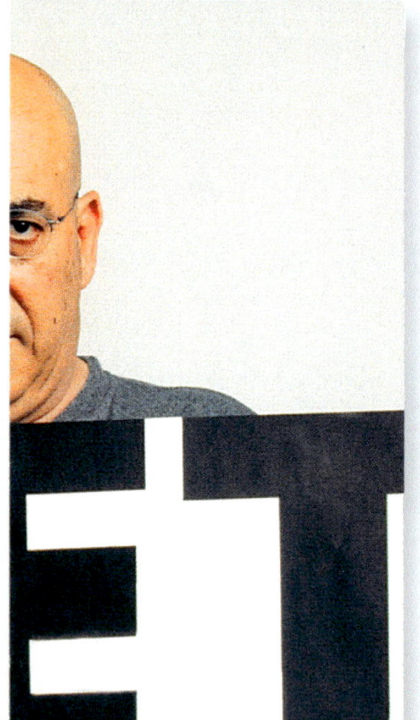

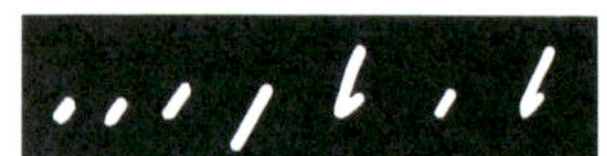

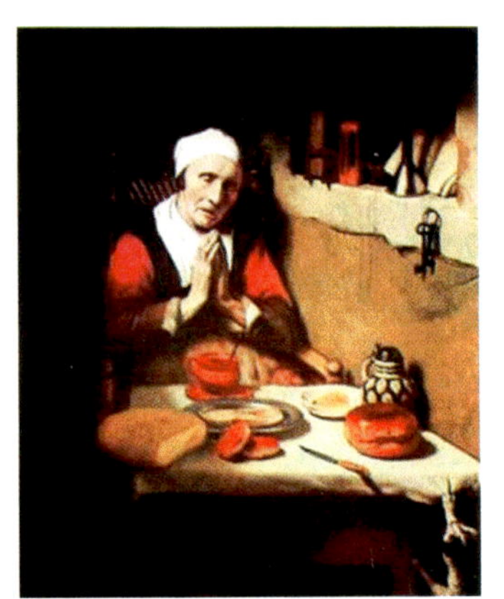

1–2   DonLeo / DonLeo and Leonard van Munster, paper 350 g, offset printing, 2001
3–5   David Tartakover, photography: Gadi Dagon, coated paper 220 g, offset printing, 2000
6–7   Goodwill / Will Holder, paper, offset printing, 2000

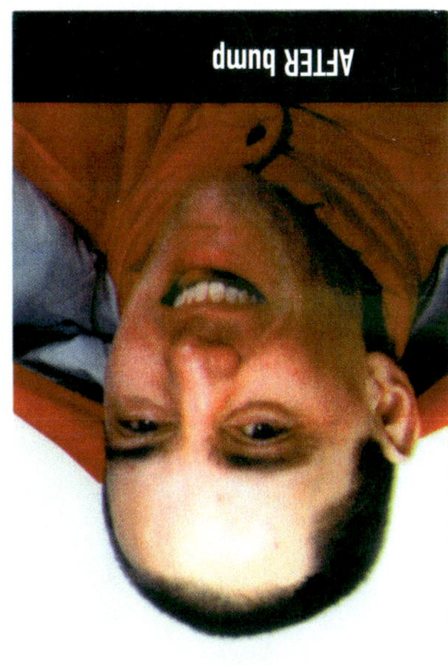

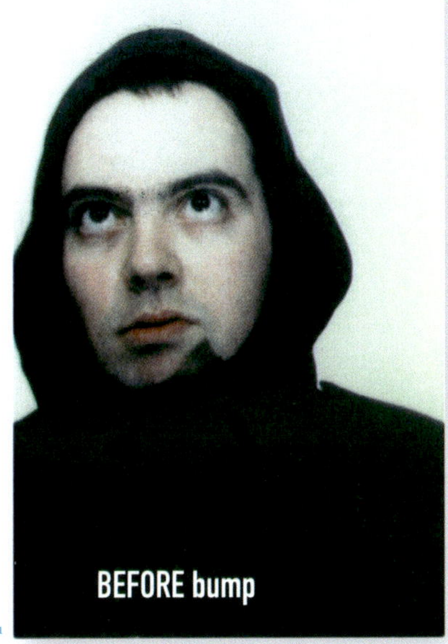

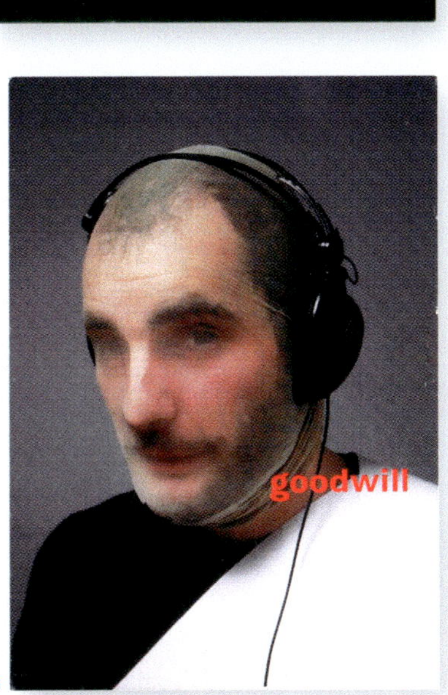

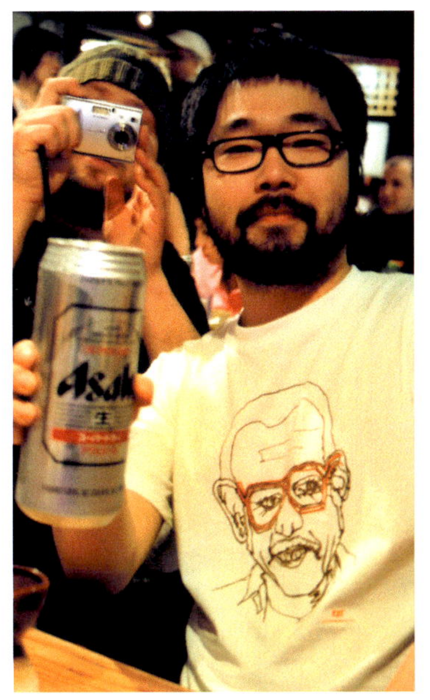

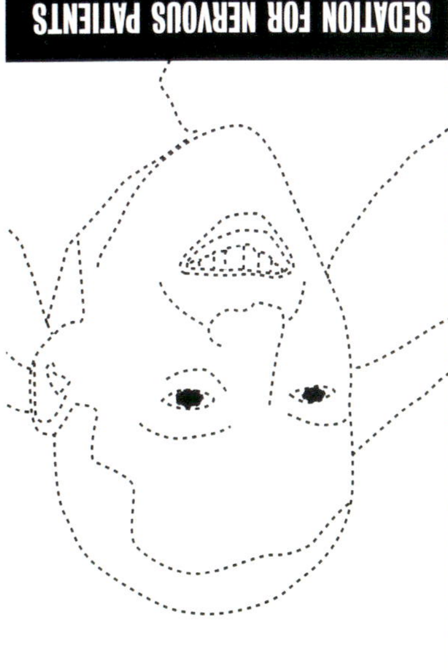

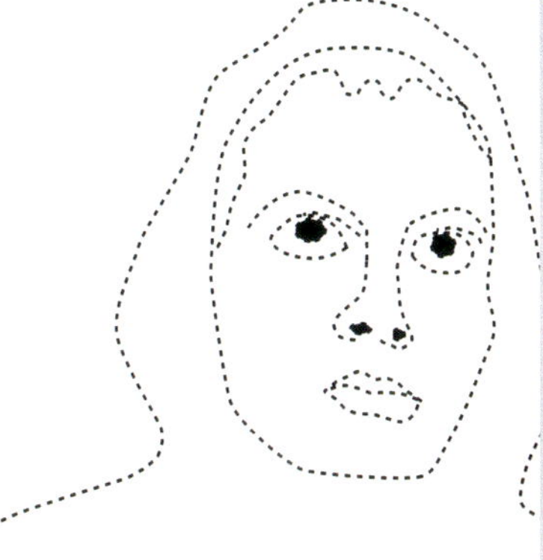

Ohyun Kwon
Bismarkstraße 38
10627 Berlin
Tel ++49.30.30604142
Mobil ++49.177.2766846
ohyun@gmx.de
www.ohyun.de

1–2   Bump Design / Mike Watson, photography: Luke Kirwan,
      paper GSM art board 150 g, offset printing, 2002
3–4   Ohyun Kwon, photography: Flexn, paper, offset printing, 2005
5   Goodwill / Will Holder, paper, offset printing, 2000

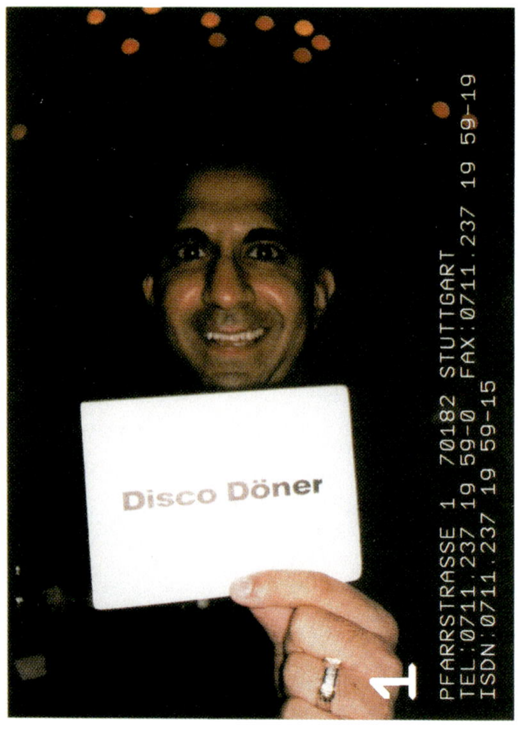

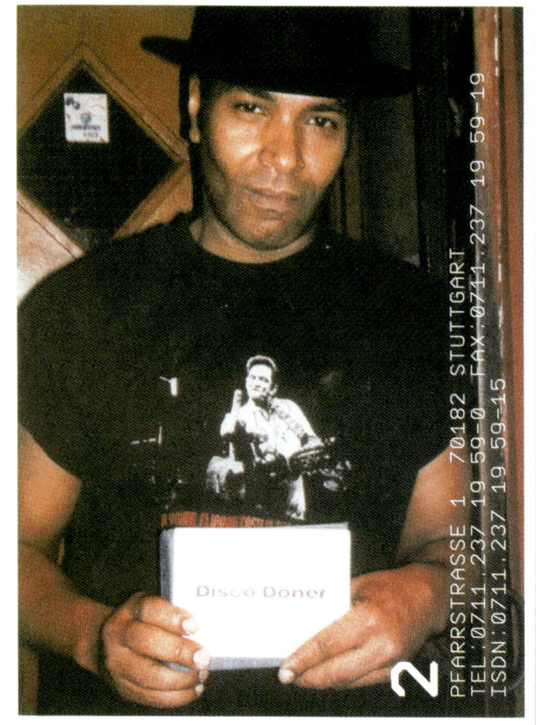

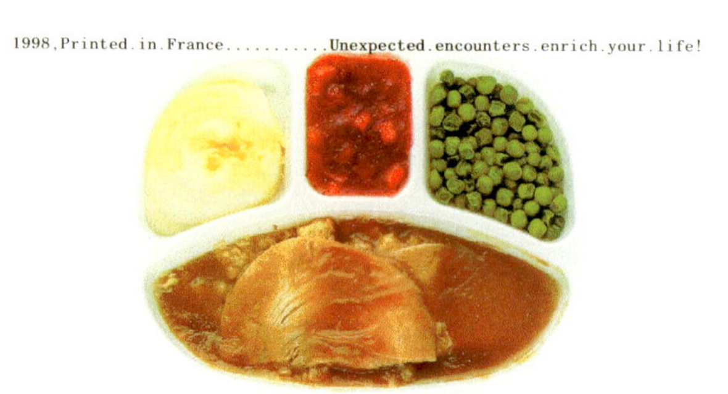

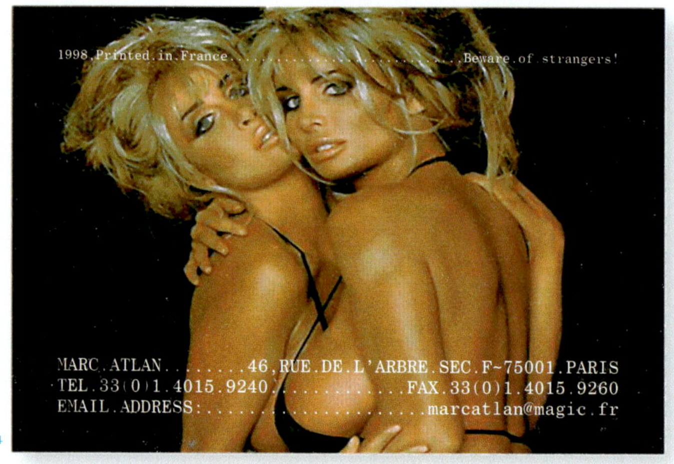

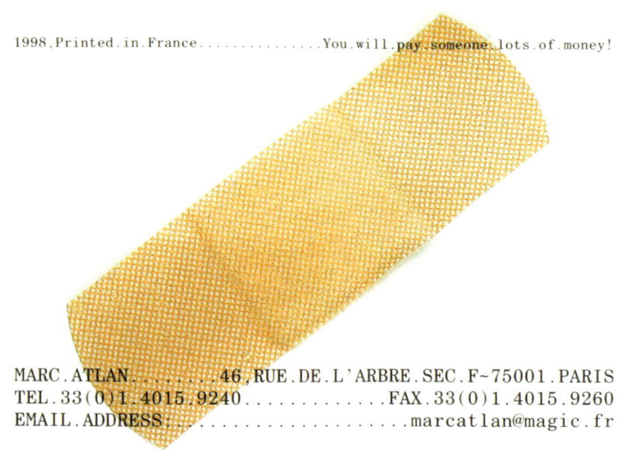

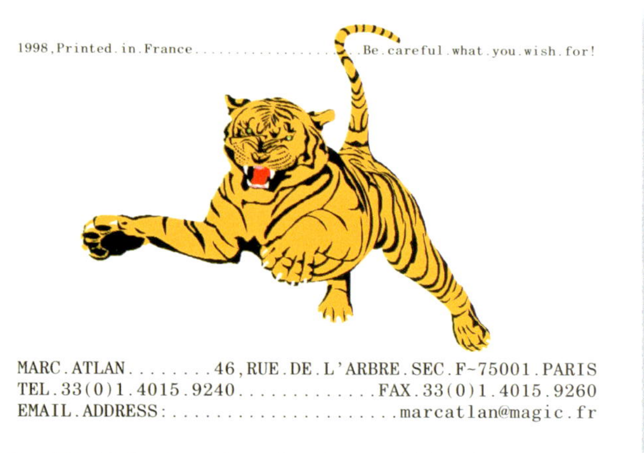

1–2 Discodoener / Pit Lederle, offset paper, offset printing, 2003
3–6 Marc Atlan, adhesive paper, offset printing, 1998

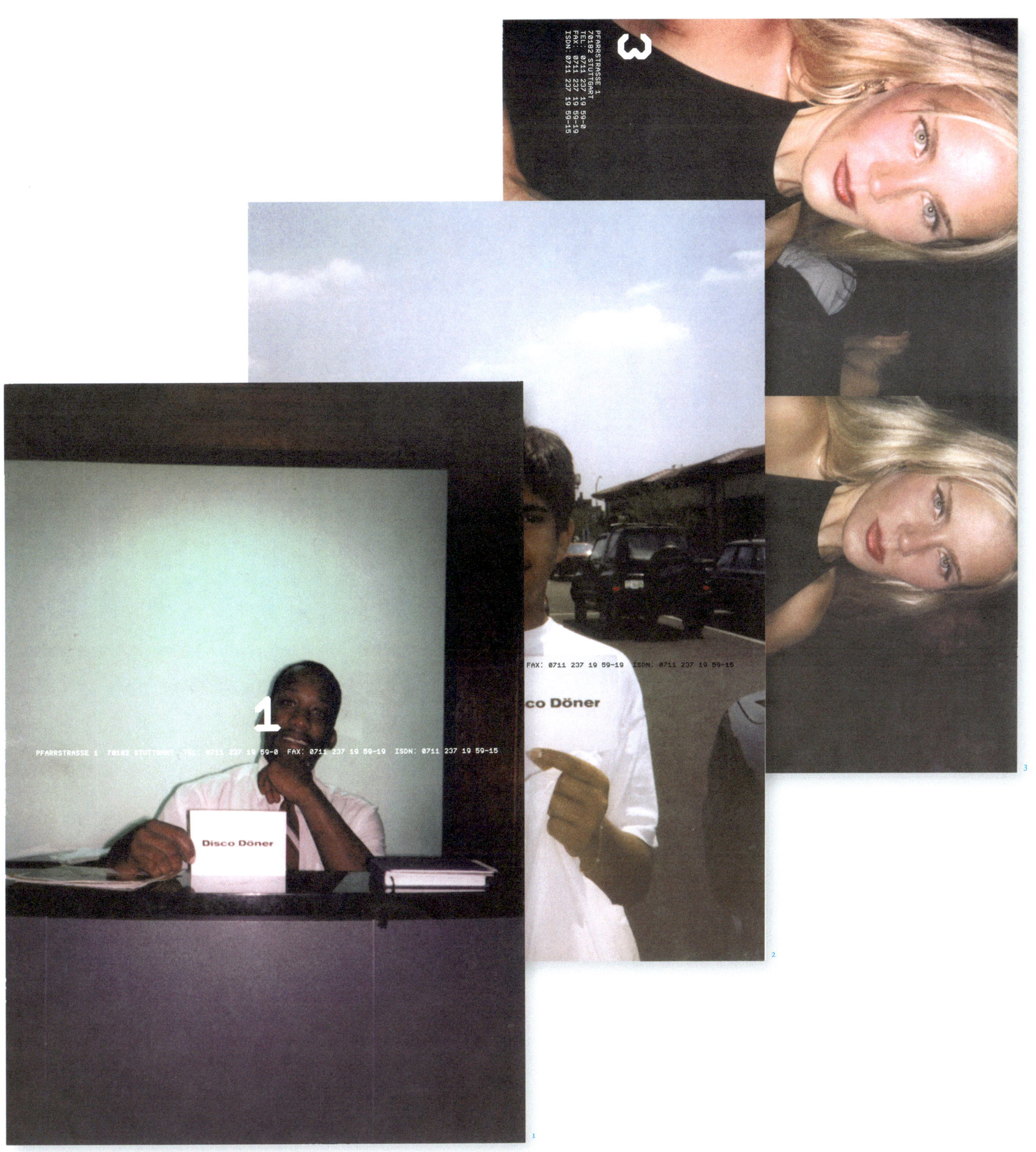

    1–3   Discodoener / Pit Lederle, offset paper, offset printing, 2003

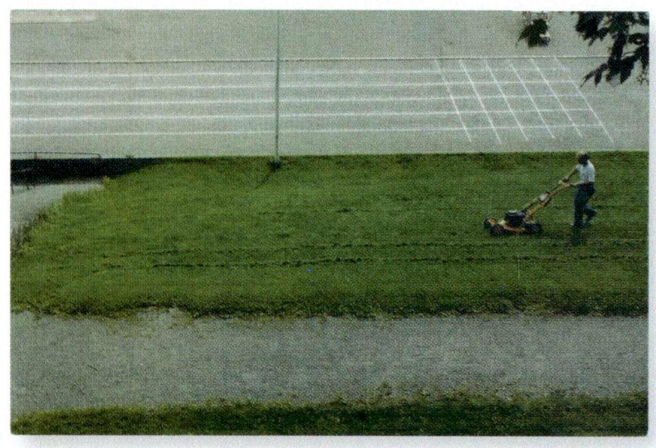

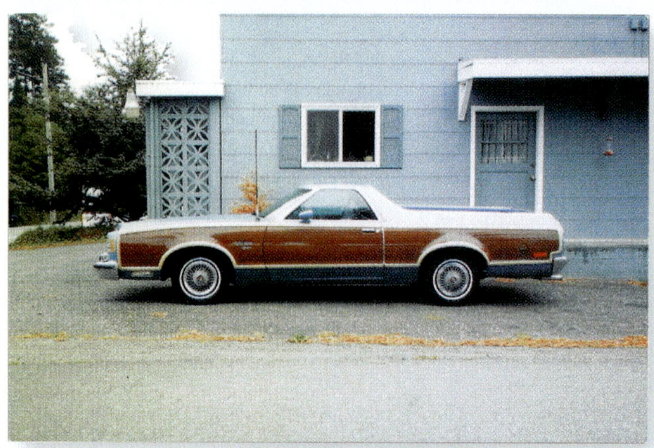

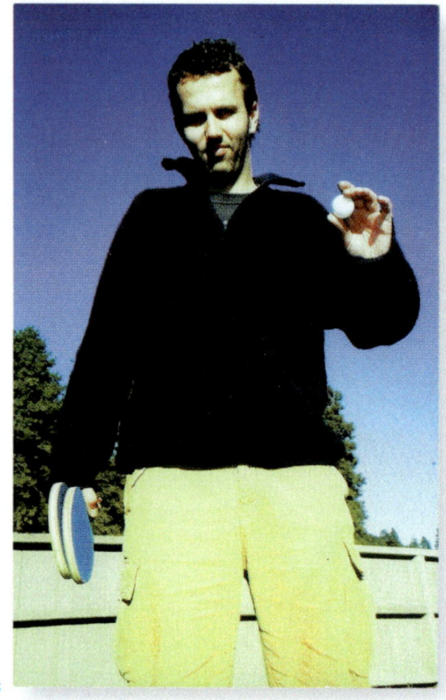

1–6   Brighten the Corners / Frank Philippin, offset printing, 1999

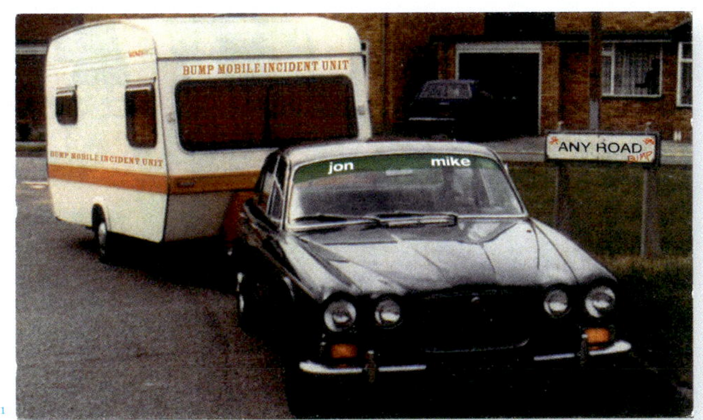

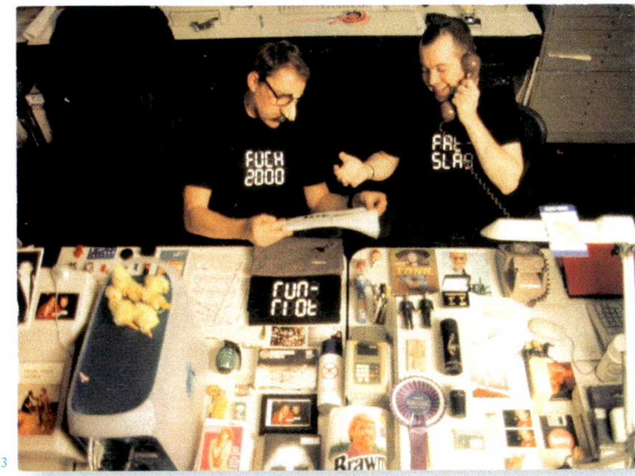

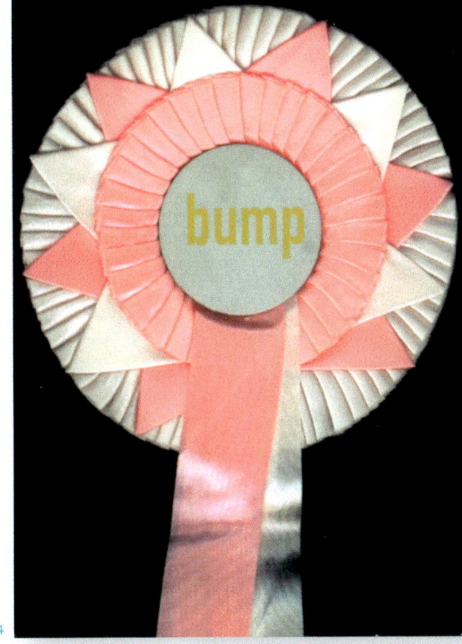

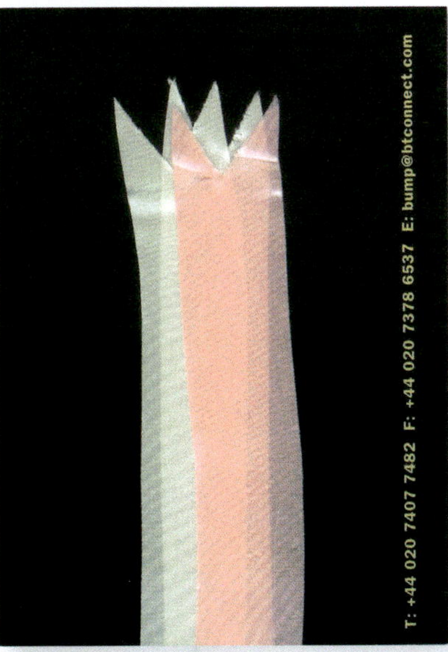

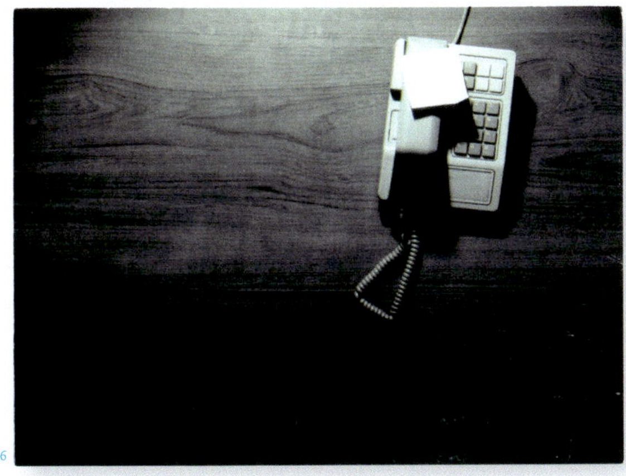

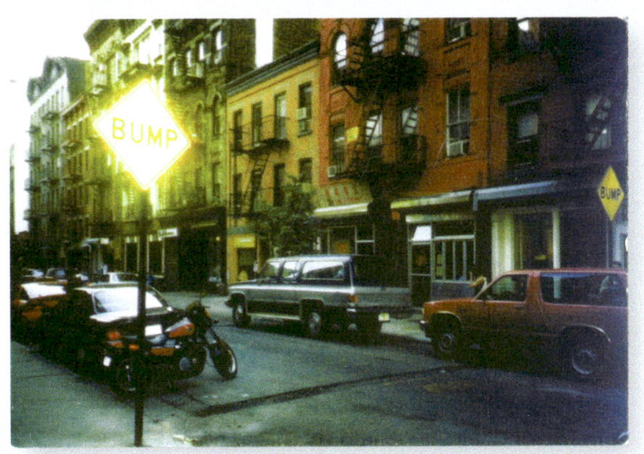

1–2   Bump Design / Jon Morgan, photography: unknown, art board 150 g, offset printing, 2002,
3   Bump Design / Jon Morgan, photography: Oliver Michaels, art board 150 g, offset printing, 2001
4–5   Bump Design / Mike Watson, photography: George Carter, Reeves 180 g, offset printing, 1999
6   Bump Design / Jon Morgan, photography: Oliver Michaels, art board 150 g, offset printing 1c, 2004
7   Bump Design / Jon Morgan, art board 150 g, offset printing, 2004

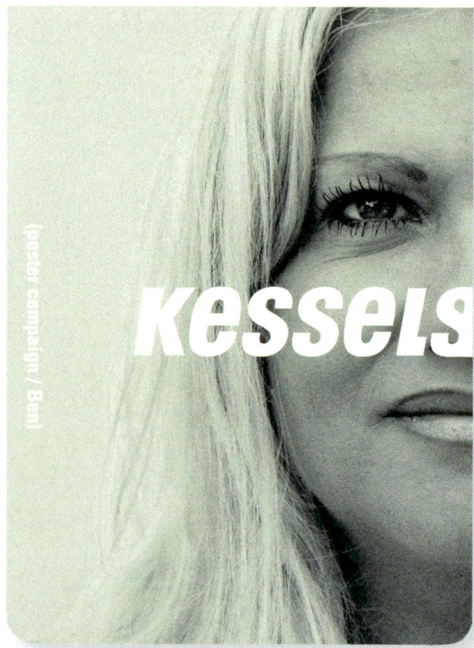

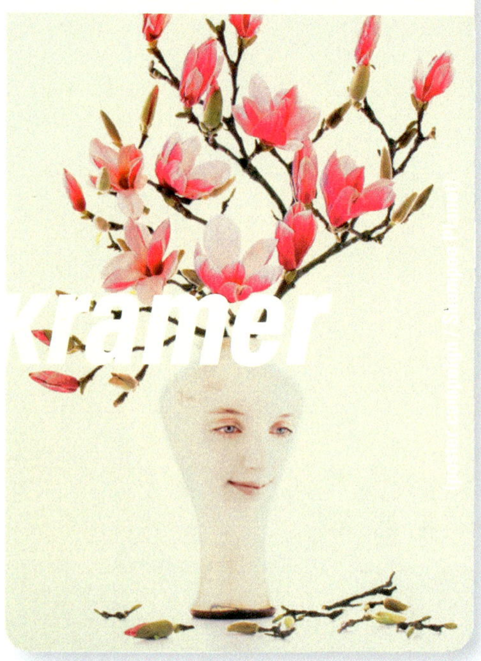

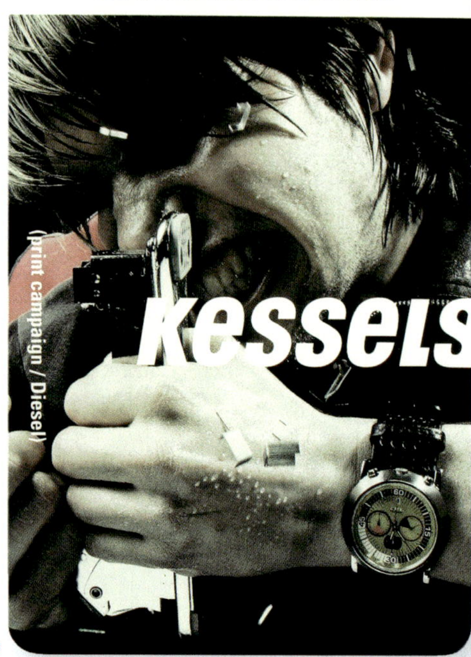

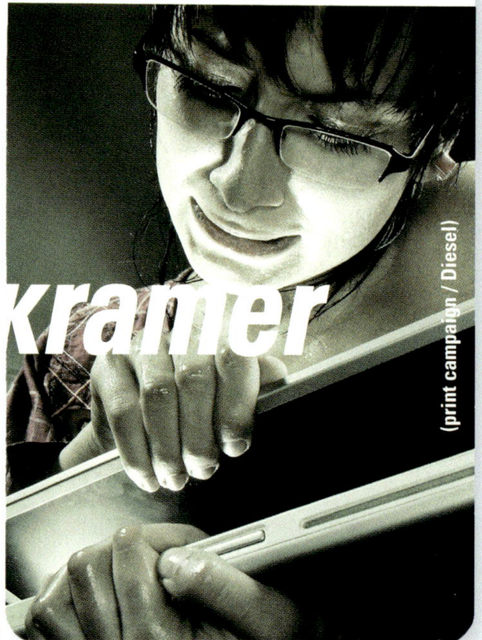

1–4   KesselsKramer, offset printing

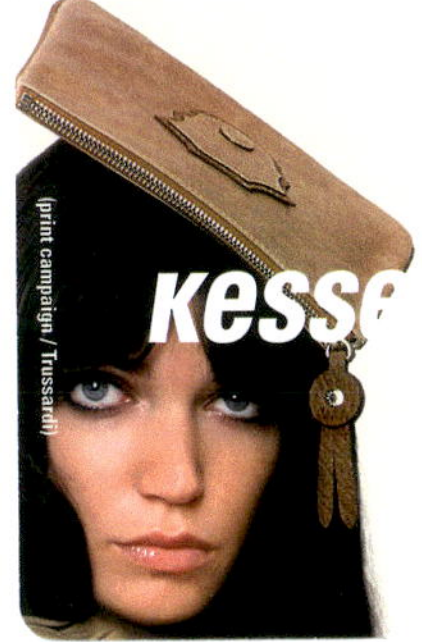

lauriergracht 39 / p.o.box 10007 /
1001 ea amsterdam / the netherlands
phone +31(0)20 5301060 /
fax +31(0)20 5301061 / church@kesselskramer.com
(print campaign / Trussardi)
kesse kramer

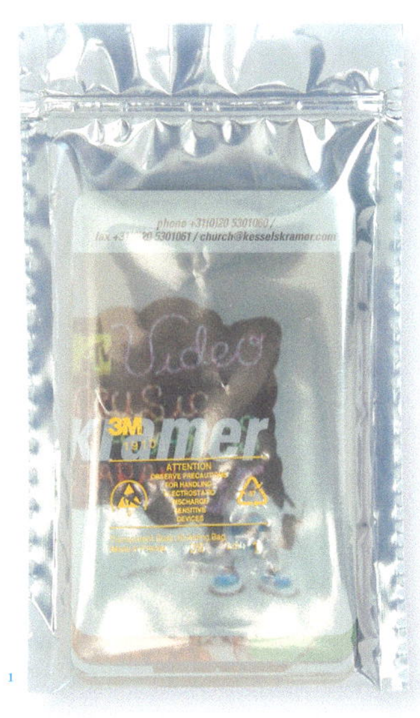

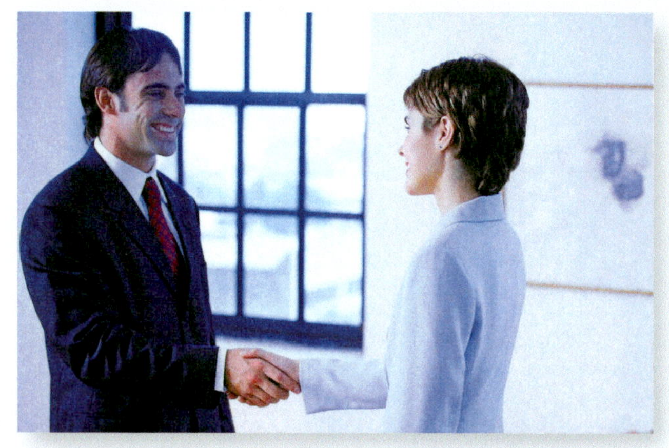

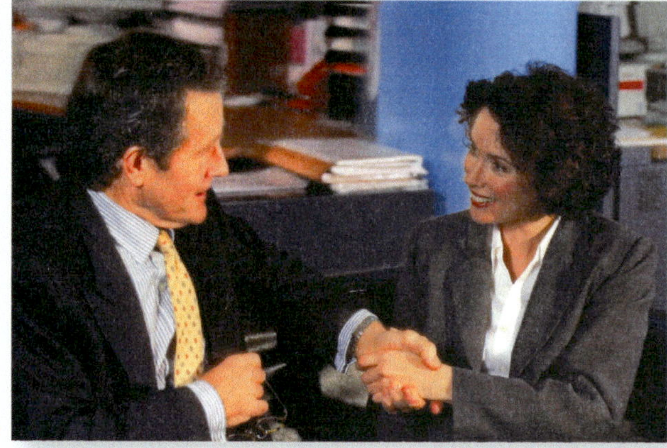

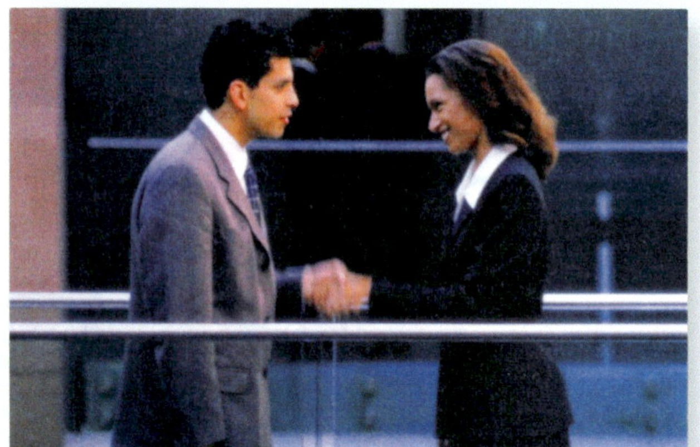

Daniel Eatock
Head of Design Partner

Office +44 (0)20 7012 6000
Mobile +44 (0)7903 869 248
Email daniel.eatock@boymeetsgirl.sj.com

boymeetsgirl S&J
Fourth Floor
159-173 St John Street
London EC1V 4RS

www.boymeetsgirl.sj.com

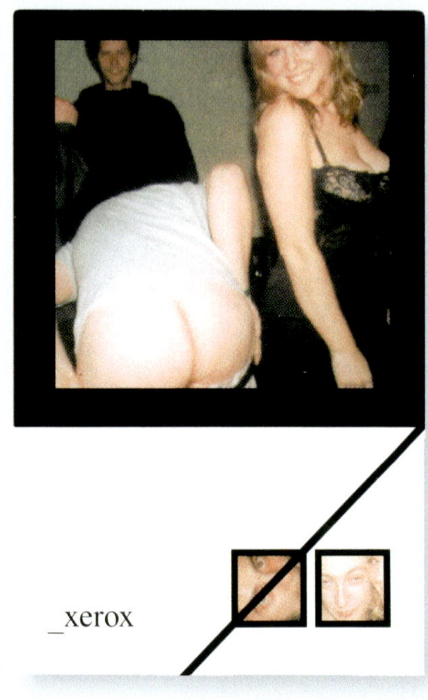

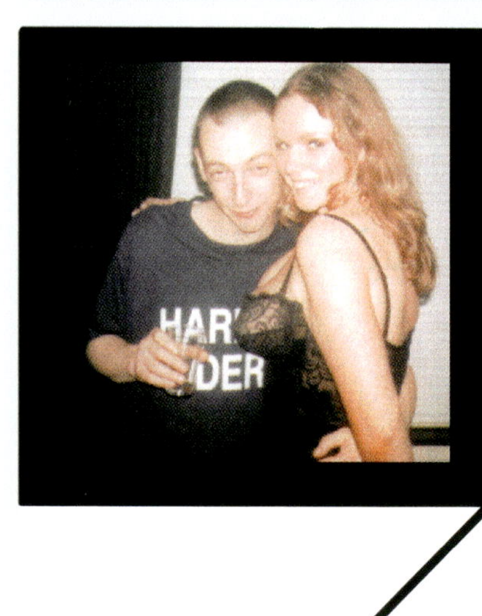

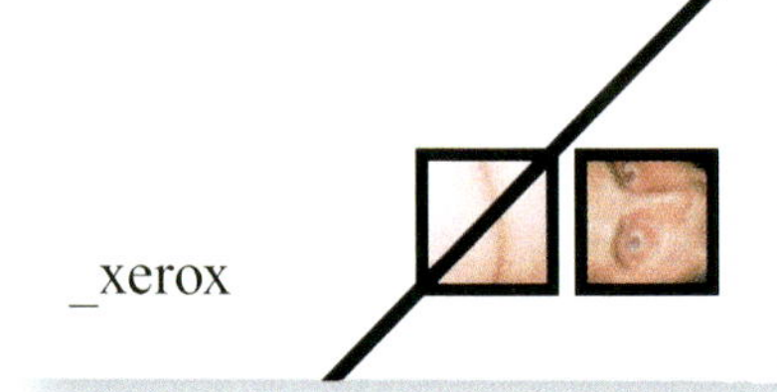

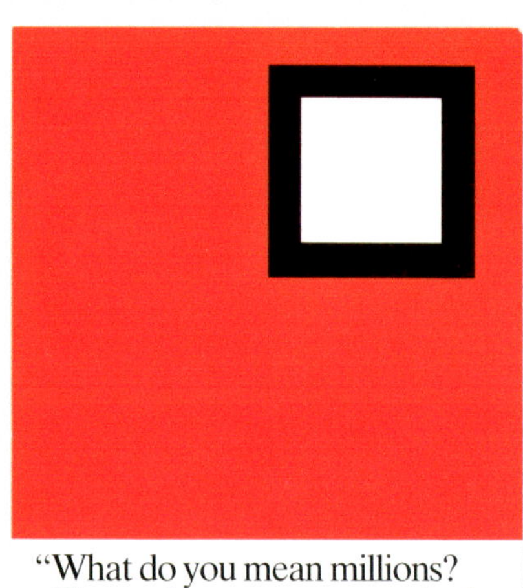

1–4   Daniel Eatock, offset printing, 2004
5–7   Goodwill / Will Holder, offset printing, 2000

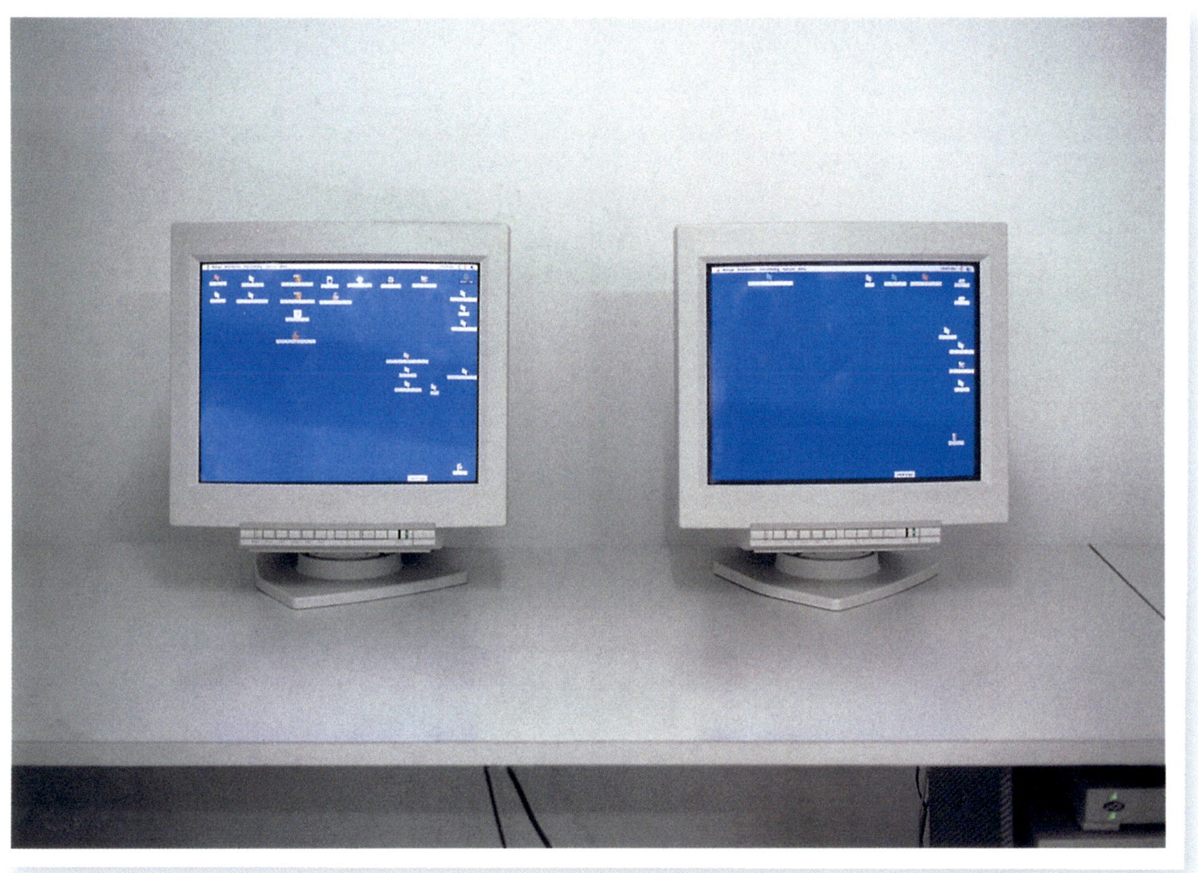

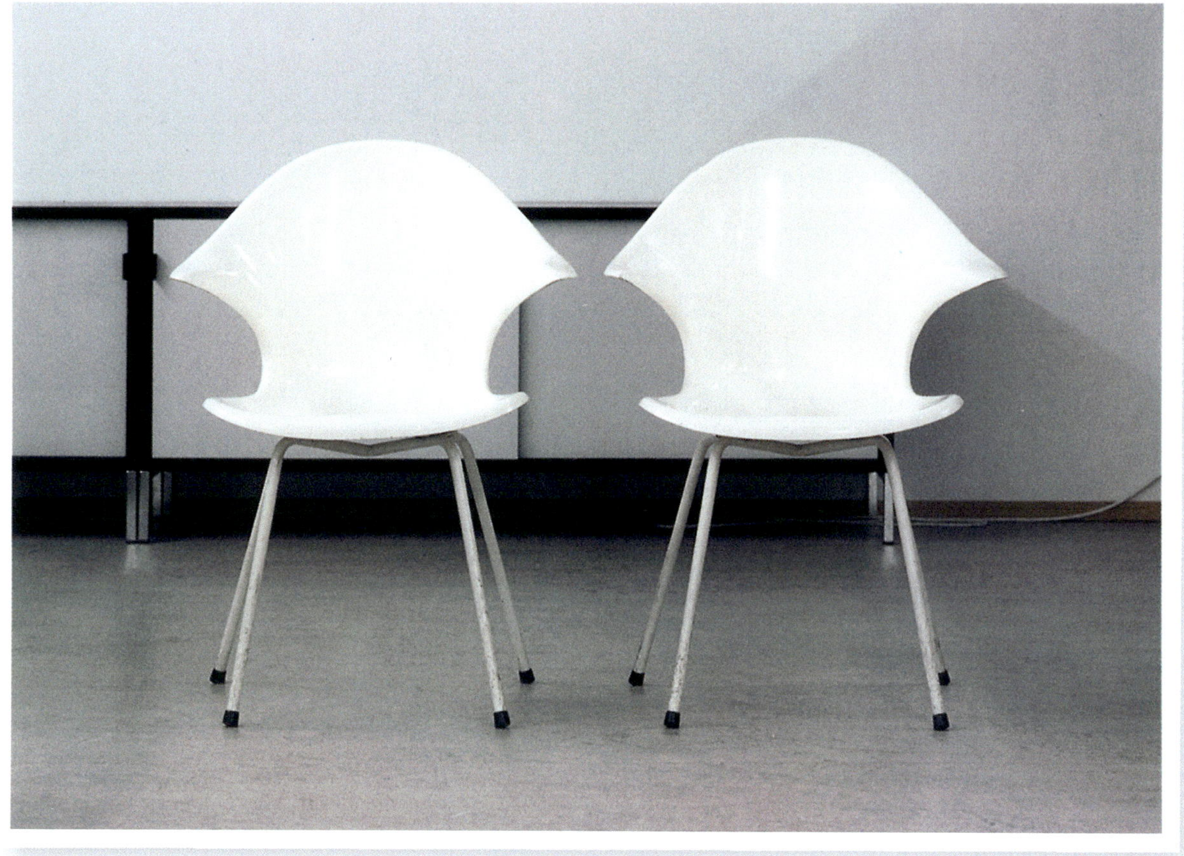

  1–2   Neeser & Müller, photography: Neeser & Müller, Invercote 300 g, offset printing, 1999

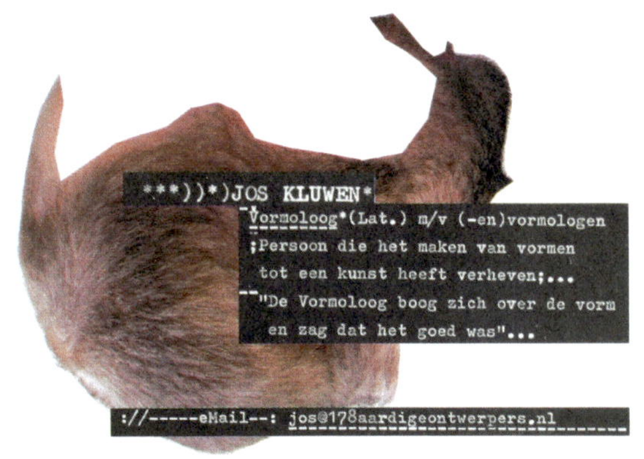

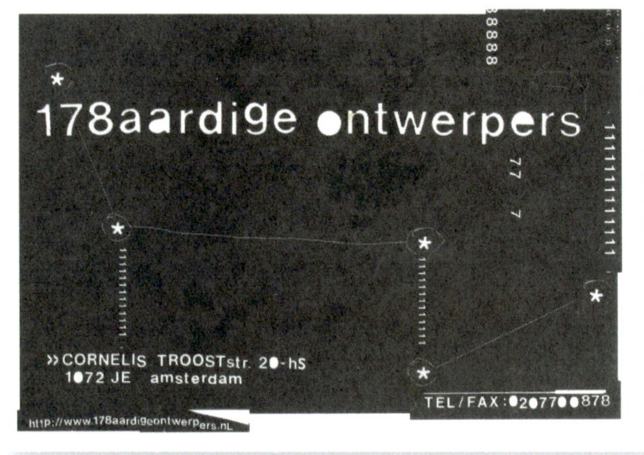

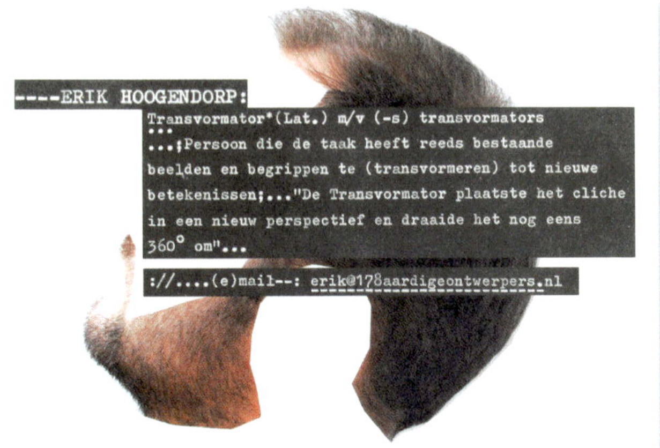

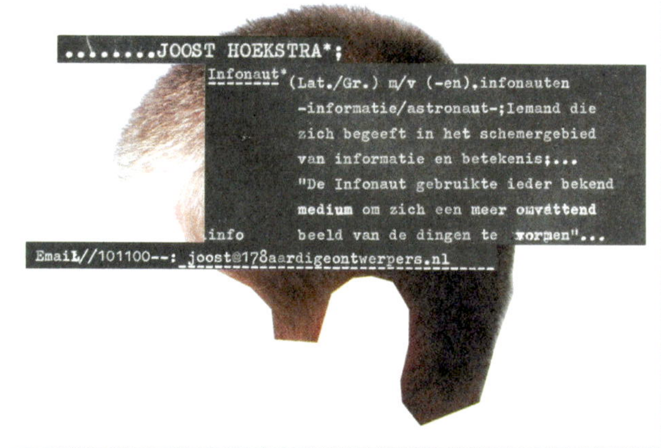

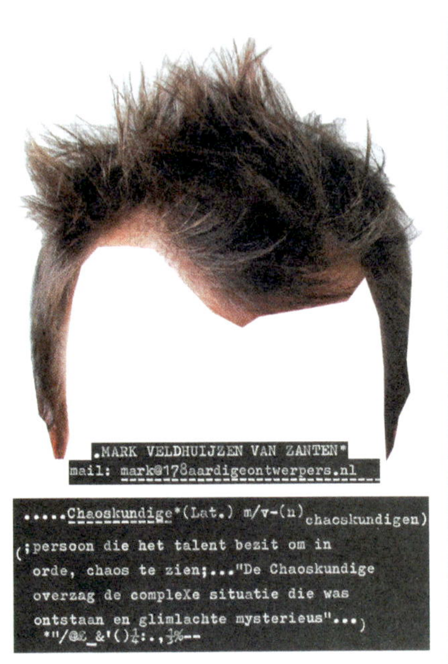

1–5   178 Aardige Ontwerpers, paper, offset printing, 2001

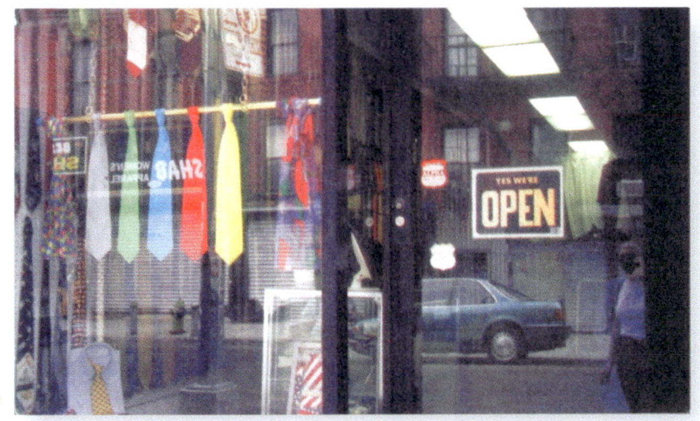

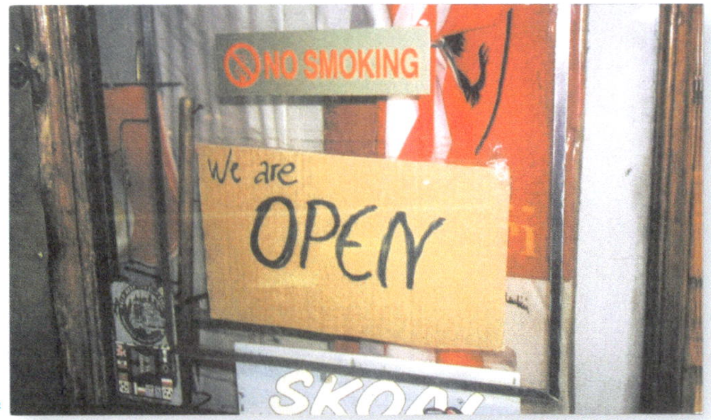

open: a design studio

180 varick street, 8th floor
new york ny 10014 usa
phone +1 212 645 5633
fax +1 212 645 8164
www.notclosed.com

mixing form + content
in two, three
and four dimensions

Scott Stowell · scott@notclosed.com

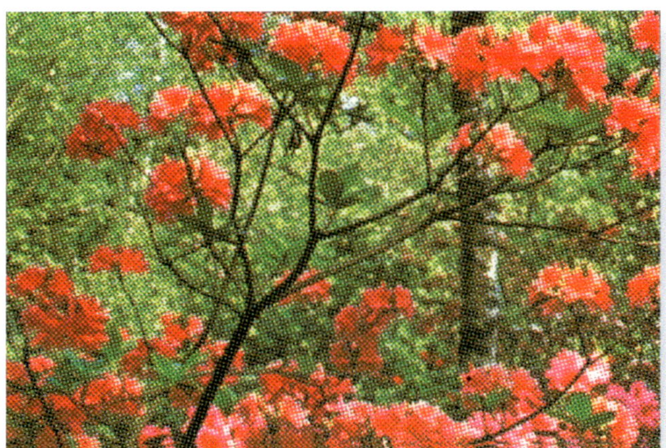

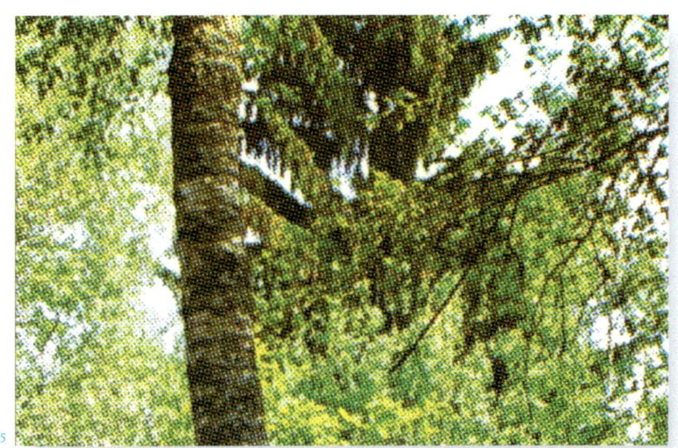

1–3   Open / Scott Stowell, photography: Susan Barber, french construction recycled white cover,
       offset printing 4/1 c, 1999
4–6   1Kilo, self-adhesive foil on plastic, laser copy, 2002

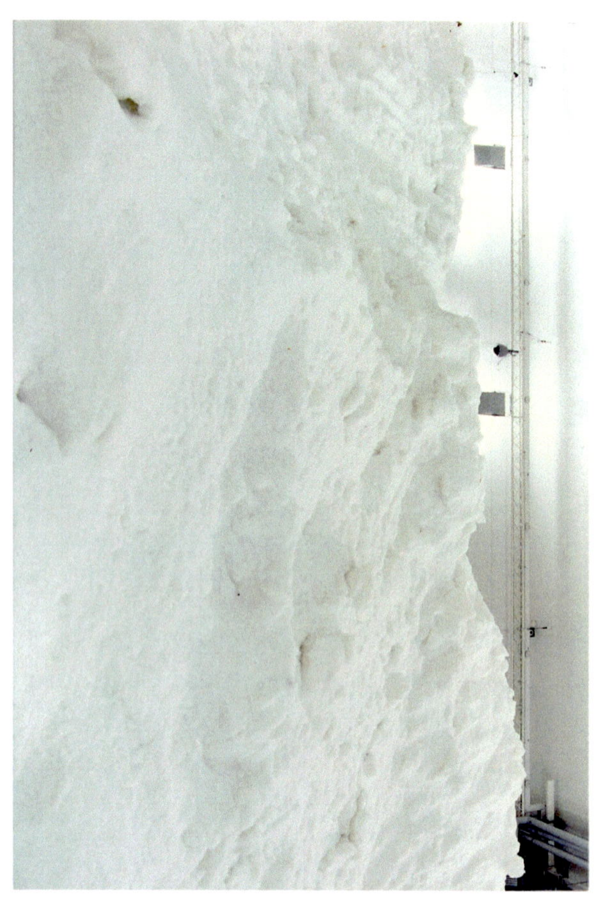

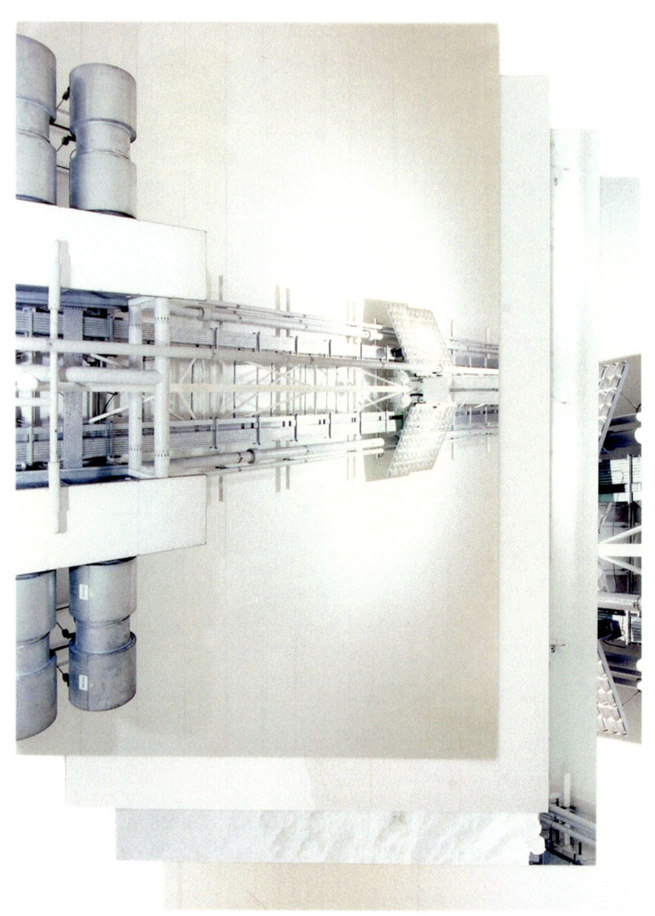

1–2   Mode / Ian Styles, Phil Costin, Darrell Gibbons,
        Artifical Christmas by Mode, 4 x A5 cards plus sleeve,
        Silk 350 g, offset printing plus spot varnish, 2003

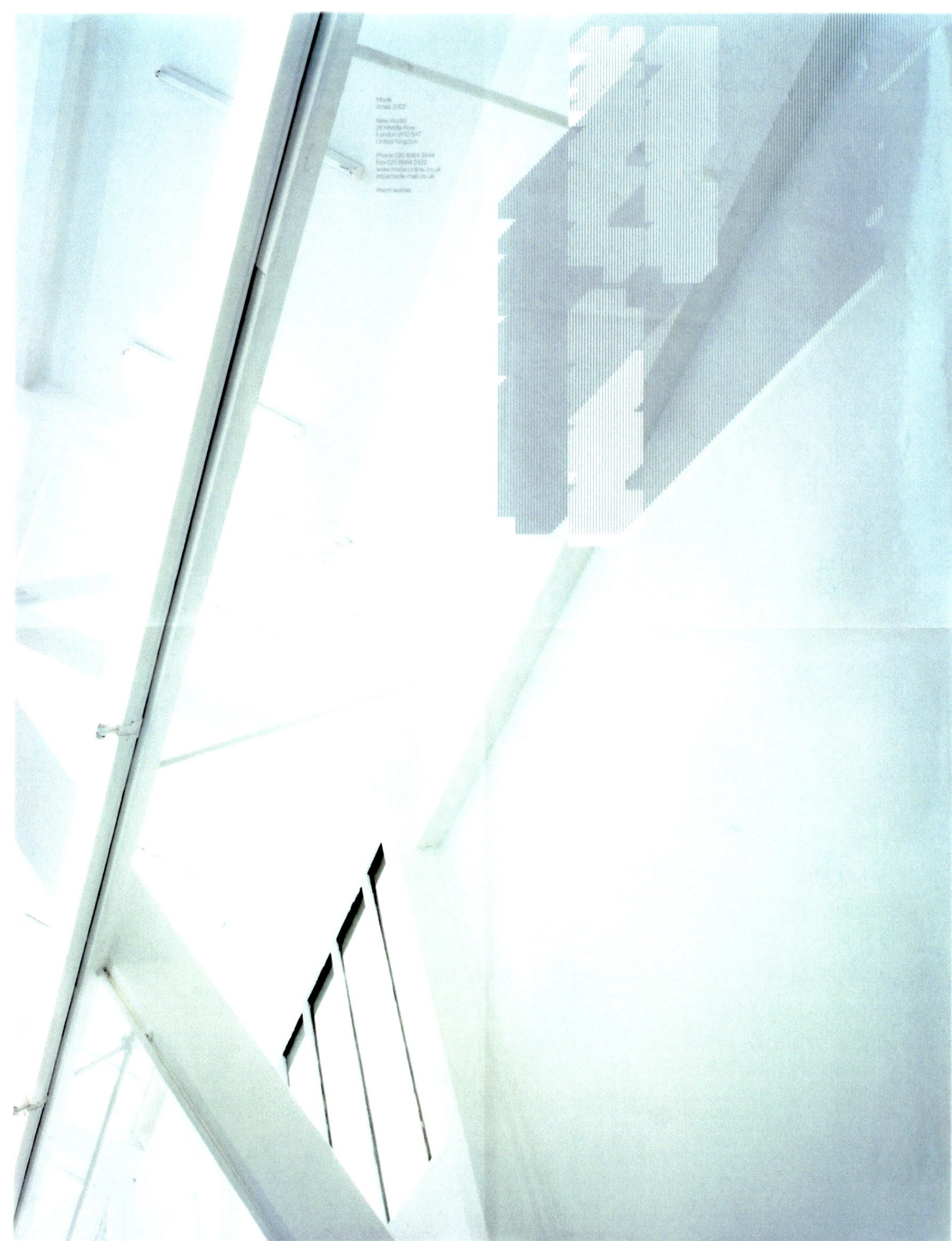

Mode / Ian Styles, Phil Costin, Darrell Gibbons, Mode Xmas 2002, Warm wishes,
445 x 565 mm folding to A4, gloss art 90 g, offset printing, gloss laminated with silver
screenprinting on top, 2002

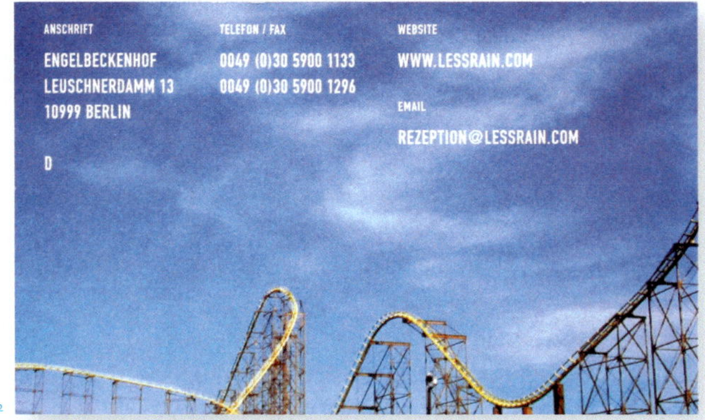

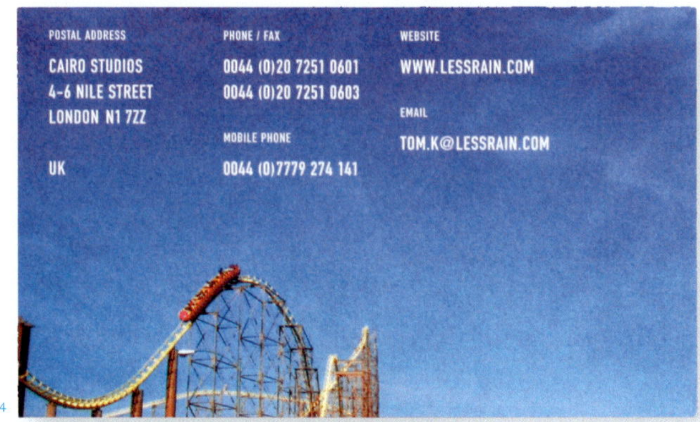

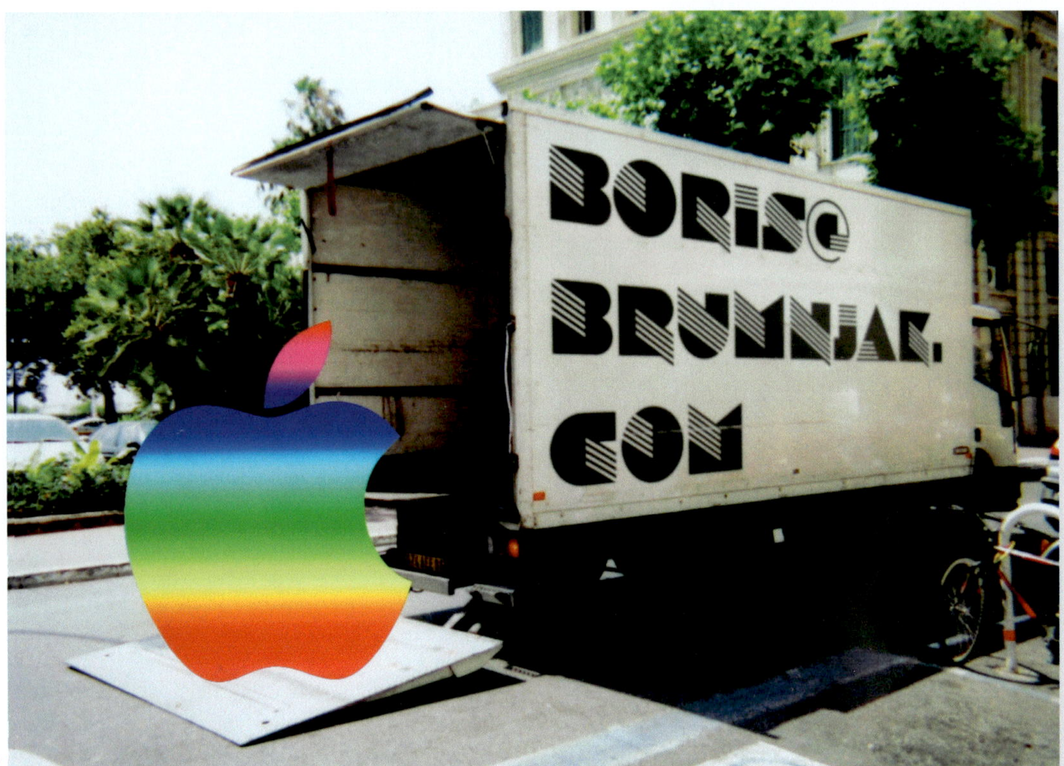

1–4   Lessrain / Lars Eberle, paper, offset printing, 2000
5   Boris Brumnjak, photo print, 2002

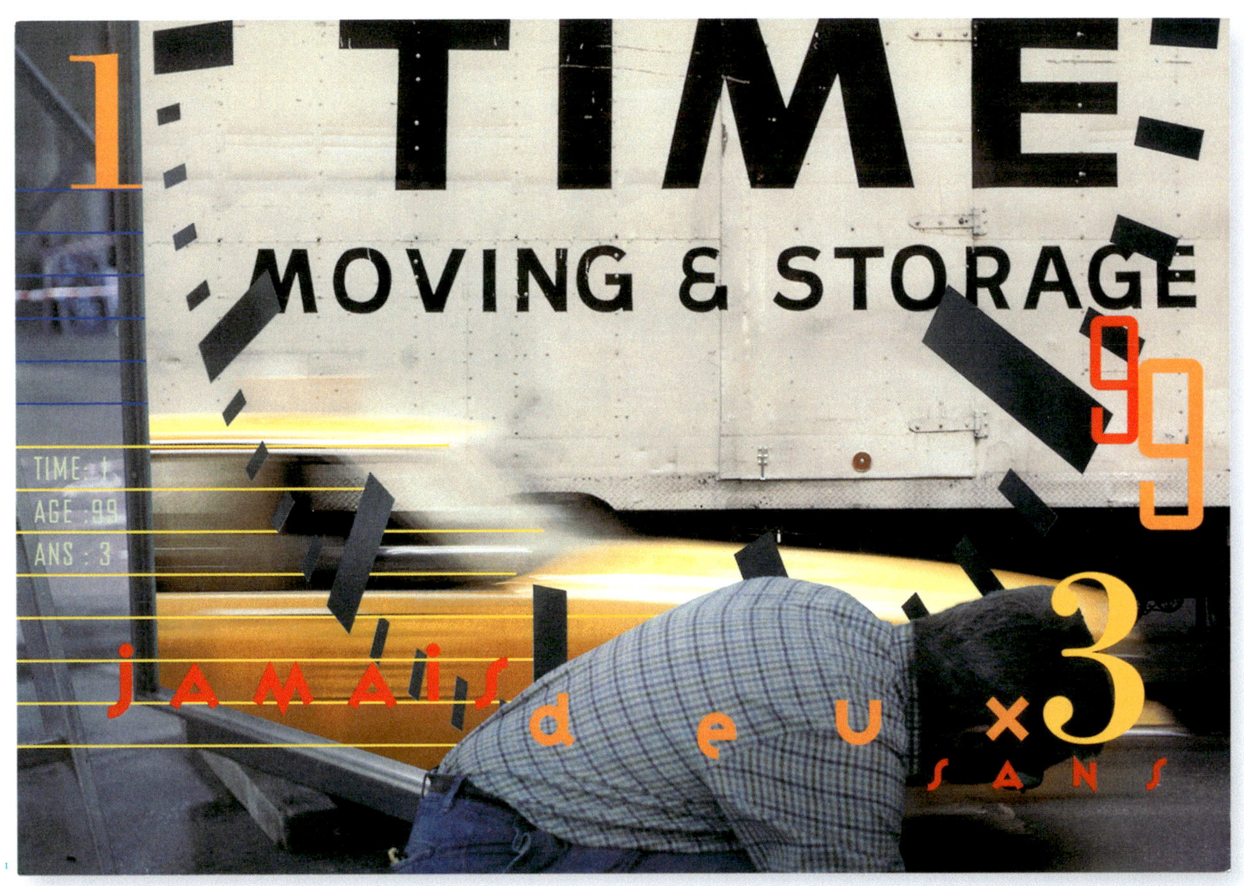

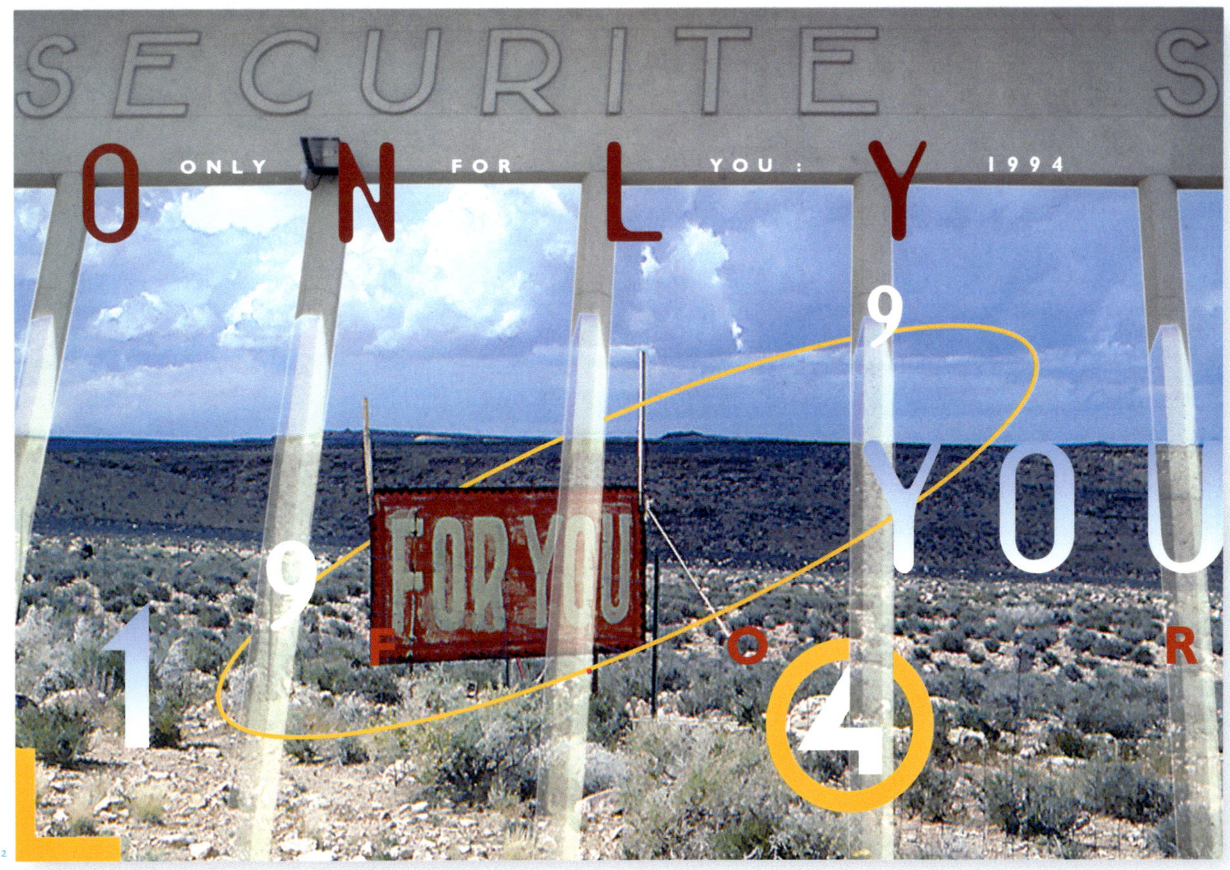

1–2   AND (Trafic Grafic) / Jean-Benoit Lévy, paper, offset printing, 1993/1994

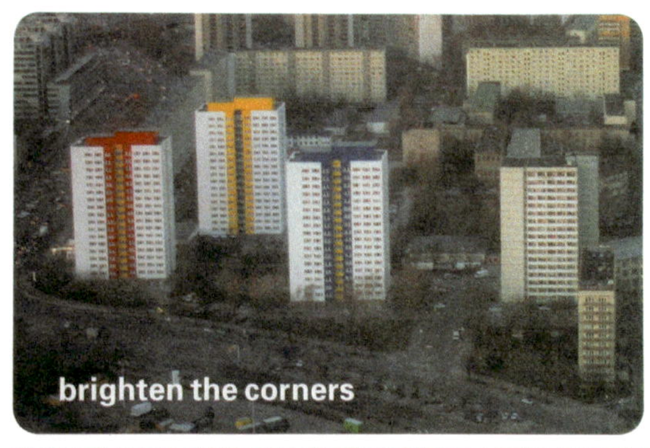

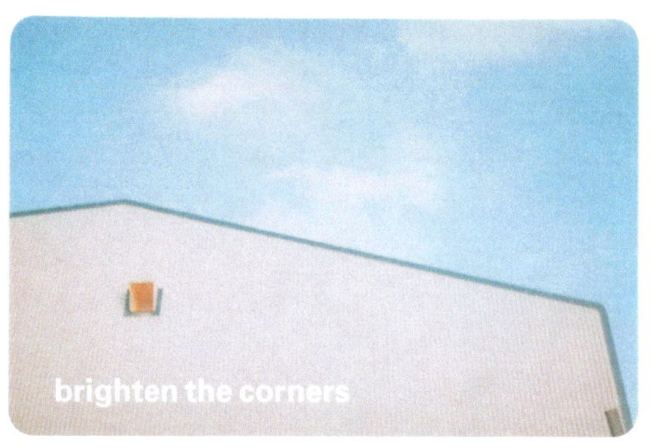

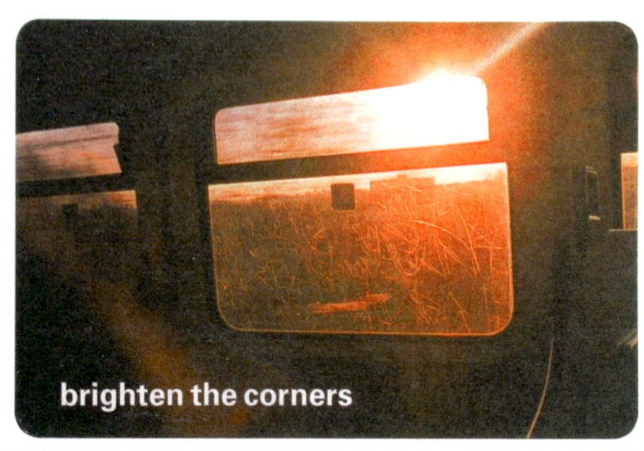

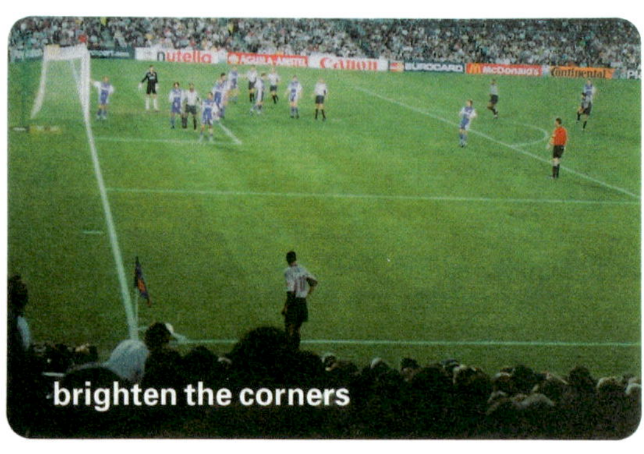

brighten the corners
studio for design

30 white's square
london sw4 7jl

frank@brightenthecorners.com
telephone 020 7627 0868
telefax 020 7627 8817

frank philippin ma rca graphic design

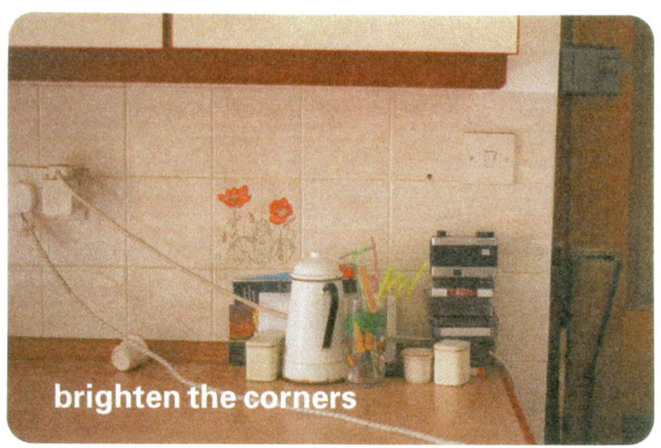

1–6   Brighten the Corners / Frank Philippin, offset printing, 2000

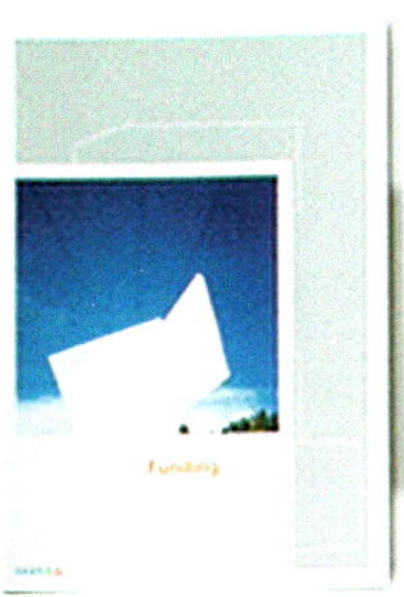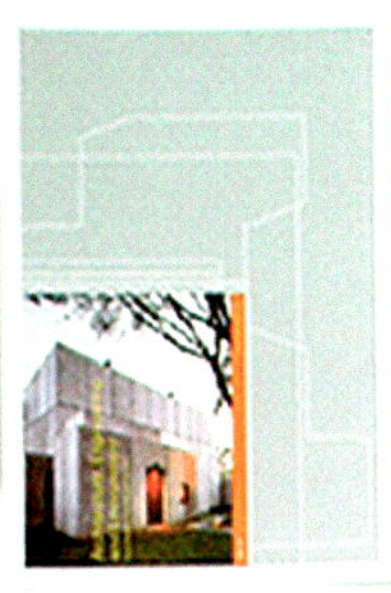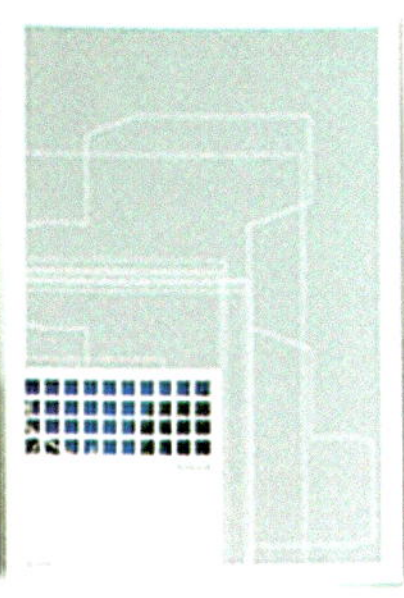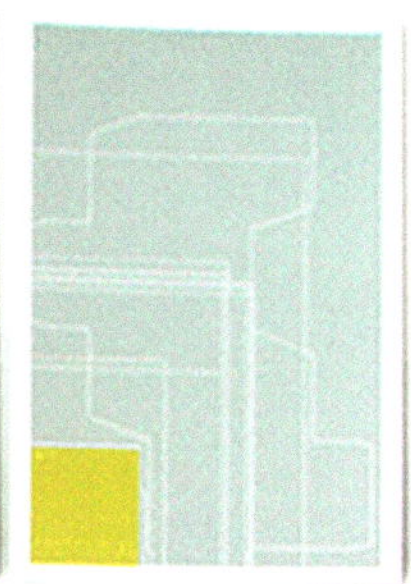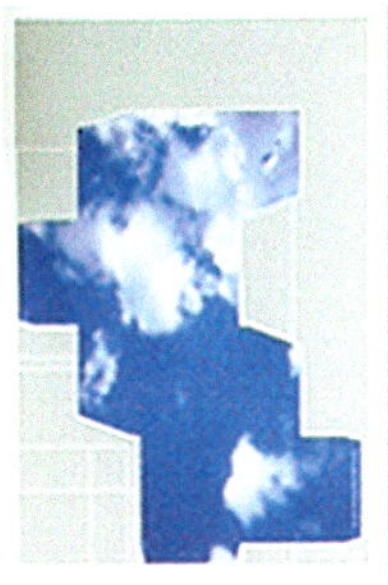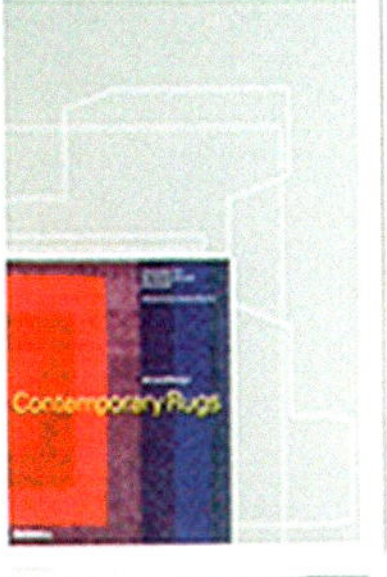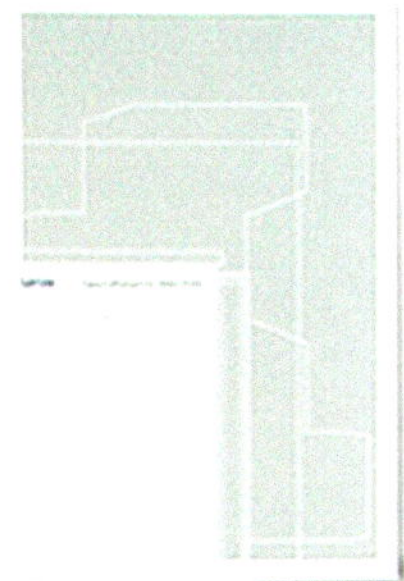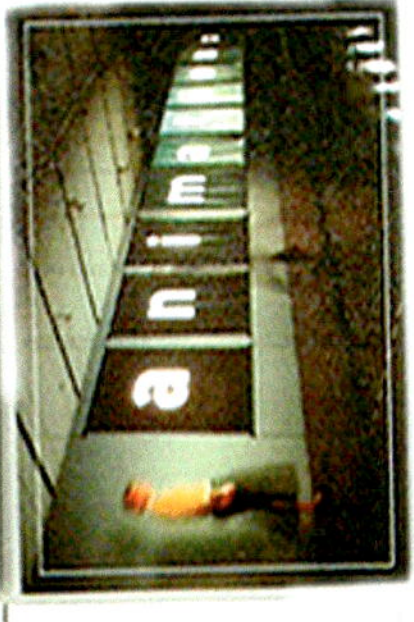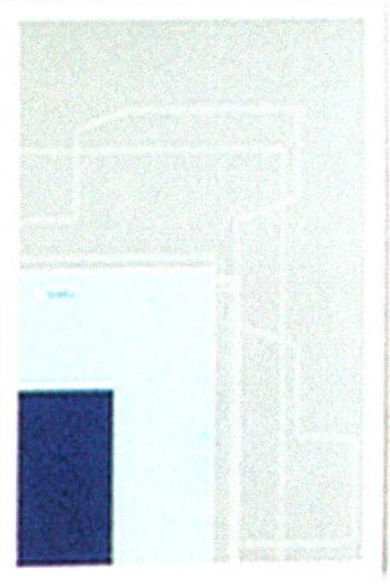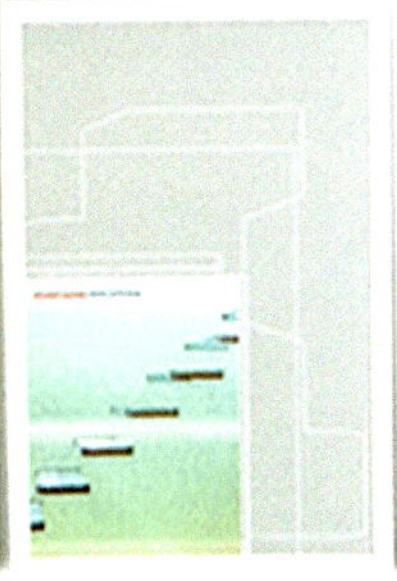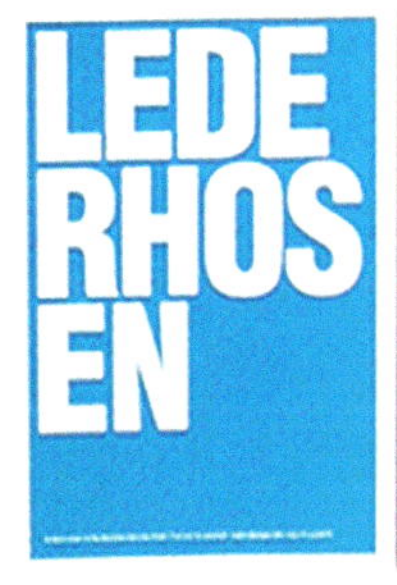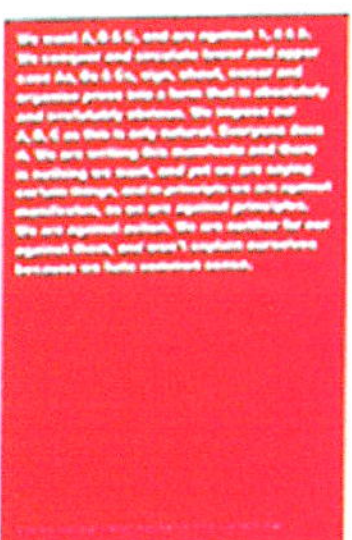

Brighten the Corners / Frank Philippin, Billy Kiossoglou, set of self-promotional cards & loose cover & A2 poster, shrink wrapped, uncoated card & super thin paper for poster & rubber band, offset printing, 2002

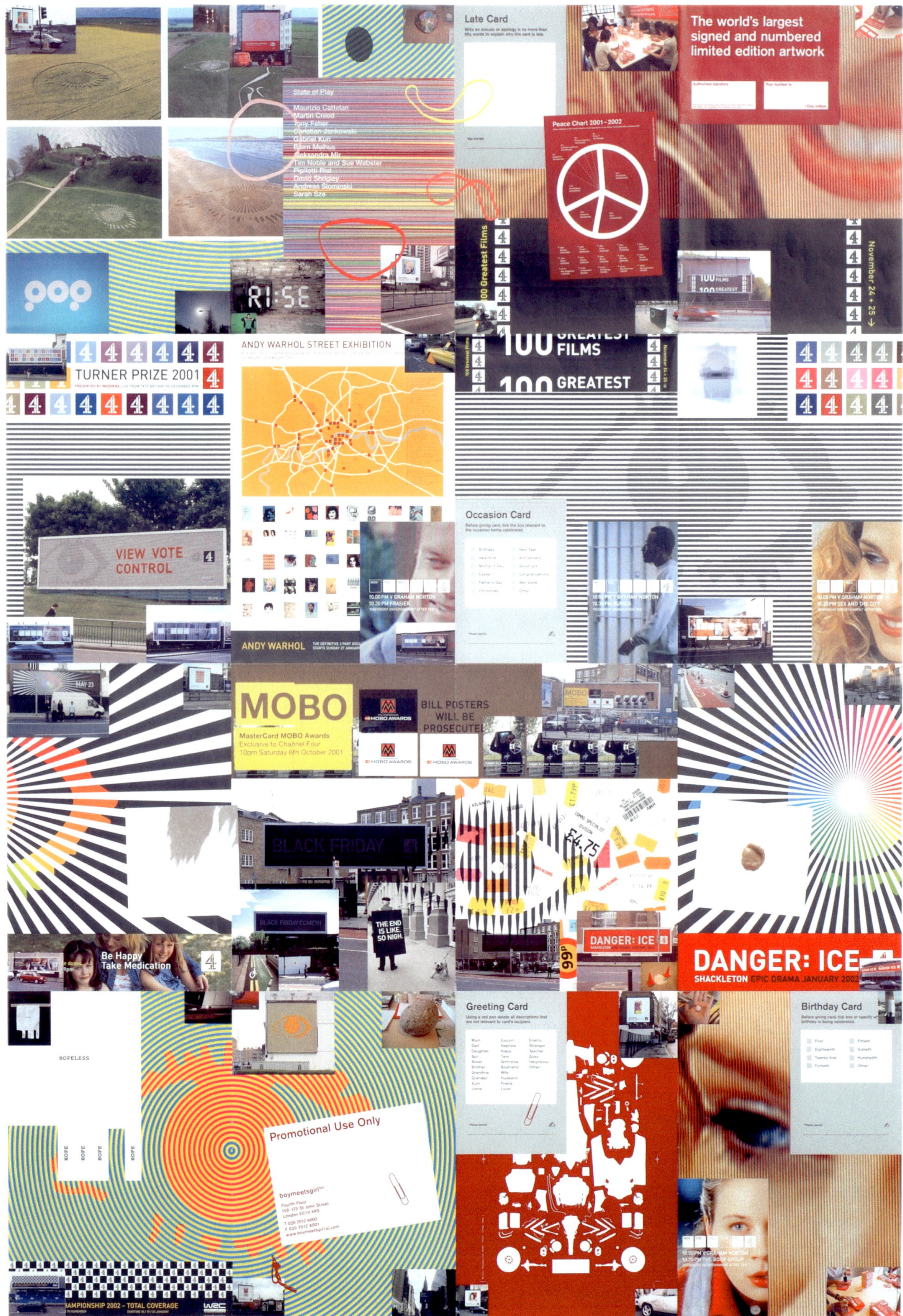

Daniel Eatock, A0 poster, offset printing

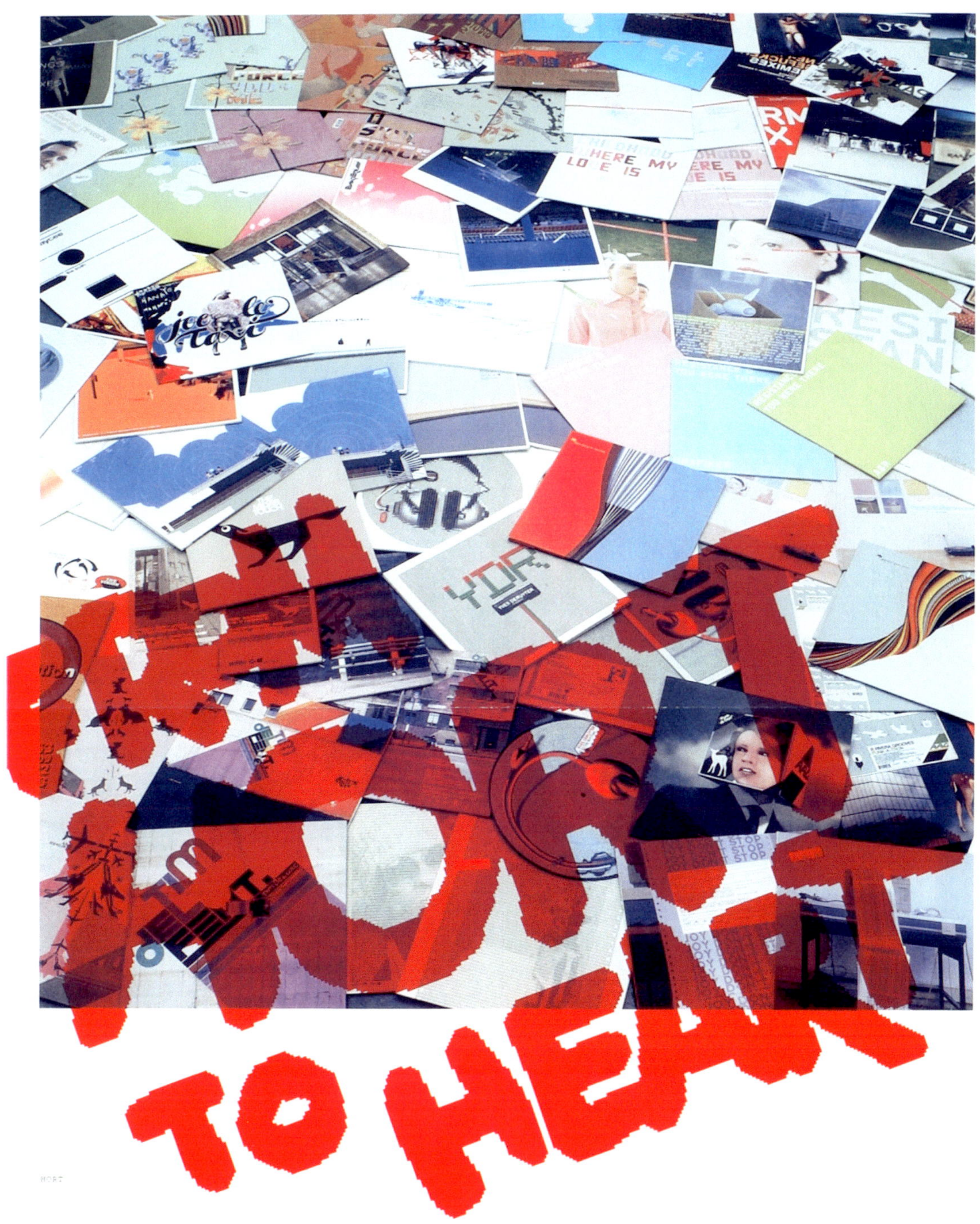

Hort, A1 poster, unvarnished paper 240 g, offset printing, 2004

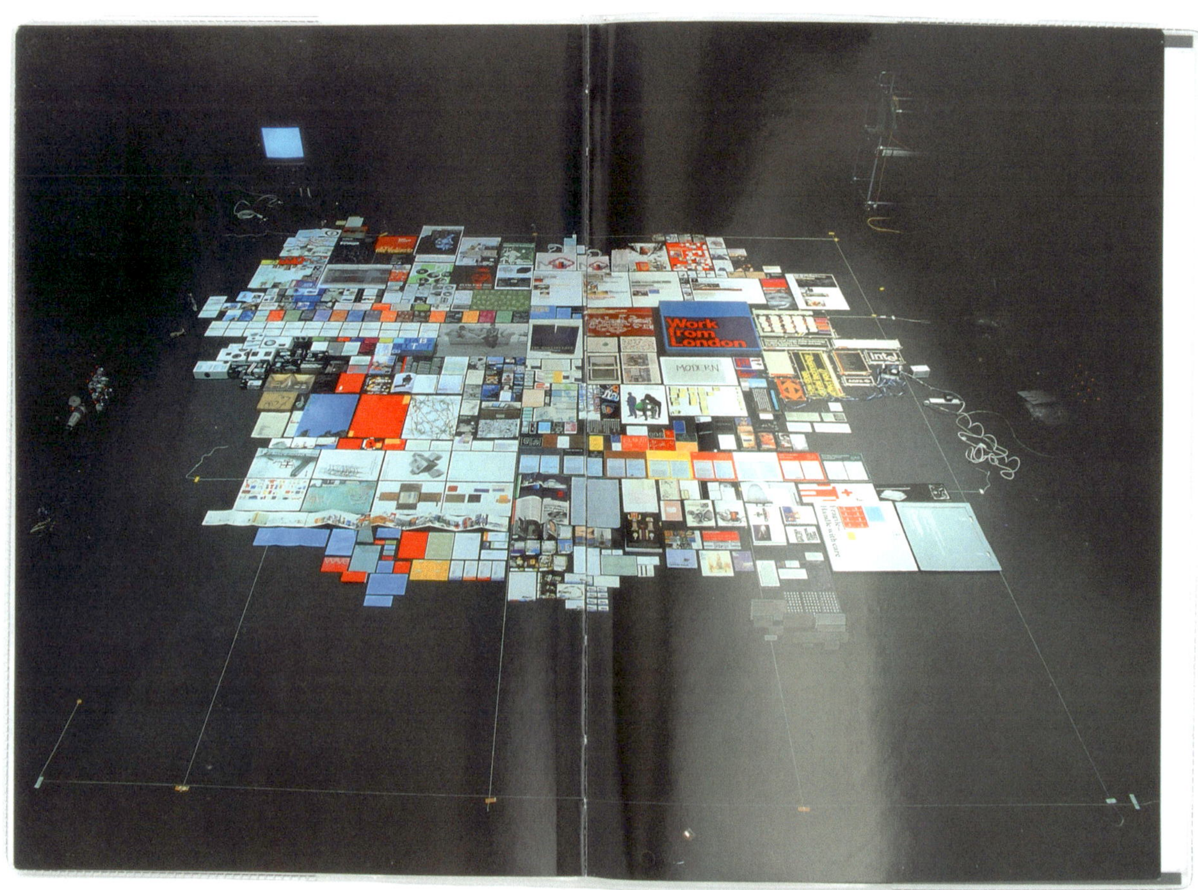
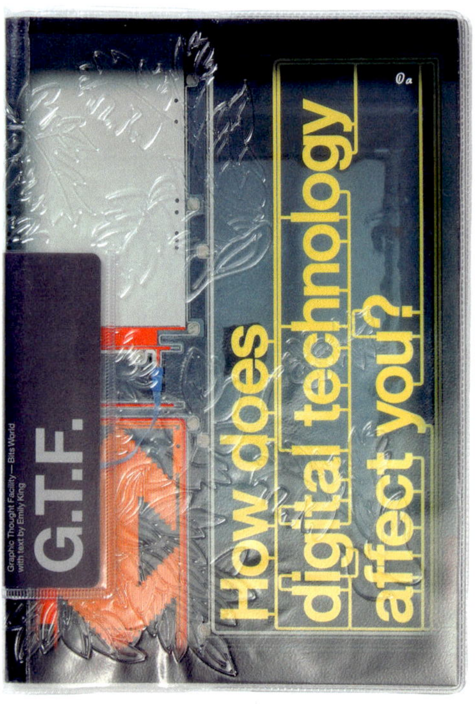

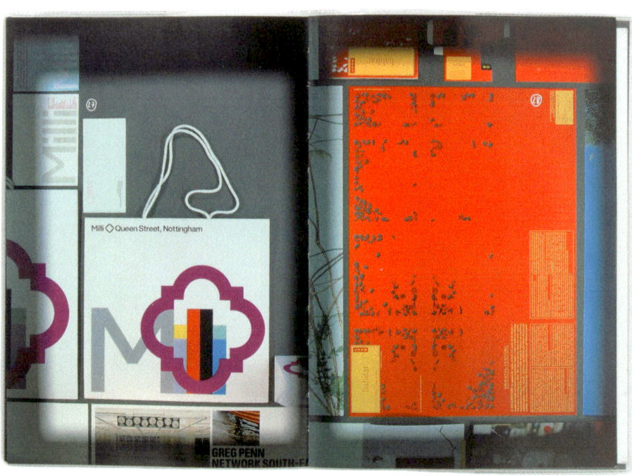

1–3   Graphic Thought Facility, photography: Graphic Thought Facility, 148,5 x 210 mm,
Zanders Ikono Gloss 170 g, and Medley Pure White 90 g, 2001

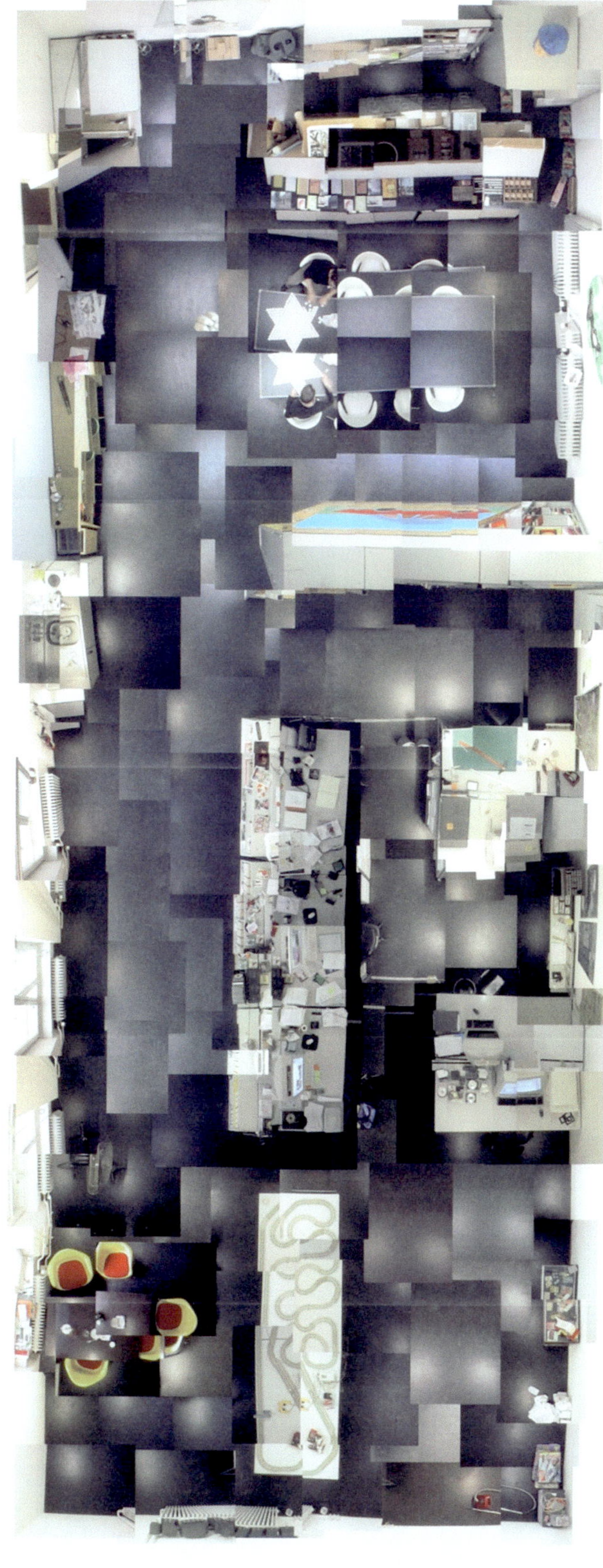

Neeser & Müller, photography: Neeser & Müller, 594 x 420 mm,
paper Euroscript 60 g, offset printing, 2004

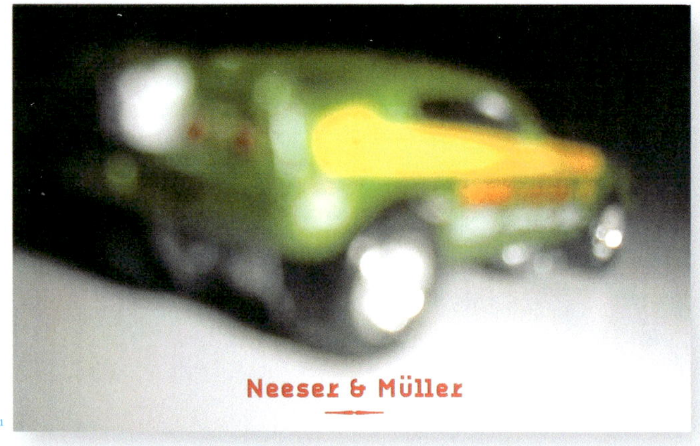

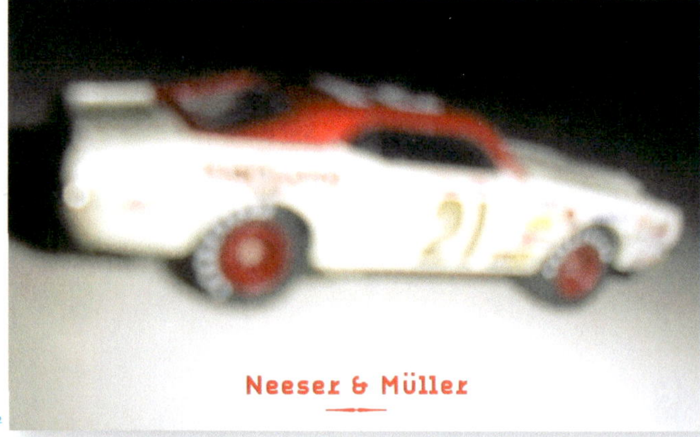

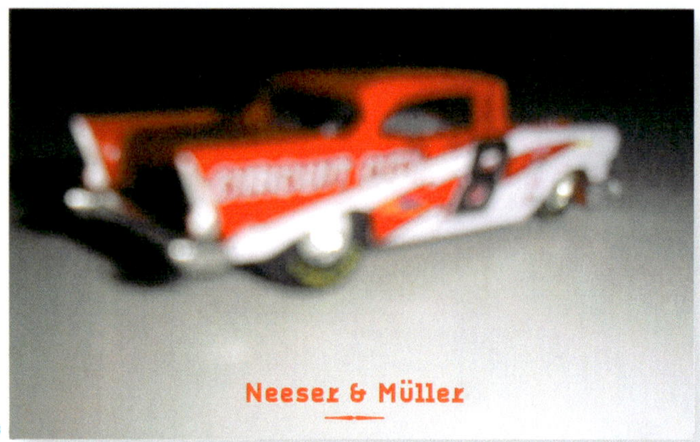

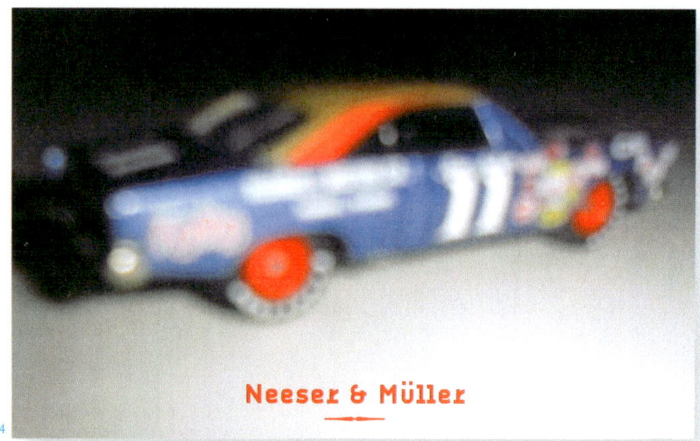

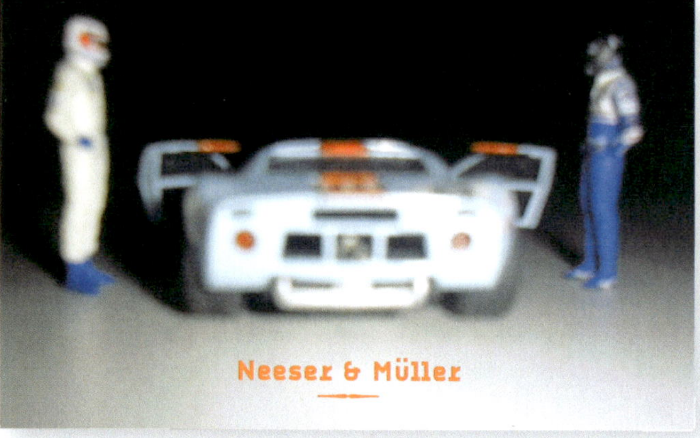

1–6   Neeser & Müller, photography: Neeser & Müller, Invercote 300 g, offset printing, 2003

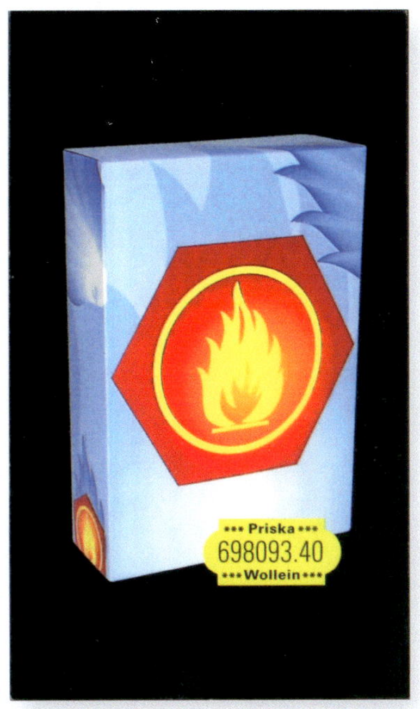

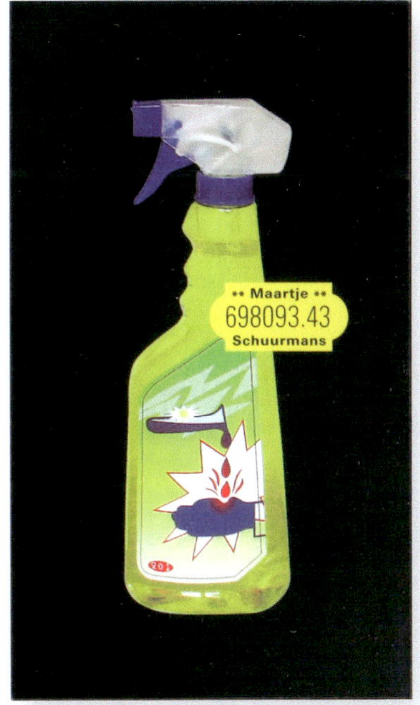

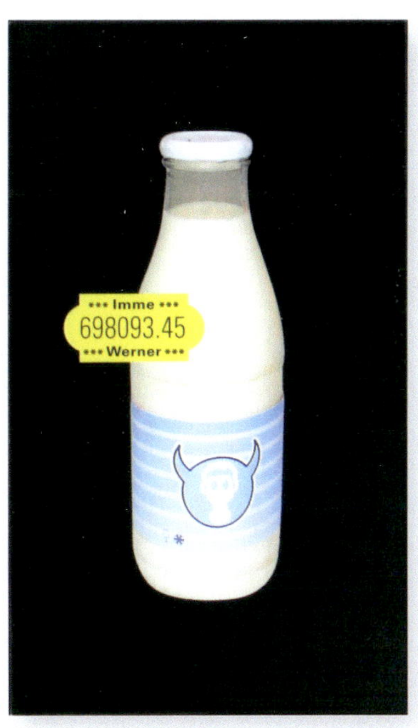

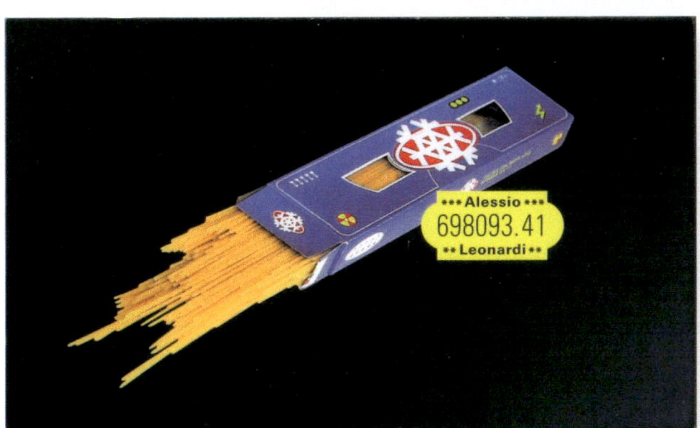

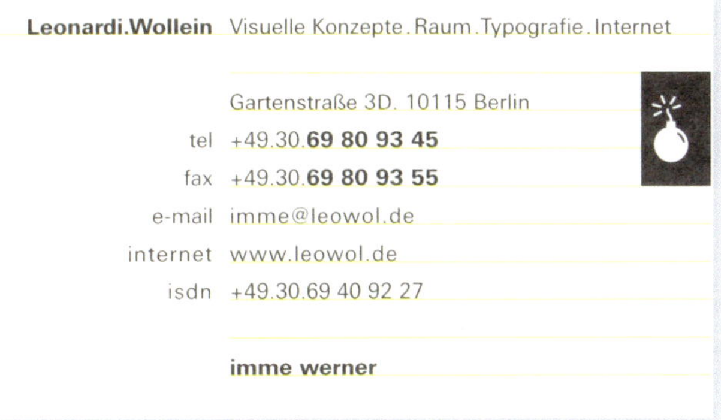

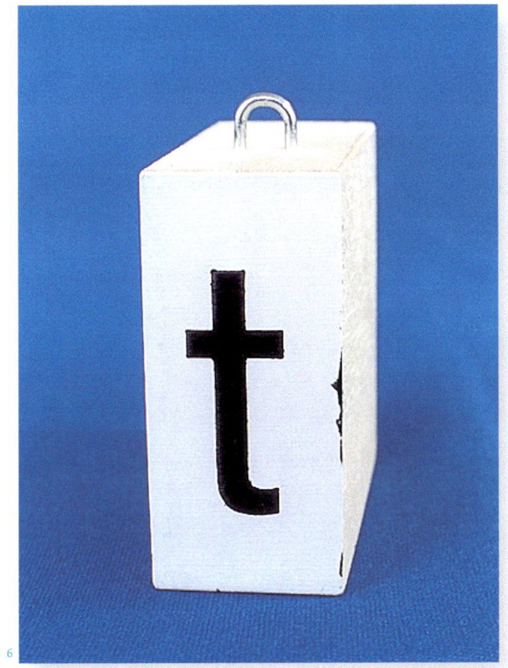

* 043 366 97 63 *

1–5   BuyMyFonts.com / Alessio Leonardi, paper, offset printing, 1997
6–7   Theres Jörger, photography: Susanne Stauss, Invercote G, 220 g, offset printing, 2002

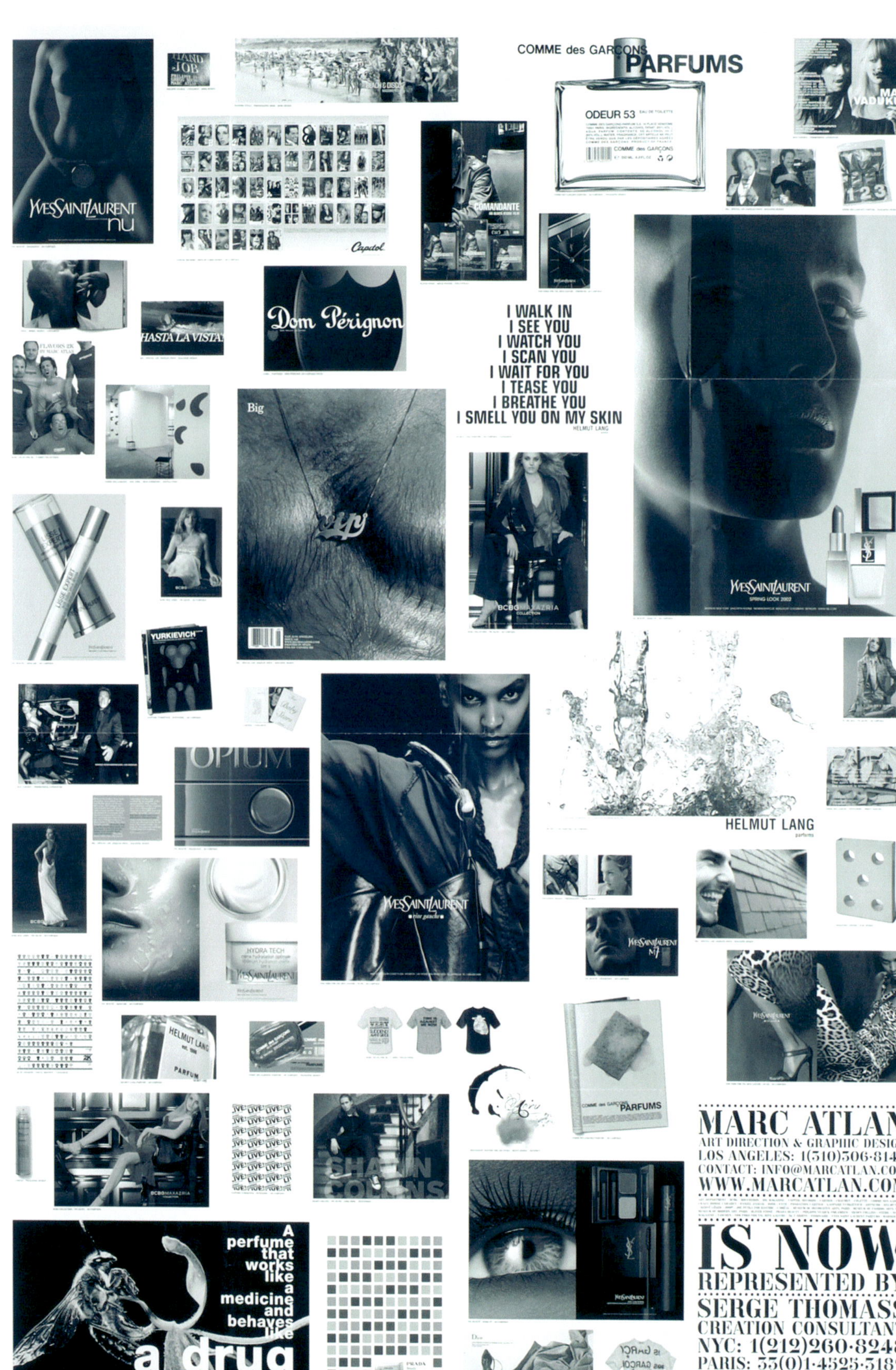

 Marc Atlan, 680 x 1010 mm, coated paper, offset printing 1c & glossy U.V. varnish, 2005

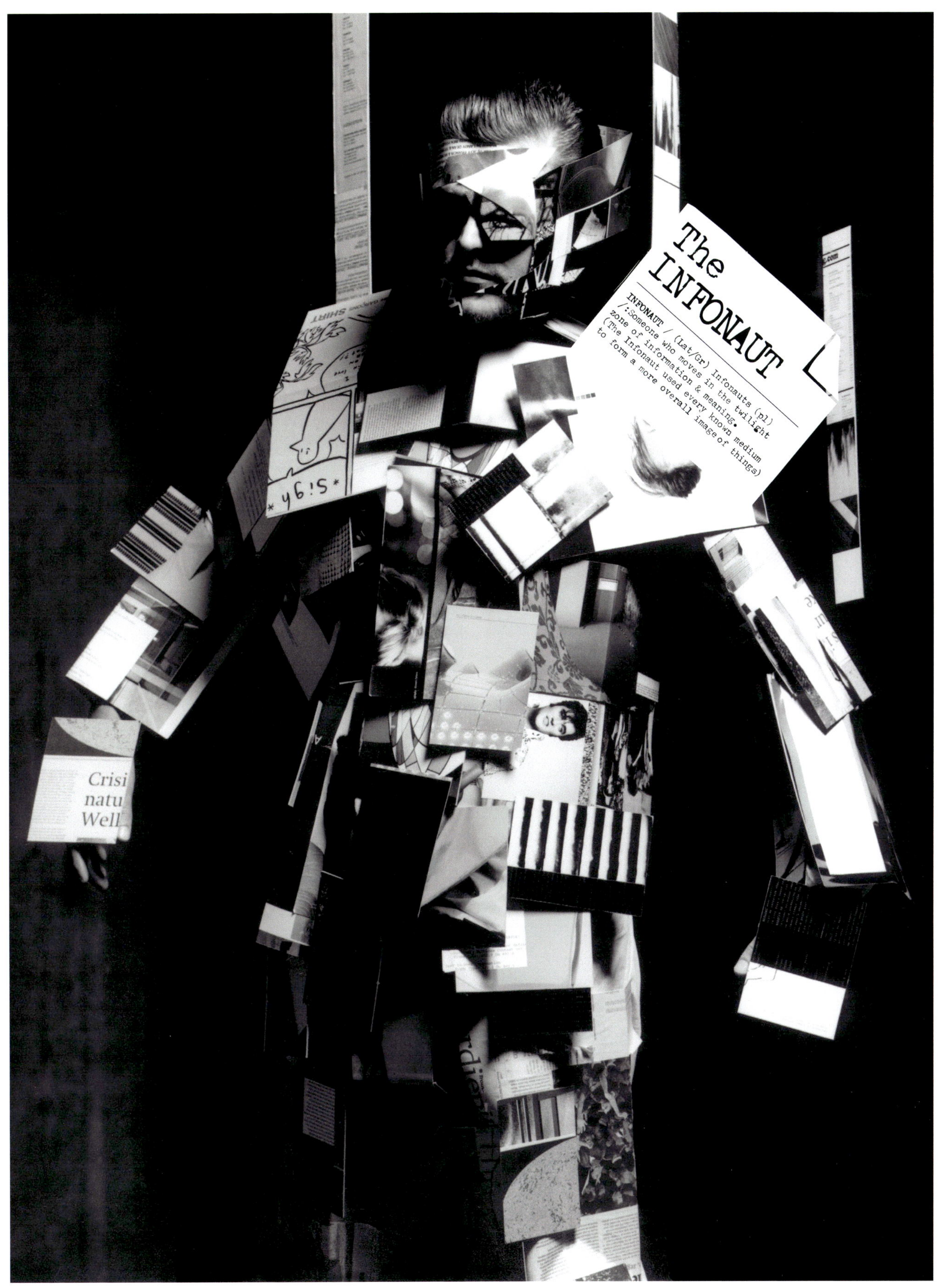

178 Aardige Ontwerpers, photography: Jouk Oosterhof, 225 x 315 mm, magazine page, offset printing, 2005

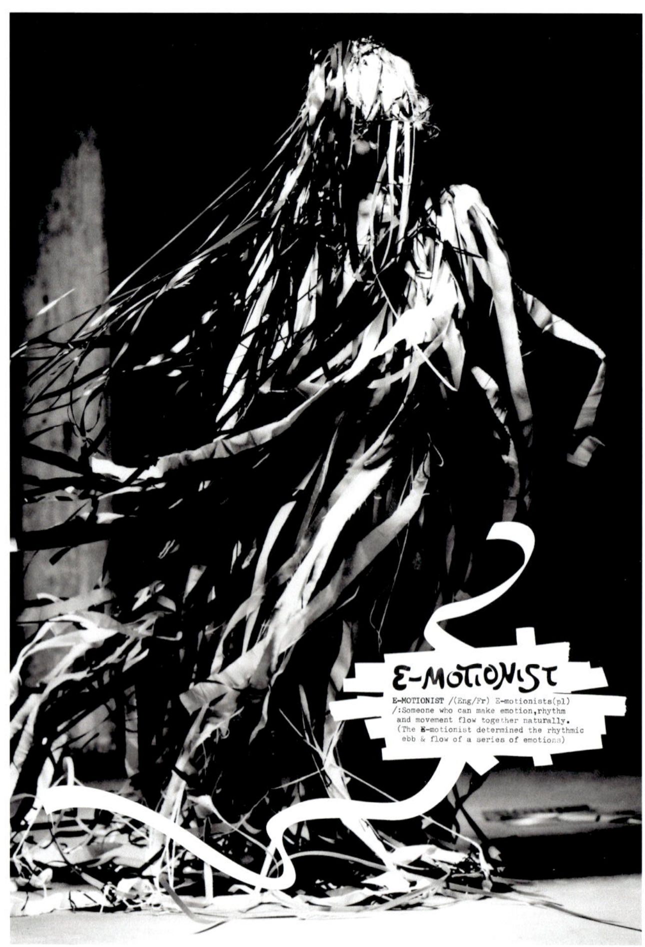

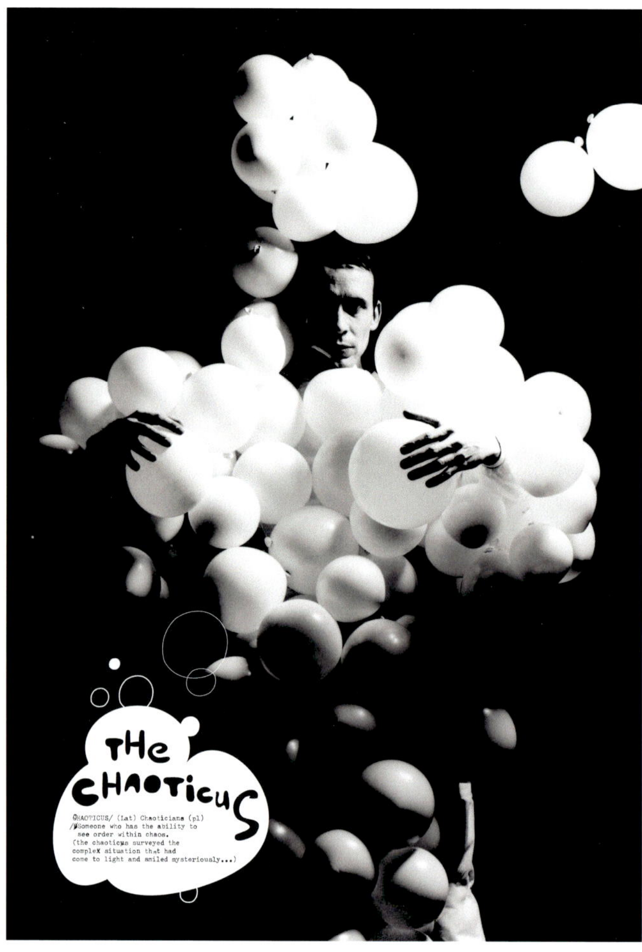

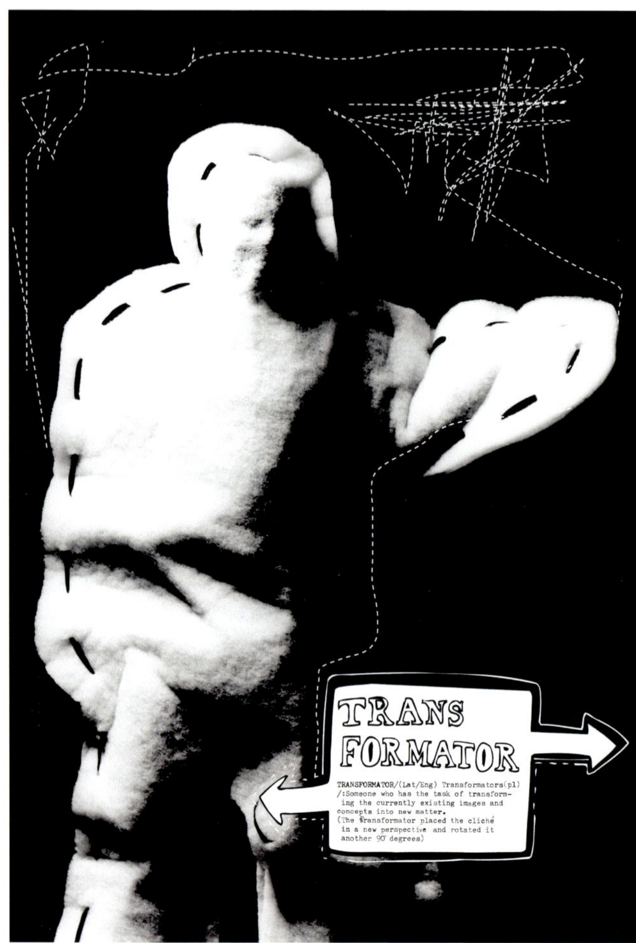

1–3   178 Aardige Ontwerpers, photography: Jouk Oosterhof,
225 x 315 mm, magazine page, offset printing, 2005

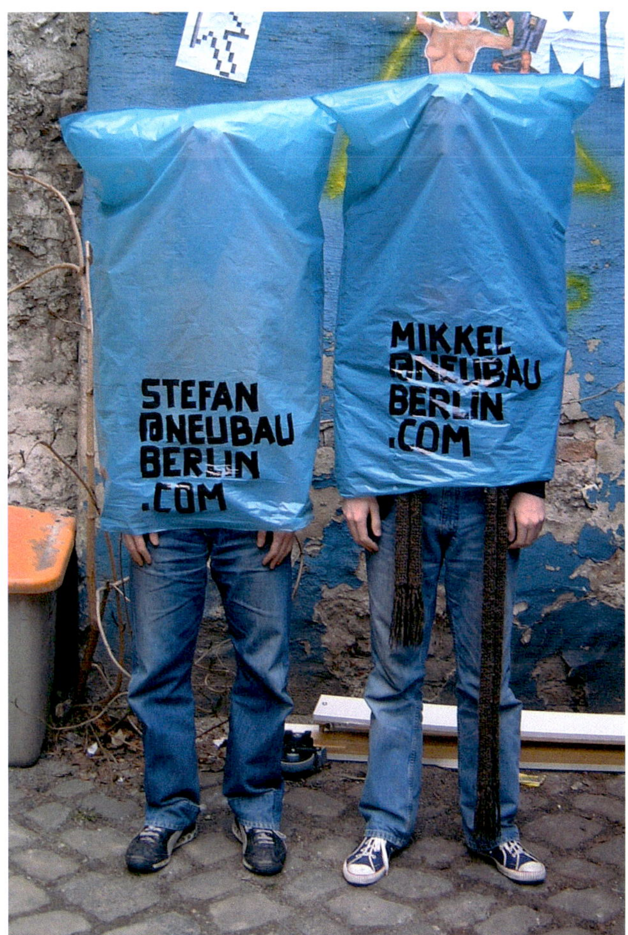

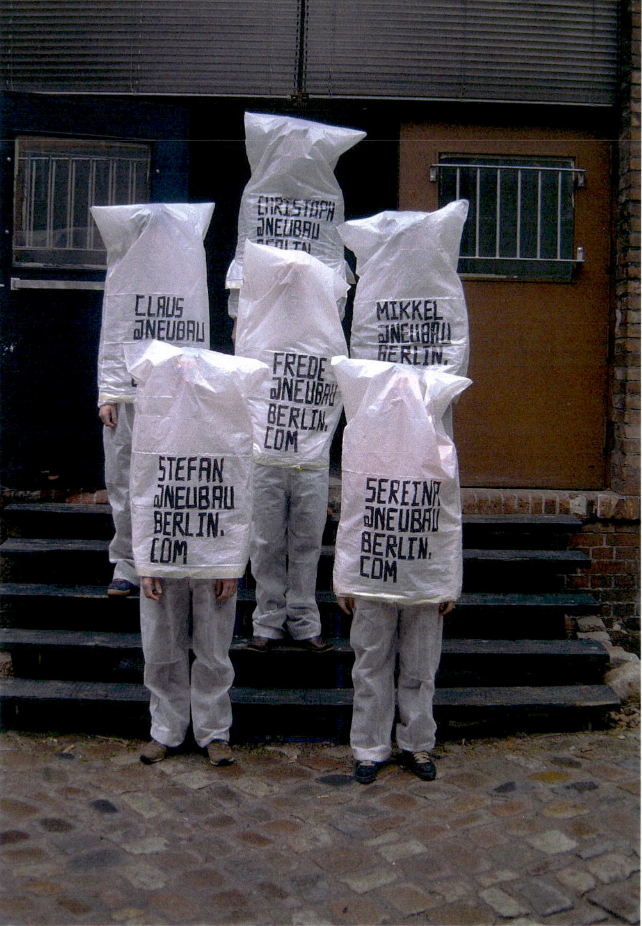

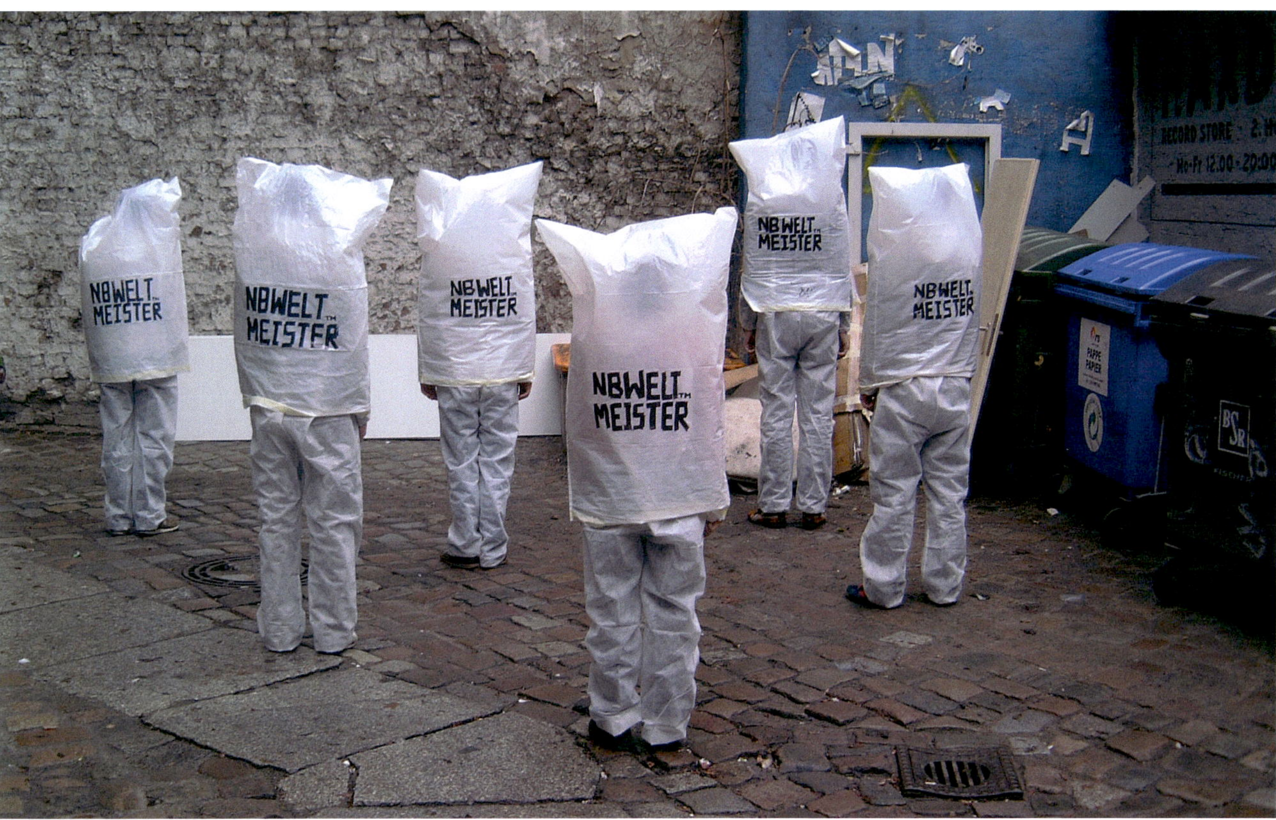

1   Neubau / Stefan Gandl, pvc, Edding 800, 2003
2–3 Neubau / Stefan Gandl, Neubau WM-Team. (Sereina Rothenberger (SUI), Christoph
     Grünberger (GER), Claus Mayr (GER), Benjamin Metz (GER), Mikkel Due Pedersen (NOR),
     Joen Szmidt (SWE), Stefan Gandl (AUT), pvc, Edding 800, 2004 / 2005

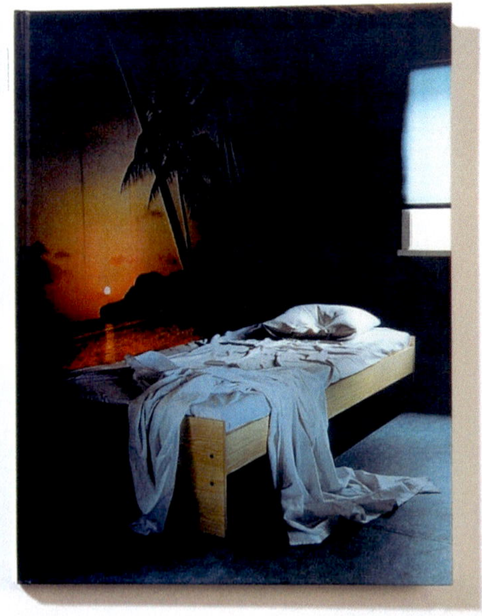

Katalog zur Ausstellung *Hybrid* im Fotomuseum Winterthur

Hardcover, 180 x 230 mm, 112 Seiten, e/d, Auflage: 3000
Herausgeber: Urs Stahel, Christoph Merian Verlag, Basel 2000
ISBN: 3-85616-125-2

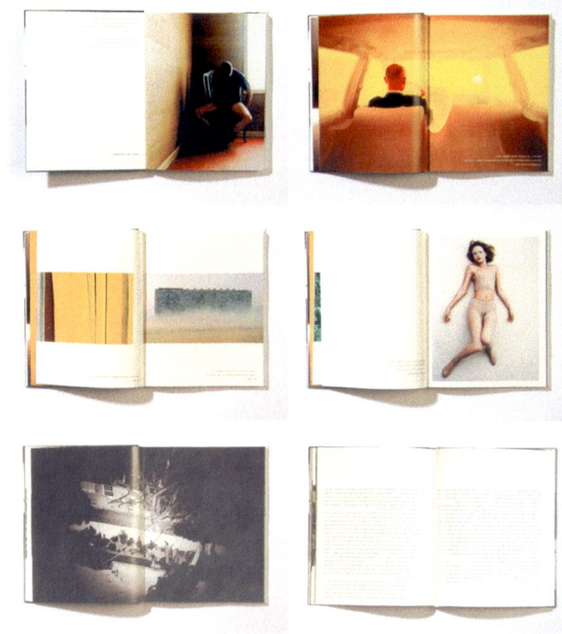

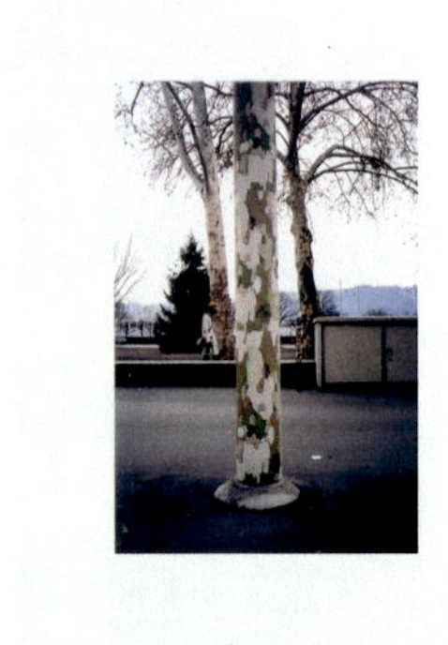

Corporate
Design

25. Januar 2005

Guten Tag Frau ███████

Wir haben von ██████ gehört, dass sie nach jeweils drei Ausstellungs-
katalogen die Gestalter wechseln. Wir erlauben uns hiermit, Ihnen
unser Portfolio zu senden. Wie sie darin sehen können, sind wir vor
allem im kulturellen Bereich tätig. Wir würden es als eine grosse
Freude und Herausforderung ansehen, Bücher für das ███████
zu gestalten. Neben unserer Leidenschaft für Grafik ist uns die
inhaltliche Auseinandersetzung mit Kunst und Künstlern ein zentrales
Anliegen.

Wir würden uns sehr freuen Sie kennenzulernen und Ihnen in einem
persönlichen Gespräch mehr über unsere Arbeit zu erzählen.

Für Ihre Tätigkeit wünschen wir Ihnen weiterhin viel Erfolg.

Mit freundlichem Gruss

Marc Kappeler

moiré – Grafik Design

Bianca Brunner, Marc Kappeler, Markus Reichenbach
Schöneggstrasse 5, 8004 Zürich
T/F +41 43 240 57 34, http://www.moire.ch, hello@moire.ch

moiré is represented in London and New York by Ling+Ling
http://www.lingandling.com

1–3   Moiré / Bianca Brunner, Marc Kappeler, Markus Reichenbach,
portfolio booklet, with individualised letter on front cover 165 x 210 mm,
adhesive binding, various papers, laser print, 2005

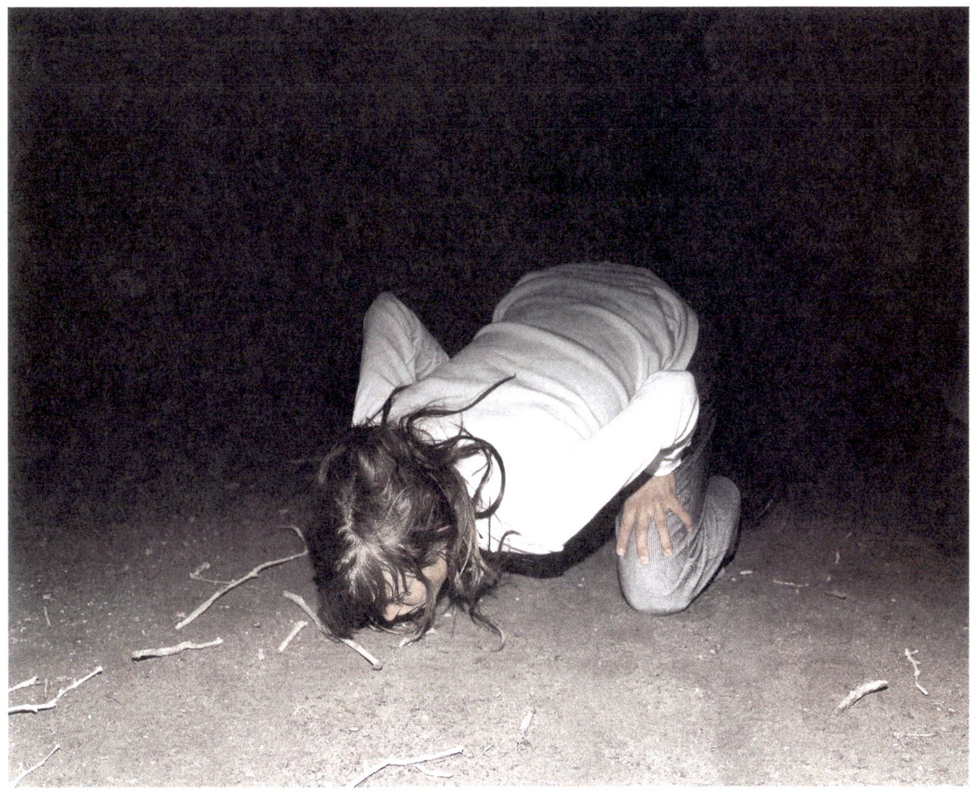

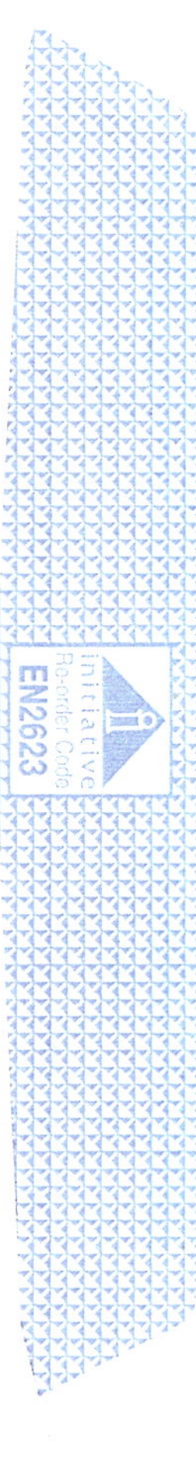

Moiré / Bianca Brunner, photography: Bianca Brunner,
228 x 162 mm, offset printing, 2004

Swiss design trio Moiré appreciate the importance of first impressions. According to their philosophy, envelopes – often the first point of contact with a designer – carry far more weight than the stationery itself, closely followed by a portfolio's title page. To this end, Moiré not only tailor their portfolio's sections and pages to the needs of each potential client, but also replace its title with a straightforward covering letter. Always aiming for the most compact and personal solution available, this understated, yet eminently effective approach is emphasised even further by the subtle contrast of paper types and printing techniques.

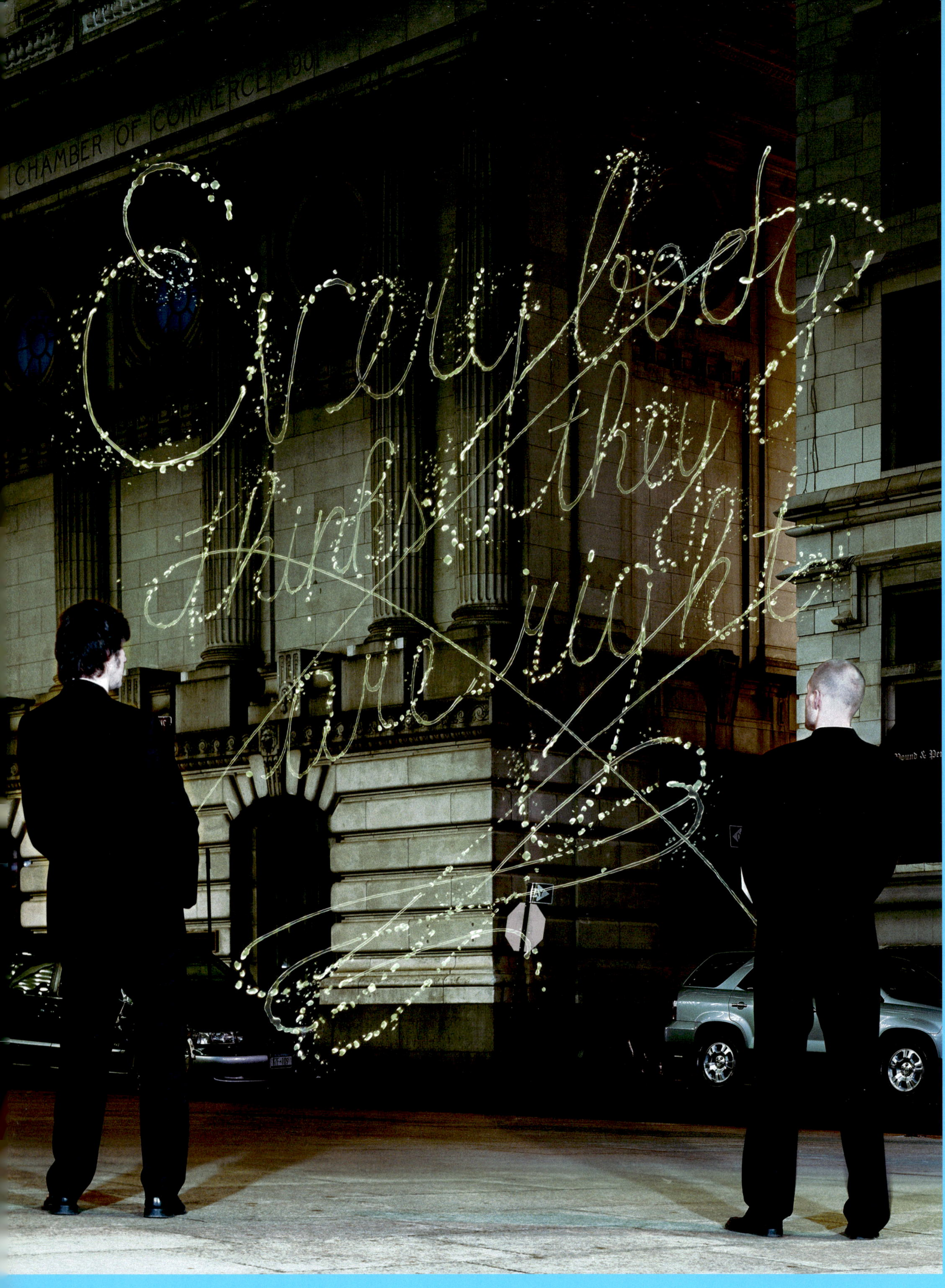

    Sagmeister Inc., Stefan Sagmeister with Matthias Ernstberger, photography: Bela Borsodi, 2005

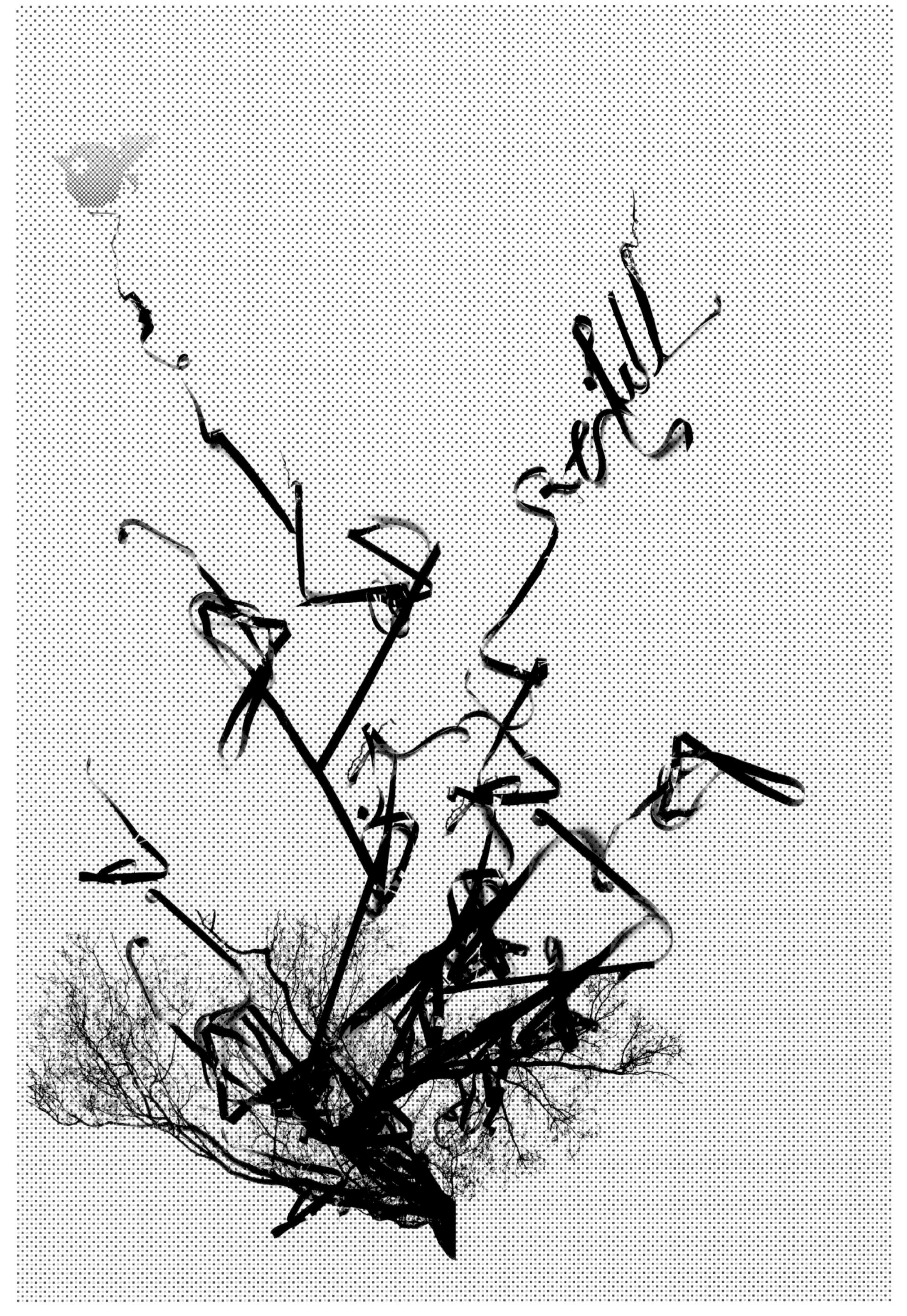

Build / Michael C. Place, postcards, offset printing, 2004

Illustration

Urs Lehni

Graphic designer Urs Lehni graduated from the Luzern School of Arts and Design in 1999. After stints at the Swiss Expo.02 and Zurich State Theatre, Lehni opened his own design office in Zurich in 2001. Besides his commissioned work, Lehni pursues a number of self-initiated projects (www.vectorama.org, www.our-magazine.ch), lectures at the Schools of Art and Design in Zurich, Lucerne and Lausanne and churns out a constant stream of business card-sized, self-contained projects featuring art, humour, cultural politics and Dadaist health manifestos, among others.

How important is self-promotion to you?

I have to admit, when I explore the work of another designer/artist/musician etc. and discover ideas or attitudes that inspire me, I do not actually care how well these people might portray themselves or how they actually go on about it. One thing I am sure off is that I do not like anything obviously ingratiating.

You show a strong penchant for the business card format – how come?

There is something to be said for almost all formats, but the obvious advantage of business cards is their size – whenever I have a printing job, there is always space for an extra card or two. Furthermore, I like the challenge of the format's innate restrictions and bureaucratic connotations. Your idea needs to be very concise and clearly formulated to still make sense when reduced to such a small size.

Do these cards – often not even featuring your name or e-mail address – serve as some kind of self-promotional measure, or what is their general purpose?

To be honest – when the situation arises, it is usually very spontaneous and I hardly ever think of self-promotion or creating a series – all cards tend to be self-contained projects. Of course, once it carries my name or number, it does become a means of self-representation. However, that's not the main reason for doing these cards, mostly it's for fun.

Any particular favourites?

Probably my own business card for the Zurich Office. Typeset in the Japanese Katakana alphabet, only numbers, e-mail and name remain legible to us Europeans. In a way, this makes sense because most people are only interested in the number anyway. Furthermore, Japanese people have their very own code of conduct when it comes to business, they "may exchange business cards even before they shake hands or bow. Be certain your card clearly states your rank. This will determine who your negotiating counterpart should be." This is the card I carry around with me most of the time. Unfortunately, as my wallet is really tiny, these cards tend to get so grubby I never really dare to hand them out to anyone.

Another "business" card seems to be the product of some ingenious teamwork – who was involved?

One day, Rafael Koch and me decided to design a card for our fictitious bureau „Blokes". Our friends always said that the two of us together reminded them of Statler and Waldorf, those grumpy old guys from the "Muppet Show". So, while one side of the card shows a picture of the two of us together, we still required the right typeface for our contact information. With an old people's home nearby, we simply decided to knock on their door. A Mr. Küttel was kind enough to supply his very best handwriting and the result made it straight onto our card. As far as I remember, we rewarded his efforts with a bottle of red wine.

So, is there an end in sight?

Not really – the moment I find some spare printing space, I will turn it into a new card.

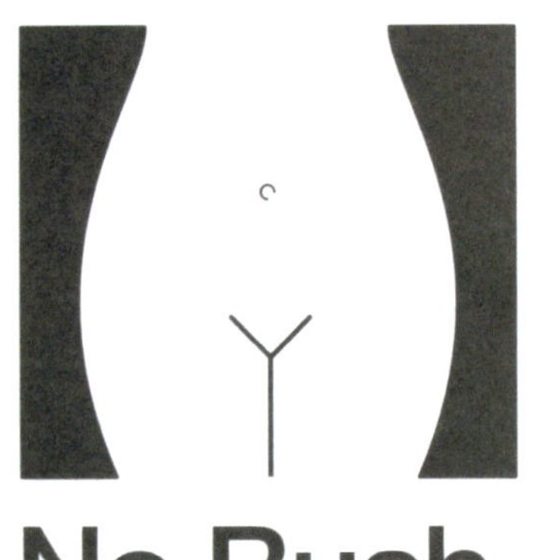

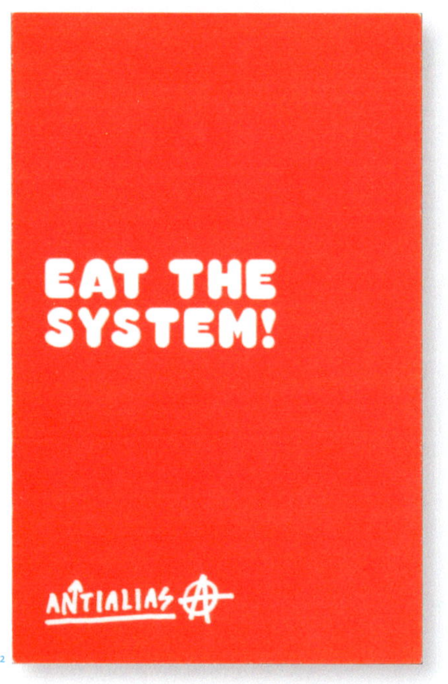

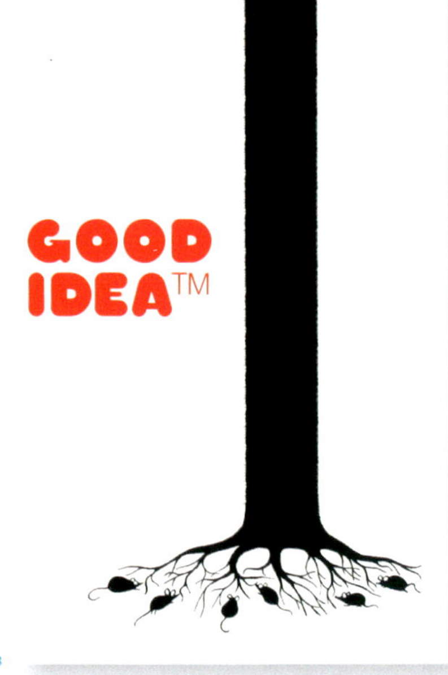

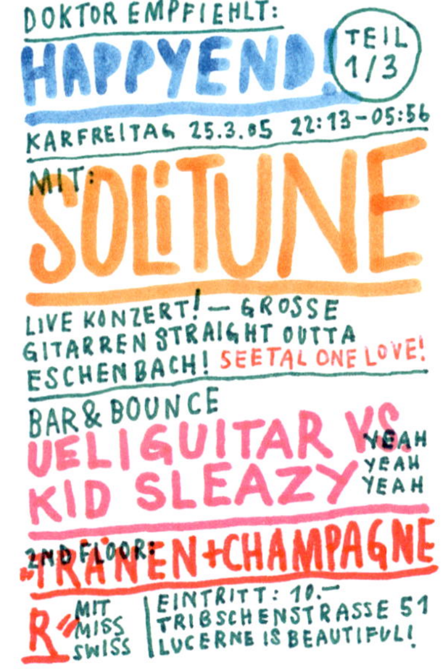

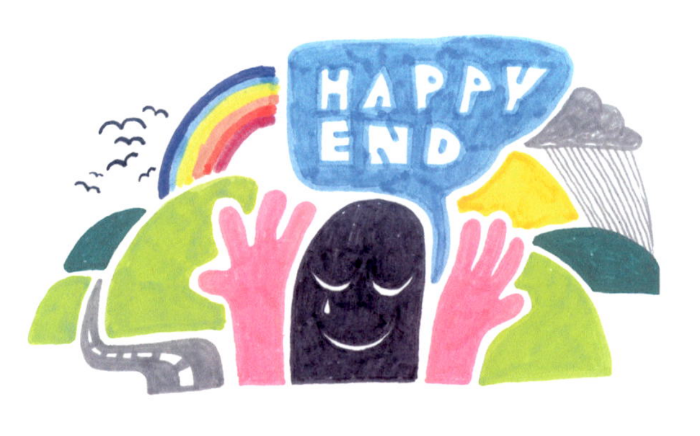

1   Urs Lehni, sticker, photocopy, 2003
2–3   Urs Lehni, Invercote, offset printing, 2002
4–5   Urs Lehni, businesscard-sized flyer, Invercote, offset printing, 2005
6   Urs Lehni, Rafael Koch, Peter Körner, Offset-paper, offset printing, 1999

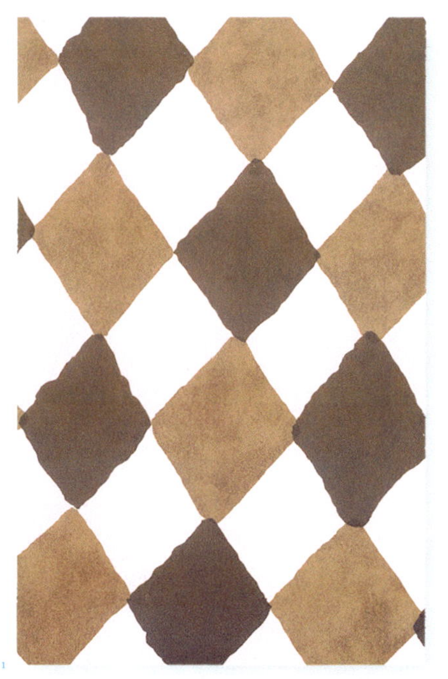

Urs Lehni
アートディレクター
ししょばこ 1574
8031 チューリッヒ
スイス

けいたいでんわ
076 348 96 80

スタジオ
01 272 95 42

でんしメール
lehni@gmx.ch

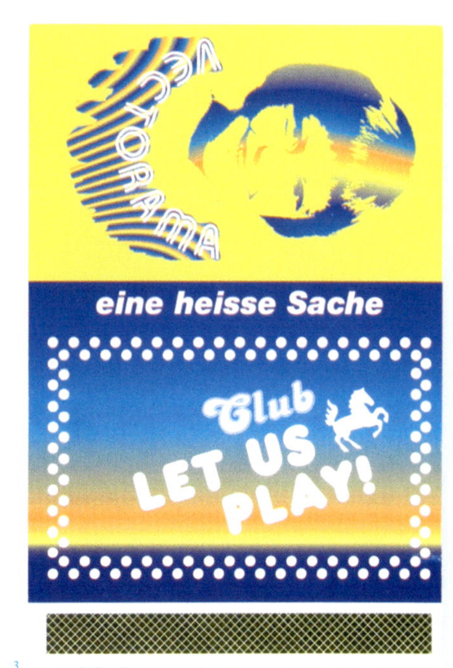

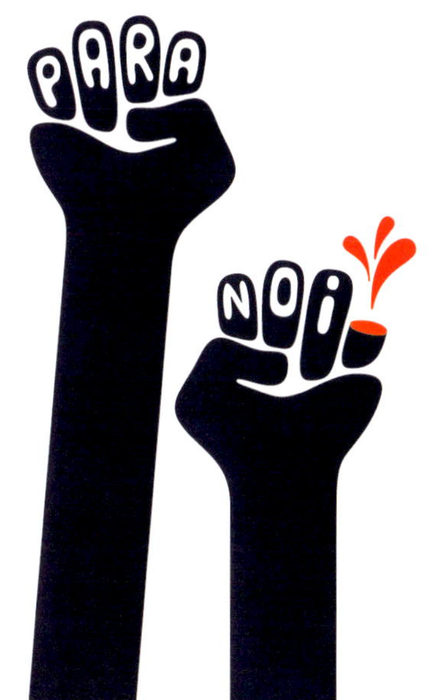

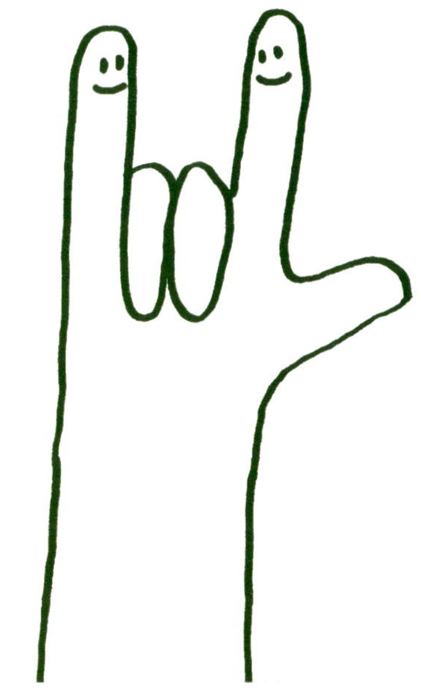

1–2   Urs Lehni, Sihl+Eika 656 Stone Quarz, matt 300 g, einseitig geprägt, offset printing
3   Urs Lehni, Invercote, offset printing, 2001
4   Urs Lehni, Invercote, offset printing, 2004
5   Urs Lehni, Invercote, offset printing, 2002
6   Urs Lehni, Invercote, offset printing, 2002

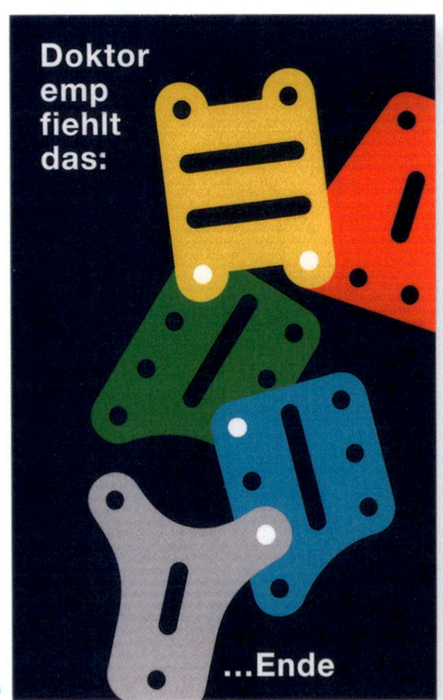

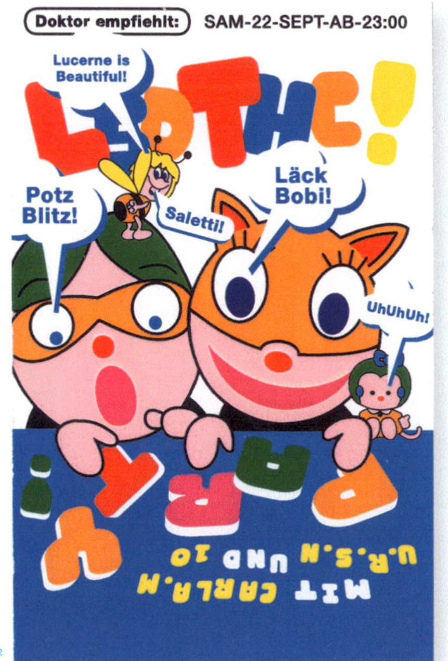

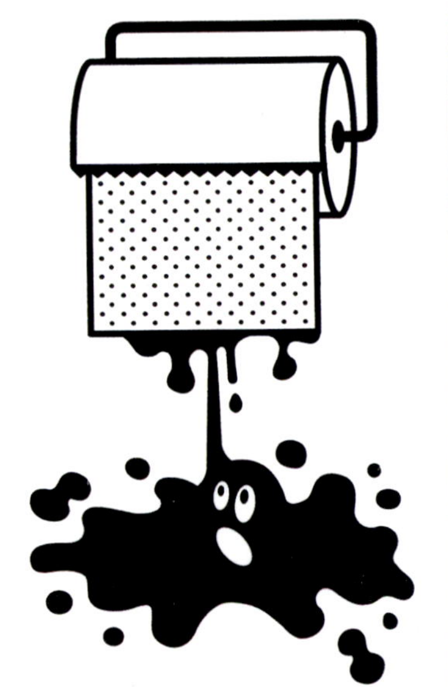

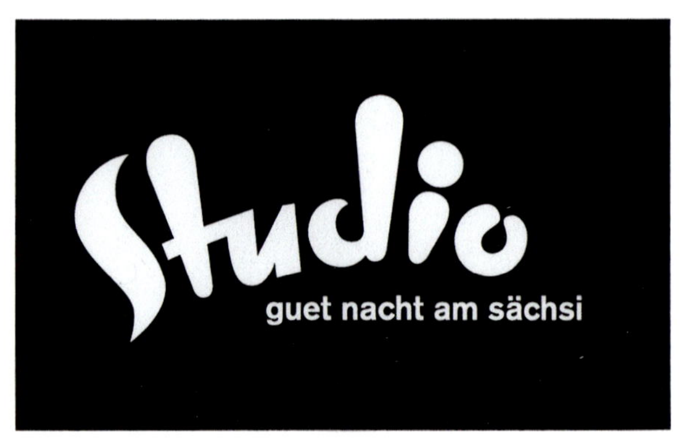

1   Rafael Koch, promotioncard for event "doktor empfiehlt", offset paper, 2004
2   Rafael Koch, promotioncard for event "doktor empfiehlt", laser print, 2002
3–4   Rafael Koch, paper, photocopy, 2003
5   Rafael Koch, informationcard for "studio-club", paper, photocopy, 2003

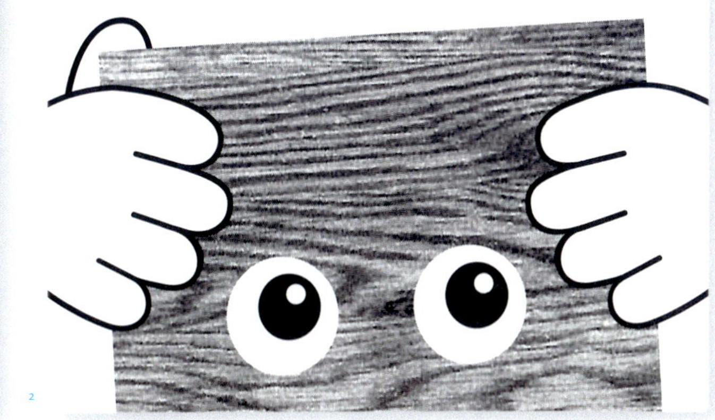

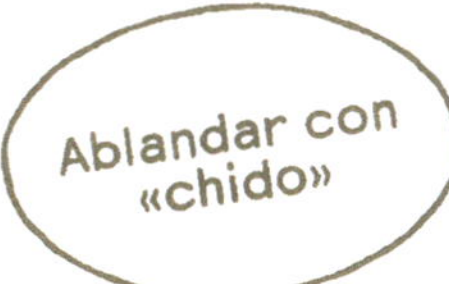

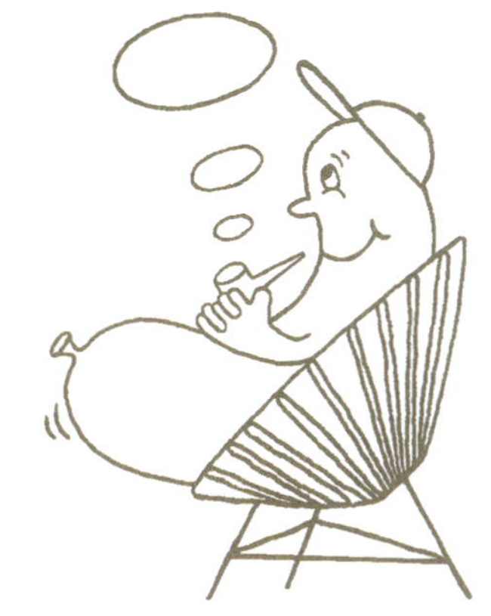

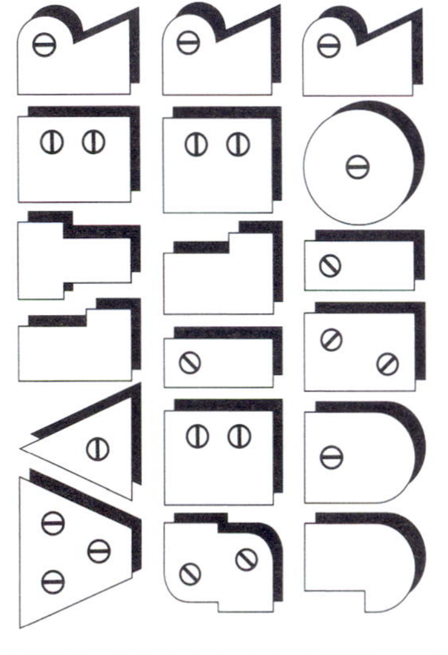

encyclopaedizer, der; [maskulin]:
Der «encyclopaedizer» ist ein gemeinschaftlich verfasstes Lexikon, bestehend aus den drei Teilen Website, Ausstellungsinterface und einem gedruckten Nachschlagewerk. Kern der Arbeit bildet eine Applikation welche auf dem Internet vorgefundene, mediale Inhalte zu enzyklopädischen Einträgen aufbereitet. Die Kombination dieser Inhalte, in Form von Text und Bild führt immer wieder zu neuen, eigensinnigen und überraschenden Definitionen.

80.254.165.121
www.encyclopaedizer.net
E08°18', N47°03', Luzern, SUI
18.01.2003, 19:00:00, Nr.1

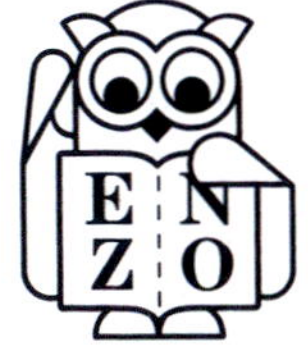

1–2 Rafael Koch, promotioncard for event "doktor empfiehlt", offset paper, 2004
3–4 Rafael Koch, promotioncard for a chair named "chido", offset paper, 2003
5   Rafael Koch, promotioncard for a product designer and close friend of mine, offset paper, 2004
6–7 Rafael Koch, promotioncard, introducing a public web project, offset paper, 2004

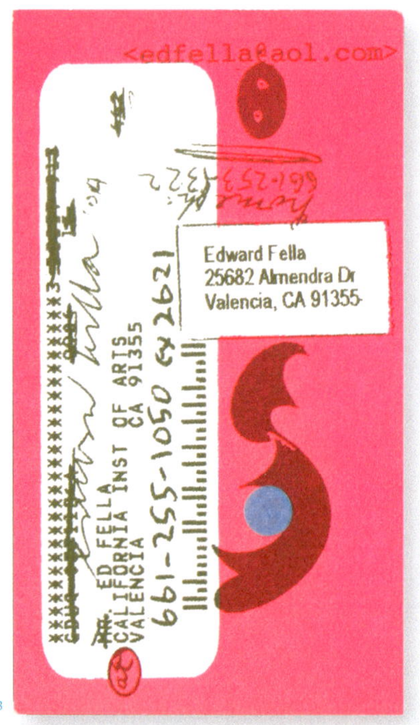

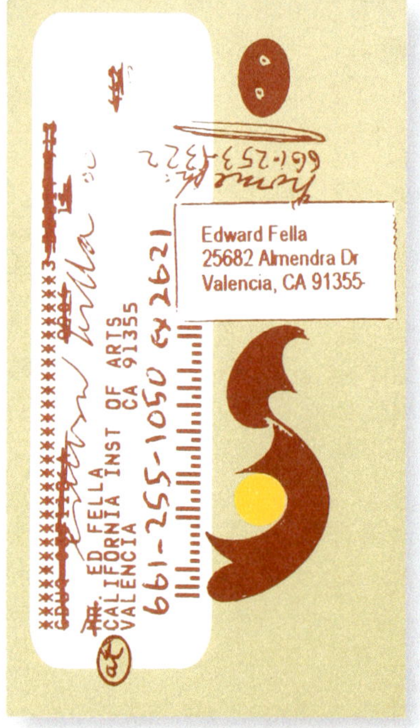

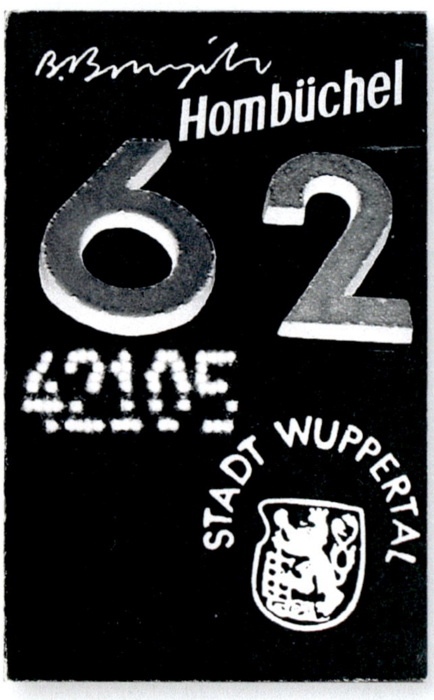

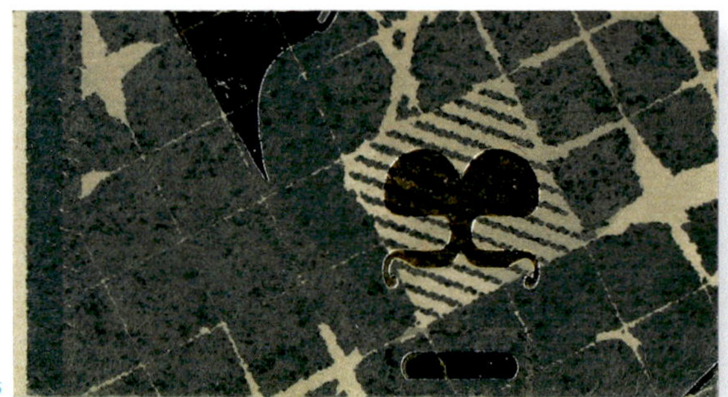

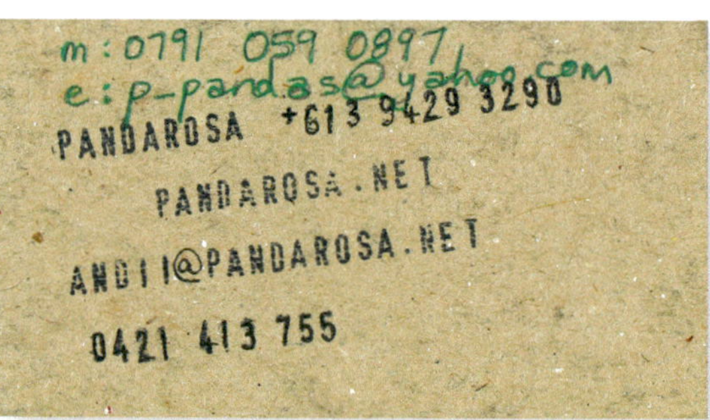

1–2   Tomoo Gokita, heavy paper
3–4   Ed Fella, paper, offset printing, 2000
5   Boris Brumnjak, paper, laser printing, 2002
6–7   Pandarosa, overprint poster for a client, silk-screen printing

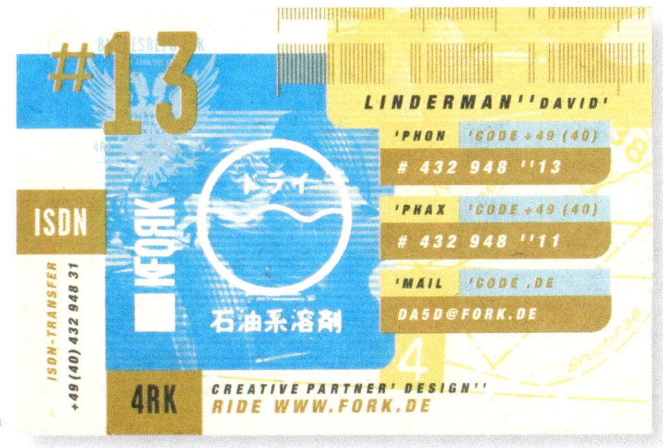

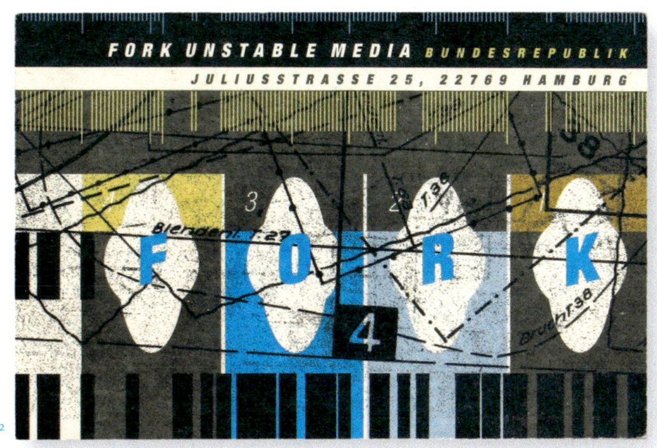

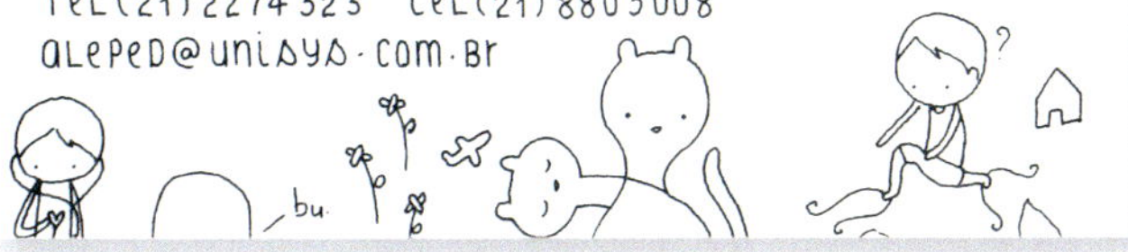

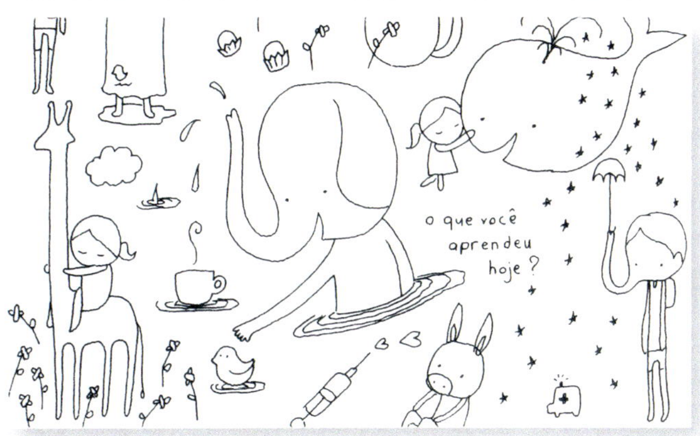

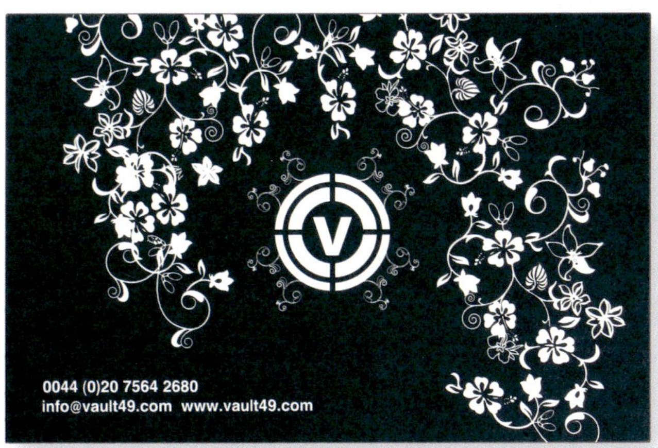

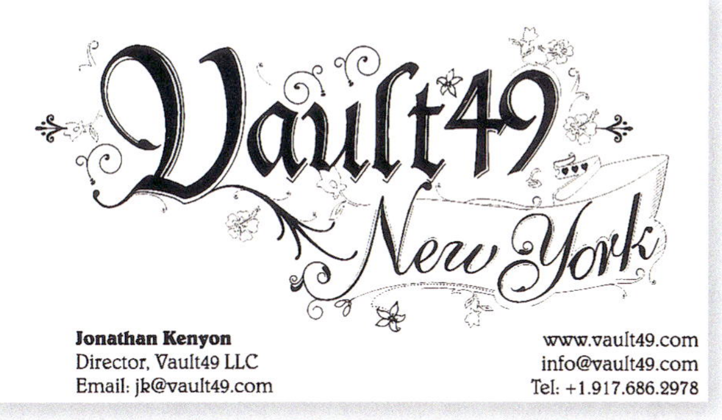

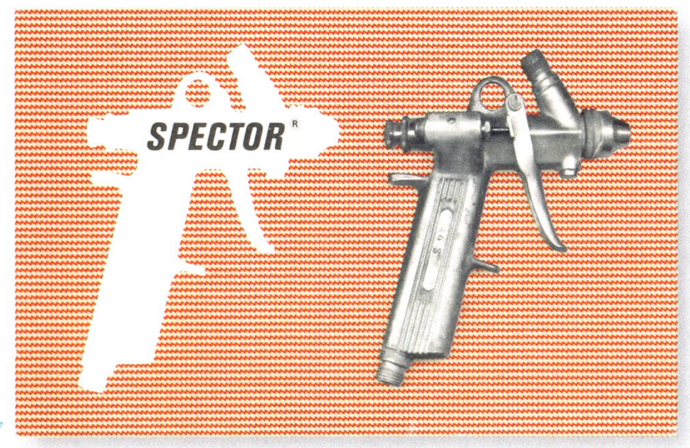

1–2   Fork Unstable Media / David Linderman, offset printing, 1998
3–4   Dra Alessandra Berliner Sznajder Pediatra, offset printing
5   Vault49, paper, offset printing, 2003
6   Vault49, paper, digital print, 2004
7   Spector / Markus Dreßen, chromo duplex board, offset printing, 1999

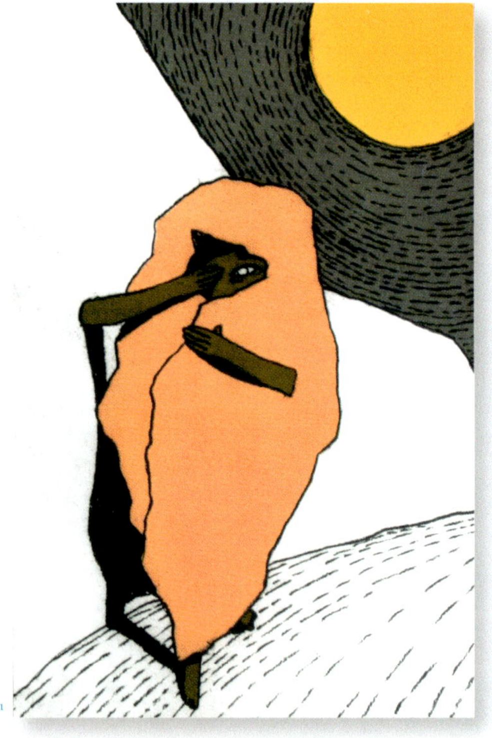

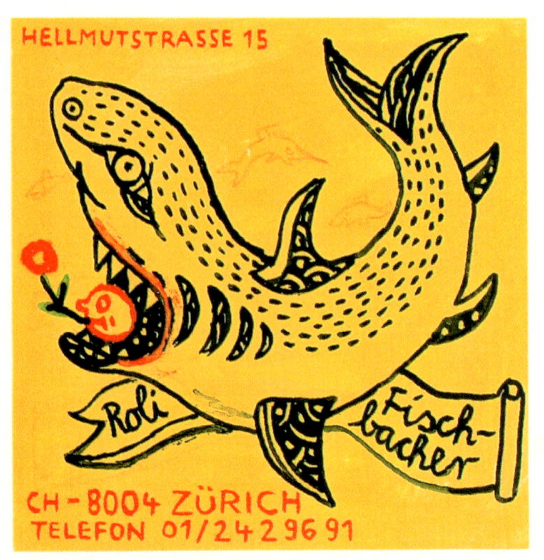

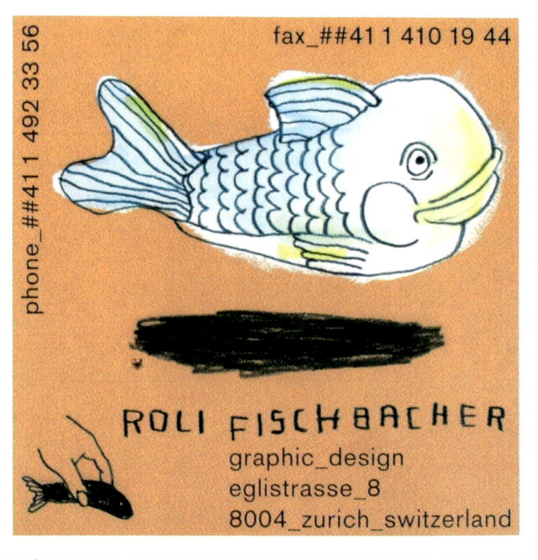

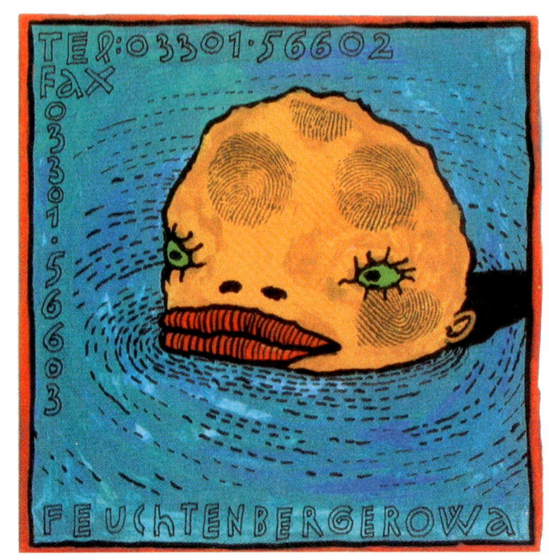

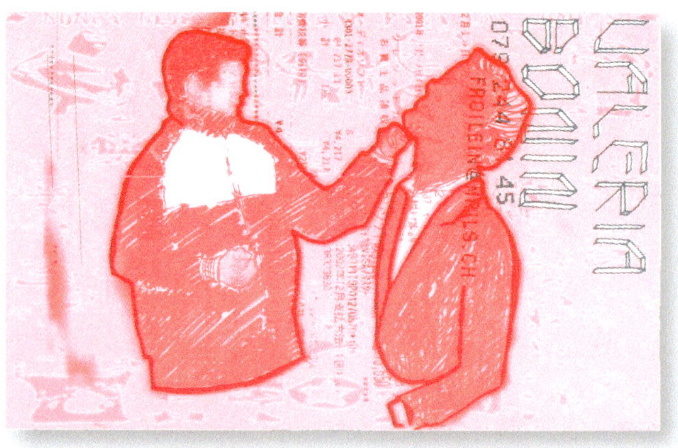

1–2   Anke Fechtenberger, offset printing and rubber stamp, 1999
3   Roli Fischbacher and Atak, self-adhesive paper, offset printing, 1997
4   Roli Fischbacher and Nadine Spengler, self-adhesive paper, offset printing, 2000
5   Anke Fechtenberger, offset printing, 2000
6   Valeria Bonin, offset paper, offset printing, 2001

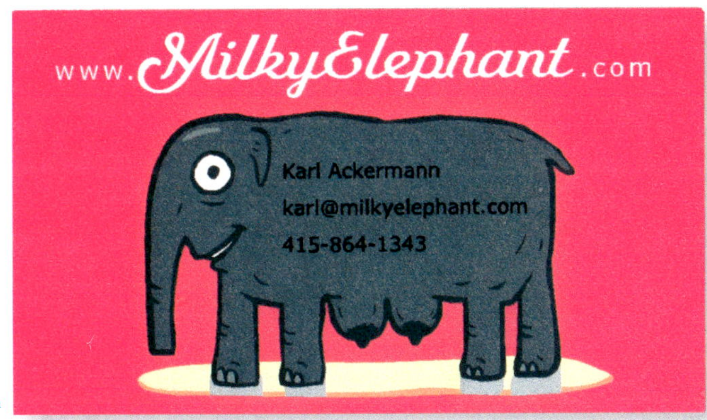

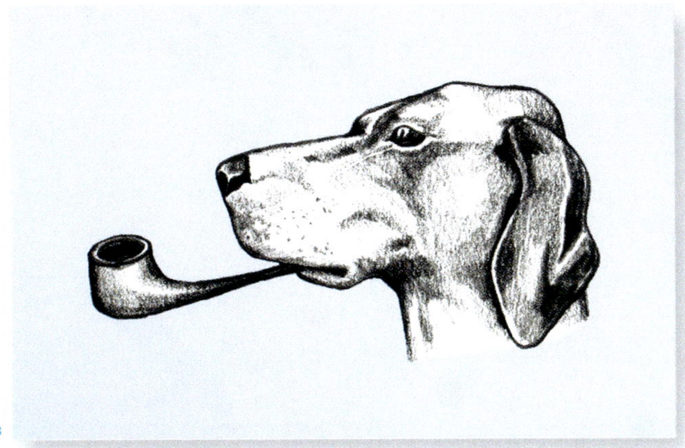

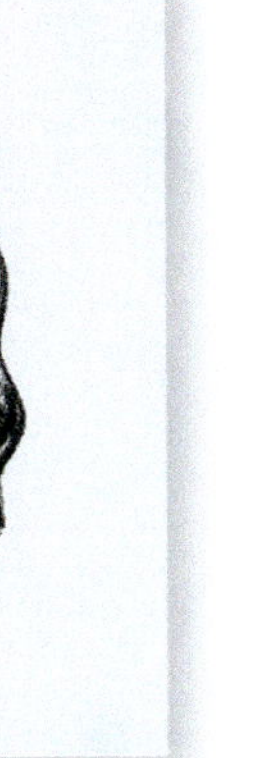

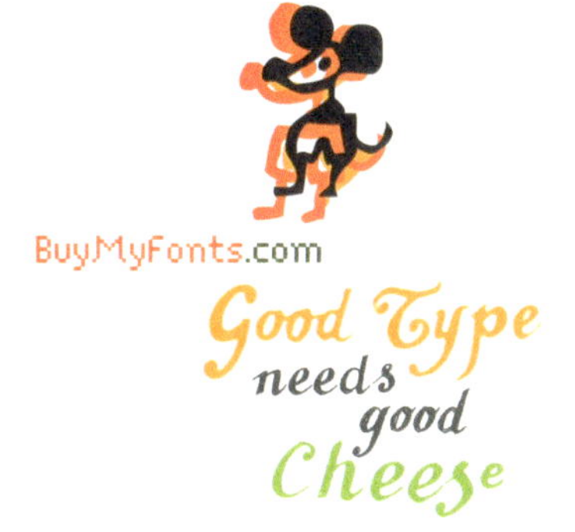

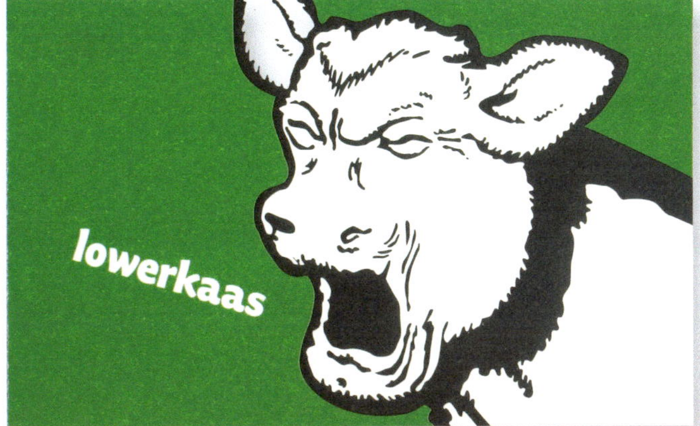

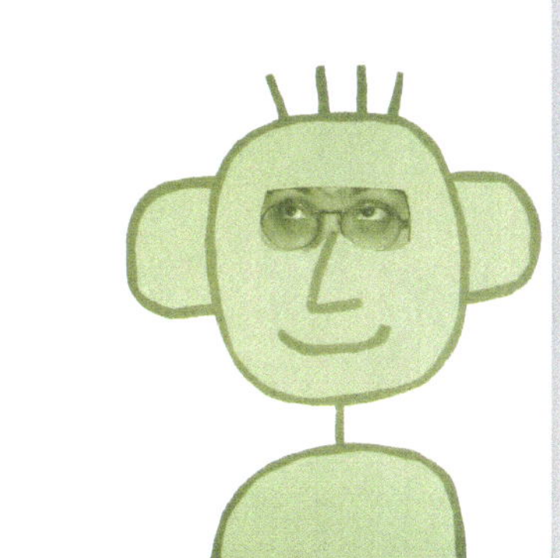

1   Milky Elephant and Karl Ackermann, thick paper, epson colour printer, 1997
2   Milky Elephant and Karl Ackermann, thick paper, epson colour printer, 1999
3   Mr. Bingo, artboard 350g, offset printing, 2001
4–5   BuyMyFonts.com / Imme and Alessio Leonardi, paper, offset printing, 2002
6–7   Underware, offset printing, 1999

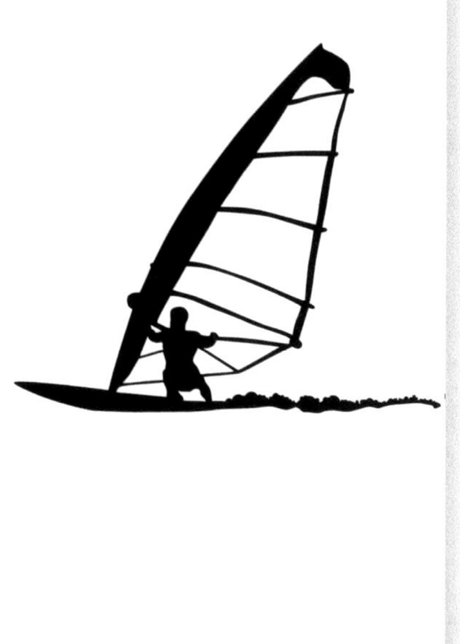

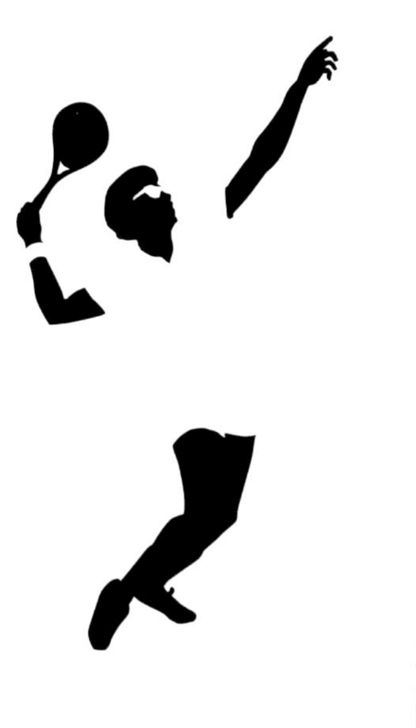

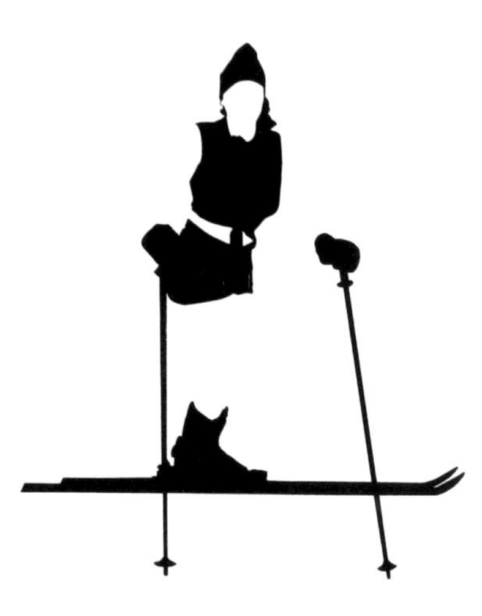

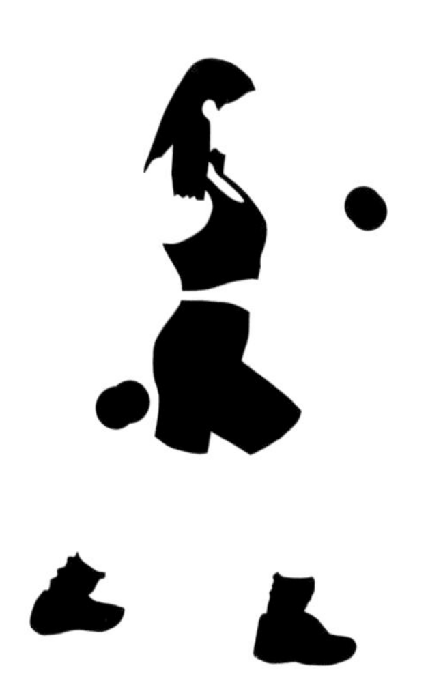

--
123buero
BUERO FUER GESTALTUNG
Timo Gaessner
Esmarchstr. 16
10407 Berlin
Germany
+49.(0)30.42020940 (TEL)
+49.(0)30.42020941 (FAX)
+49.(0)172.3950069 (MOBILE)
timo@123buero.com
www.123buero.com

1–6   123Buero / Timo Gaessner, cardboard 300 g, offset printing, one-sided finishing, 2002

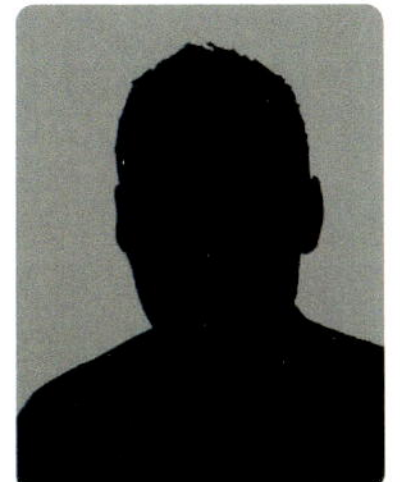

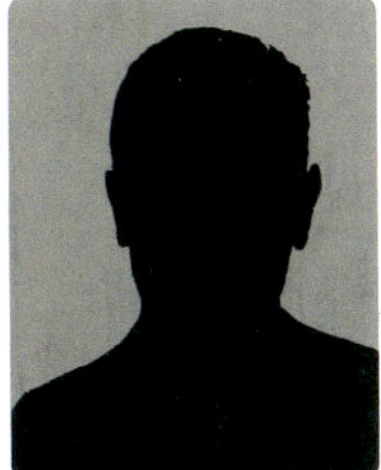

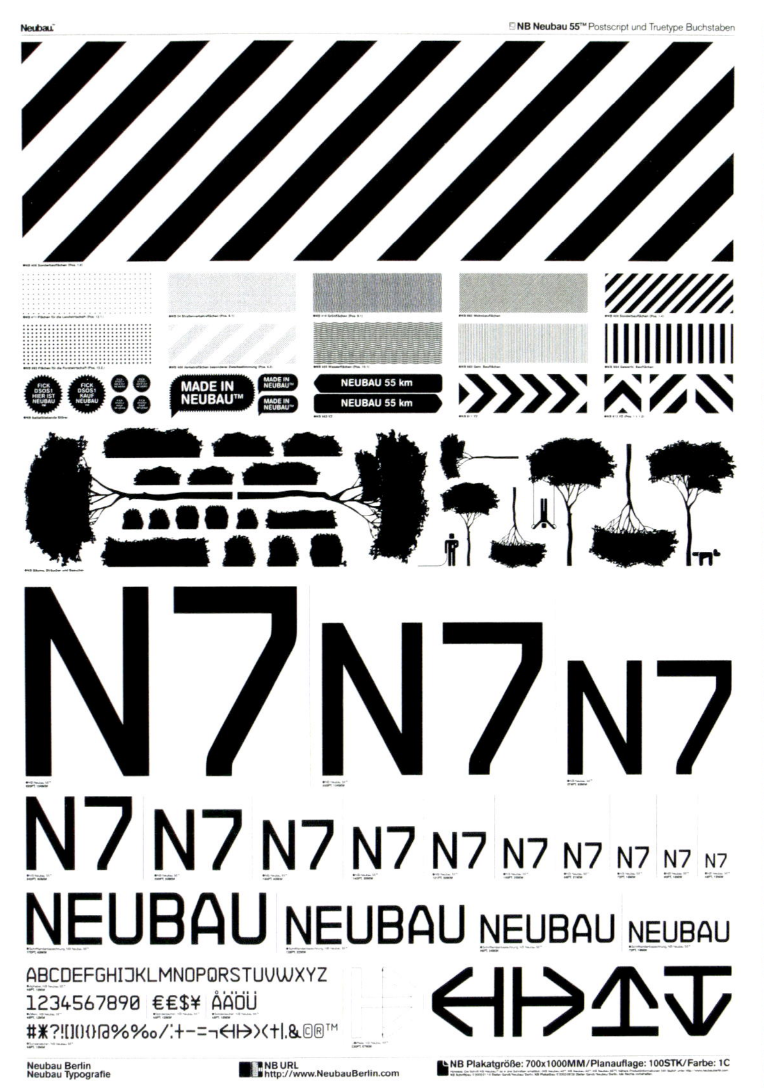

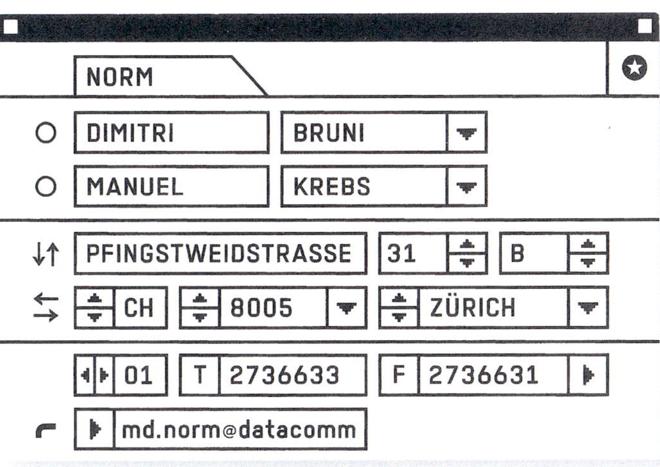

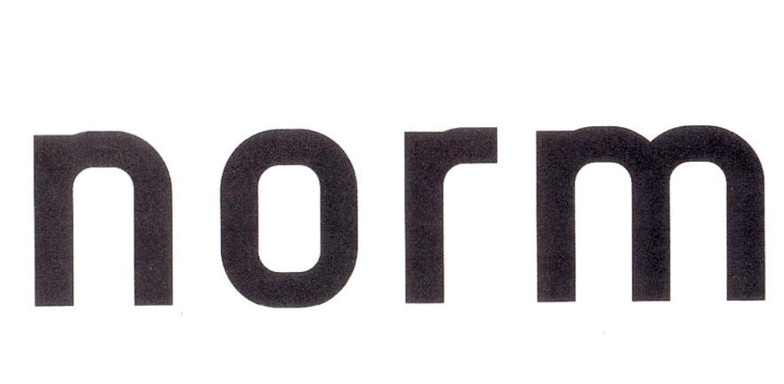

1–2   Norm, Ikonogloss paper 200 g, offset printing, 2002
3   Neubau / Gandl, cardboard 250 g, offset printing, 2002
4–5   Norm, chromo cardboard 300 g, offset printing, 2000

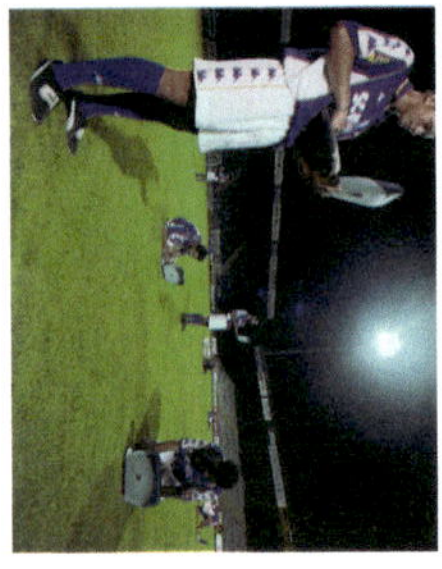

VECTORAMA.ORG
A MUTLIUSER PLAYGROUND –
PLAY IT ONLINE WITH NINE OTHER
USERS AT THE SAME TIME.

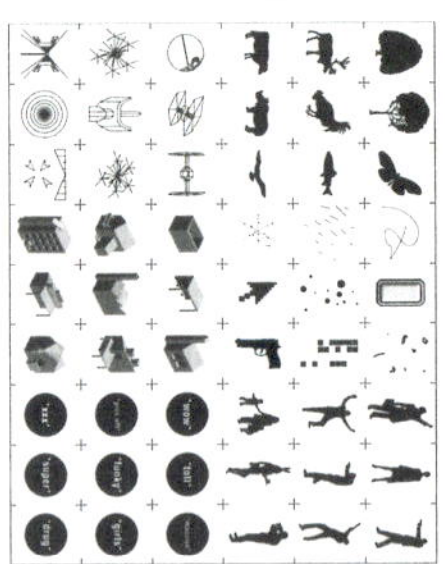

VECTORAMA.ORG
CHOOSE FROM A WIDE RANGE OF
VECTOR-DRAWINGS AND ARRANGE THEM
ON THE PLAYGROUND.

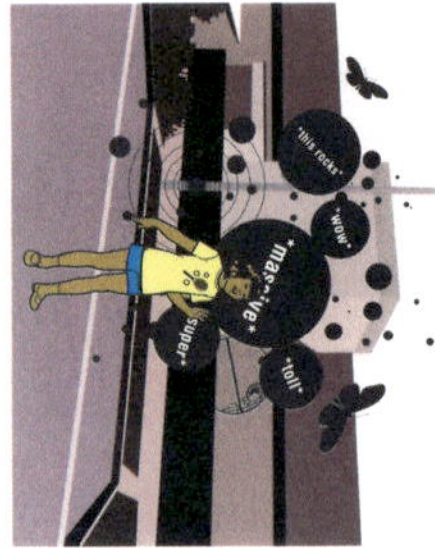

VECTORAMA.ORG
MOVING, SCALING, ROTATING AND COLORING
ITEMS ON THE PLAYGROUND COULD LEAD
TO PICUTERS LIKE THIS…

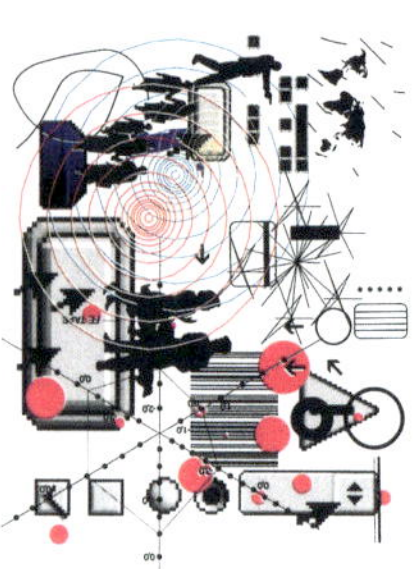

VECTORAMA.ORG
…OR PICTURES LIKE THIS. IT'S UP TO YOU.

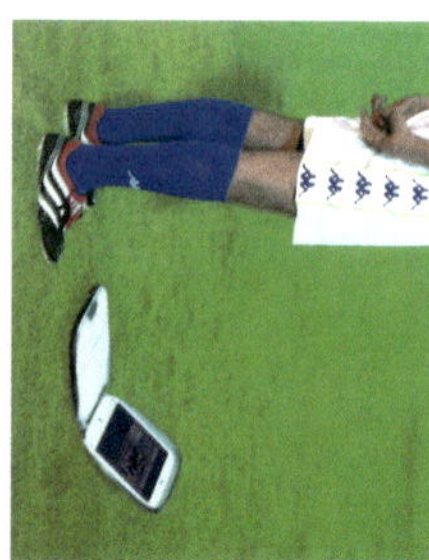

VECTORAMA.ORG
LET US PLAY.

CONTACT HTTP://WWW.VECTORAMA.ORG

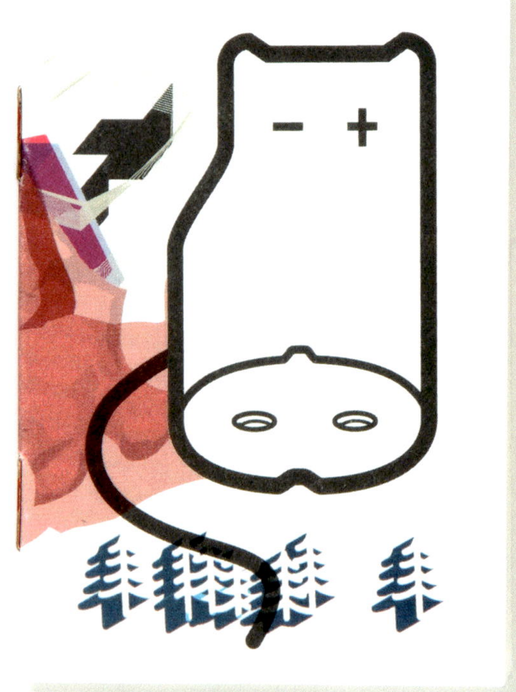

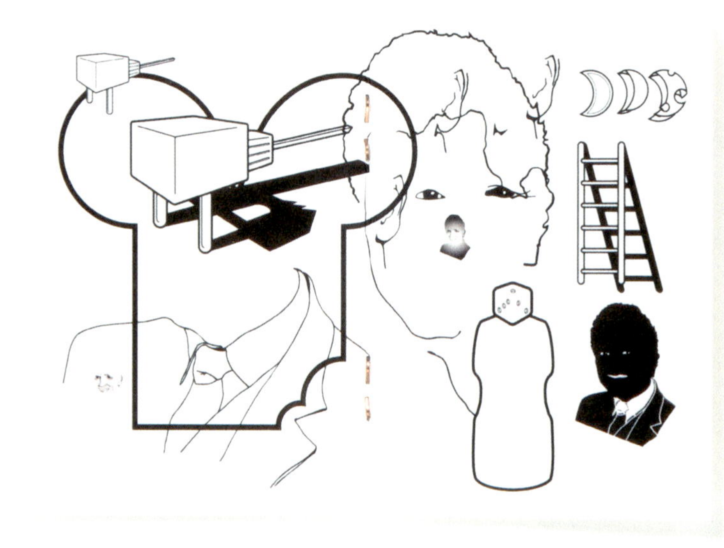

1   Urs Lehni, 425 x 55 mm, offset printing, 2001
2–3   178 Aardige Ontwerpers, 65 x 92 mm, paper 250 g, offset printing, 2000

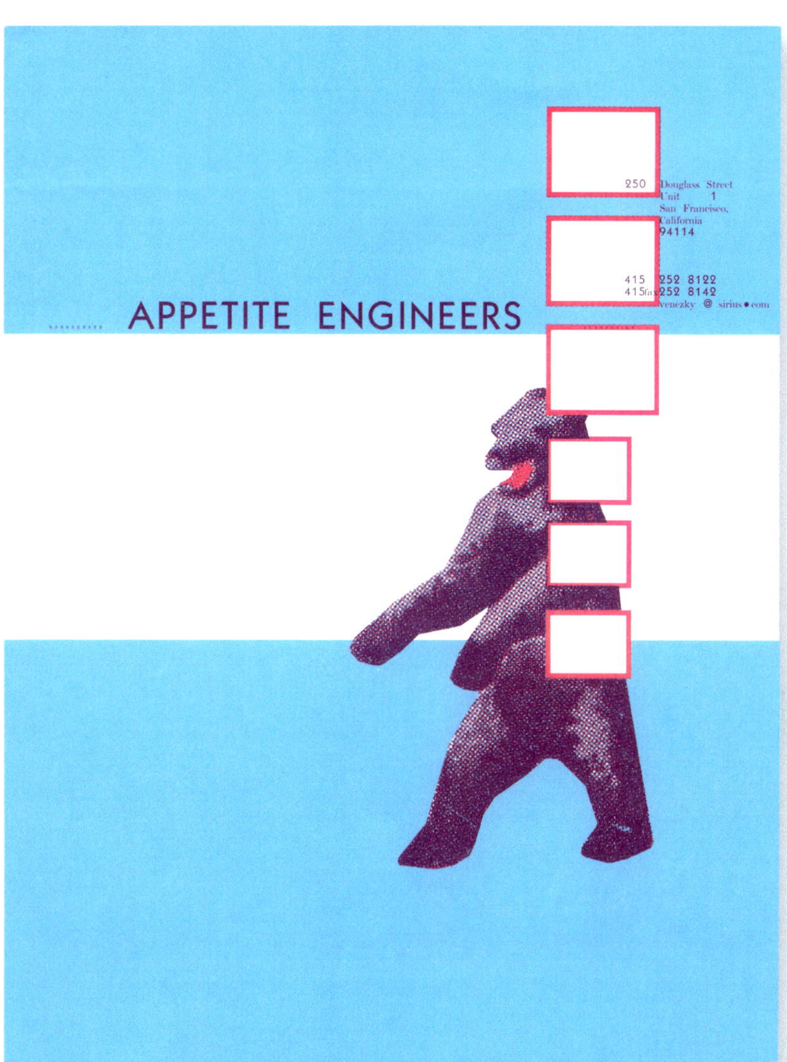
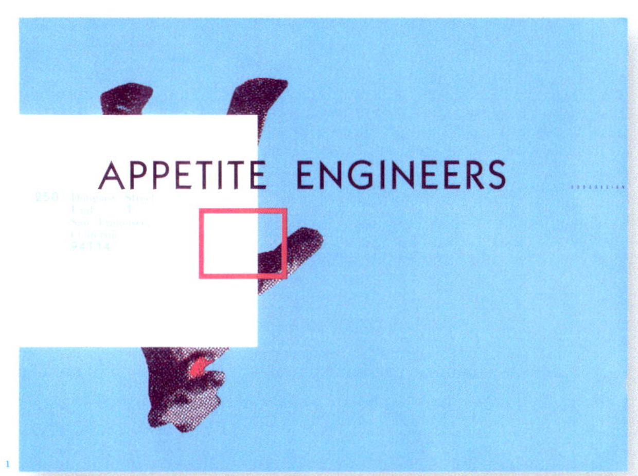
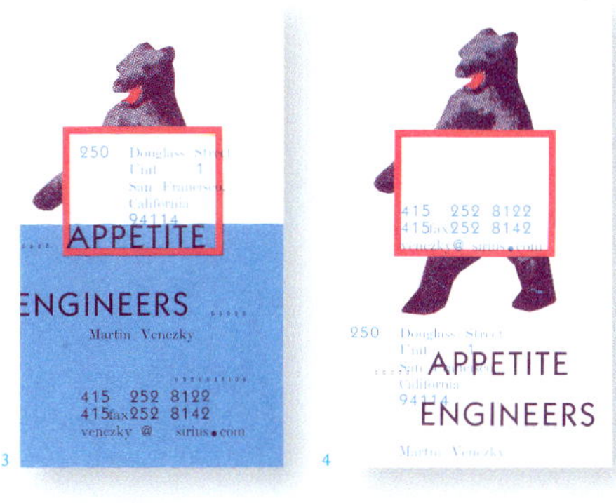
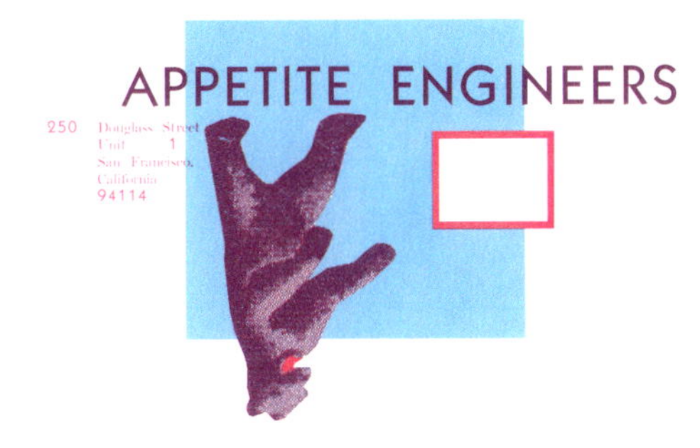

1–5   Appetite Engineers / Martin Venetzky, offset printing, 1998

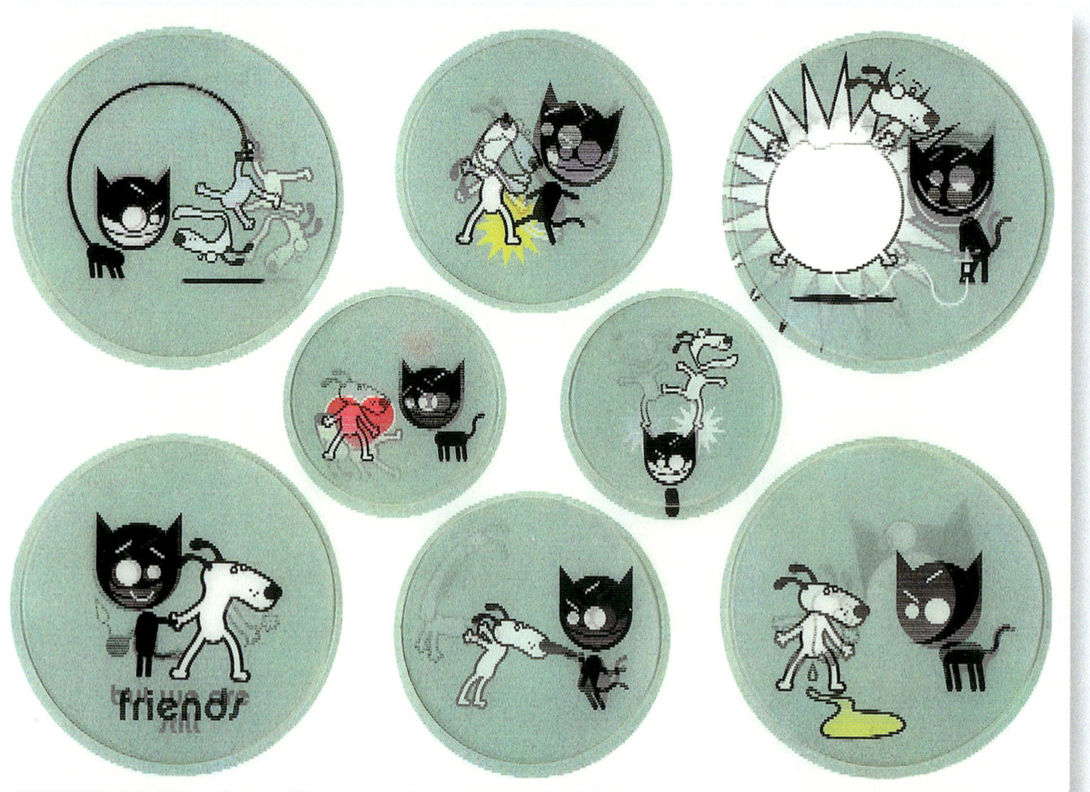

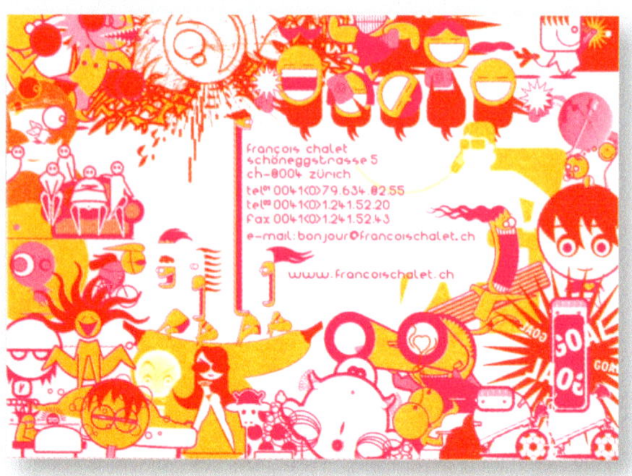

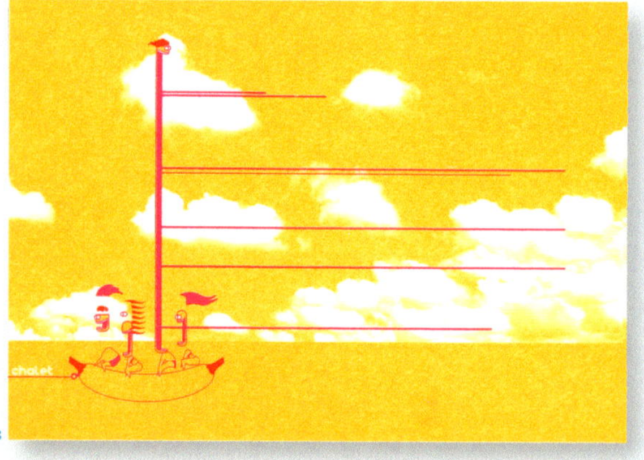

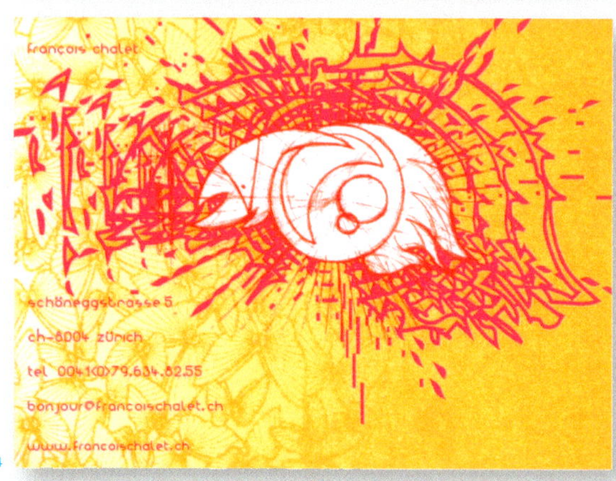

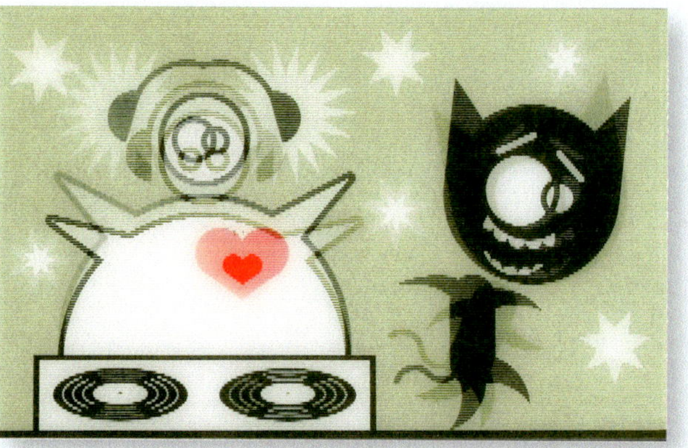

1   François Chalet, adhesive cardboard with special foil, offset printing, 2004
2–4 François Chalet, heavy adhesive offset paper, offset printing, 2000
5   François Chalet, cardboard with special foil, offset printing, 2002

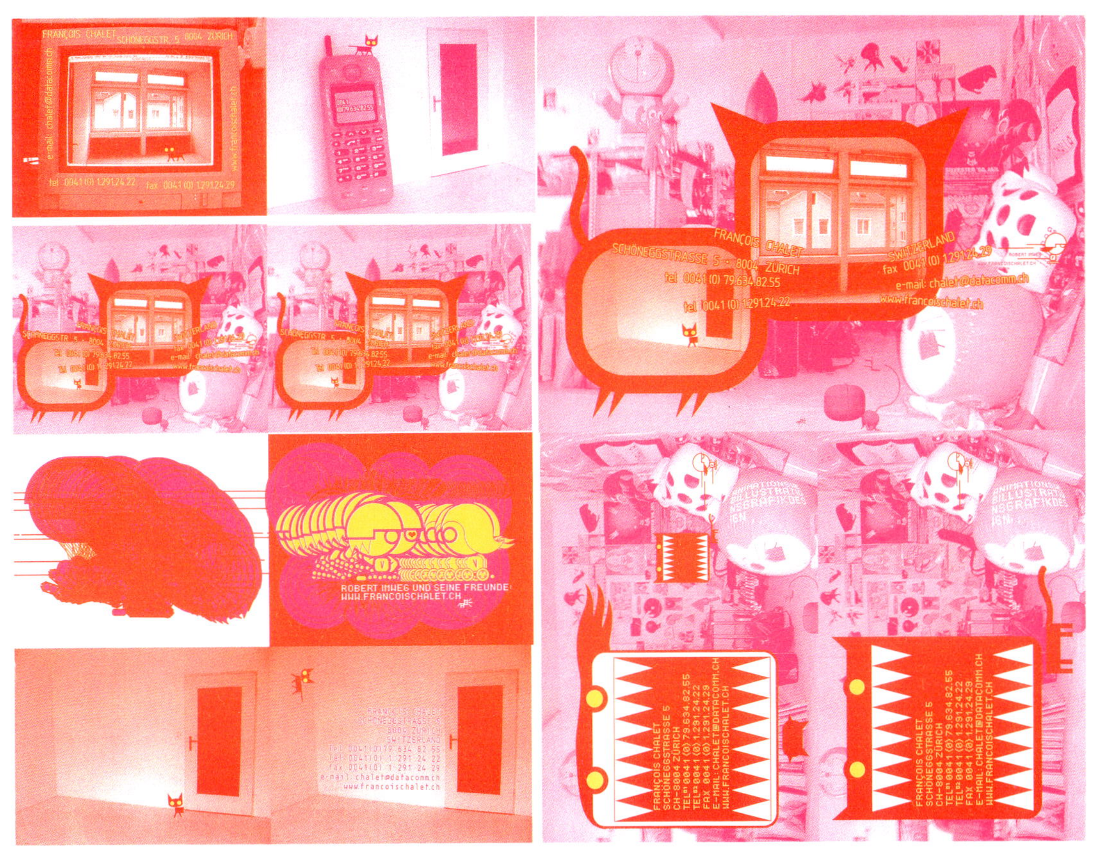

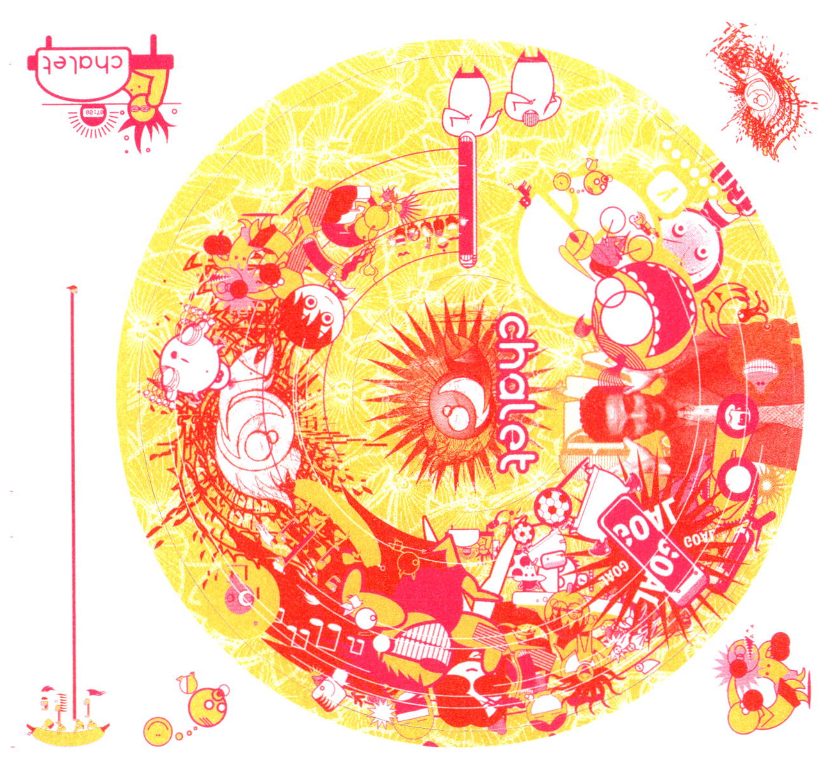

1   François Chalet, A5, adhesive offset paper, offset printing, 2001
2   François Chalet, 150 x 130 mm, heavy adhesive offset paper, offset printing, 2000

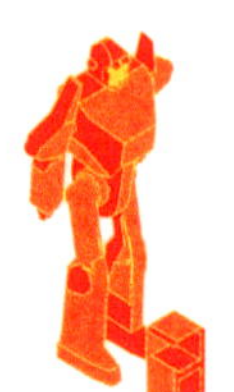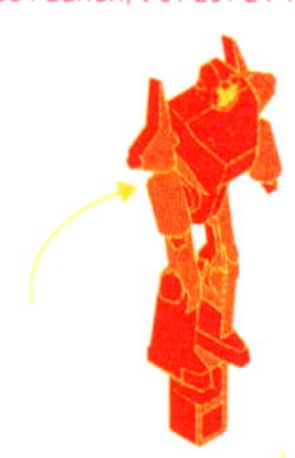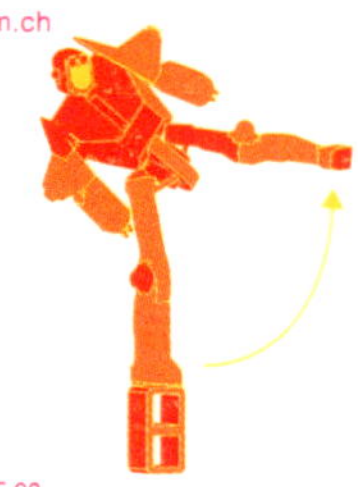

just want to mention some good balance and strength exercises that you can try that will help build up your legs and overall agility. the only tools or
equipment you will need is a concrete BLOCK of about 6 or 8in. for more kicksinformation:
martin woodtli, schöneggstrasse 5, 8004 zürich, t 01 291 24 19, f 01 291 24 29, n 076 396 69 63, martinwoodtli@datacomm.ch

EXERCISE 01.

this is very simple & basic. this will develop jumping and
overall balance in the legs. repeat until you can't do anymore.
with feet together, stand behind the block and just jump
onto the block without busting your ass.

EXERCISE 02.

just hop on the block like EX. 01.
bend the knees a bit and do a
front snap kick, alternating legs.
do this shit with intent.

EXERCISE 03.

this kick will be harder to perform,
but you should try it anyway.
prefom a sidekick with speed and power.
the emphasis is control first.

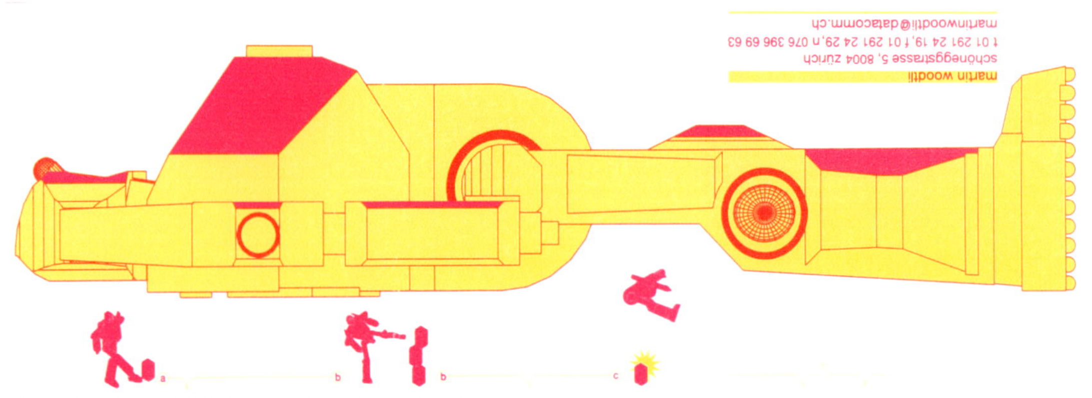

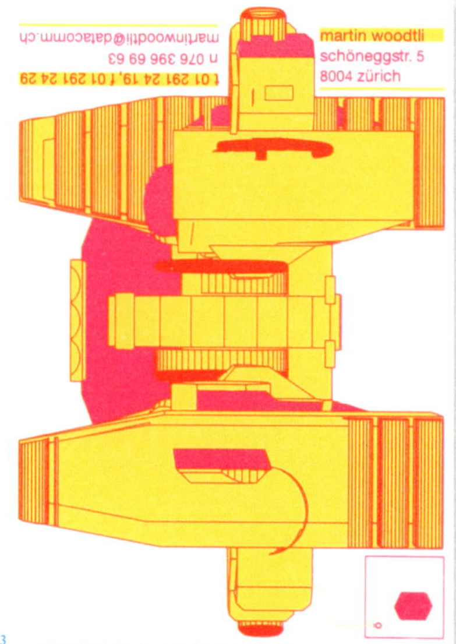

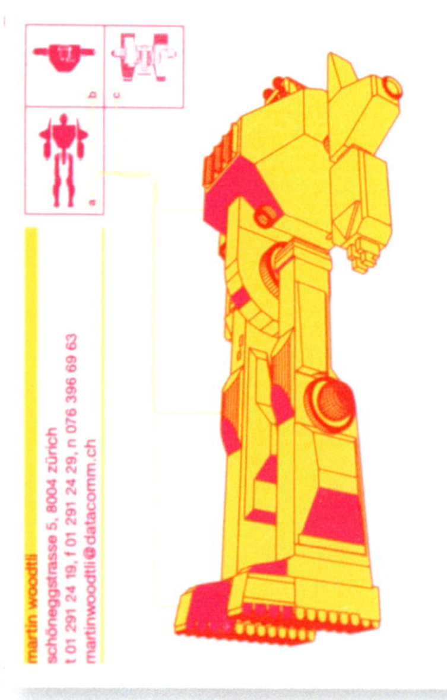

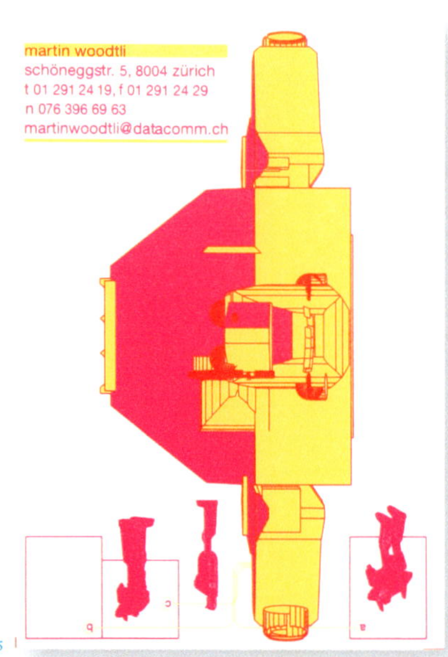

1–5   Martin Woodtli, adhesive paper, offset printing 2c, 1999

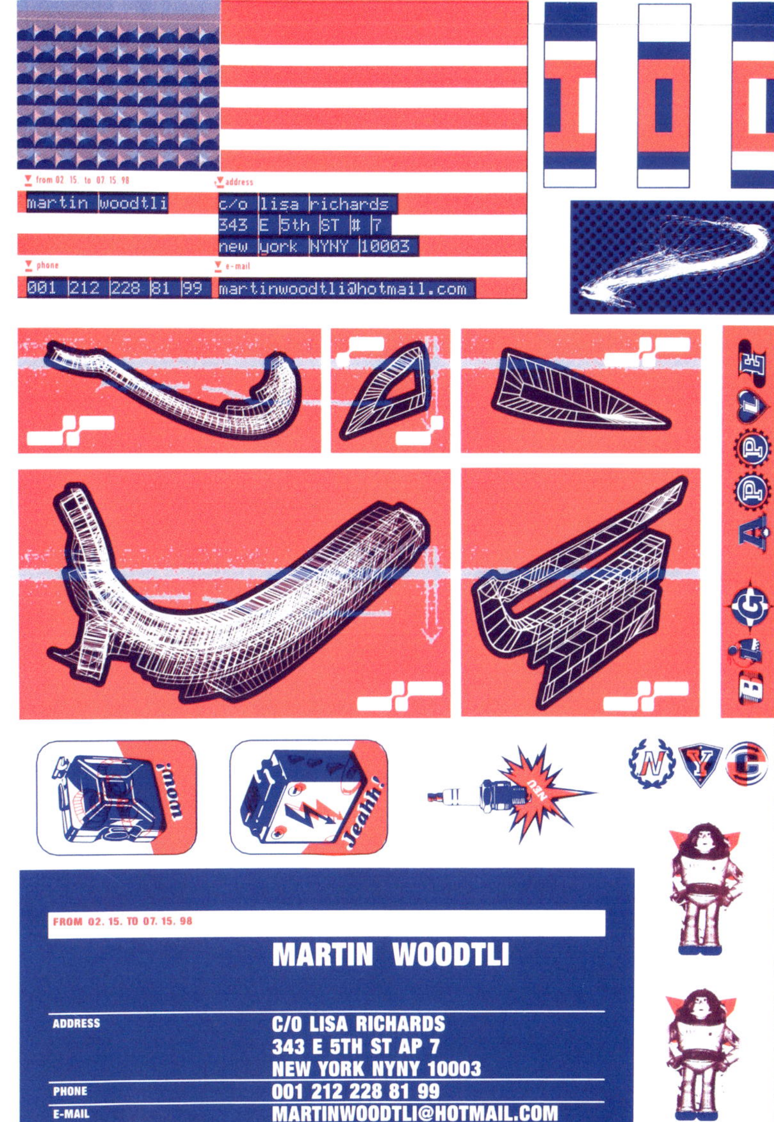

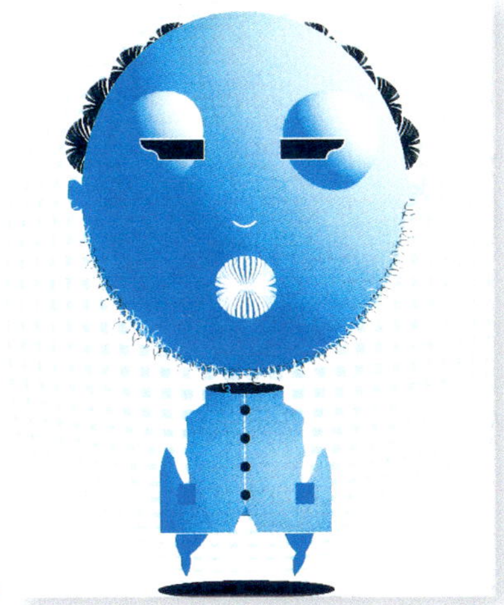

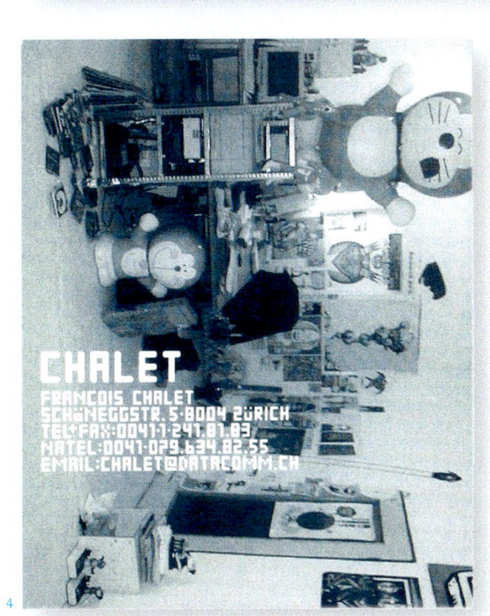

1–2   Martin Woodtli, adhesive paper, offset printing 2c, 1998
3–4   François Chalet, offset printing, 2001

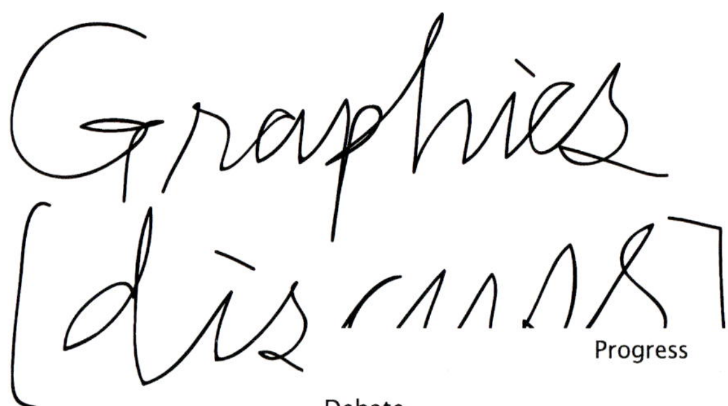

TUESDAY 8 JUNE 2004 7PM

TICKET 110

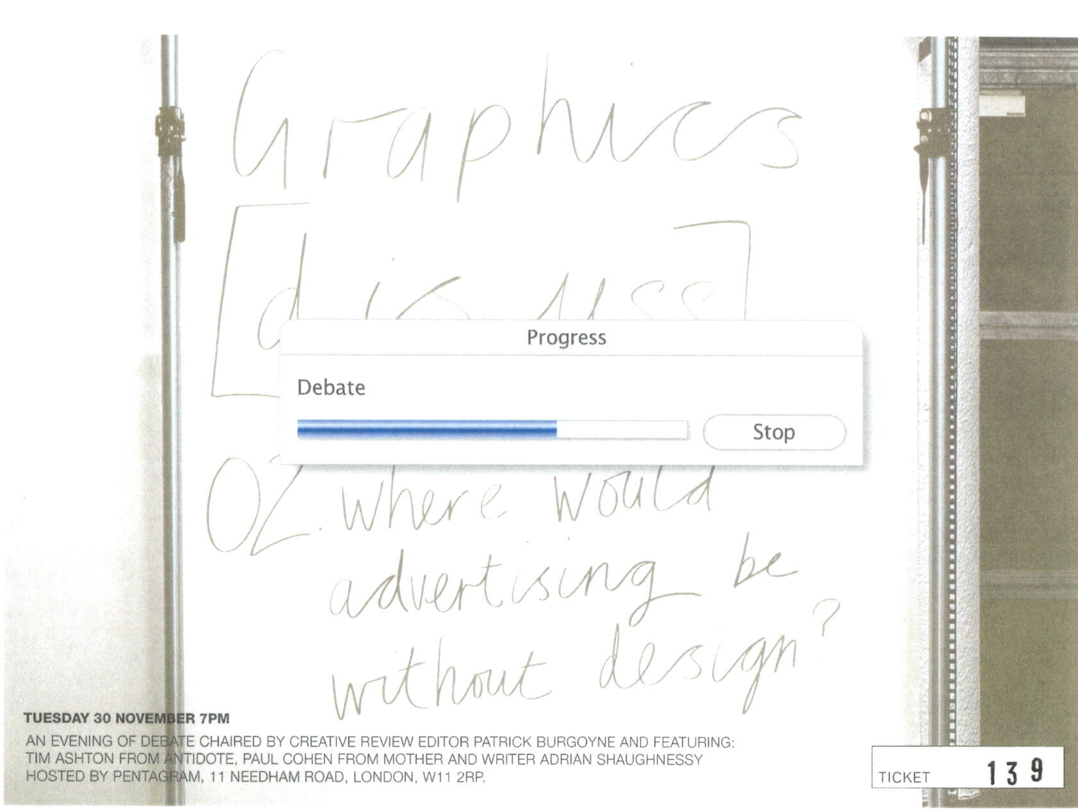

TUESDAY 30 NOVEMBER 7PM
AN EVENING OF DEBATE CHAIRED BY CREATIVE REVIEW EDITOR PATRICK BURGOYNE AND FEATURING:
TIM ASHTON FROM ANTIDOTE, PAUL COHEN FROM MOTHER AND WRITER ADRIAN SHAUGHNESSY
HOSTED BY PENTAGRAM, 11 NEEDHAM ROAD, LONDON, W11 2RP.

TICKET 139

1   Pentagram Design Limited / Angus Hyland with Sharon Hwang, 2004
2   Pentagram Design Limited / Angus Hyland with Charlie Hanson, photography: Nick Turner, 2004

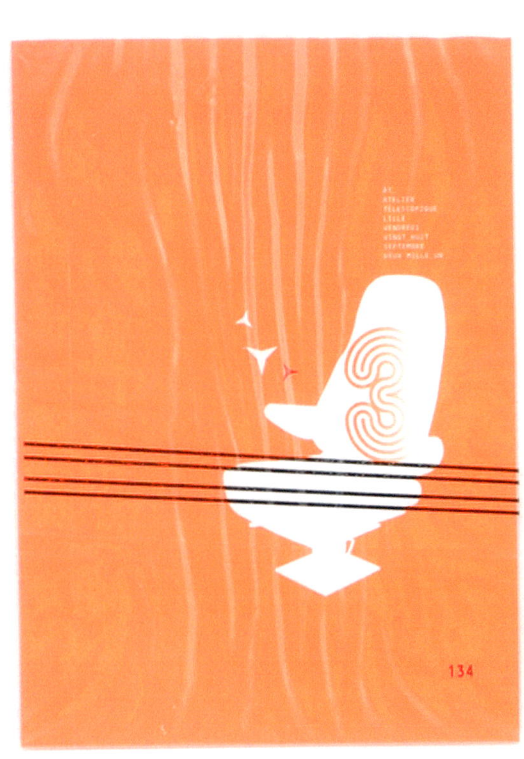
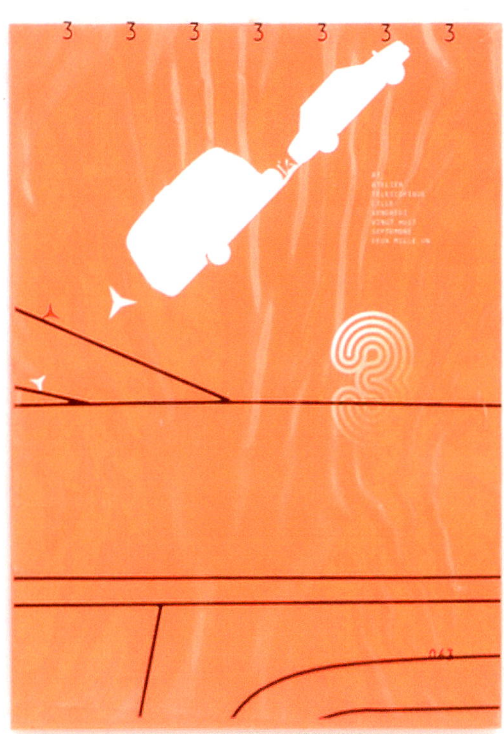
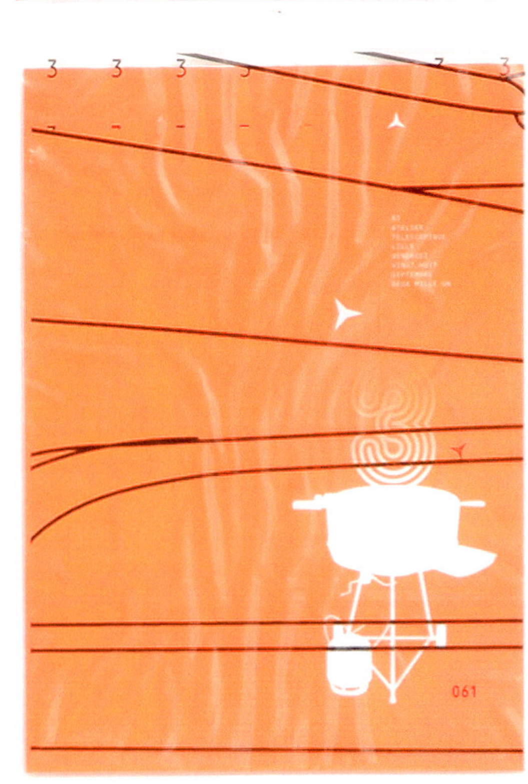

1–3 Atelier Télescopique, 160 x 210 mm, paper and plastic pocket, offset printing, 2001

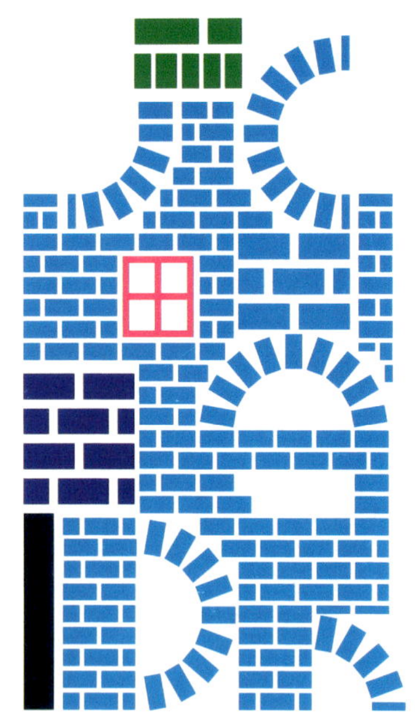

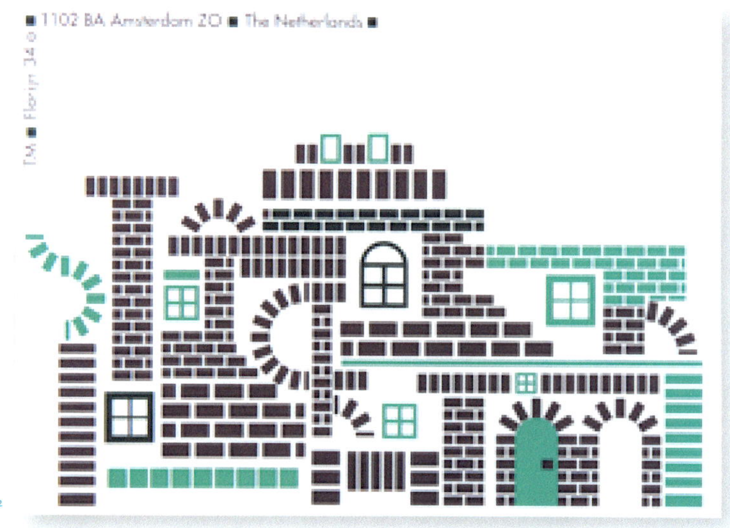

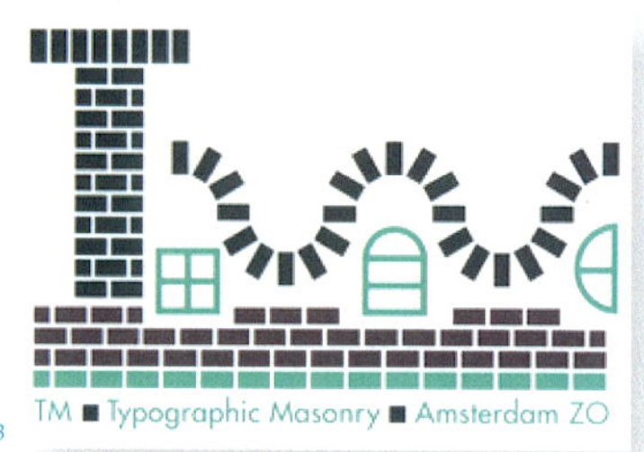

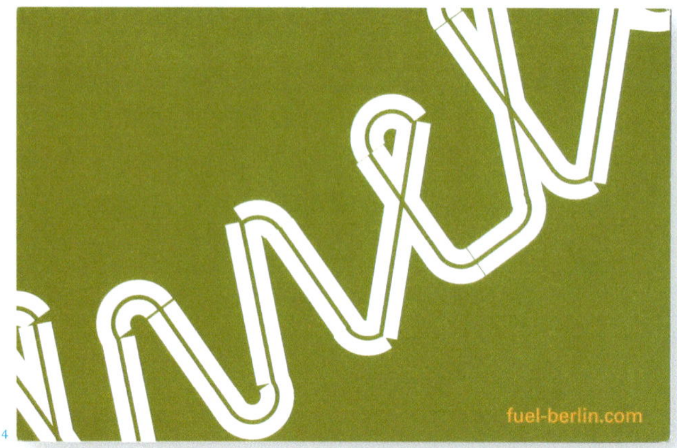

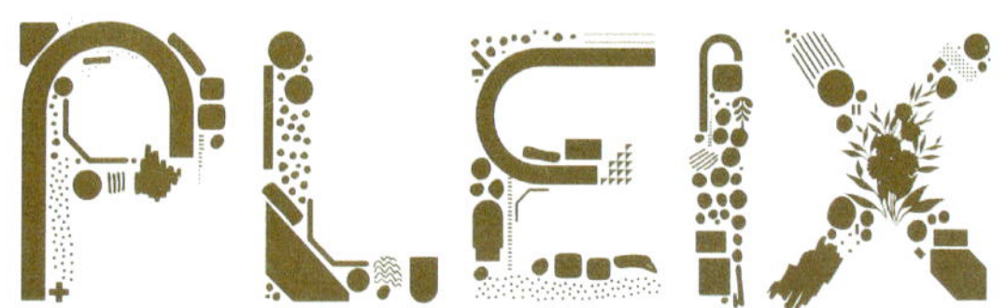

1–3   Richard Niessen, sticker, offset printing, 2003
4–5   Fuel-Berlin / Vasili Trigoudis, cardboard, offset printing, 2003
6   Pleix / Genevive Gauckler, paper 300 g, offset printing, 2003

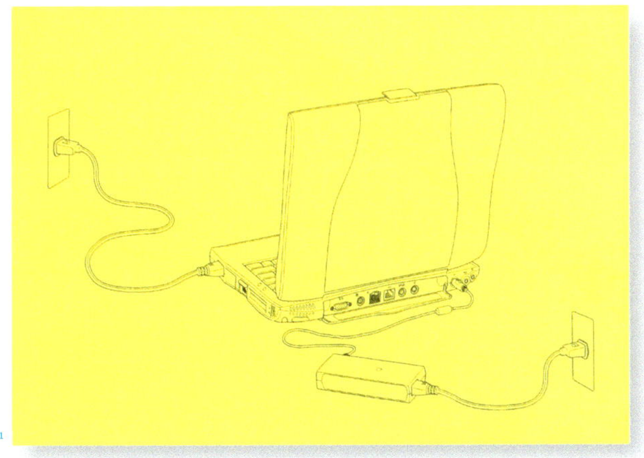

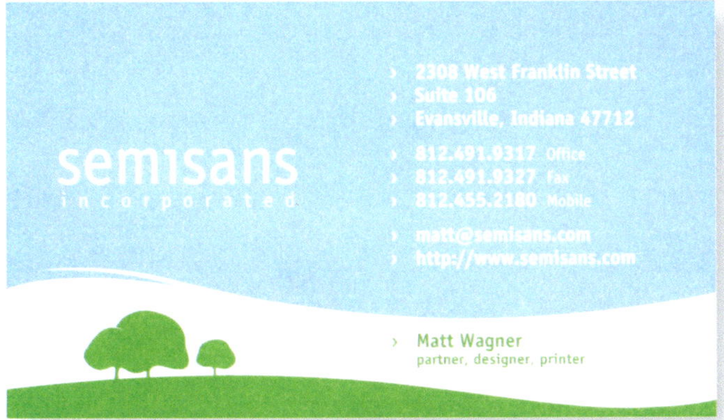

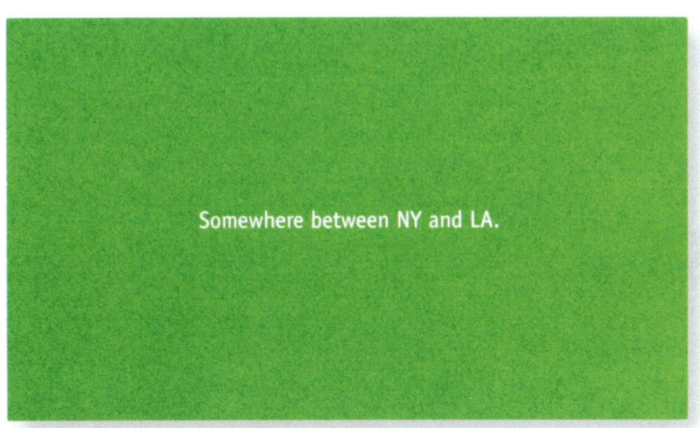

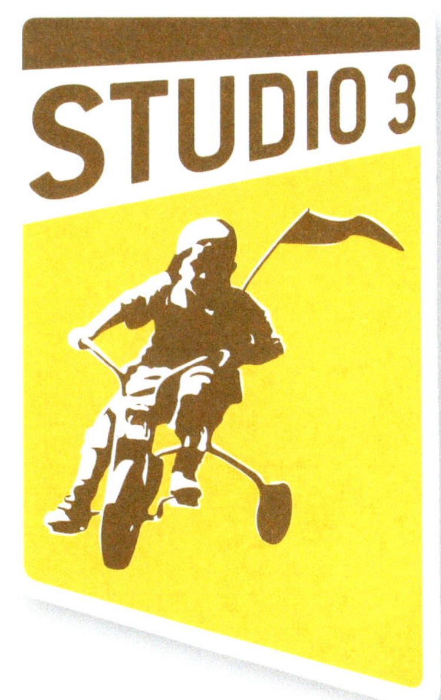

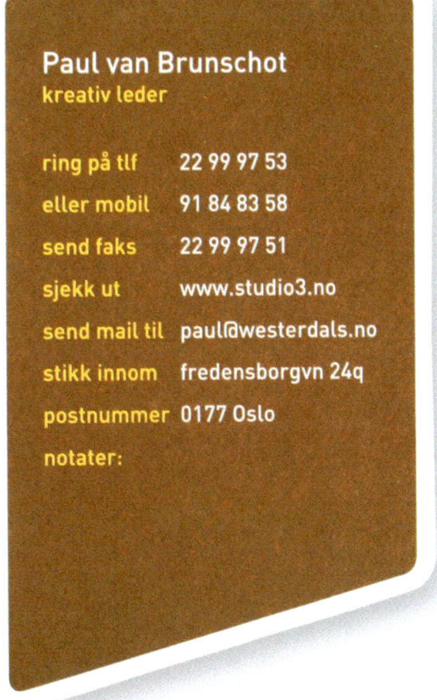

1–2   Prill Vieceli / Alberto Vieceli, Tania Prill, chromolux, offset printing, 2001
3–4   Semisans, Inc. / Matt Wagner and Aaron Tanner, French @ Smart White, offset printing, 2004
5–6   Studio 3 / Maren Johnsen, paper, offset printing, 2002

grafisch ontwerpstudio

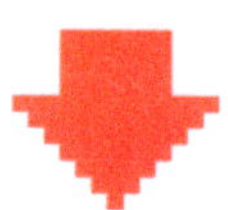

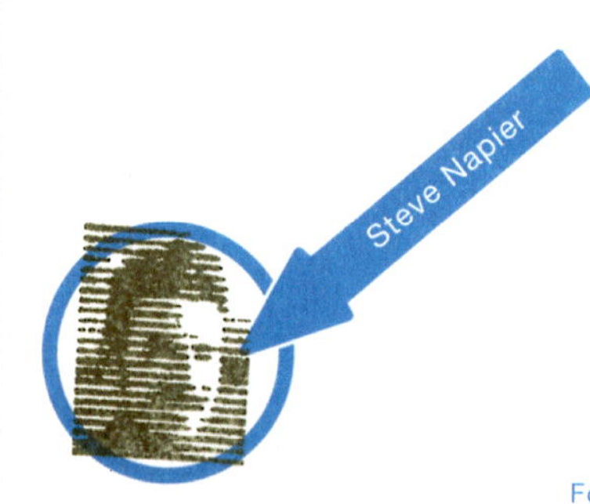

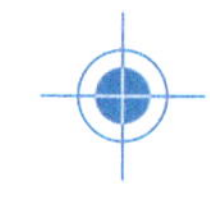

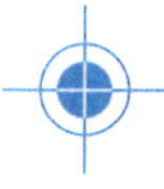

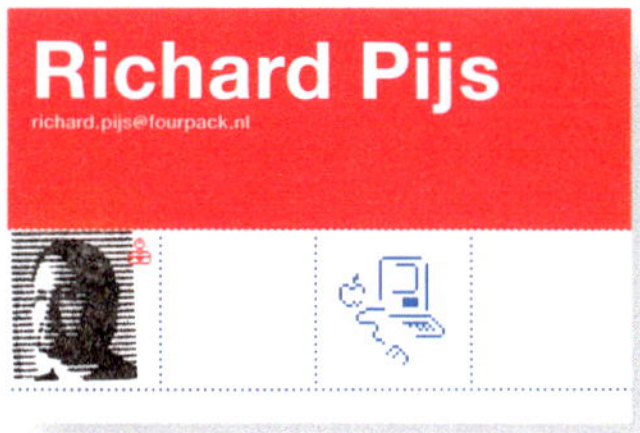

Dutch design team FoURPAcK ontwerpers (four members, four design disciplines) love to go postal – a homage to the timeless clarity of Dutch design, their strictly coherent, yet instantly lovable range of promotional materials goes far beyond the usual assortment of business cards, envelopes and letterheads to encompass ubiquitous use of rubber stamping, perforated package stickers, countless icons and even a matching paper sash to hold it all together.
In their strong fusion of illustration and graphic design, FoUR-PAcK's self-imposed restriction to just a few pure colours (cyan, white and a variant of red fluor) carries the added advantage of lossless enlargement.

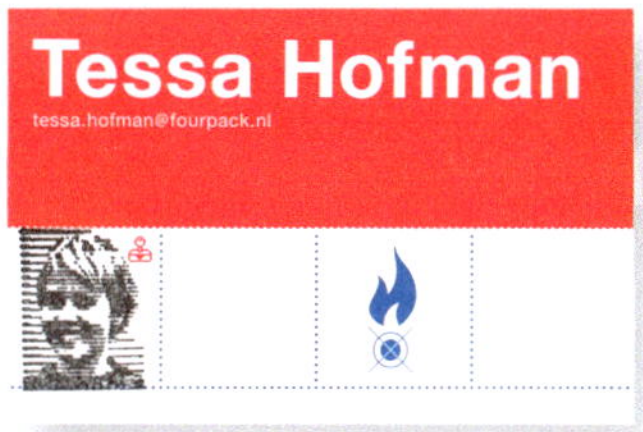

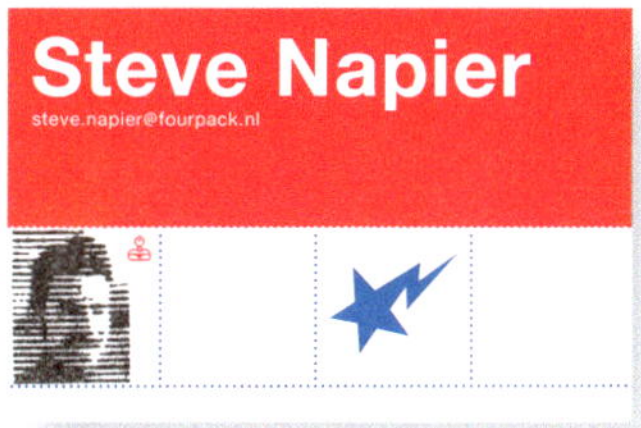

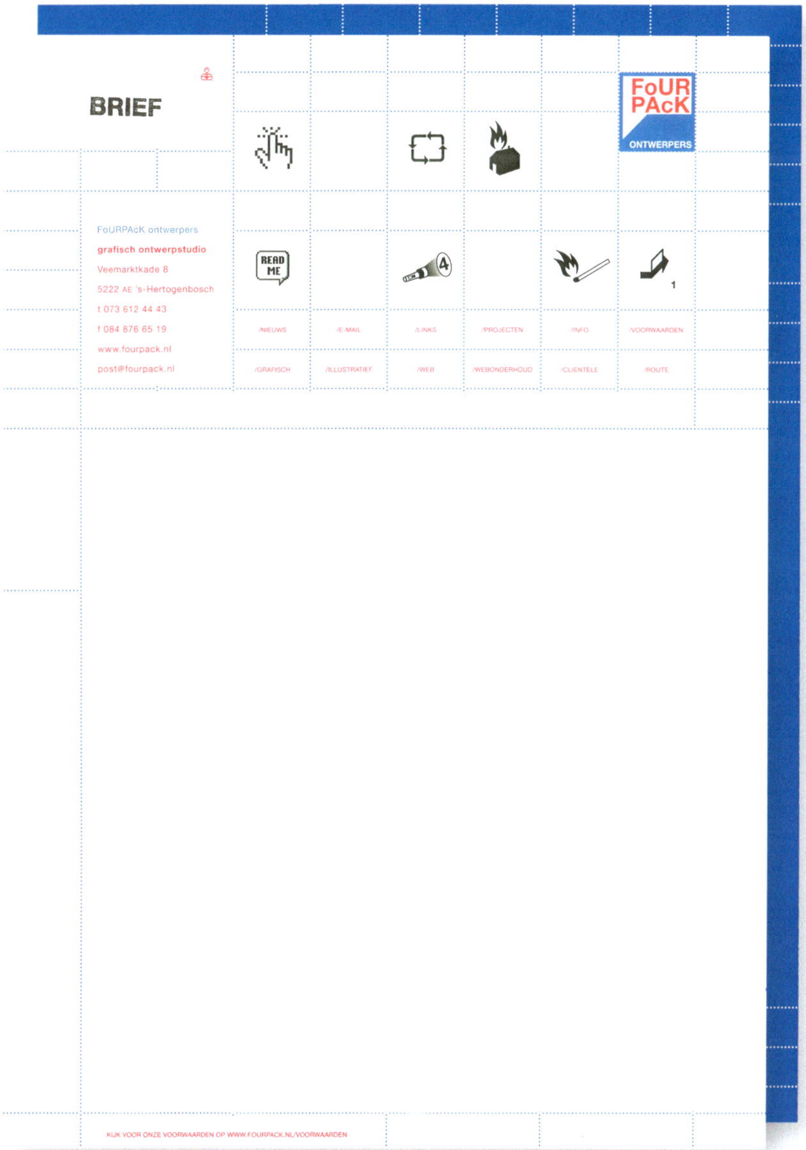

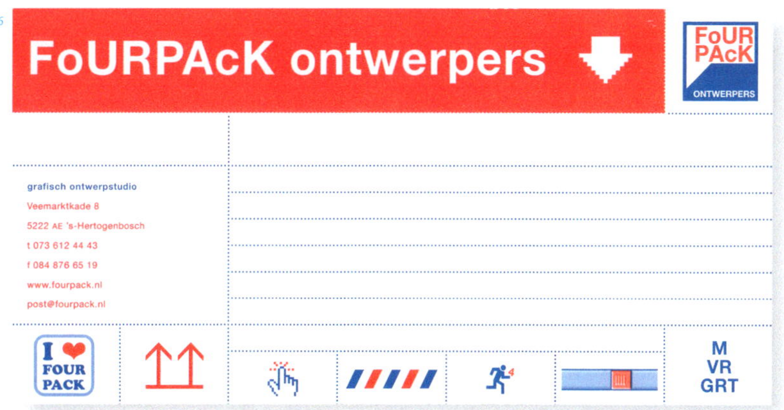

1–6   Four Pack Ontwerpers, rubber stamp and perforations, paper, offset printing, 2003

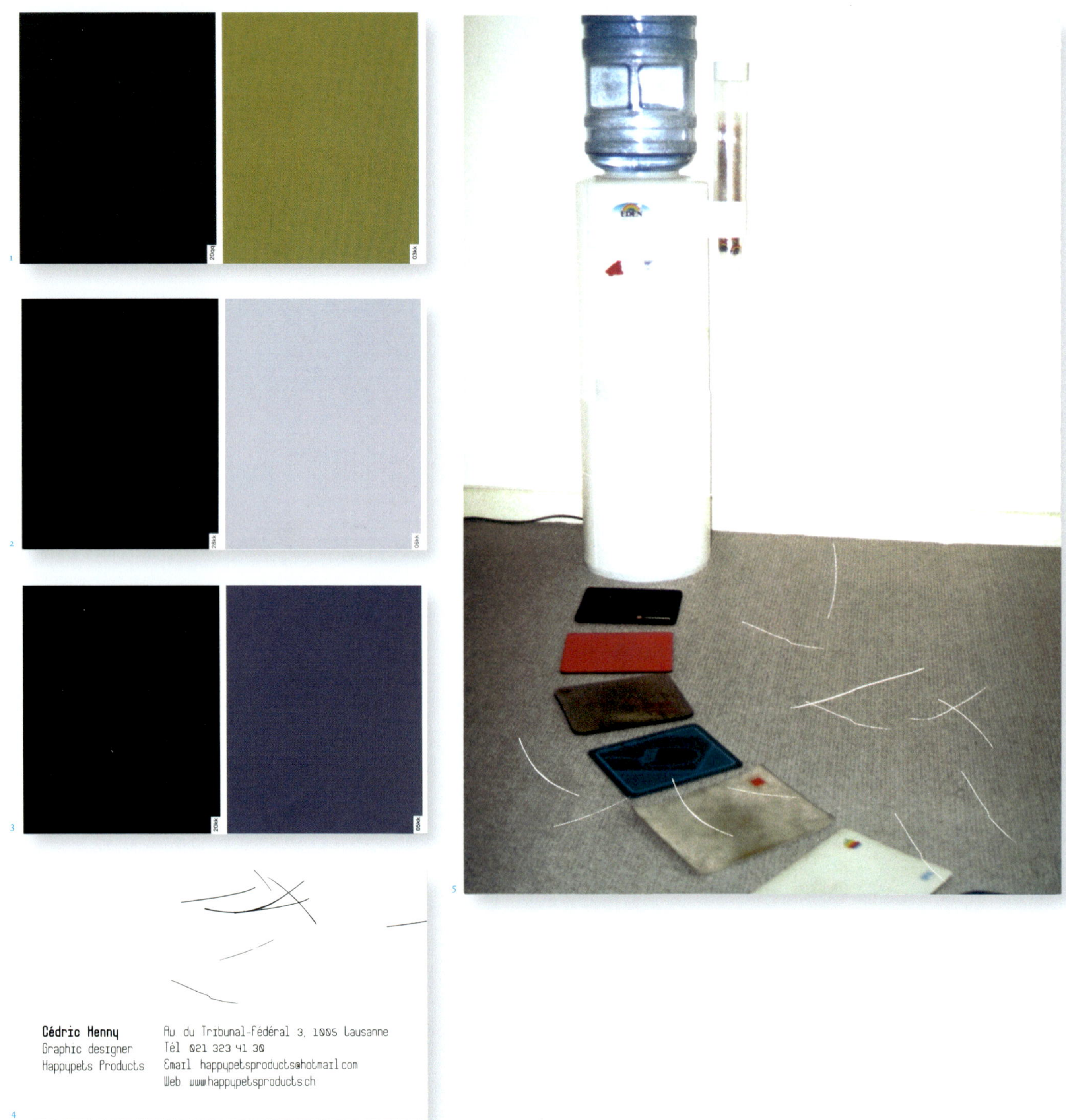

1–4   Happypets, 80 x 50 mm, Invercote, offset printing, 2000
5   Happypets, 105 x 150 mm, Invercote, offset printing, 2000

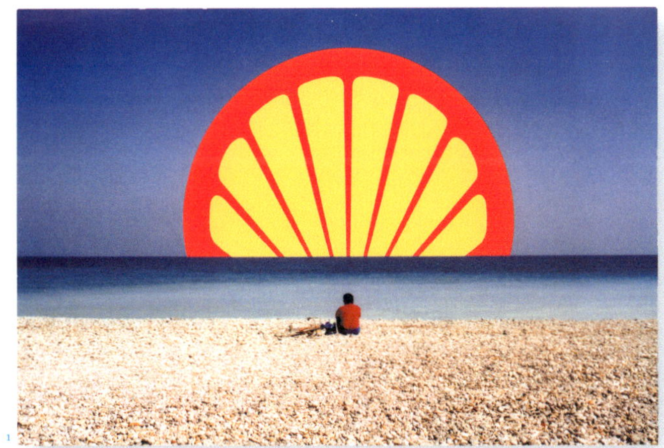

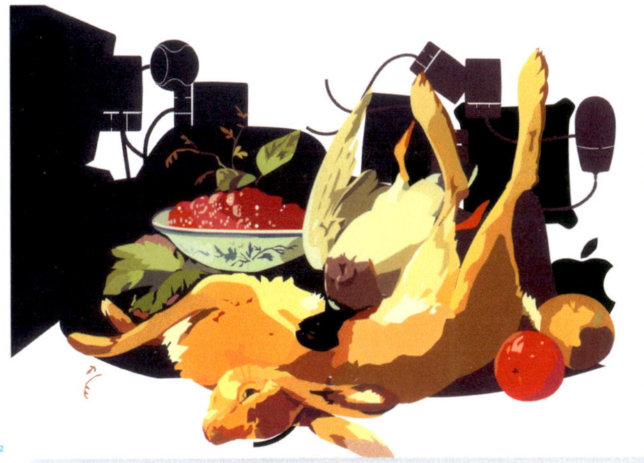

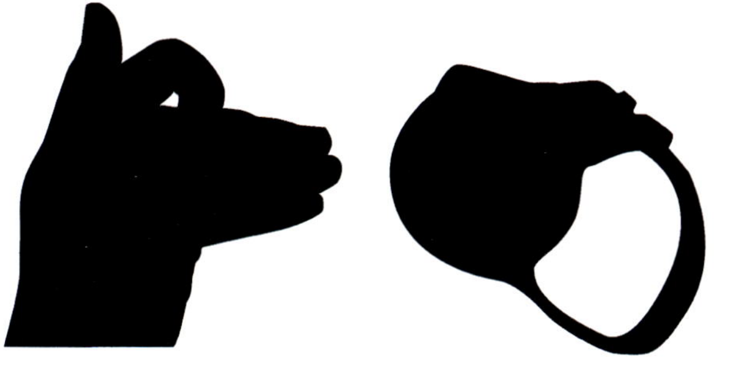

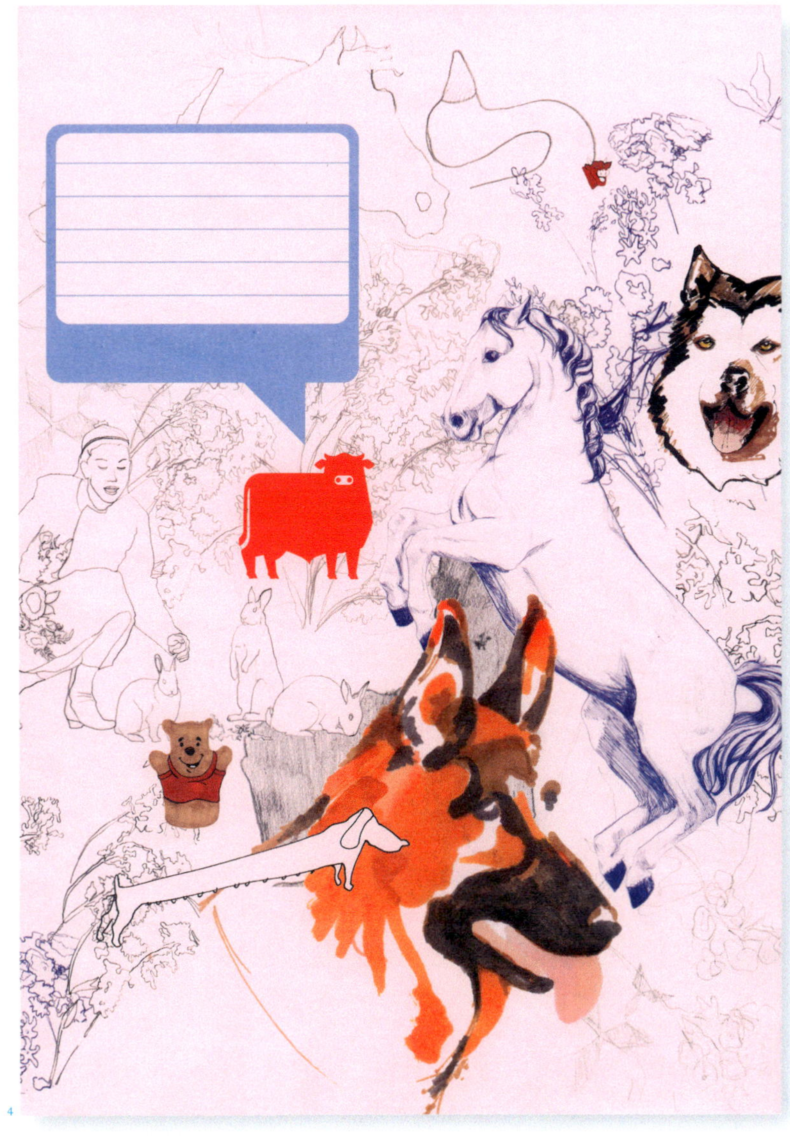

1   Happypets, 175 x 118 mm, offset printing, 2001
2–3   Happypets, 150 x 105 mm, Invercote, offset printing, 2000
4   Happypets, A4, Gmund colour pink, flexo, 2001

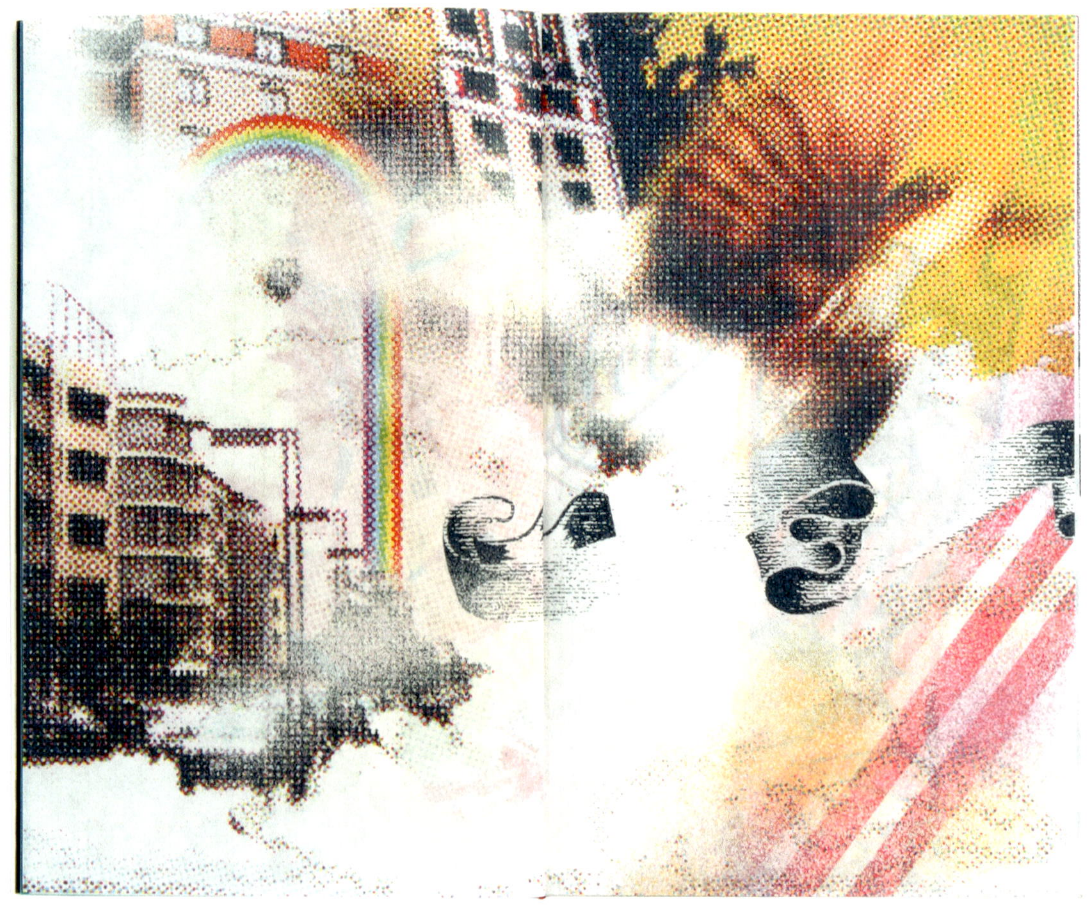

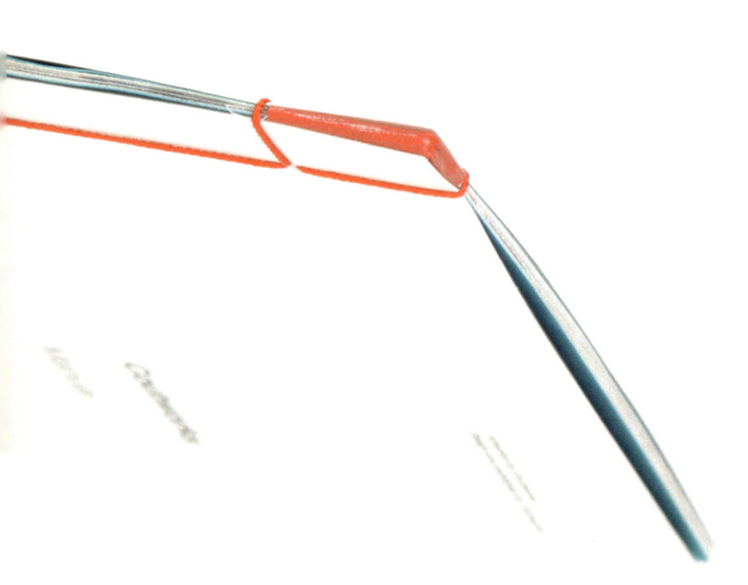

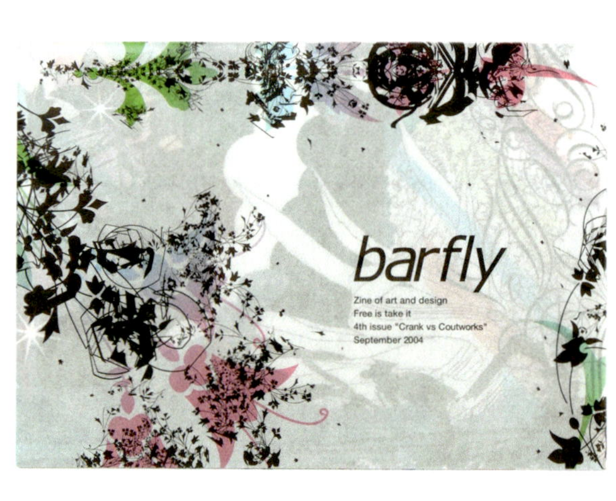

1–2   Coutworks / Daisuke Sato, Kazumasa Morizumi, paper, laser print, 2005
3   Coutworks / Daisuke Sato, Kazumsa Morizumi, Shin Kikkawa, paper, offset printing, 2004

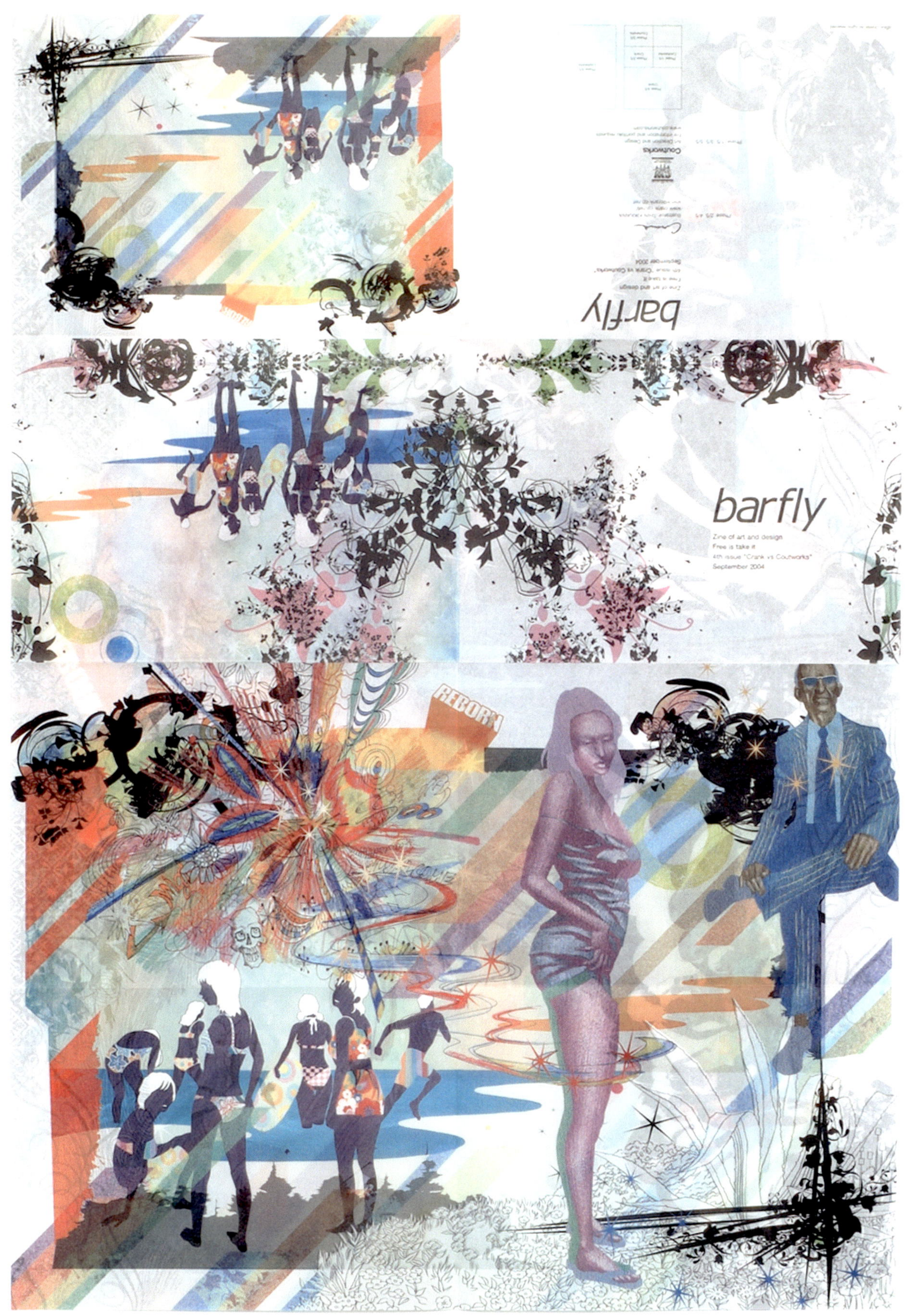

Coutworks / Daisuke Sato, Kazumsa Morizumi, Shin Kikkawa, paper, offset printing, 2004

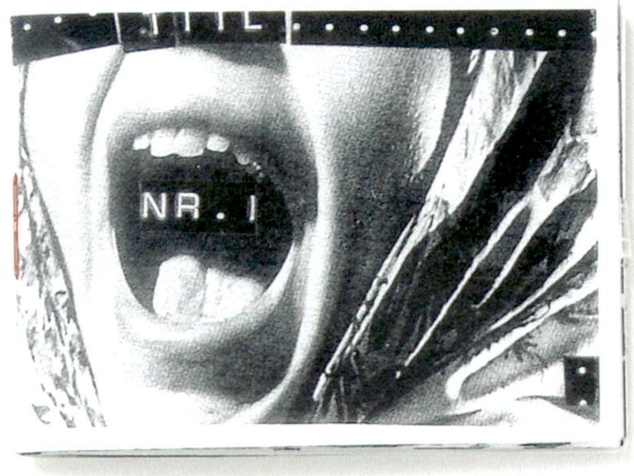

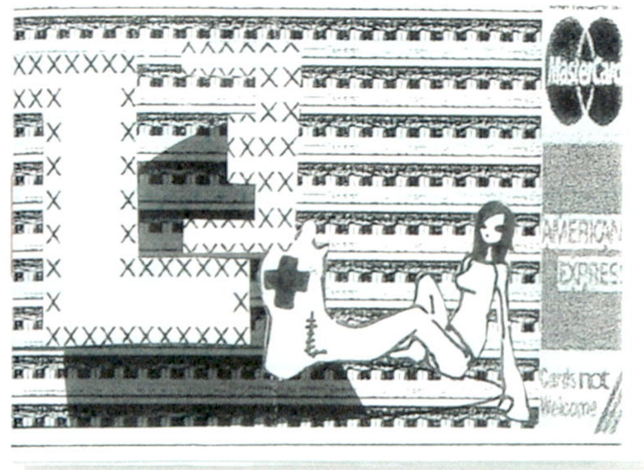

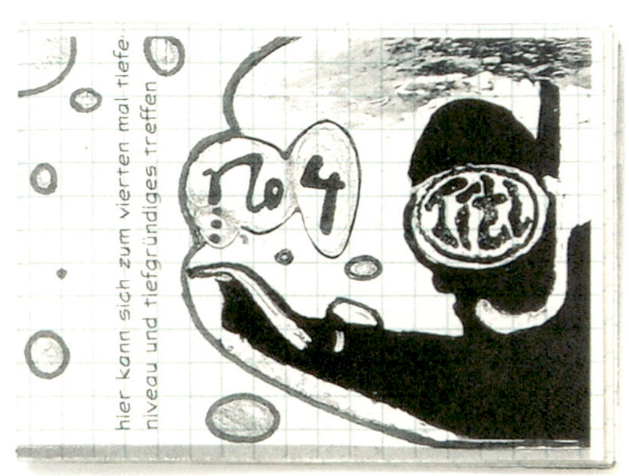

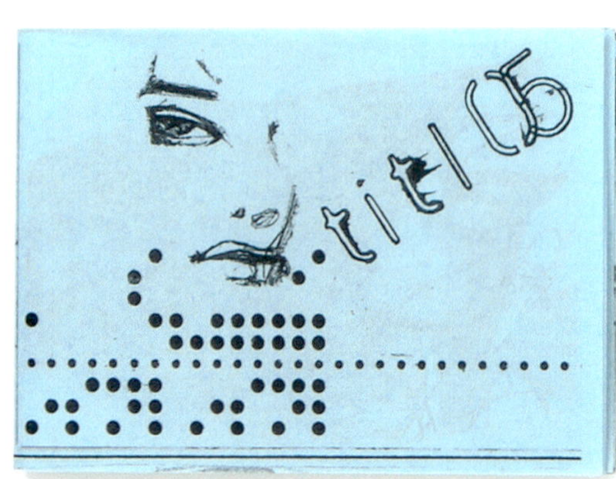

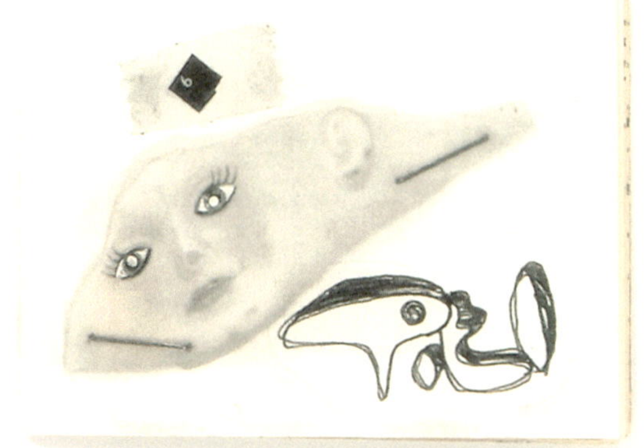

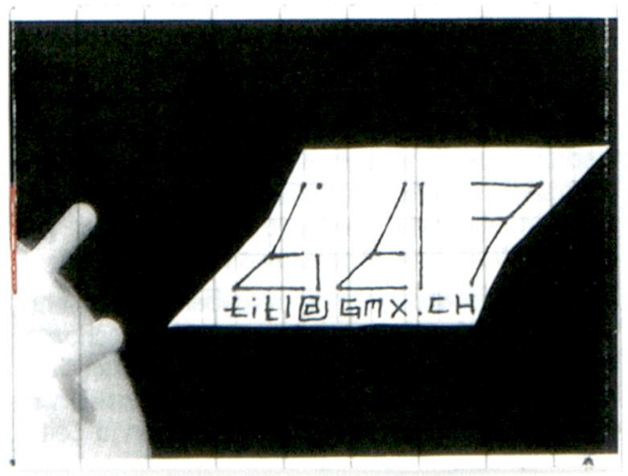

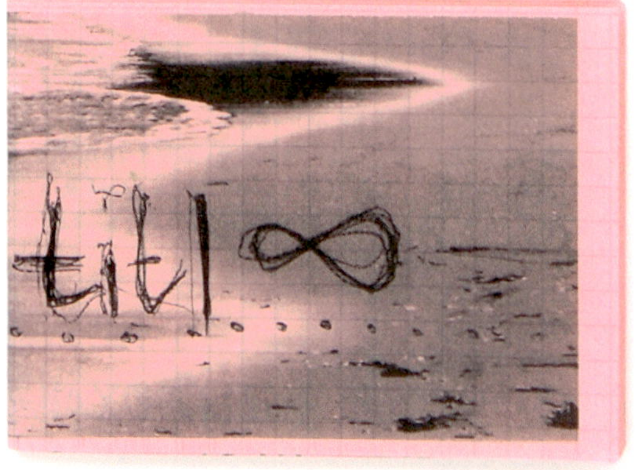

 Elen Rolih with Roman Glaus, folded 74 x 52 mm, paper, copied and cross hatched, 2001

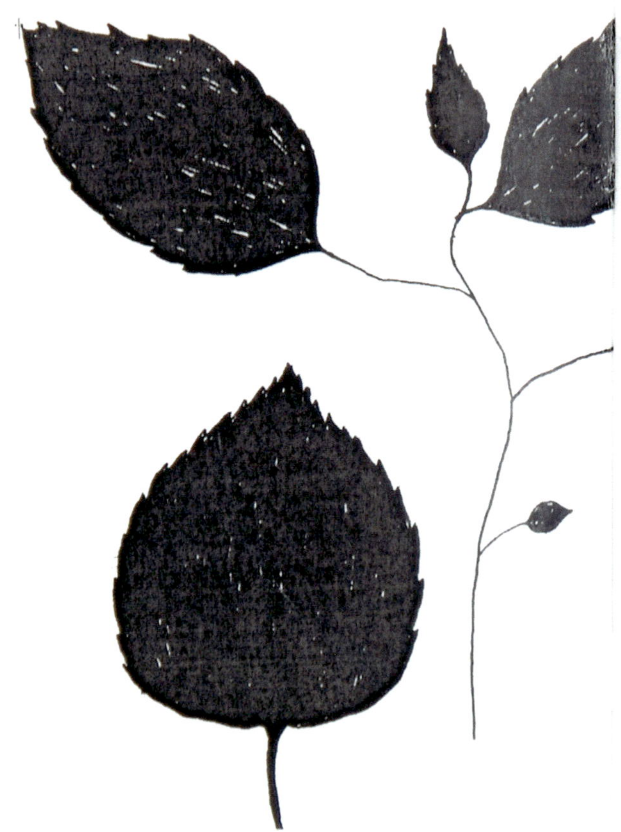

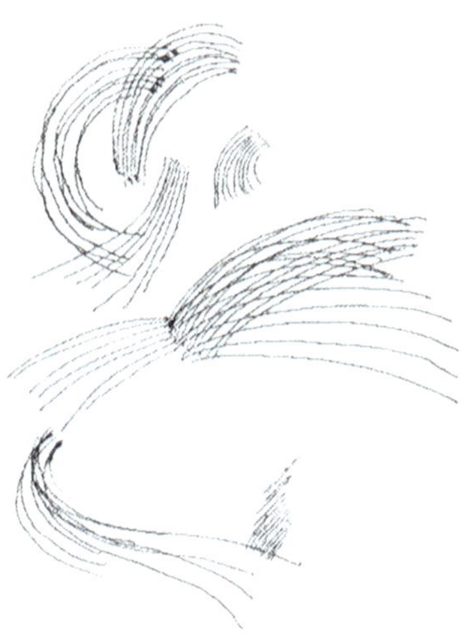

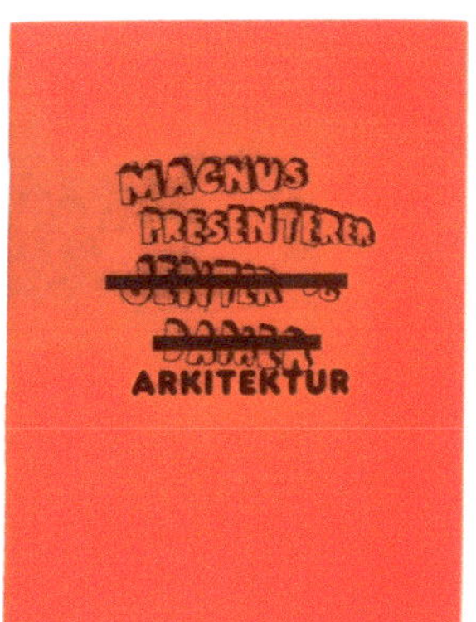

1–2   Grandpeople, 80 x 115 mm, black and white photocopy, 2003

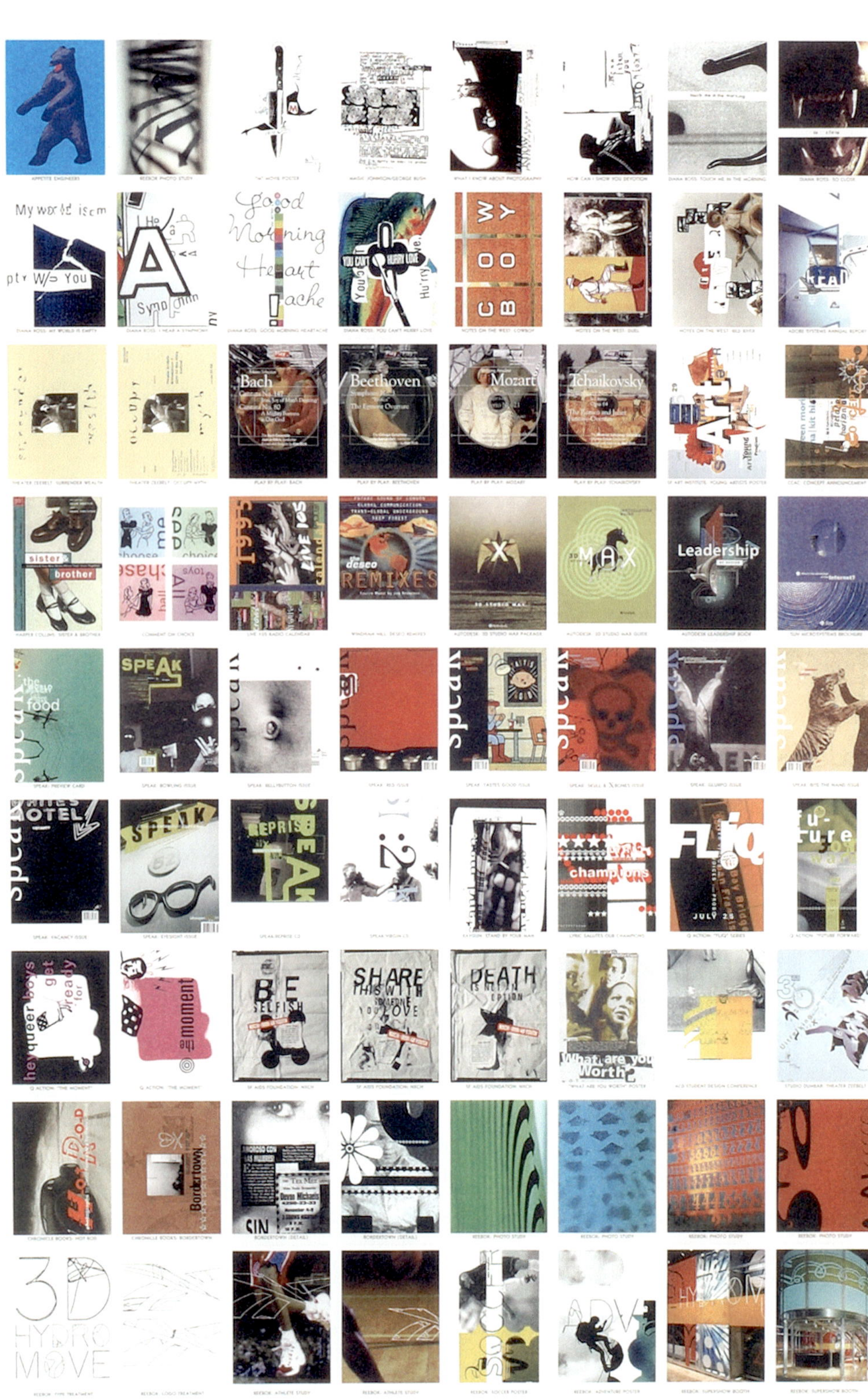

 Appetite Engineers / Martin Venetzky, gummed and perforated sheet, offset printing, 1998

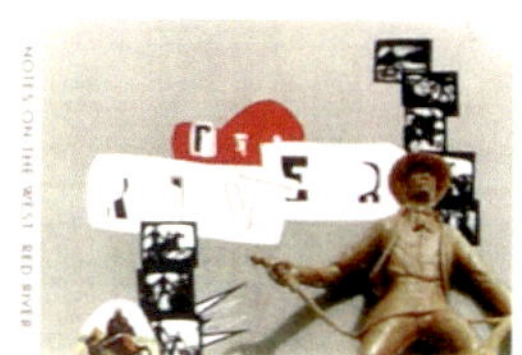
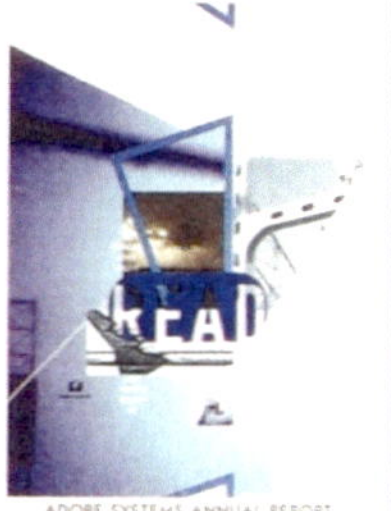
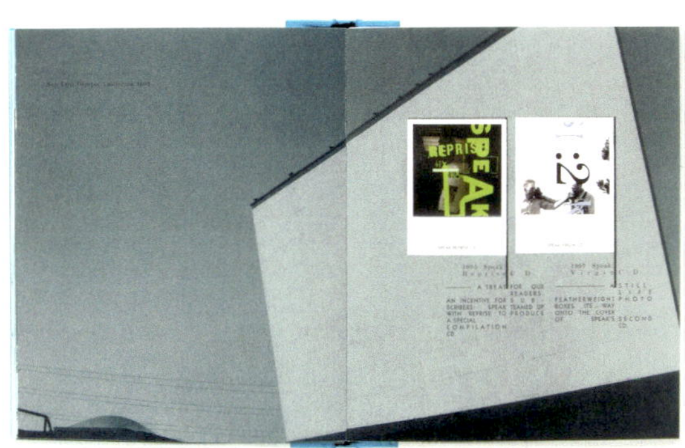
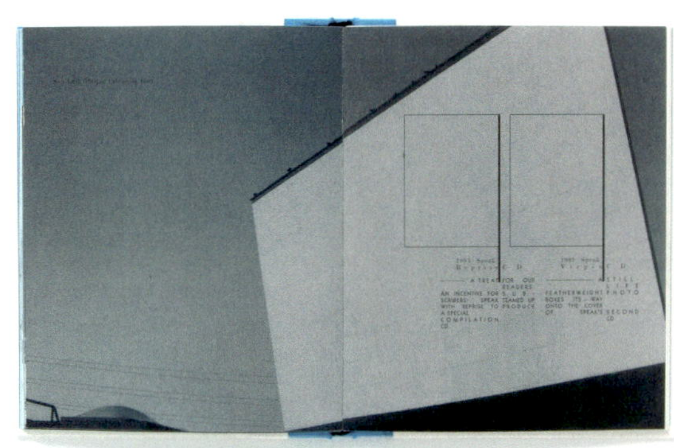

 1–3 Appetite Engineers / Martin Venetzky, book spread with stamps affixed, offset printing, 1999

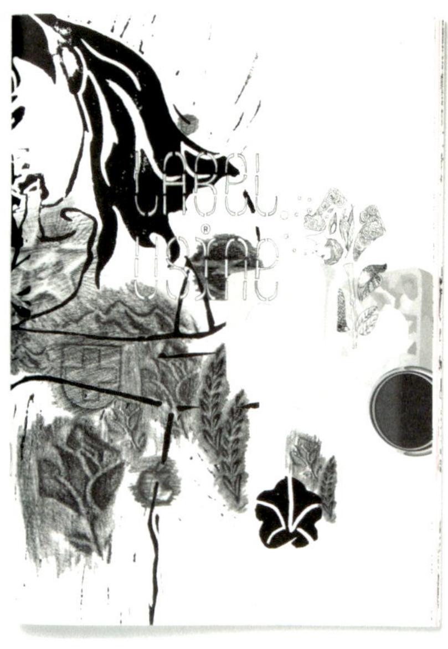

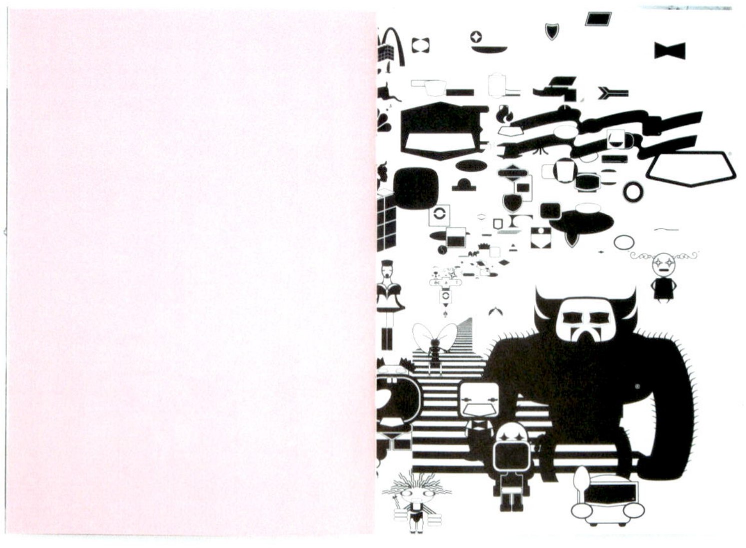

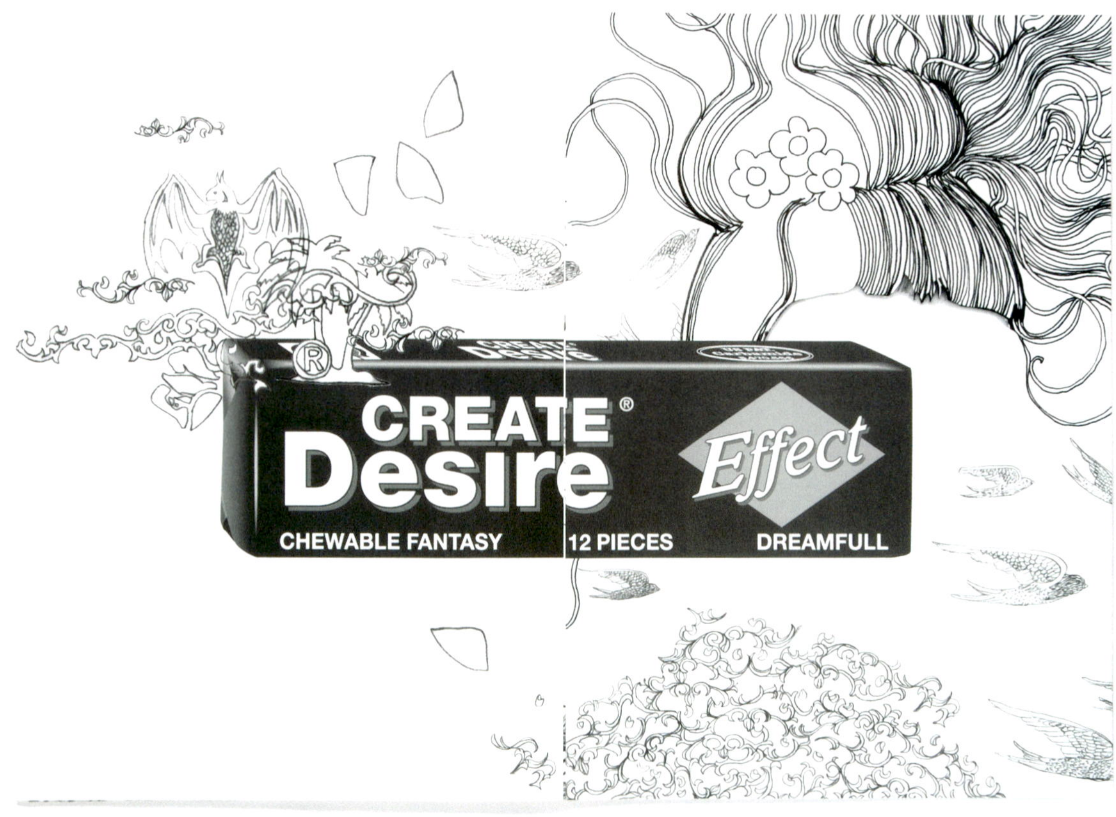

    1–3   Happypets, 160 x 220 mm, z-offset 140 g, offset printing, 2002

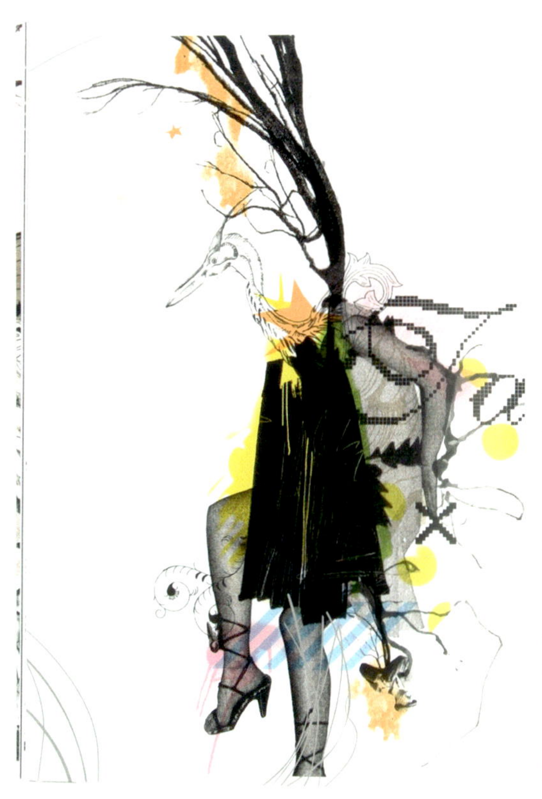

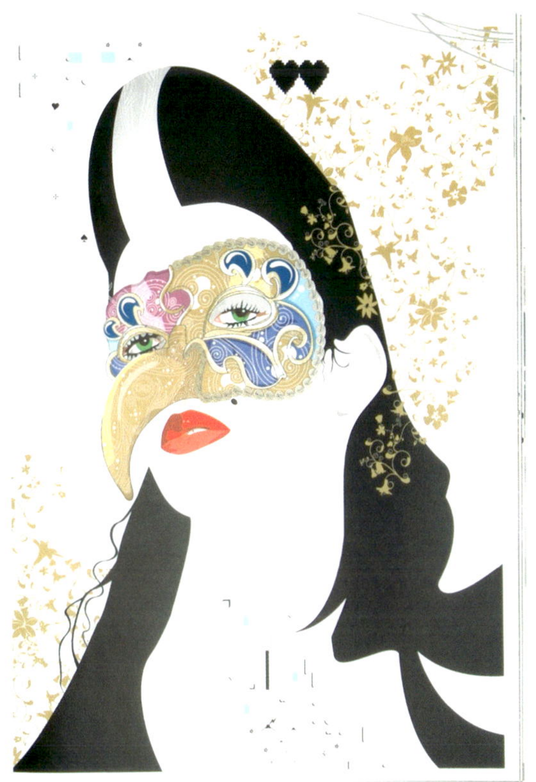

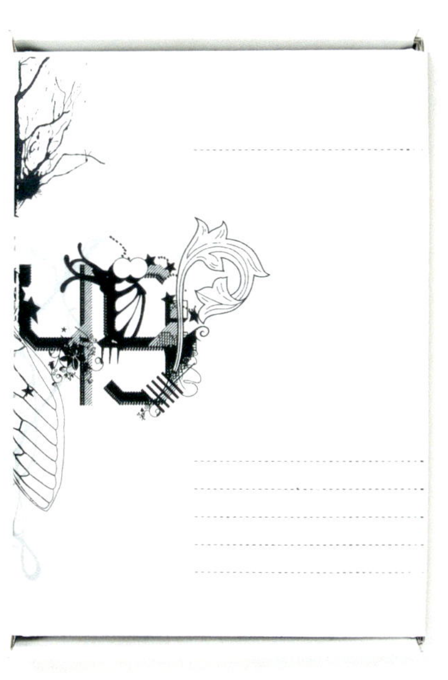

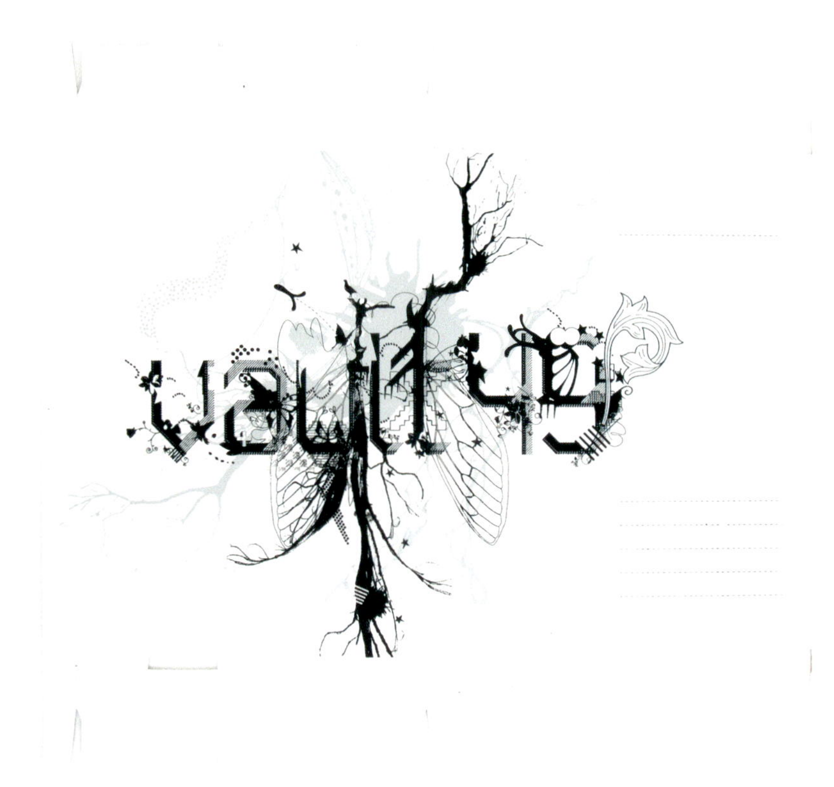

1   Vault49, 150 x 210 mm, mat varnished, medium-weight paper stock, offset printing 5 c , 2003
2–3   Vault49, box, cardboard, silk-screen printing, 2003

BOOK SMARTS #2

SEMI-SURVIVAL GUIDE TO THE FUTURE

SILENCE IS A POWERFUL STATEMENT.

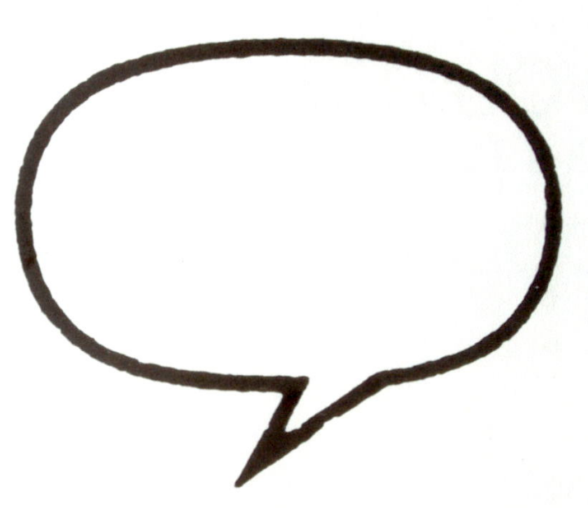

  1–2 Anthony Burrill, Text: Chad Rea, wire bound books, cheap paper, offset printing, 2004

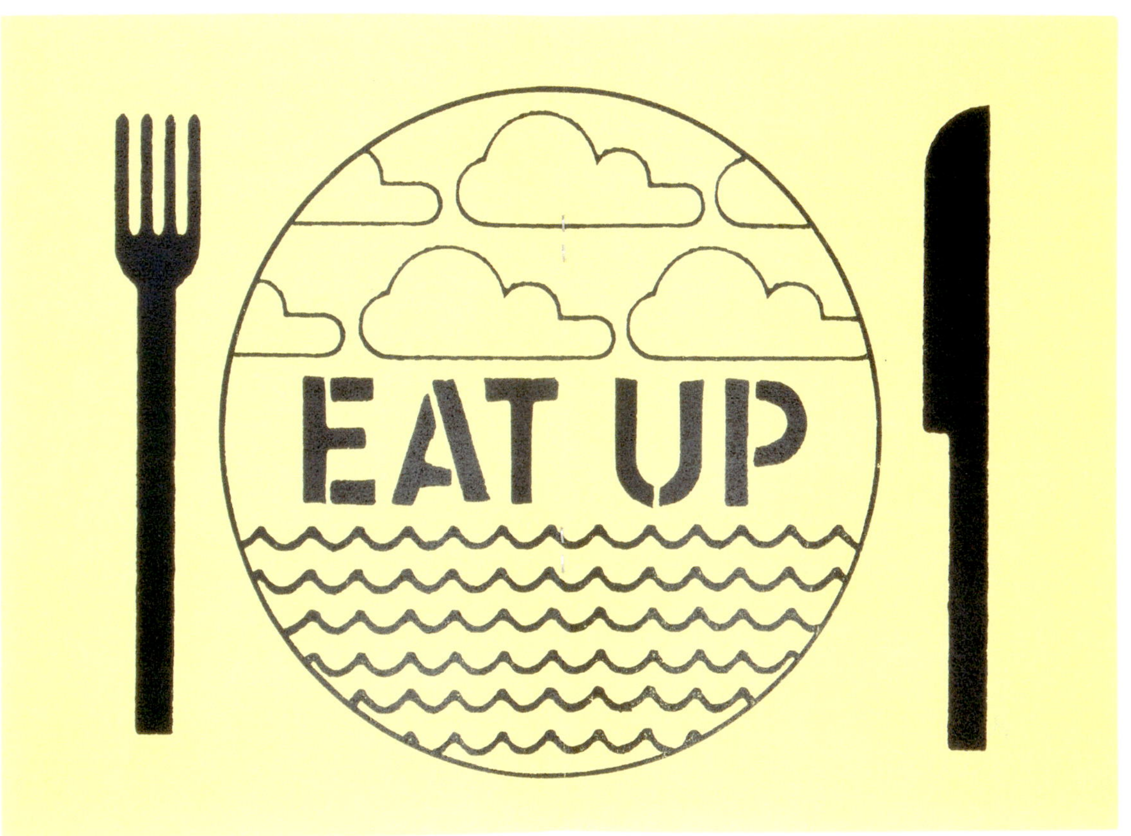
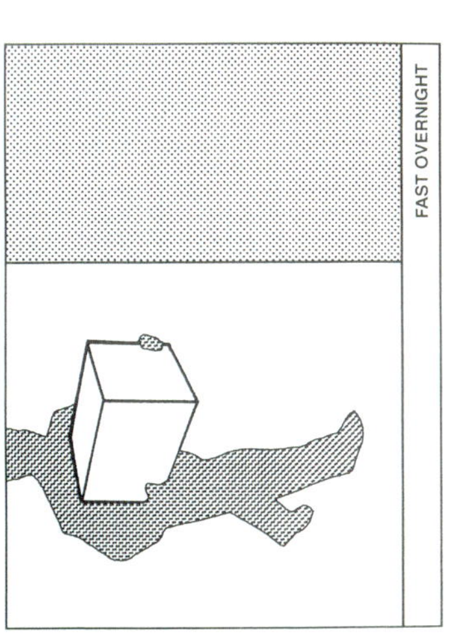

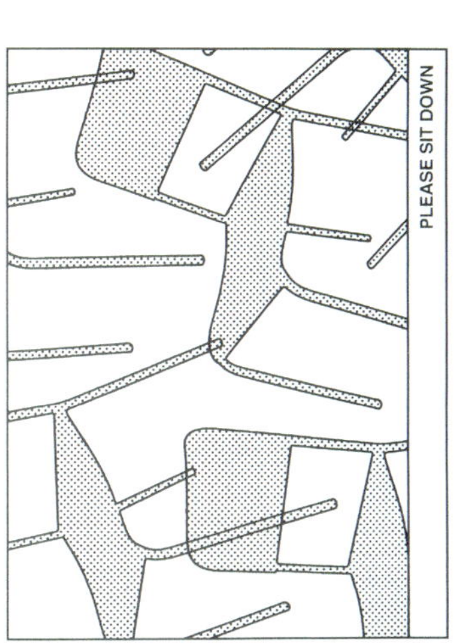

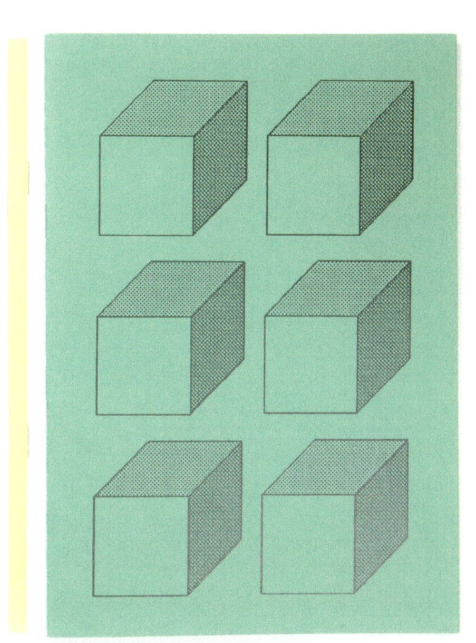

    1–3   Anthony Burrill, self-published book, cheap paper, photocopy, 2002

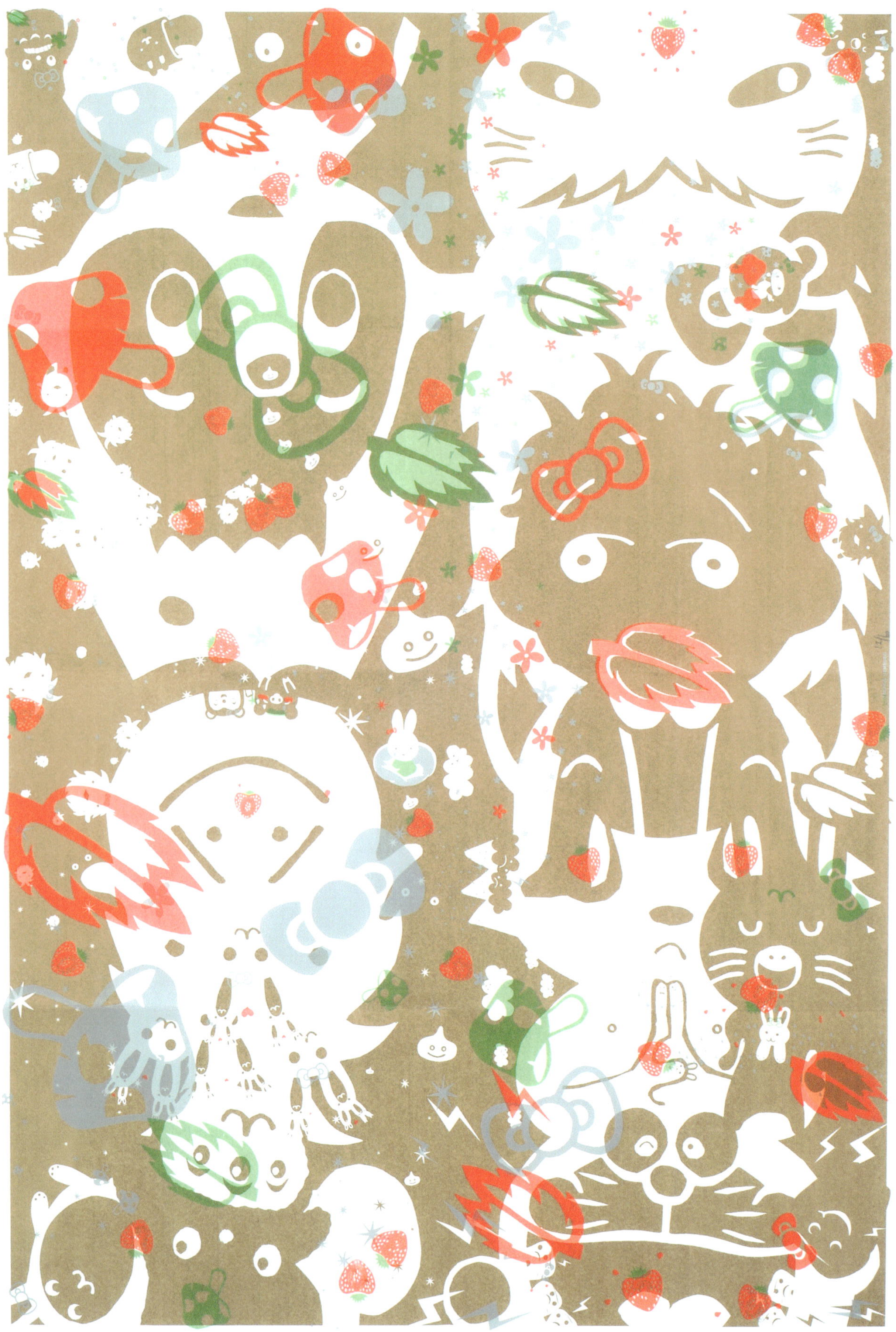

 Harmen Liemburg, A 0, silk-screen printing, 2004

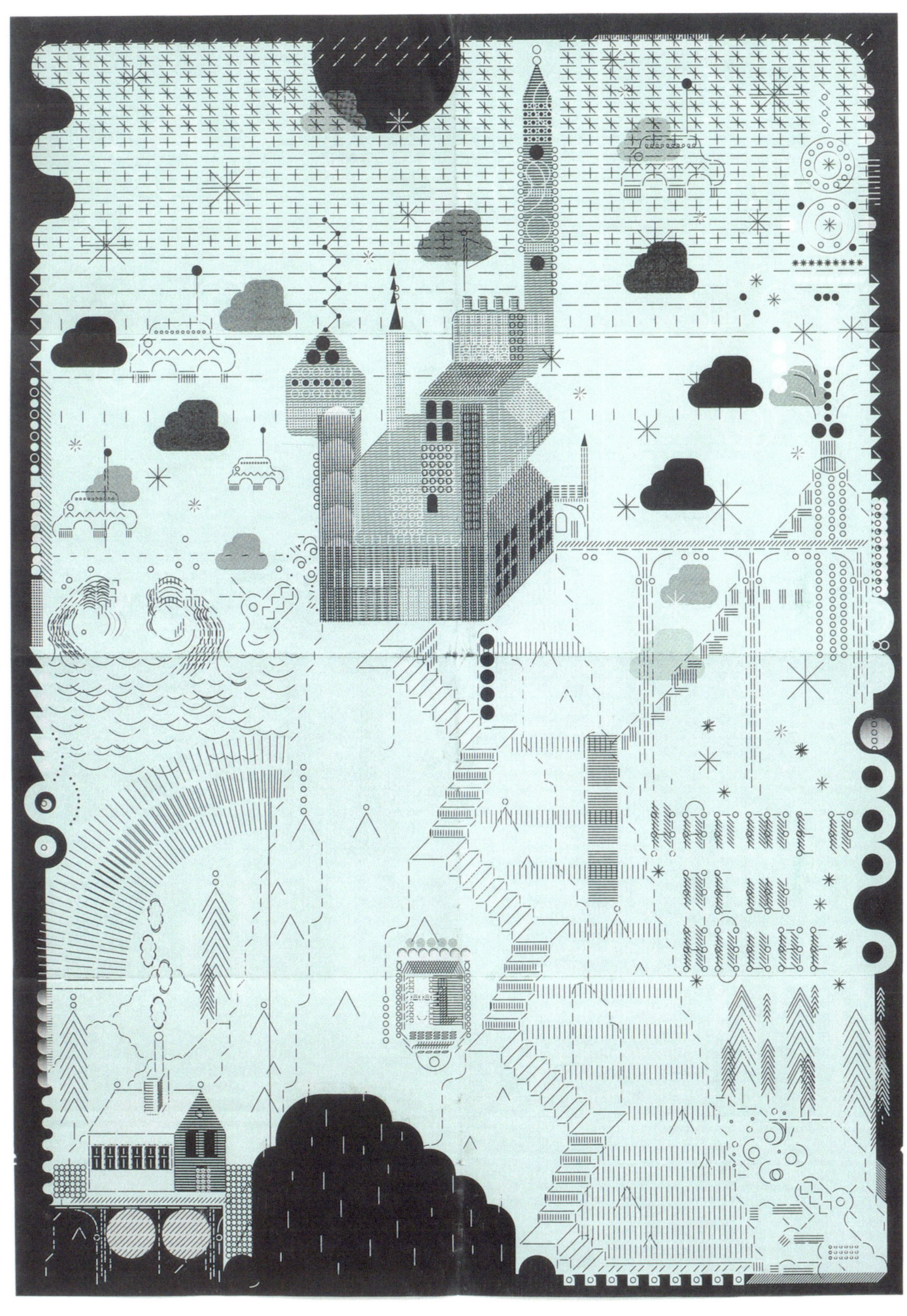

Harmen Liemburg and Richard Niessen, 50 x 70 cm, silk-screen printing, 2001

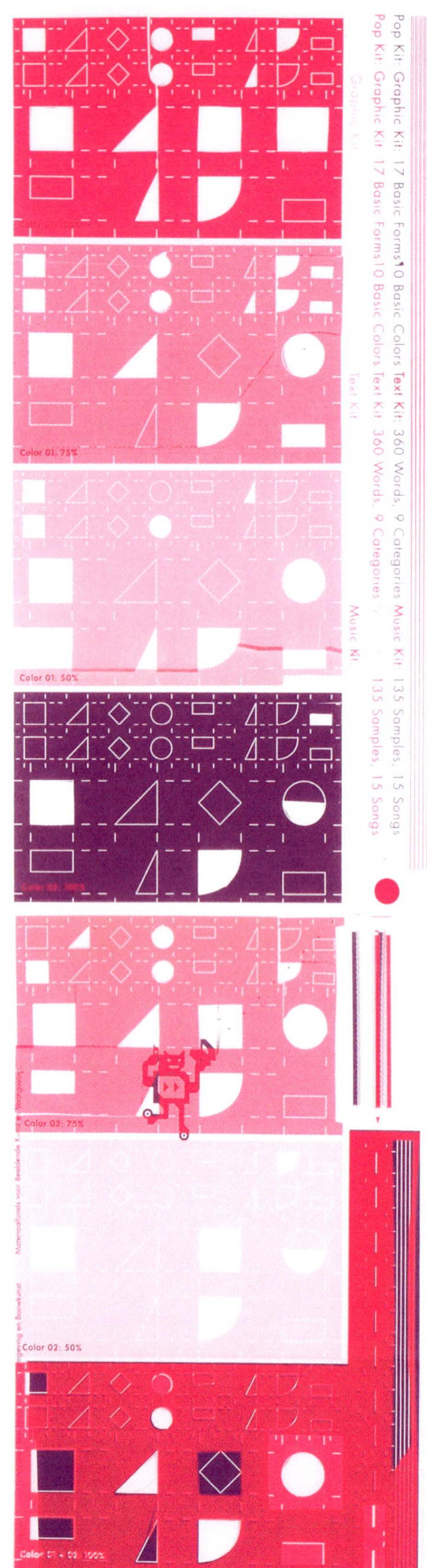
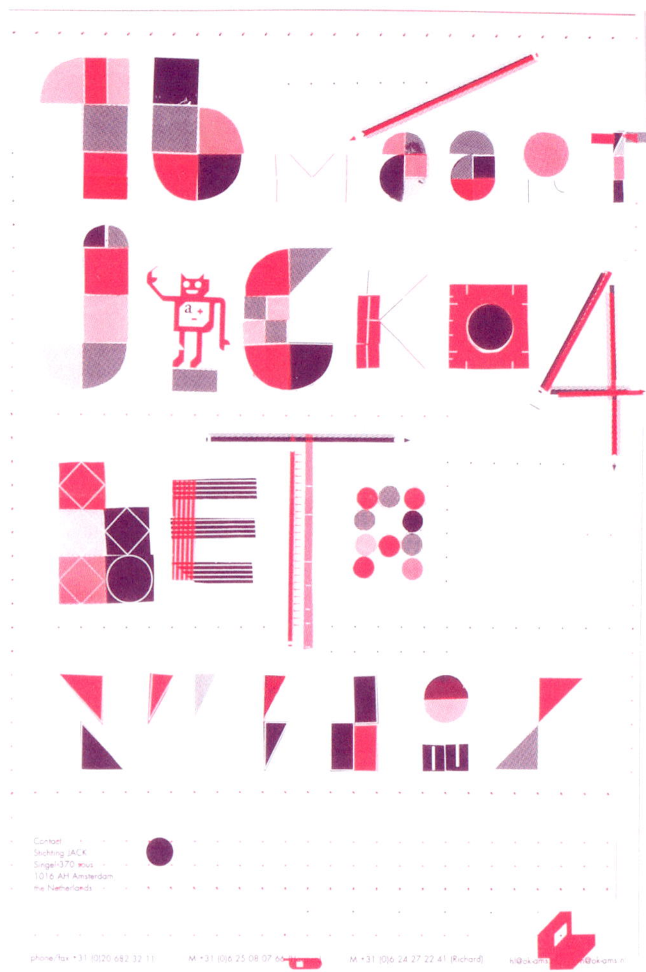
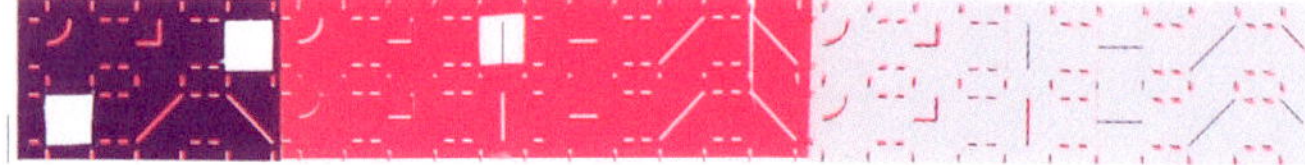

 Harmen Liemburg and Richard Niessen, A 1, silk-screen printing, 2001

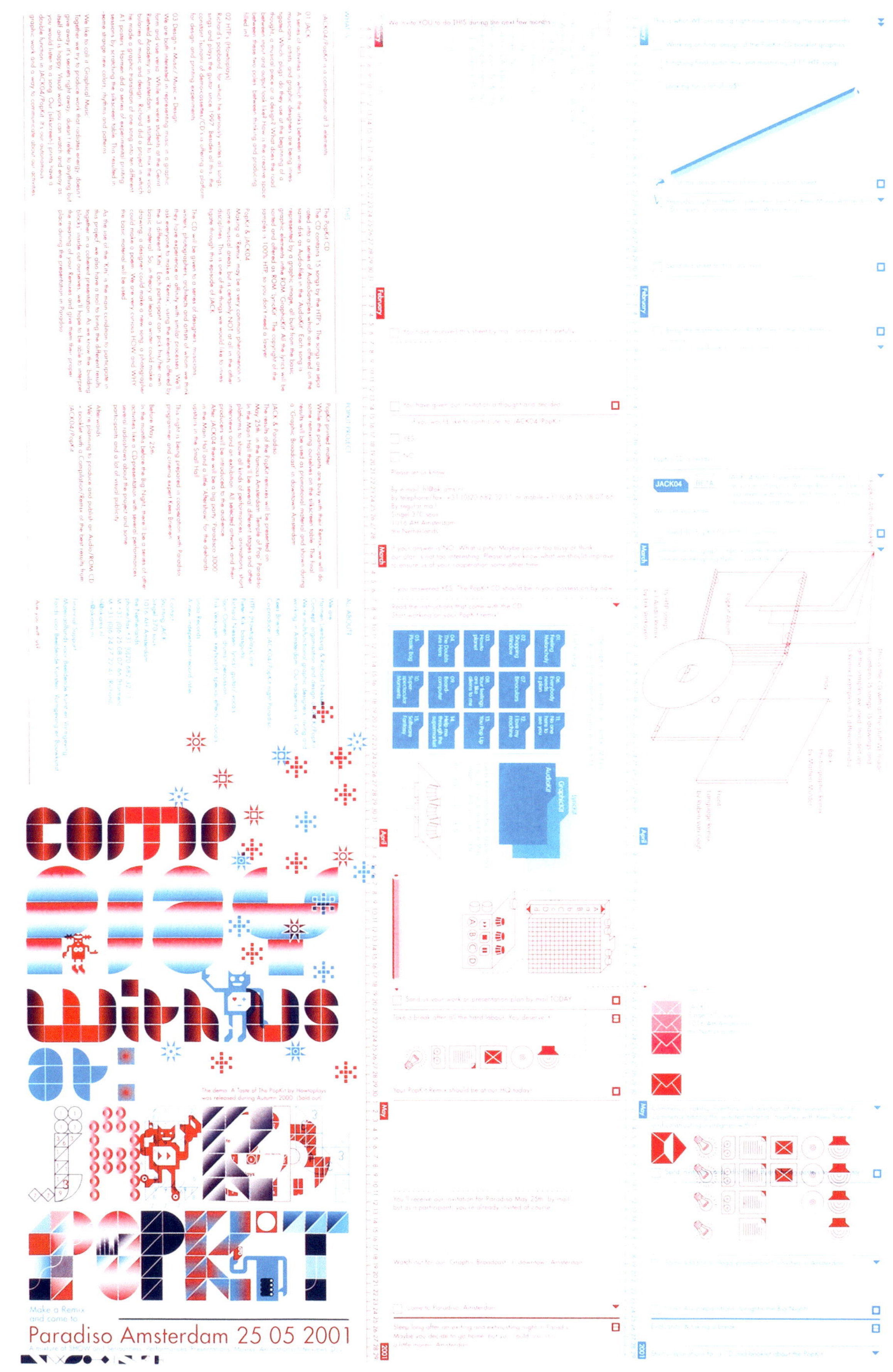

Harmen Liemburg and Richard Niessen, A 1, silk-screen printing, 2001

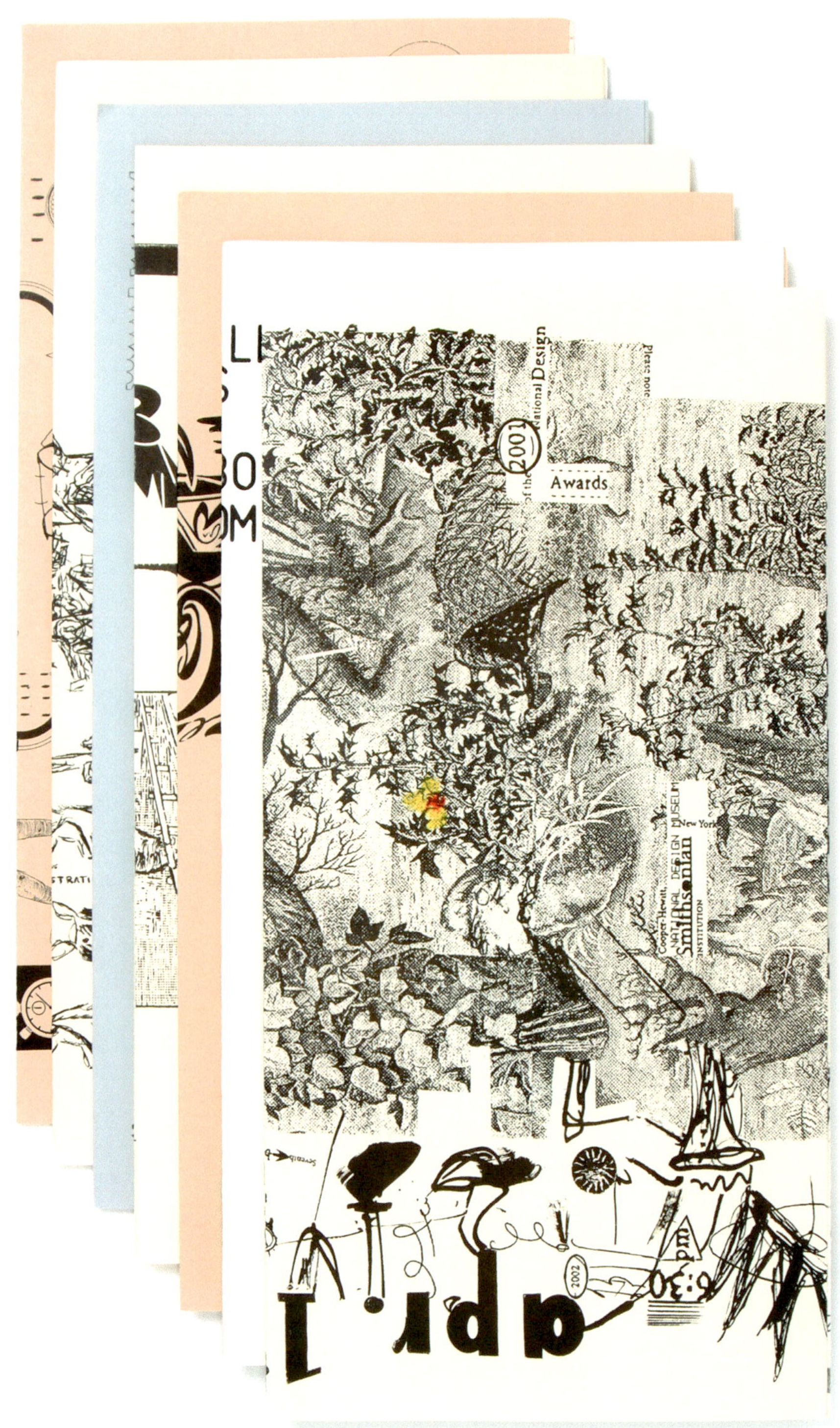

Best-known for his intricate drawings and unusual use of space and layout, Ed Fella's business cards serve as a perfect example of refreshingly spontaneous "non-design". When opportunity knocked with two last-minute slots in a student business card print run (a bargain at twelve dollars for 500), Fella simply scraped off a magazine address label, added a signature, a few handwritten phone numbers, a quickly drawn flourish and a fast colour break. The second and by no means inferior version is the work of his non-designer wife, who claimed: "If it's that simple, I'll do it myself!".

    Ed Fella, 280 x 430 mm, paper, offset printing, various dates

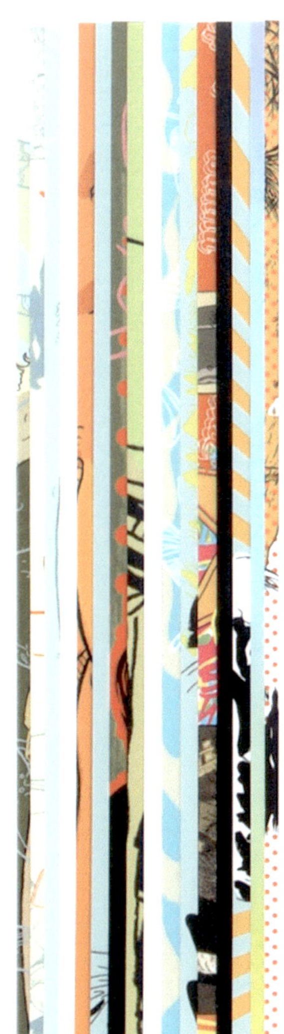
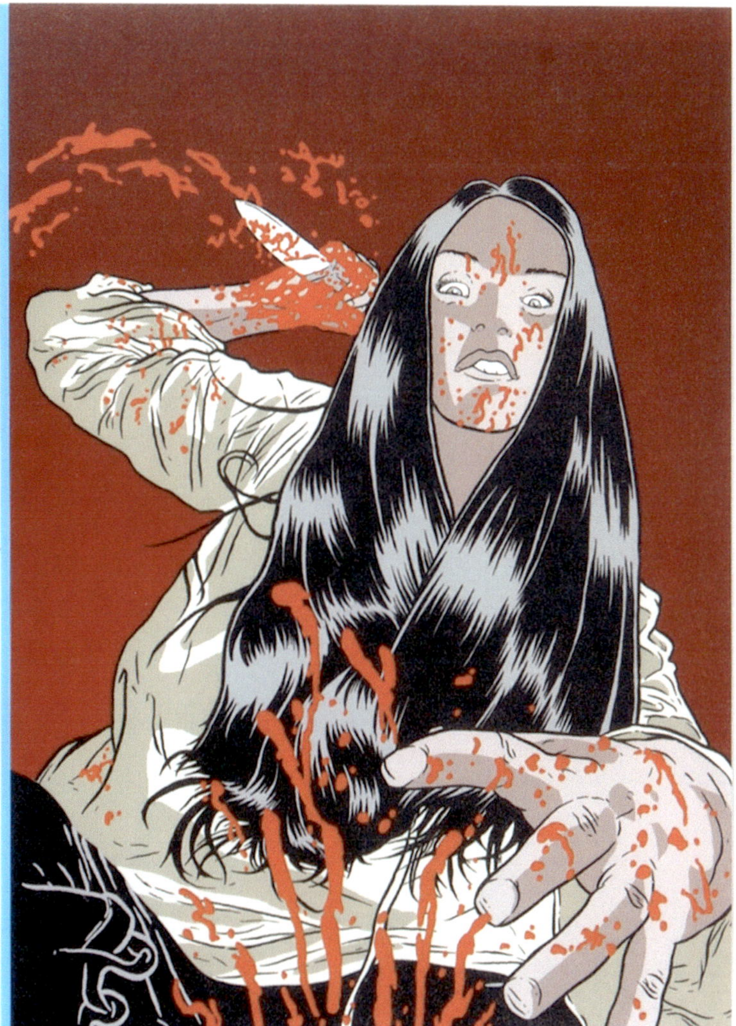

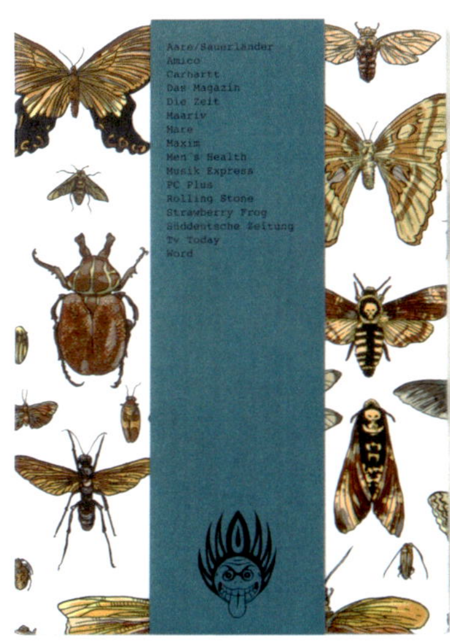

1–2   Jan Feindt, cardboard, digital printing, 2005

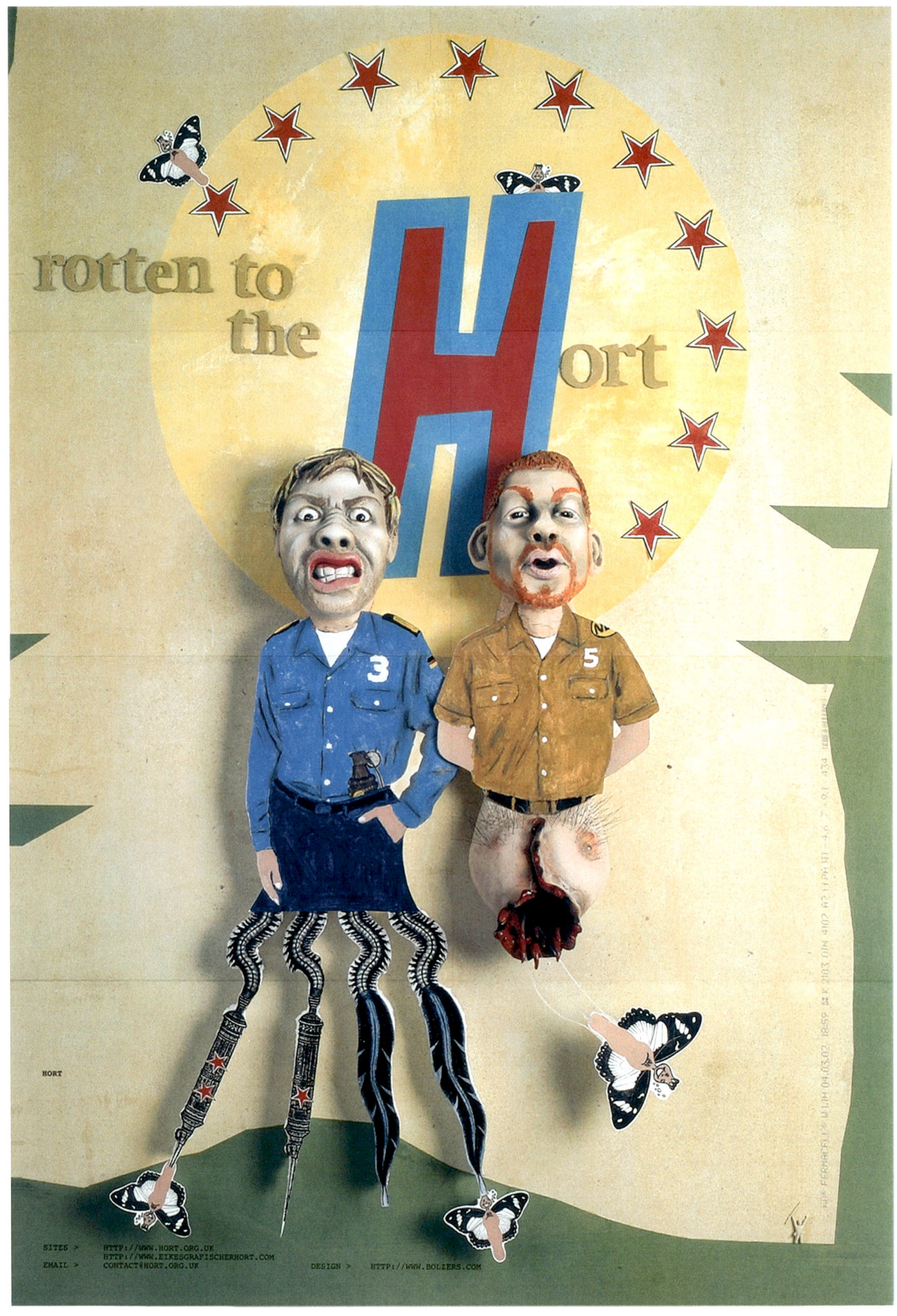

 Hort / bolzers.com, A 1, unvarnished paper 240 g, offset printing 4c, 2004

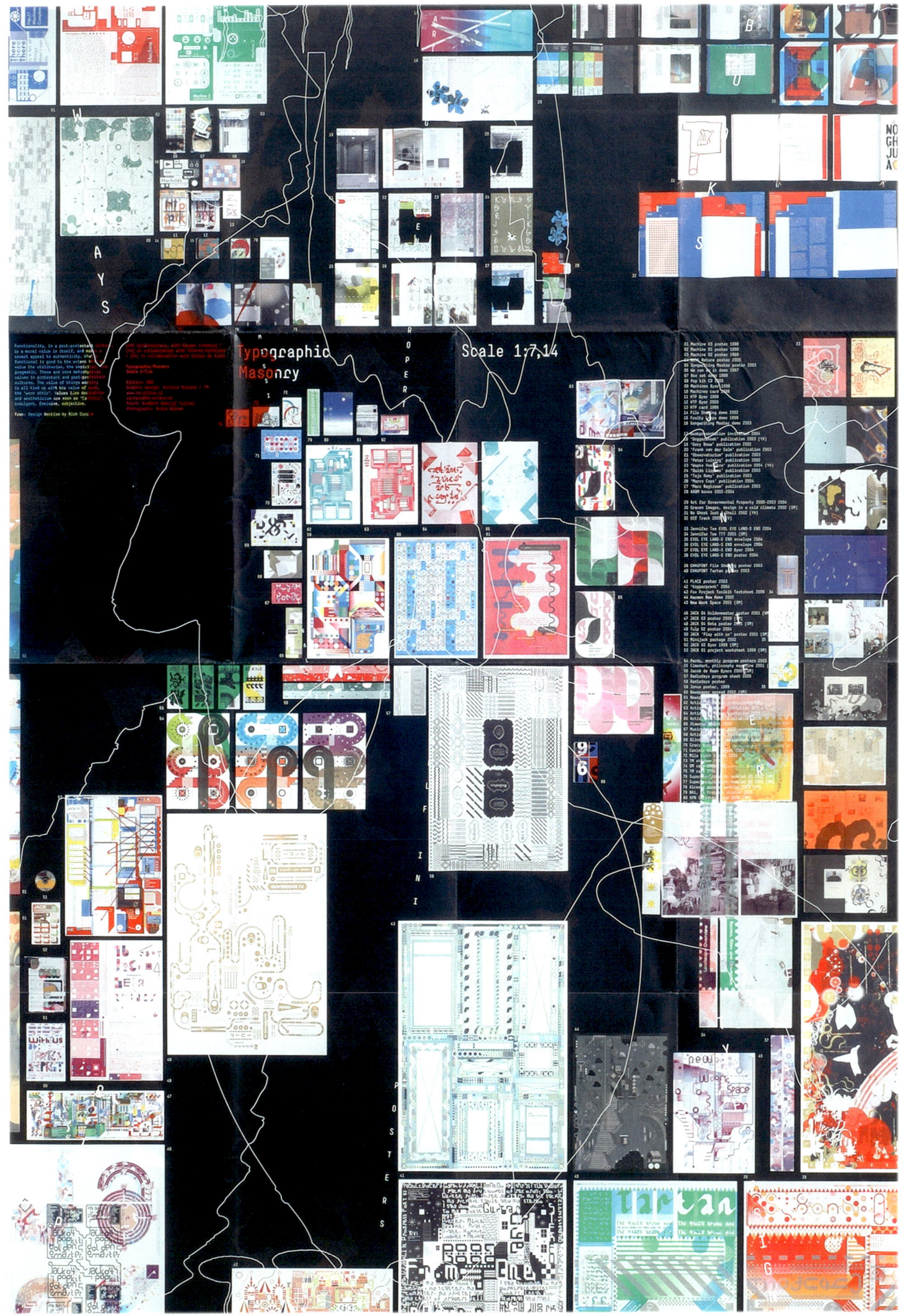

Richard Niessen, A0, offset printing, 2005

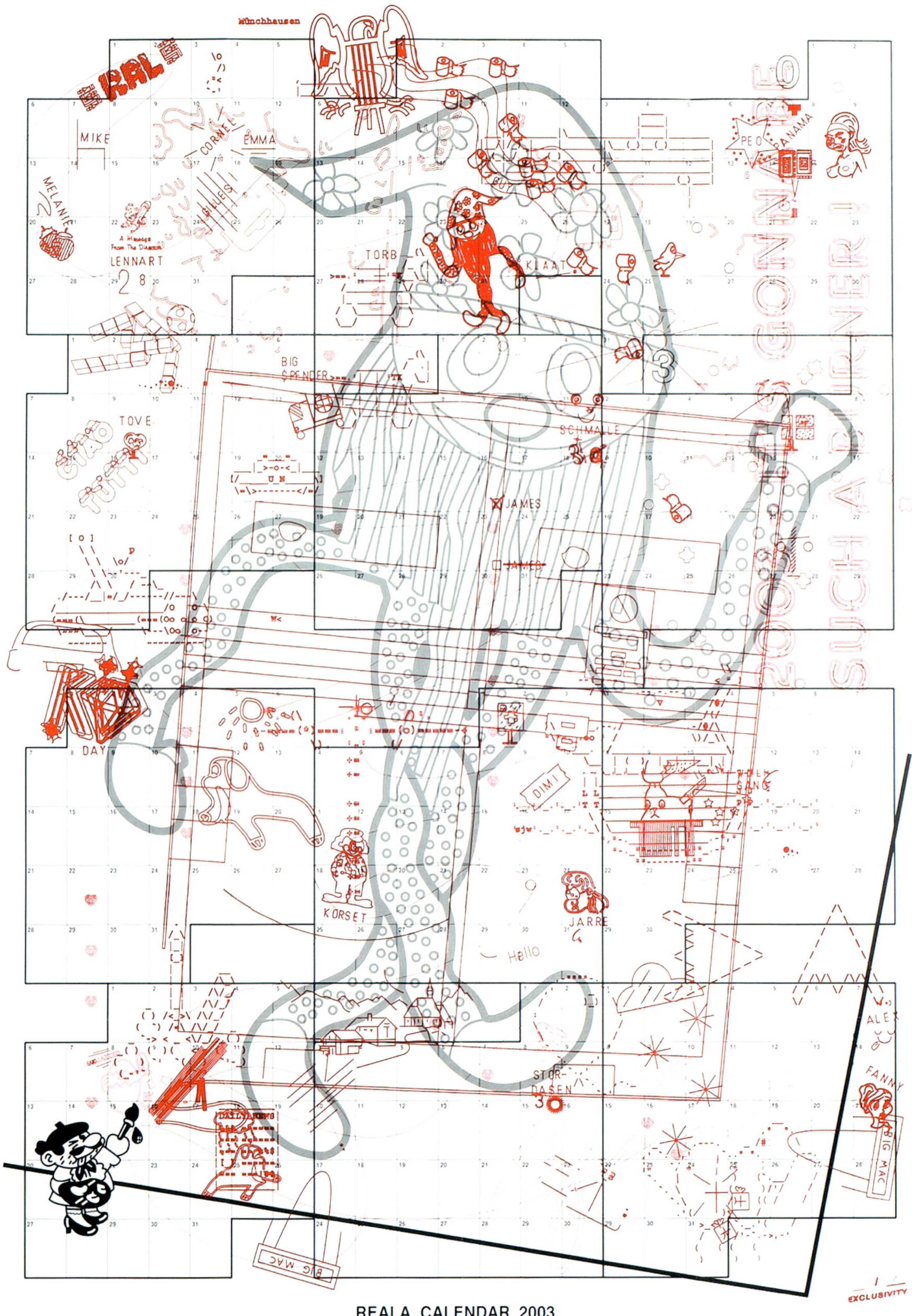

REALA_CALENDAR_2003

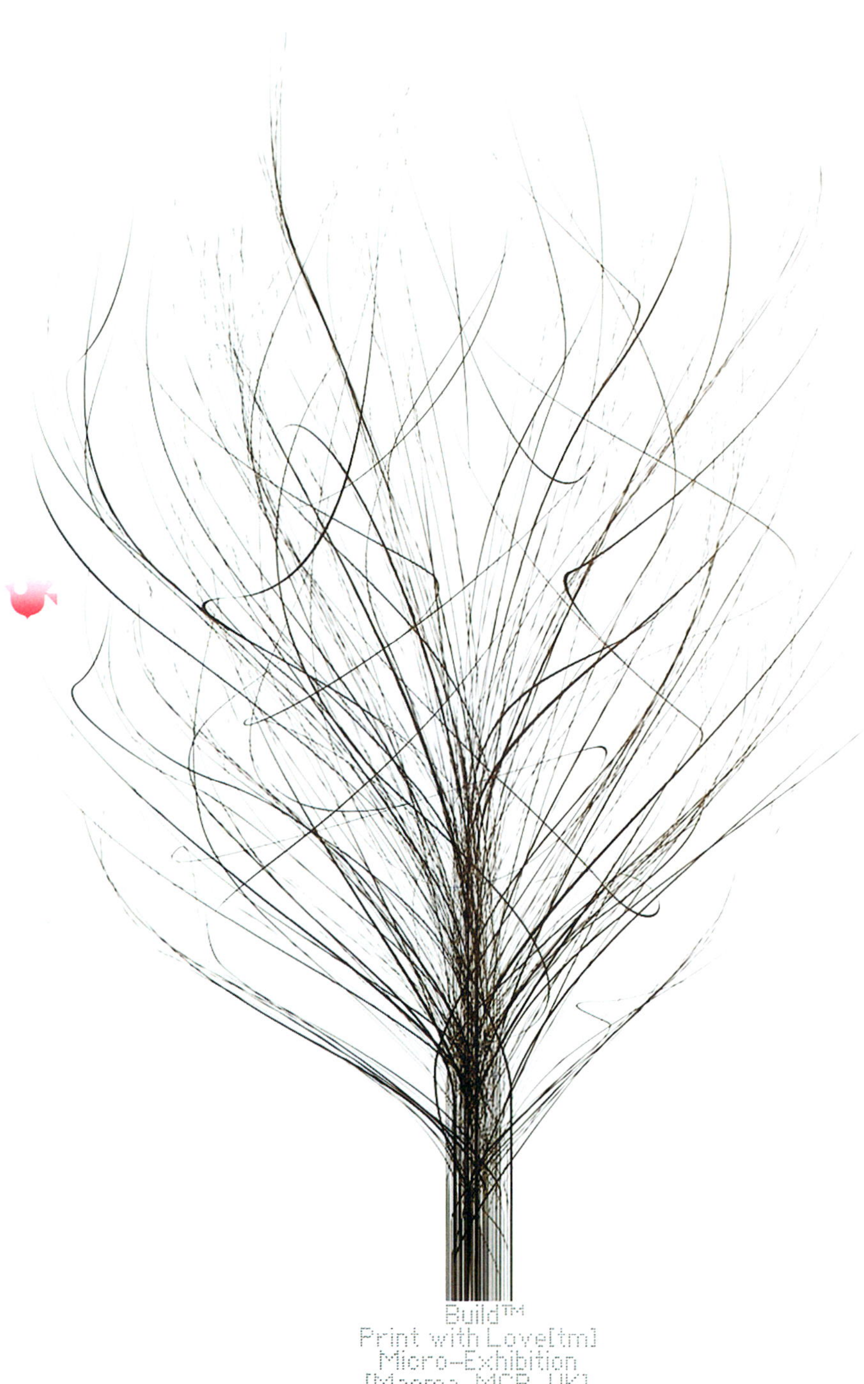

 Build / Michael C. Place, offset printing, 2004

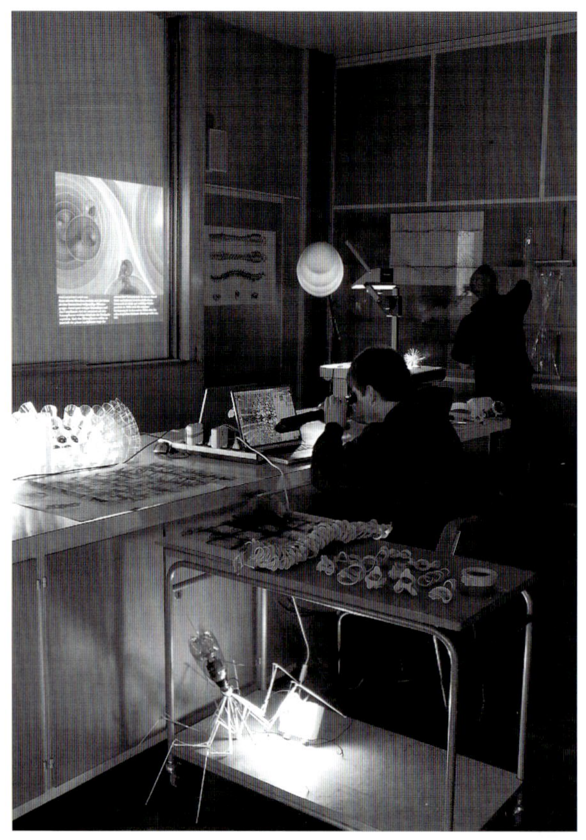

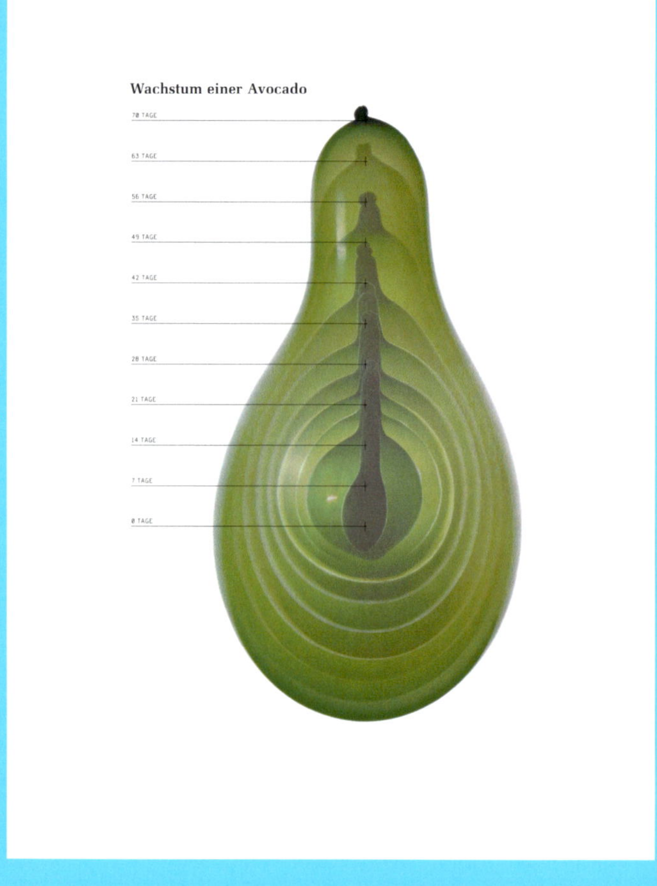

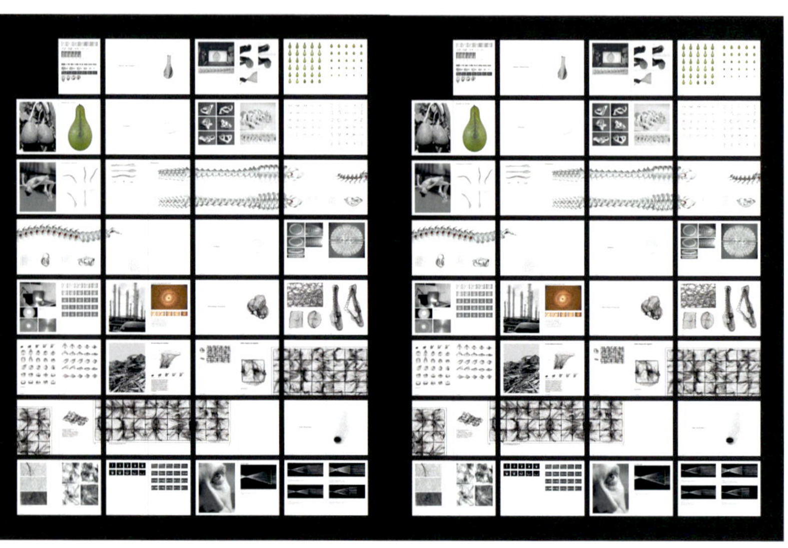

All surface but by no means superficial, Silo's 120 page book "Visuelle Erklärungen" ('Visual Explanations', published in a very limited edition of 12) marks the Swiss design collective's deliberate return to earnest research in the design profession. With the aim of devising a method to create graphics for visual explanation, Silo analysed a wide range of different objects and materials. The resulting selection of ultimately nonsensical information graphics might place umbrellas in a zoological setting to visualise the flight phase of a mallard, yet it remains a homage to clear, elegant representations of facts.

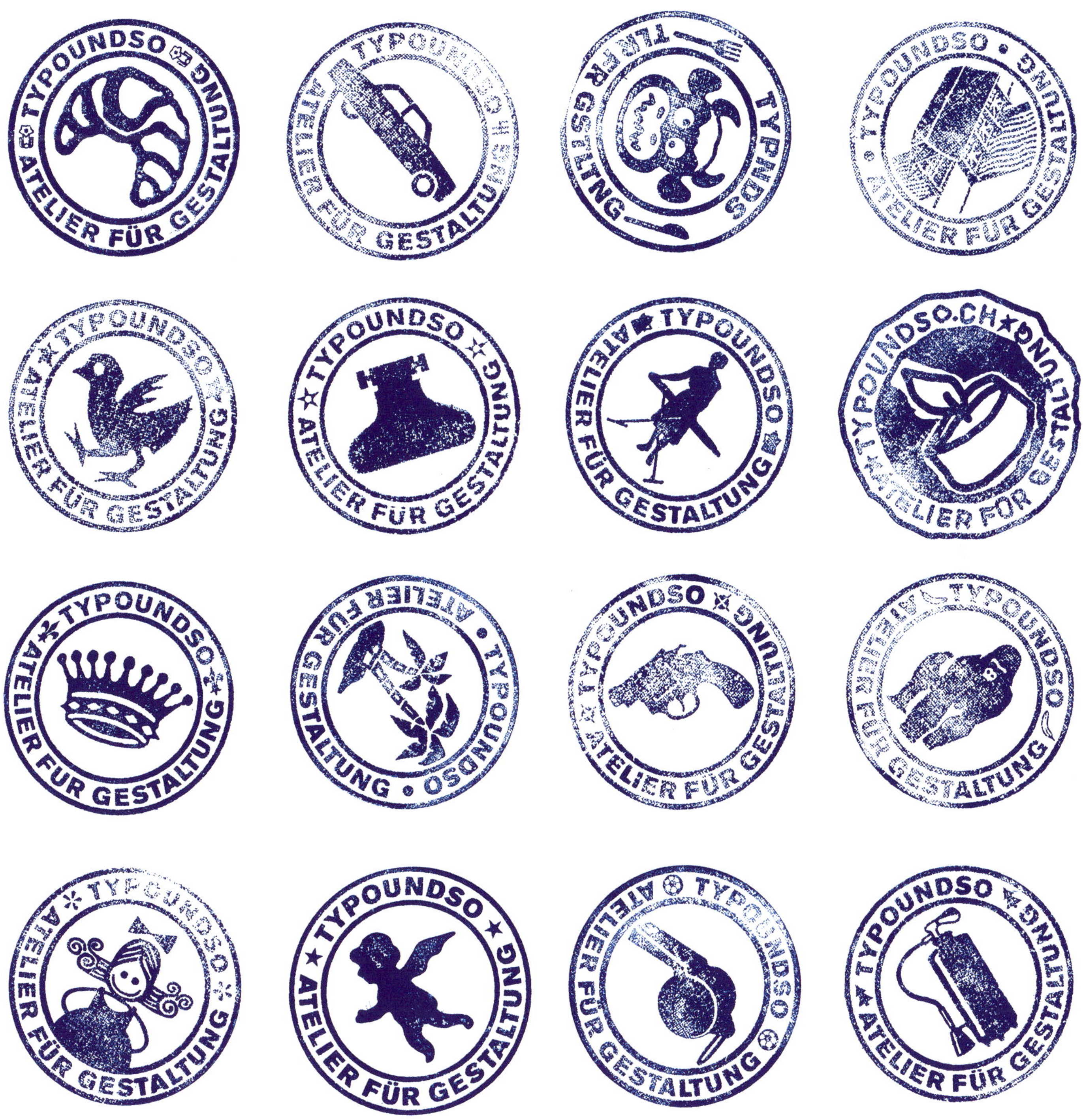

 Typoundso / Marc Philipp and Eva Bommeli, stamp, 1996–2005

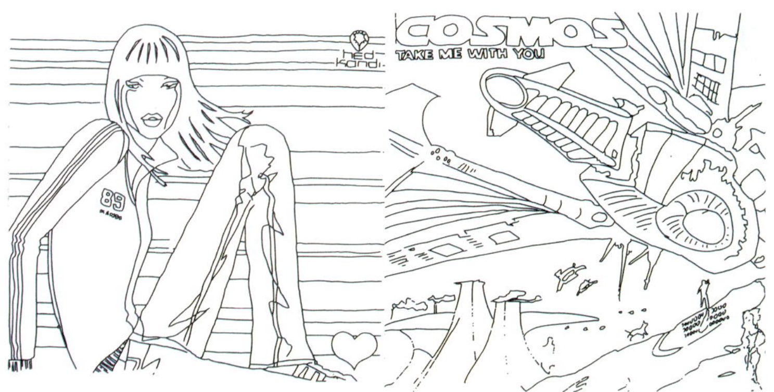

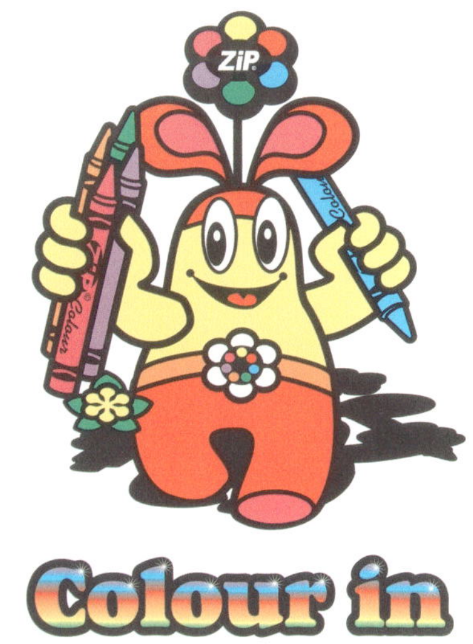

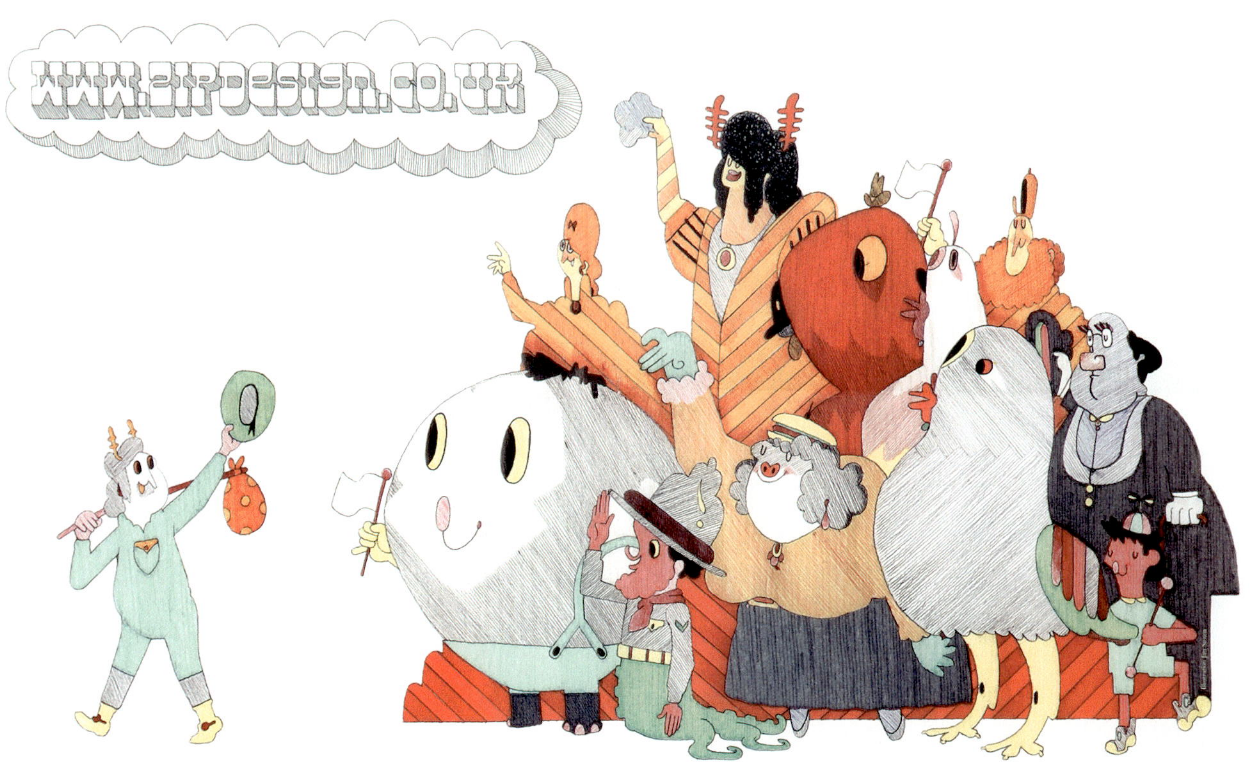

1–2   Zip Design / Peter Chadwick, cover illustrated by Sean Sims, 240 g one sided cartboard
with spot gloss UV varnish, offset printing, 2002
3   Zip Design / Peter Chadwick and Chrissie Abbott, illustrated by Jim Stoten,
A3 poster, recycled stock, newspaper, offset printing, 2005

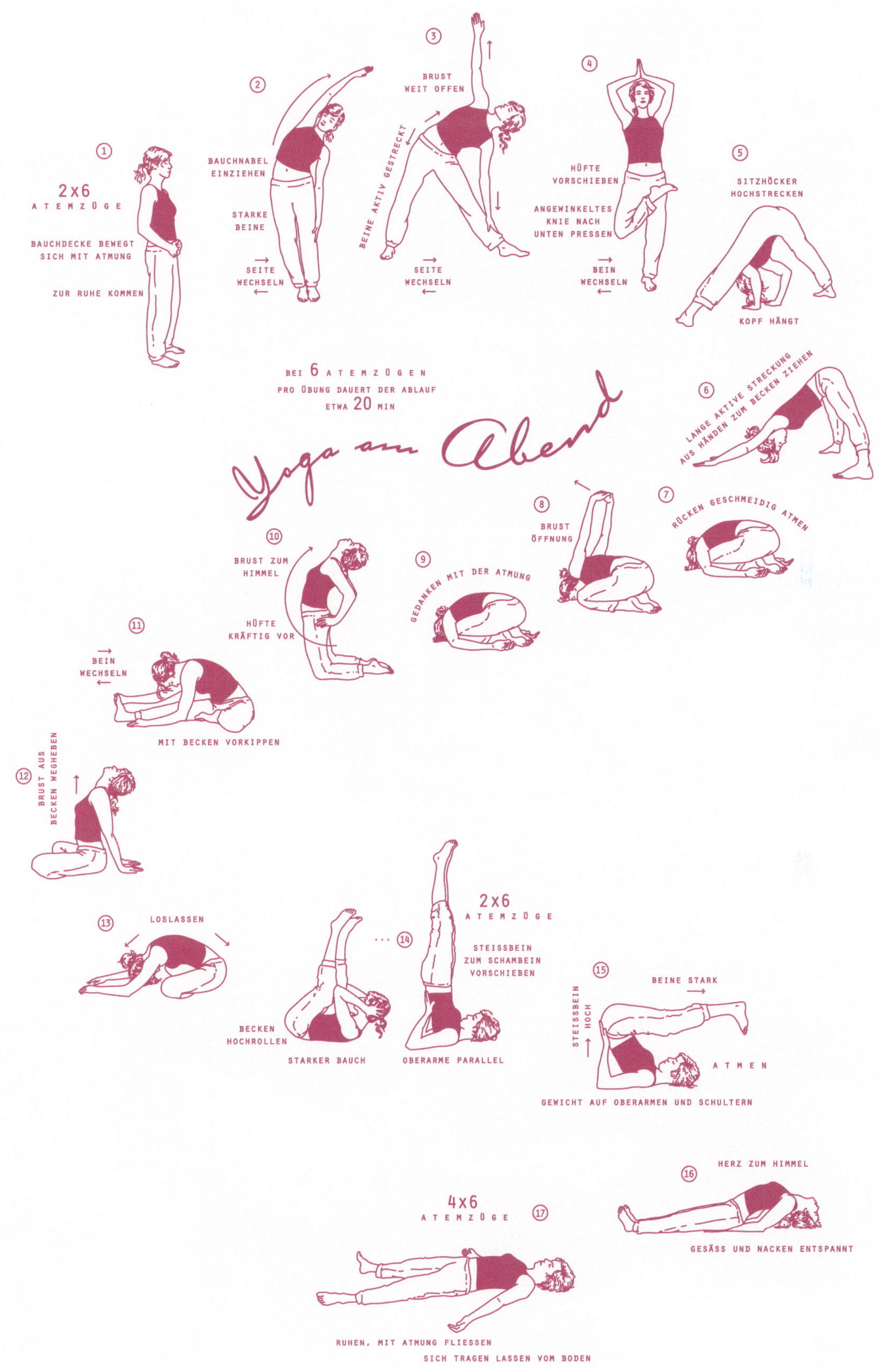

Claudia Blum / Sara Zeiter and Claudia Blum, serigraphy: Eliane Gossweiler, A3, cardboard, 2005

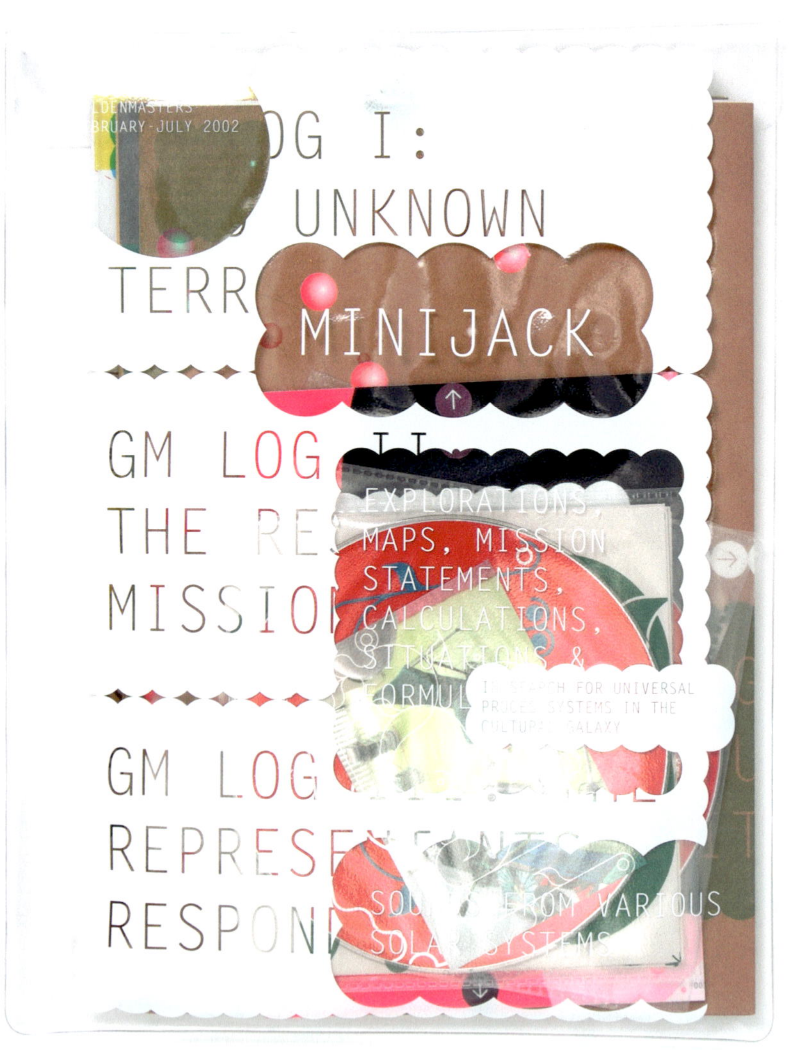

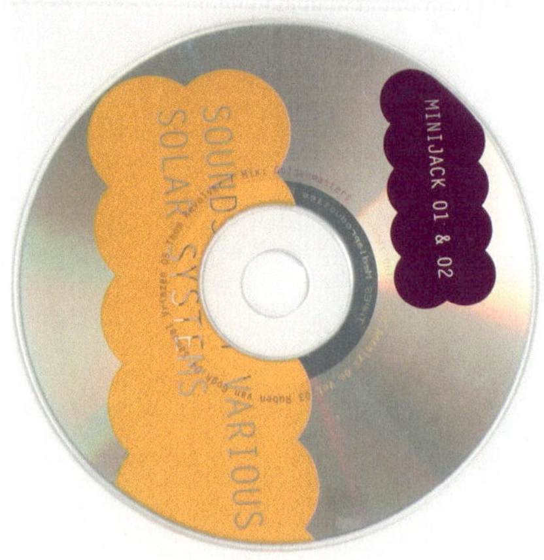

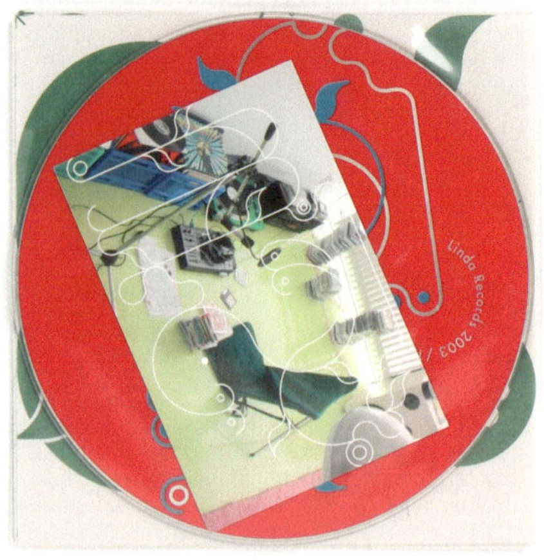

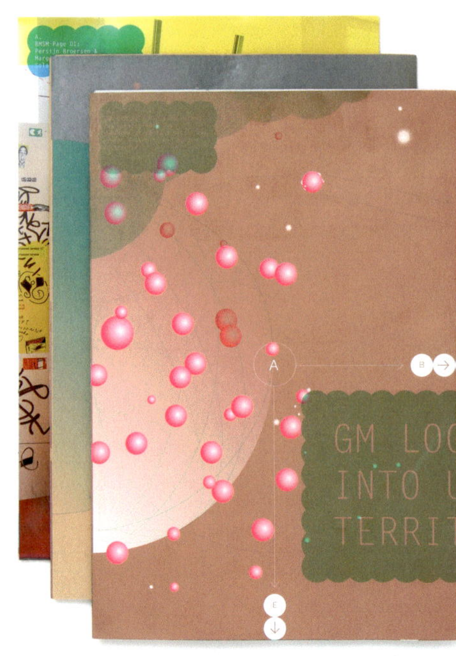

1–3   Richard Niessen, 2001

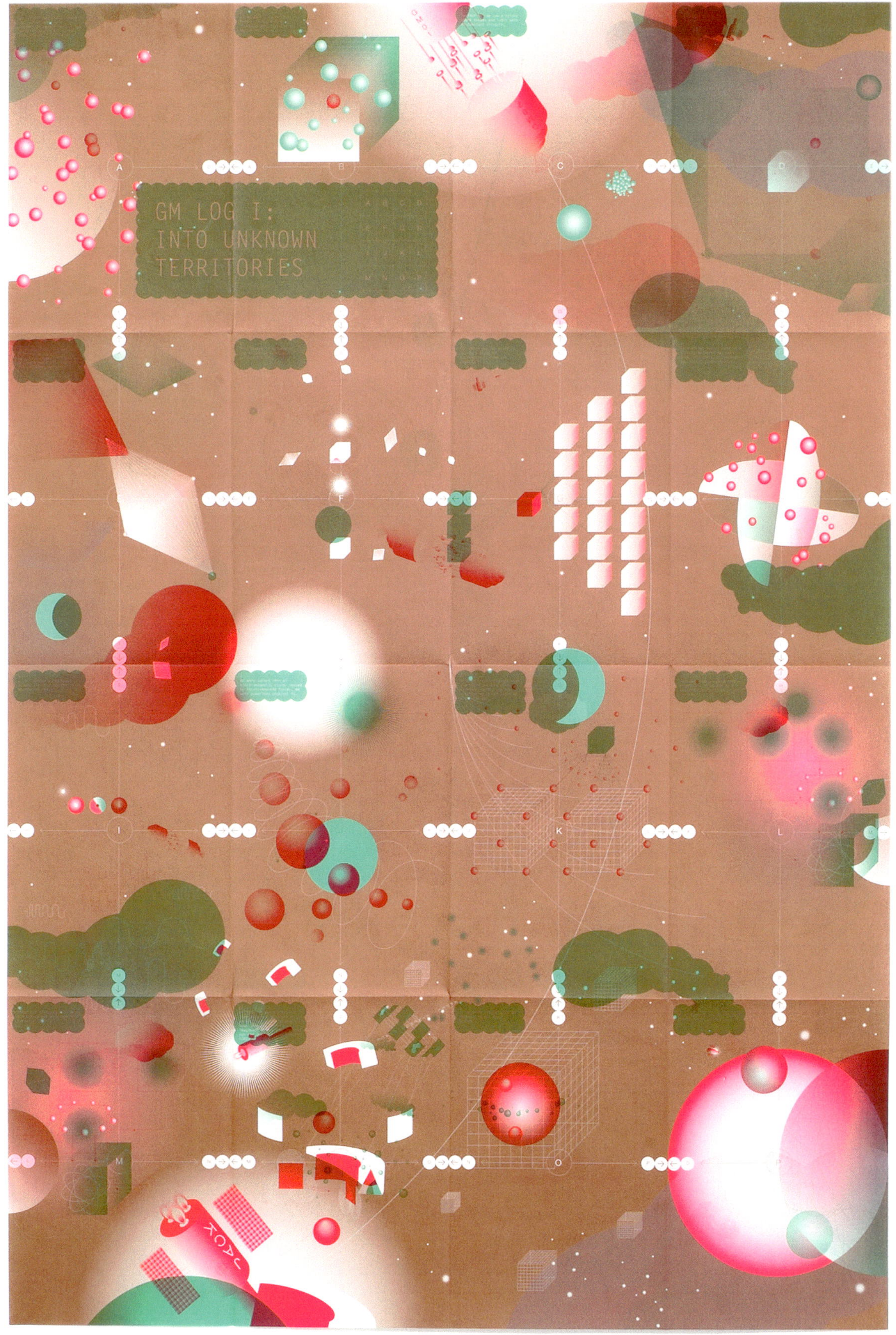

Richard Niessen, A1, offset printing 2001

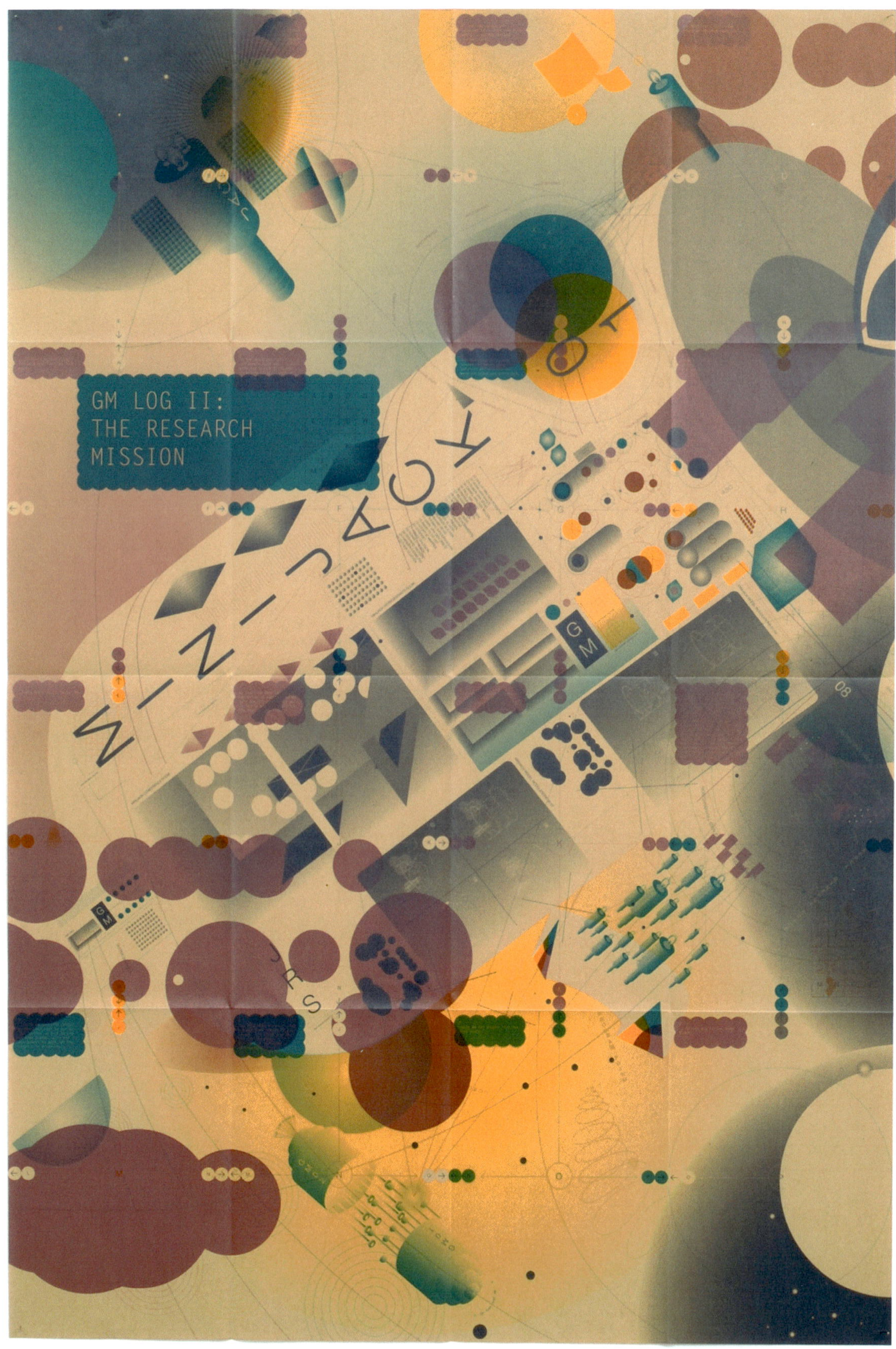

    Richard Niessen, A1, offset printing 2001

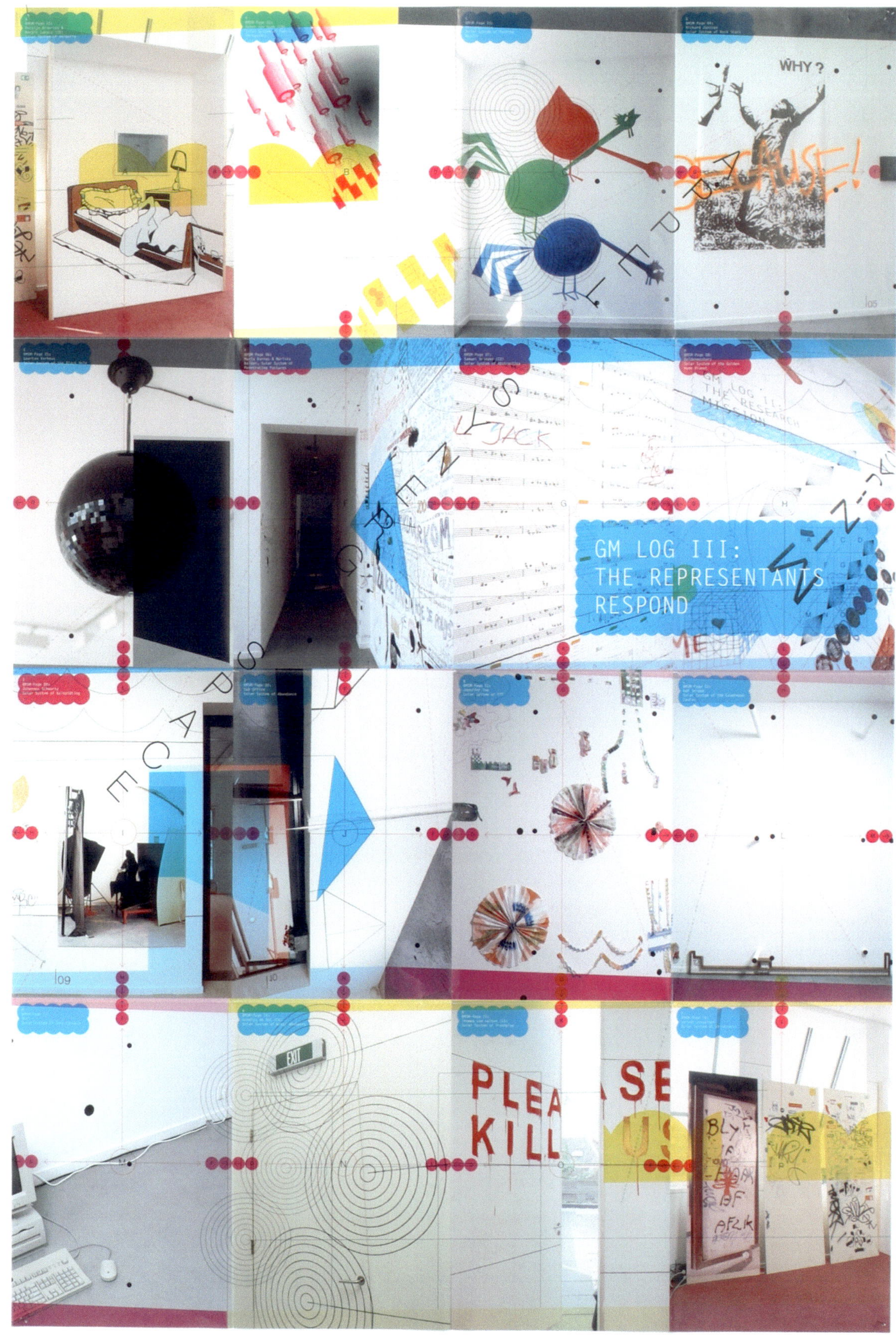

Richard Niessen, A1, offset printing 2001

Interview:
Juli Gudehus

Berlin-based Juli Gudehus, a true hunter and gatherer when it comes to weird and wonderful materials, considers herself a multi-disciplinary joker or the "cartilage between the joints – you might be able to do without it, but badly so".
With clients ranging from the German Bundestag to weekly newspaper "Die Zeit", Gudehus "advises, coordinates, designs, researches, gets upset, gets excited, writes, collects, connects, learns, teaches and, ultimately, tackles boundaries".

What is your general take on self-promotion?

I do not like the word per se – it reminds me of a peacock showing off its plumage. Essentially, the people and institutions I work with want me for exactly what I am, for my unique thoughts and reactions. Of course, I have some "classic" means of self-representation – the stationery and measures I use when I cannot be present in person. Yet the way I see it, I do not use them to represent or promote myself, they ARE part of myself. It's as simple and difficult as that.
Generally speaking, I think that in order to be successful, any method needs to be clear and individual without being pretentious – the actual means by which you achieve this are unimportant.

Could you tell us a little bit about the idea behind your range of calling cards and stationery?

It all started more or less unintentionally when water damage spoiled my great-grandmother's postcard collection. As I did not have the heart to throw them all away, I simply decided to reuse them.
My obvious strength lies in the combination of sensuality, playfulness, systematics and my ability to react to ever-new situations – and all this is reflected in the design of my letters and business cards.
In the beginning, it was stamped postcards and their more chunky successors (sometimes up to half an inch thick – doormat, car tire, styrofoam), later I designed some split versions consisting of one half found object and one half laser-printed information on cardboard. My move to Berlin triggered the current sticker idea.

How many different variations did you come up with?

Although some might look similar, none are identical because I know how great it feels to receive a letter made just for you. Not personalised, but personal. In this way, my overall philosophy is reflected in each and every communication.

I have many favourites, some of whom I find it very hard to part with, yet they keep changing all the time. Take the wallpaper of legendary Cologne café Hallmackenreuther, for example – every card smelt of smoke for years. And people went crazy for them. Right now, I love this quaint, chequered cupboard paper. In addition, I use sand paper, model railway astroturf, Lisa (light-collecting foil that glows at the edges), felt, tar board and lots and lots of fantastic found objects: typing exercises, children's drawings, foreign wrappers, old book covers…

So, how do you decide who gets which version?

With the stationery, I always take my time to select the right sheet. I ask myself – who would appreciate this design most? Reused homework from 1972, flower wrapping or Czech paper bags… and who is likely to be put off? Does the stationery reflect what I am trying to convey?

For the business cards, there is a different system. As the proud owner of more than forty handbags, I soon got tired of repacking the contents and went about filling each bag with the same essentials: small mirror, lip care, aspirin, pen, paper… and business cards. These are designed to match each respective bag in colour, style, pattern or material.

What kind of reactions do you get?

Most people adore them; some have even started a collection. Furthermore, they seem to serve as a great reminder – whenever I speak to someone after a few years, they always seem to remember who I am.

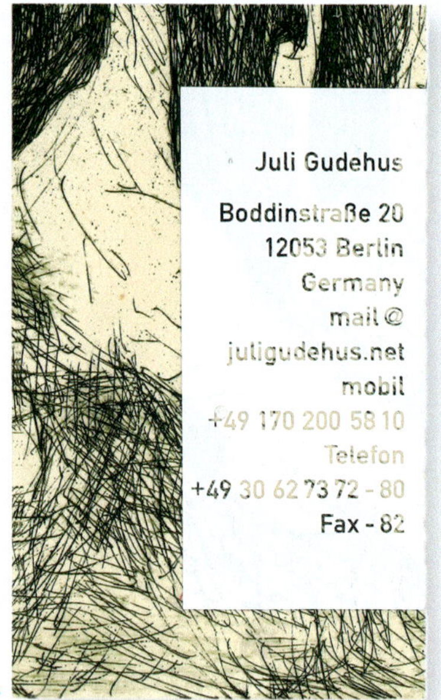

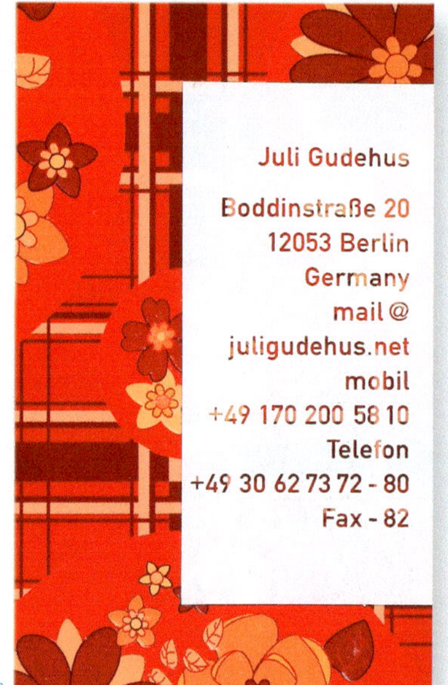

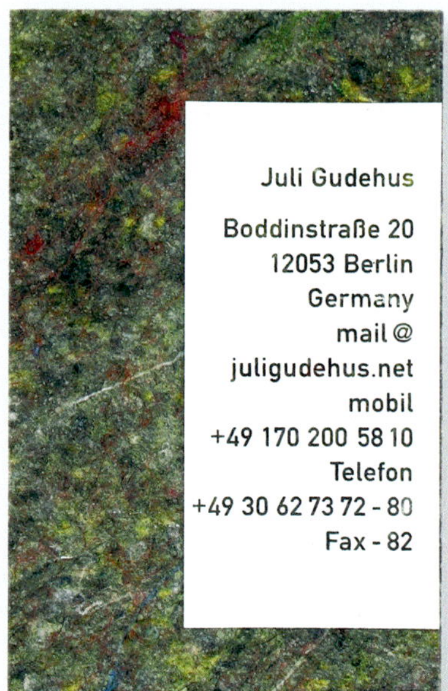

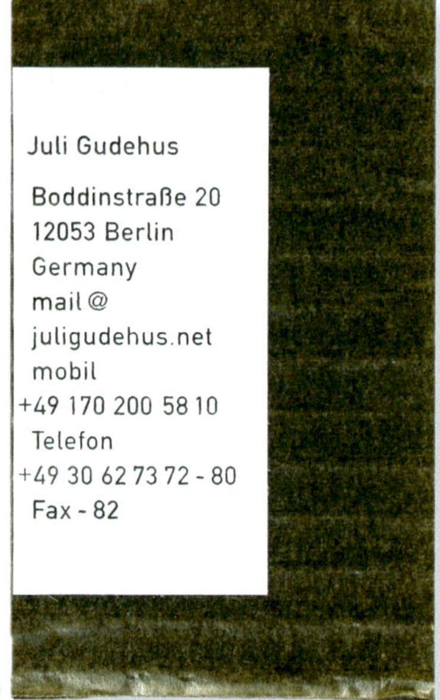

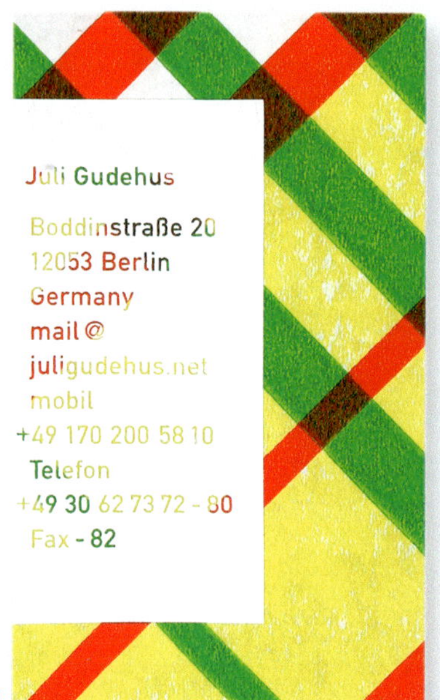

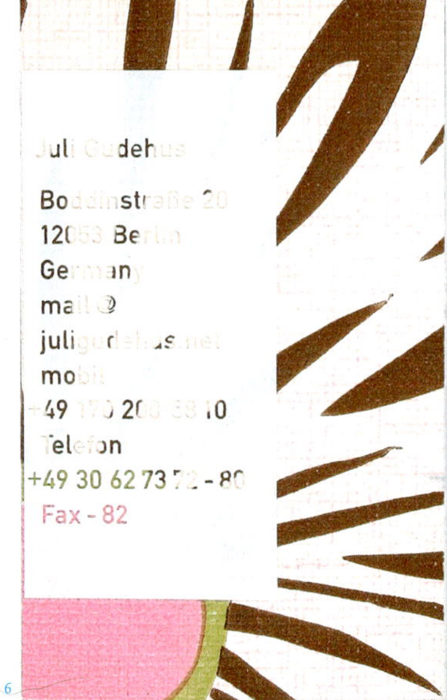

1–6   Juli Gudehus, different papers, sticker, silk-screen printing, 2002

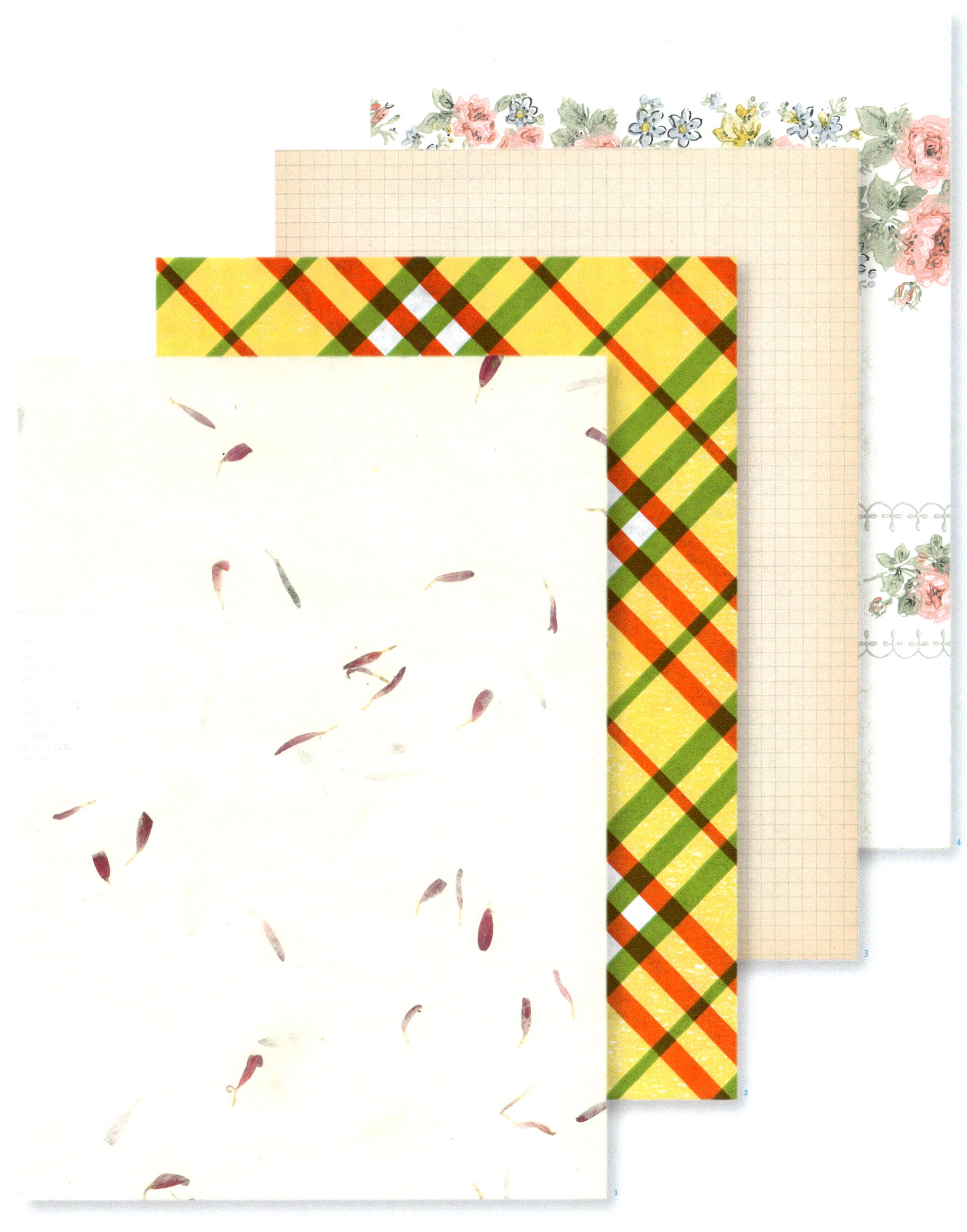

1–4   Juli Gudehus, wallpaper, sticker, silk-screen printing, 2002

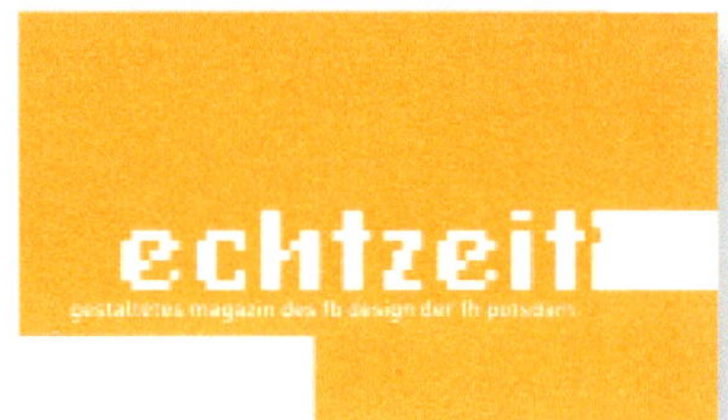

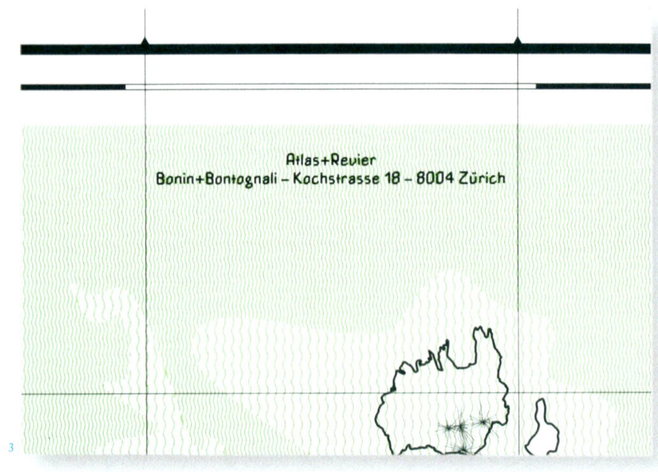

1–2   Redaktion "echtzeit" / Svenja von Döhlen, Borries Schwesinger, misprinted sheets,
       offset printing 1c, 2004
3   Bonbon / Rahel Arnold, Valeria Bonin, Diego Bontognali, paper, offset printing, 2001
4   1Kilo, printed on perforated coupon, laser print, 2003
5   Emmi Salonen, 2004

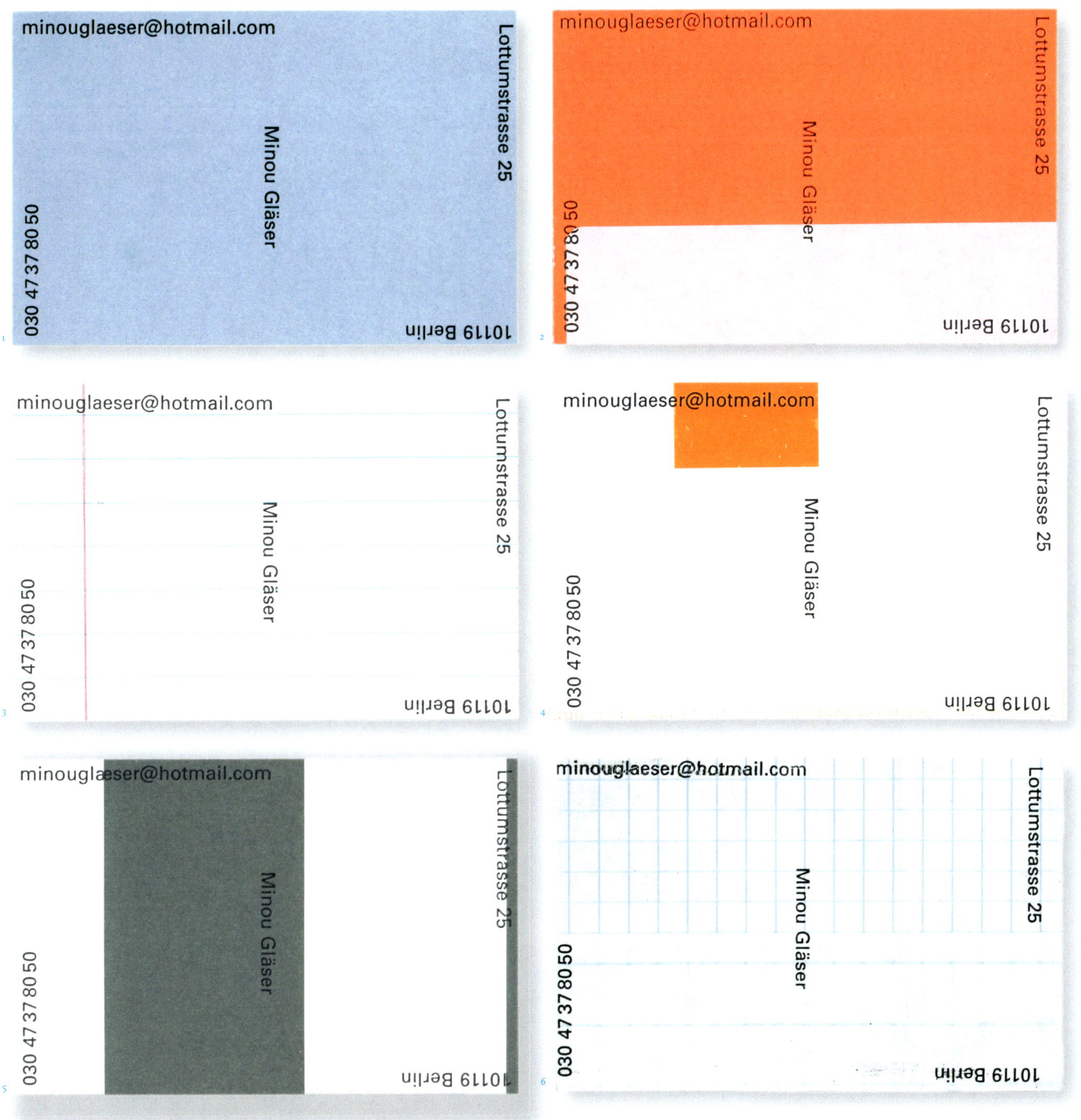

1–6   Minou Gläser, misprinted paper and rest paper, laser print, 2002

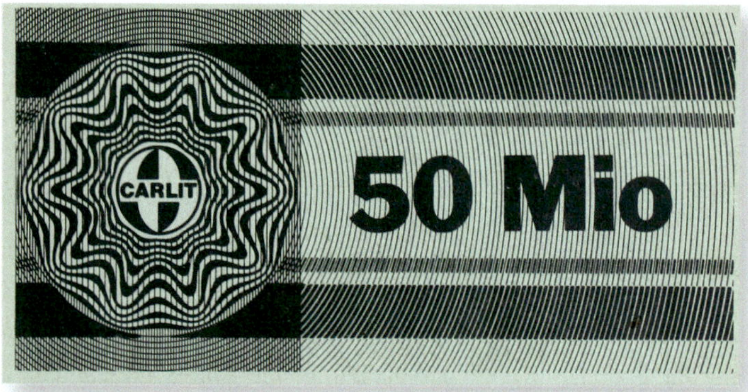

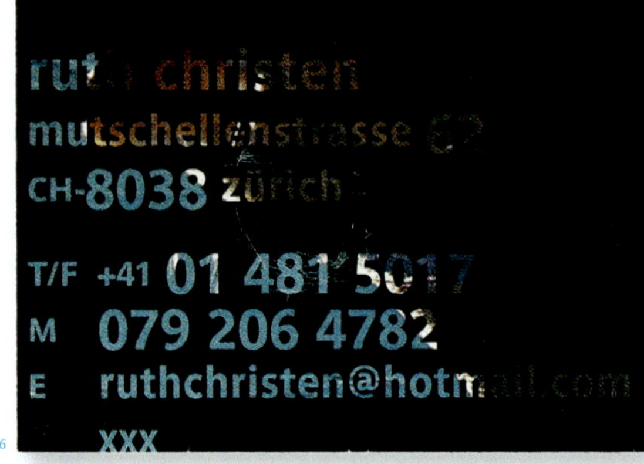

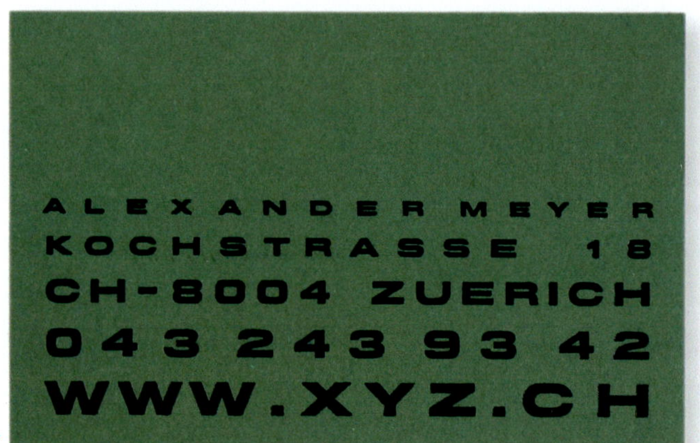

1　Alexander Meyer, Rebecca Pfaffhauser, poster paper, silk-screen printing, 2001
2　Alexander Meyer, paper, lead composition, 2003
3–4　Alexander Meyer, Carlit, Monopoly
5　Alexander Meyer, paper, laser print, 1999
6　Donat Raetzo and Ruth Christen, recycled magazine pages, laser print, 2000
7　Alexander Meyer, paper, lead composition, 2005

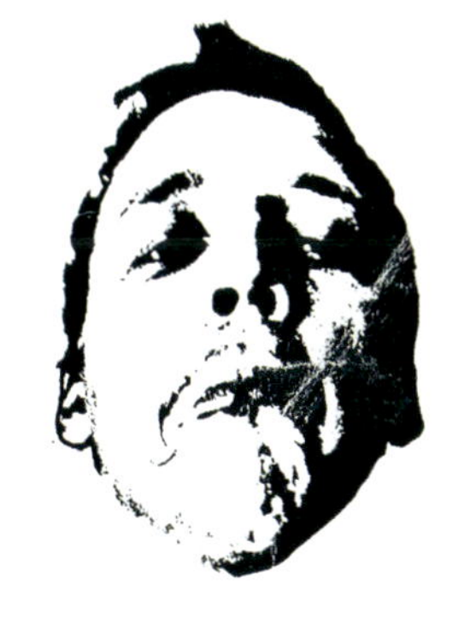

www.MADEYE.info
peter@madeye.info

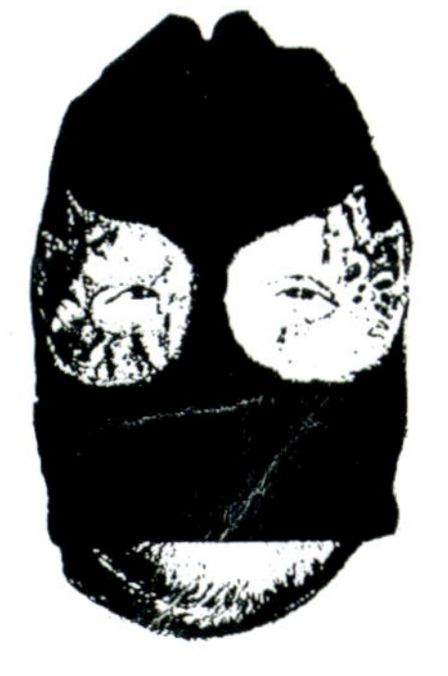

www.MADEYE.info
jakob@madeye.info

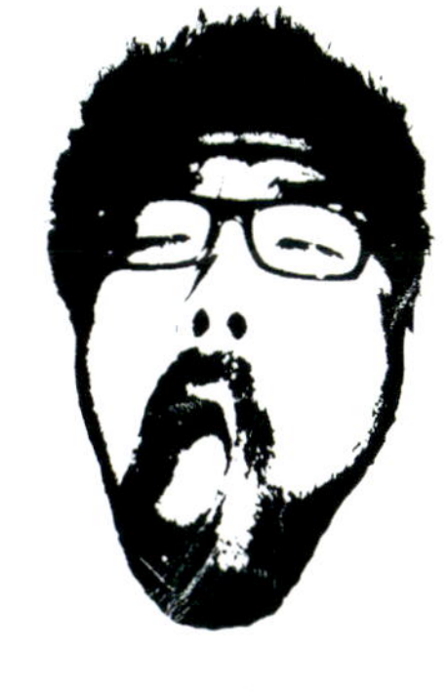

www.MADEYE.info
ohyun@madeye.info

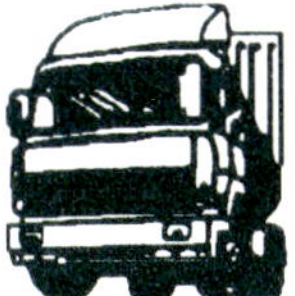

XXXXXXXXXXXXXXXXXX
XXXXXXXXXXXXXXXXXXX
XXXXXXXXXXXXXXXX
XXXXXXXXXXXXXXXXX
XXXXXXXXXXXXXXXX
XXXXXXXXXXXXXXXXXXXXXXXXXXX
anthony burrill 020 8674 3707

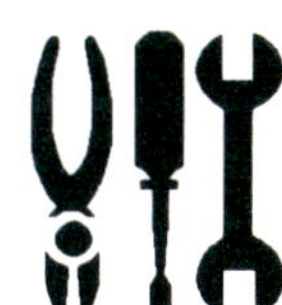

OOOOOOOOOOOOOOOOOO
OOOOOOOOOOOOOOOOO
OOOOOOOOOOOOOOOO
OOOOOOOOOOOOOOOOOO
OOOOOOOOOOOOOOOOO
OOOOOOOOOOOOOOOOOOOOOOOOOOOO
www.friendchip.com

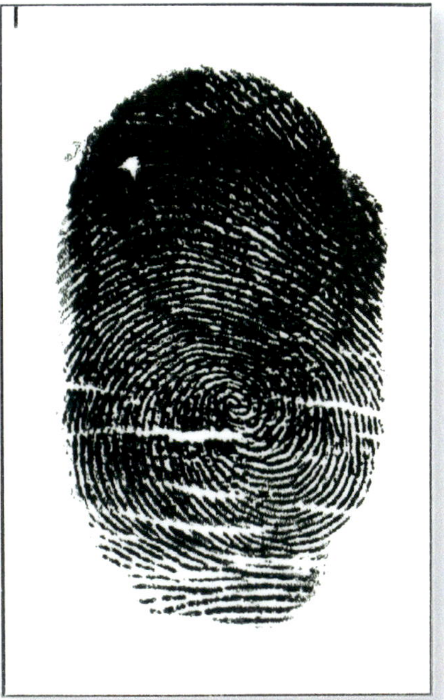

lvispresleydshingiskhando
navanheinzg.konsalikpius
XXVX.marlboromanromanp
olanskijackieobertivogtsa
Dginalollogrigidaherrhitl
ermuttertheresajonnyrott
enundzaballaheinzrühman
nmamaclarazetkinrosavon
praunheimarnieschwarzen
eggerdrmedthengistsoulou
kidsecaptainahabdickcock
leyschönbohmjörgphilipho
chtiefcheguevarasarahyou
ngrübezahlbrigittemirach
tbakerludwigwittgenstein
antoninabenignalilithhan
dloschristophergruszkaop
anophreteteignazbubisme
laniebrunobeatnicolaseng
elsczernydaguerrederliebe
gottilienastasebrittawass
erfilterjosefbeuysvanessa
redgravediepolizeijeangen
etronaldmcdonaldbrunofis
hermelbrooksfriedlichküp
persbuschlaurelandhardyd
ollyschlegelstraße14doila
r10115berlinjekyllandhyd
e030/2820518leokirchacht
ernbuschhelgagötzejulesv
ernemuhamadalimariacalla

1–3   Ohyun Kwon and Jakob Kanior, sticker-paper, laser print, 2002
4–5   Anthony Burrill, business cards cheap card, self-service kiosk in a railway station, 2002
6–7   Christopher Gruszka, photocopy, 1998

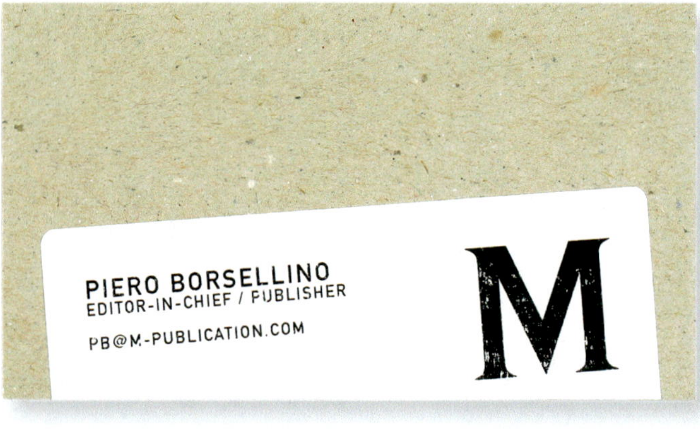

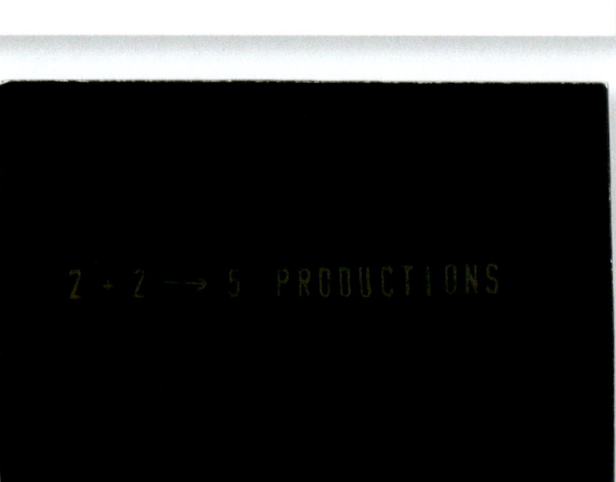

1–2   M-Publication, sticker, stamp
3–4   Boris Brumnjak, paper, 300 g, laser print, 2002
5–6   2+2-5 Productions, stamp
7   Boris Brumnjak, type writer on silver cardboard, 2000

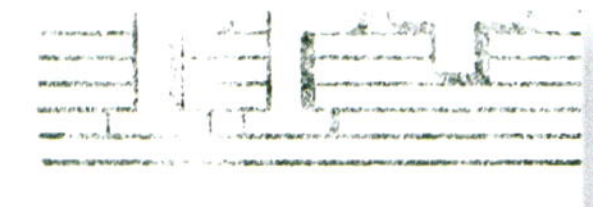

Boris Brumnjak
Visuelle Gestaltung
Prisdorferstrasse 14b

D-13581 Berlin

MetaDesign

Leibnizstrasse 65 · 10629 Berlin

⋯⋗ Herrn
Boris Brumnjak
Prisdorfer Straße 14 b
13581 Berlin

Transport Deutschland
Dieselstr. 2-4
D 42489 Wülfrath
ID-Nr:
KD-Nr: 0

Brumnjak
Boris
Prisdorferstraße 14B
D 13581 Berlin

Diesel Deutschland GmbH

UFFIZI FEDERAL DA C
CH-3003 BERN

Boris Brumnjak
Visuelle Gestaltung
Prisdorferstrasse 14b
De-13581 Berlin
Deutschland

Boris Brumnjak
Graphic Design
Prisdorferstrasse 14B
13581 Berlin
Germany

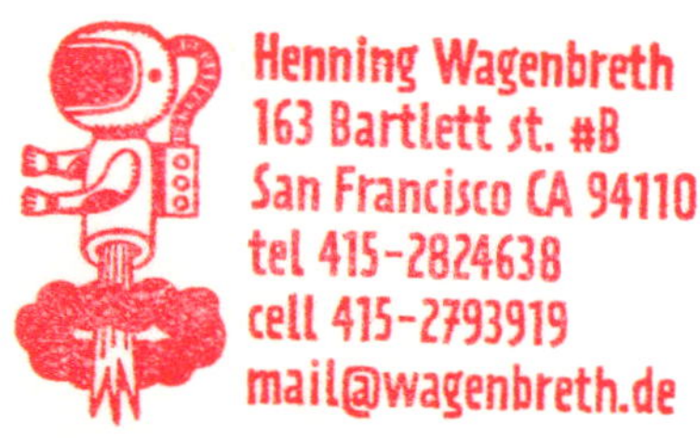

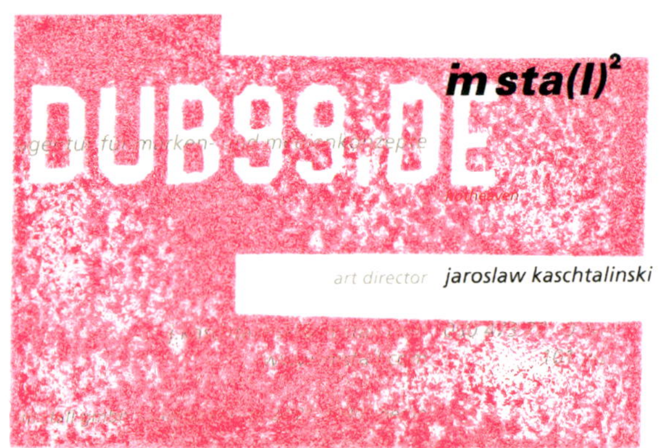

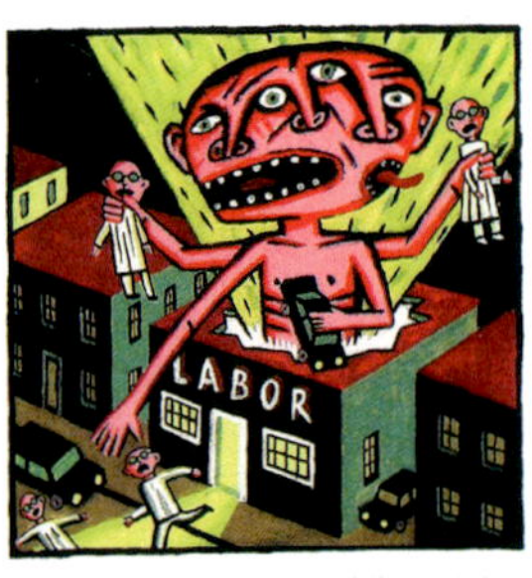

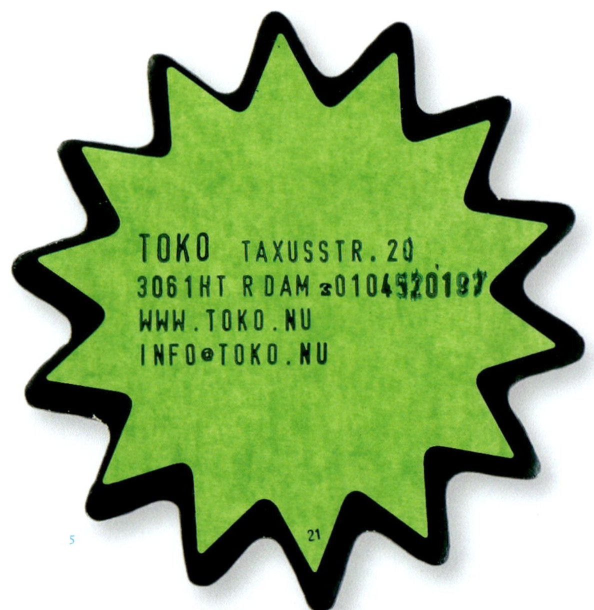

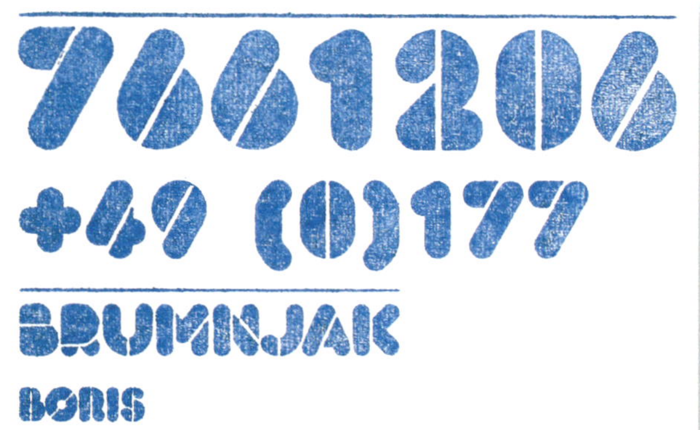

1   Robert A. Schaefer, Gmund paper, rubber stamp, 1999
2   Henning Wagenbreth, card stock, rubber stamp, 2000
3   DUB99 / Jaroslaw Kaschtalinski over Claudius Lazzeroni, cardboard, offset printing and rubber stamp, 2000, overprint 2002
4   Henning Wagenbreth, card stock, rubber stamp and printed »post« stamp, 2001
5   Toko / Eva Dijkstra, paper, rubber stamp, 2002
6   Boris Brumnjak, paper, rubber stamp, 2004

Neubau. Screen. Print. Broadcast & Typography.

Stefan Gandl [Name] Stefan@NeubauBerlin.com [Email]
http://www.NeubauBerlin.com [URL] +49.30-695.371.9-21 [Telephone]
+49.30-695.371.9-26 [Facsimile] Paul-Lincke-Ufer 44A [Street]
2.HH, Fabrik/Aufgang B [Building] 10999 Berlin [AreaCode] Germany [Country]

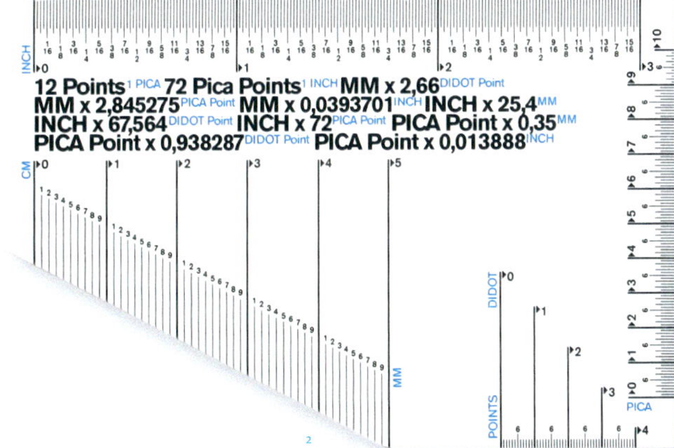

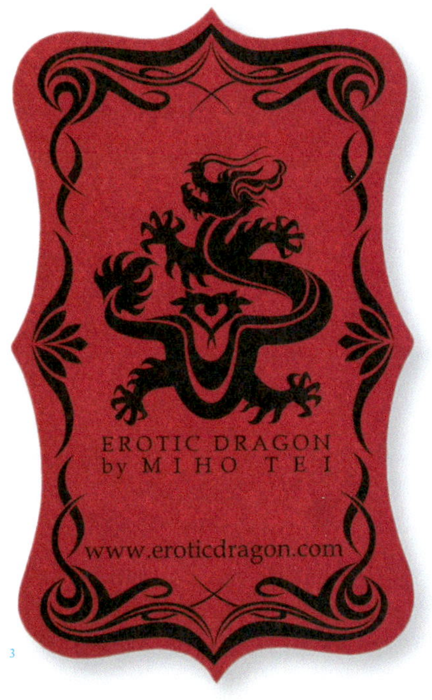

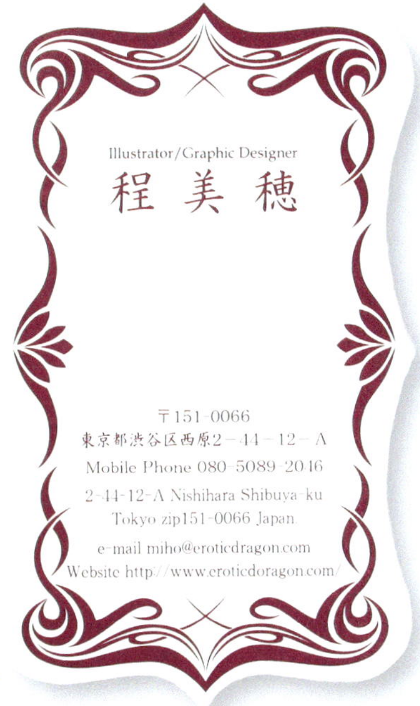

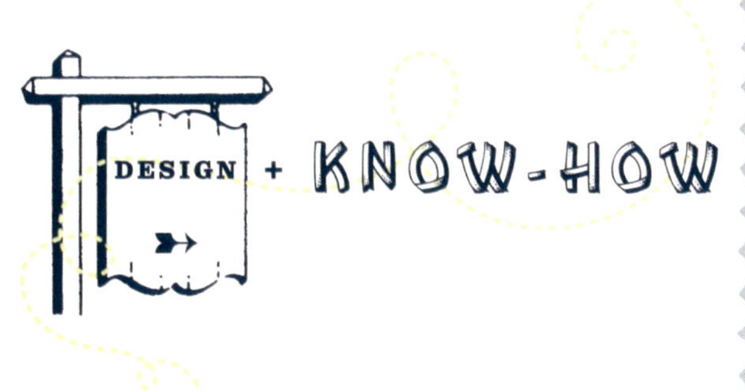

1–2   Neubau, Stefan Gandl, paper, 195 g, offset printing, 2001
3–4   Erotic Dragon, offset printing, 2003
5–6   Martine Trélaün, offset printing

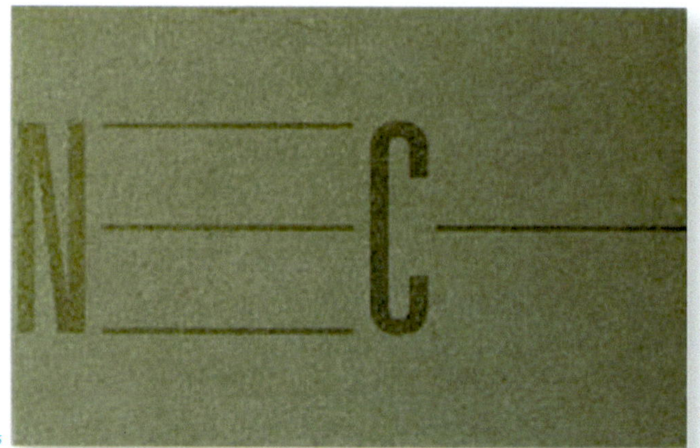

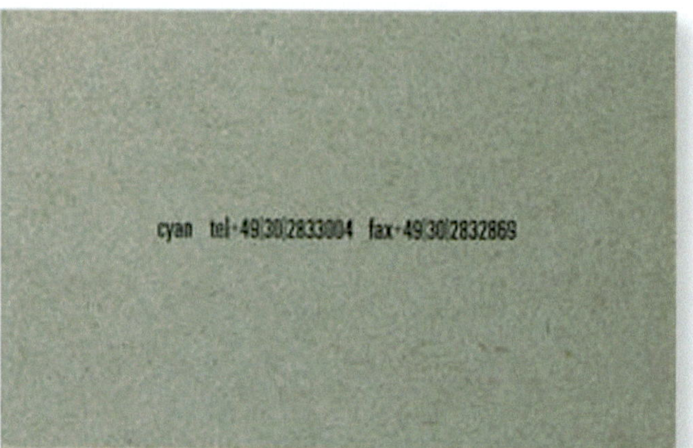

1–2   Matthias Hoene / Samuel Baker and Inca Starzinsky, grey cardboard, silk-screen printing, 2004
3–4   Non-format / Kjell Ekhorn and Jon Forss, white lined grey chipboard, silk-screen printing, white ink, 2003
5–6   Cyan, grey cardboard, offset printing, 1992

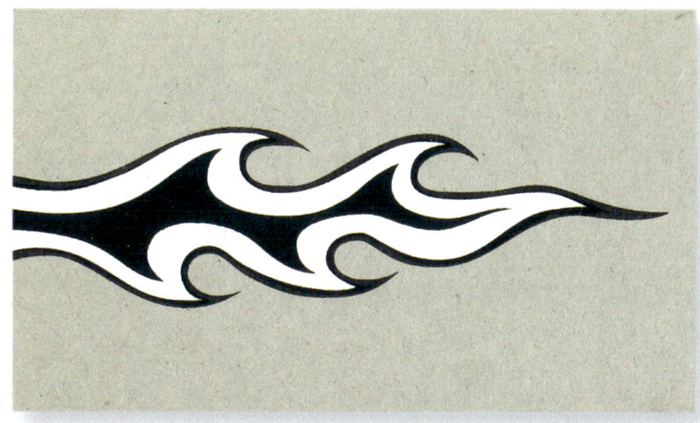

1   Karlssonwilker Inc. / Hjalti Karlsson and Jan Wilker, cardboard, with silver front, silk-screen printing 2c, 2001
2   Karlssonwilker Inc. / Hjalti Karlsson and Jan Wilker, cardboard, silk-screen printing 2c, 2001
3–4   Karlssonwilker Inc. / Hjalti Karlsson and Jan Wilker, cardboard, with silver front, silk-screen printing 2c, 2001
5   Non-format / Kjell Ekhorn and Jon Forss, uncoated white cardboard, offset printing, 2002
6–7   Jakob Kanior, pink cardboard, silk-screen printing, 2000

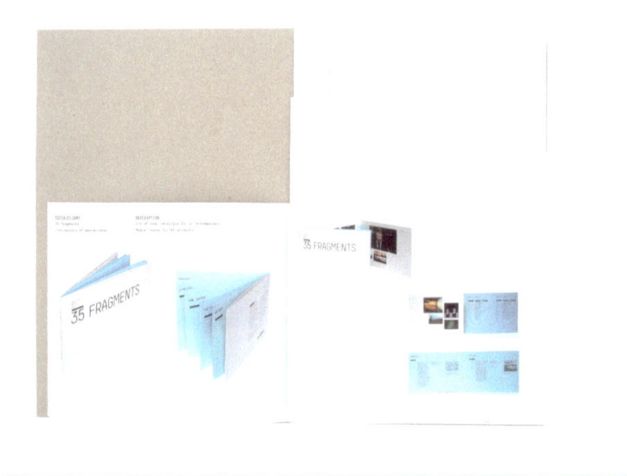

1–2 Emmi Salonen, A4, recycled cardboard with sticker, 2005
3   Emmi Salonen, matt white paper 100 g, 2005
4   Emmi Salonen, different size notebook papers, 2005

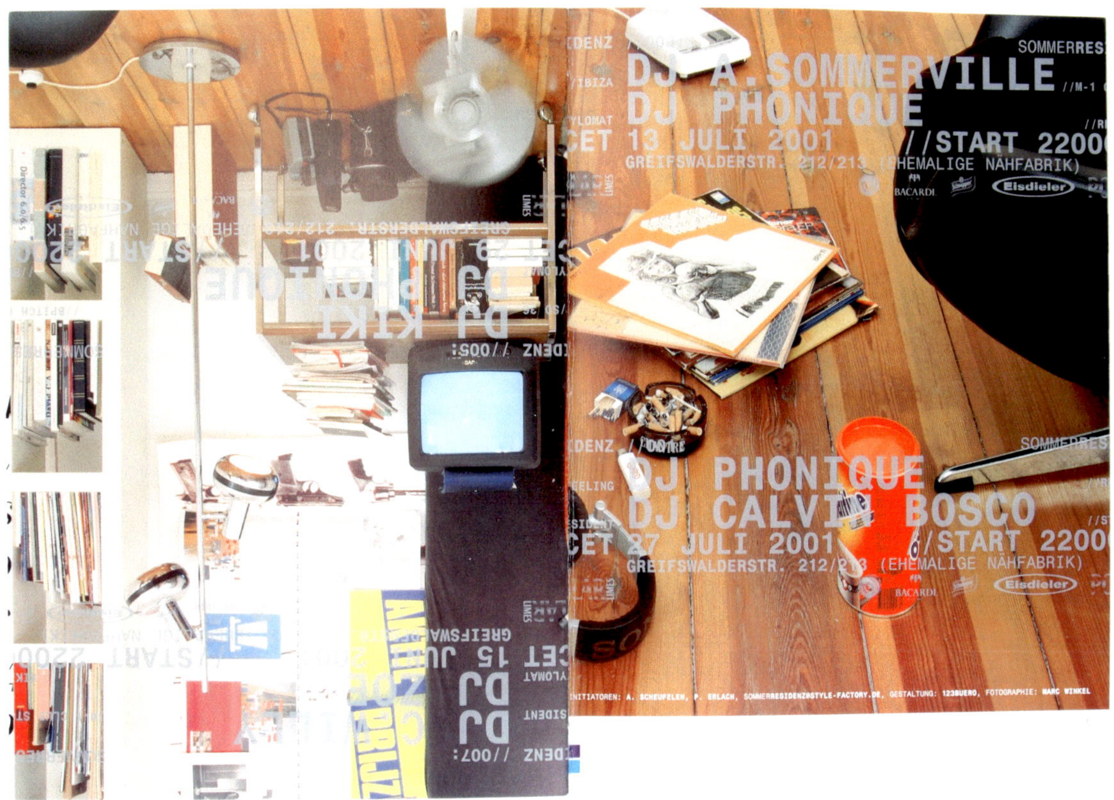

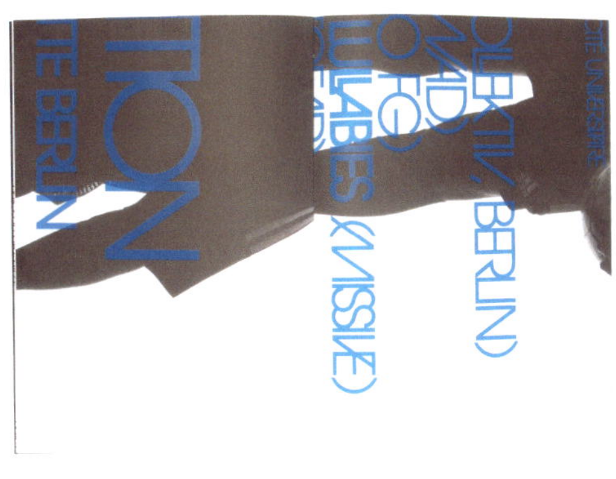

Originally printed in a limited edition of two (one of which has sadly gone missing), 123buero's remaining sample book accompanies designer Timo Gaessner wherever he goes. A clever addition to his website and regular portfolio, where all work is clearly documented, this lighter and more compact, text-free version serves as an effective teaser and introduction to his trademark style by assembling a collection of intriguing fragments, cut-up print sheets and sensuous paper types to allow any prospective client to see, feel and experience Gaessner's style first-hand.

1–3   123Buero / Timo Gaessner, various paper, offset printing, silk-screen printing and Xerox, 2003

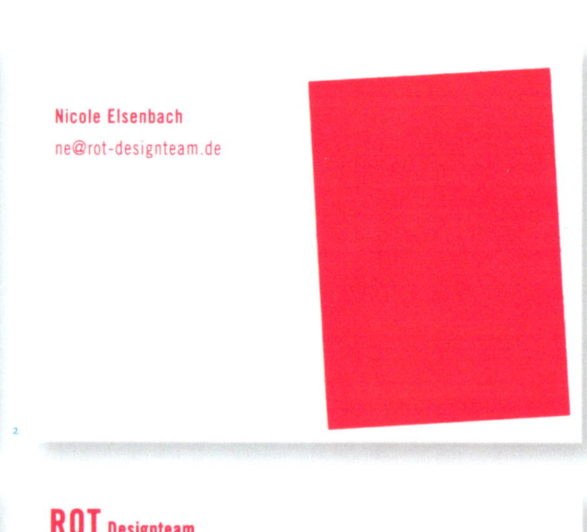

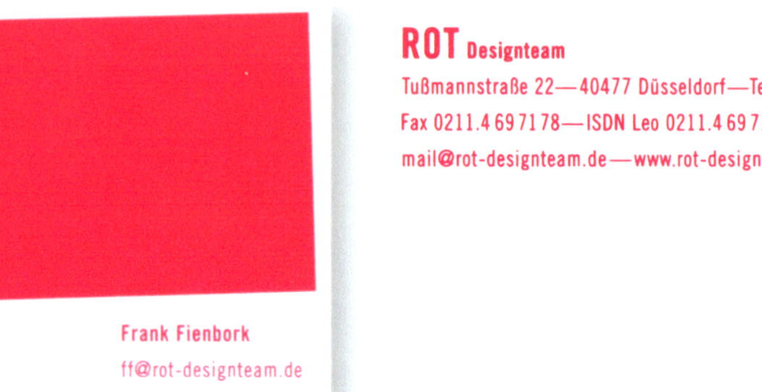

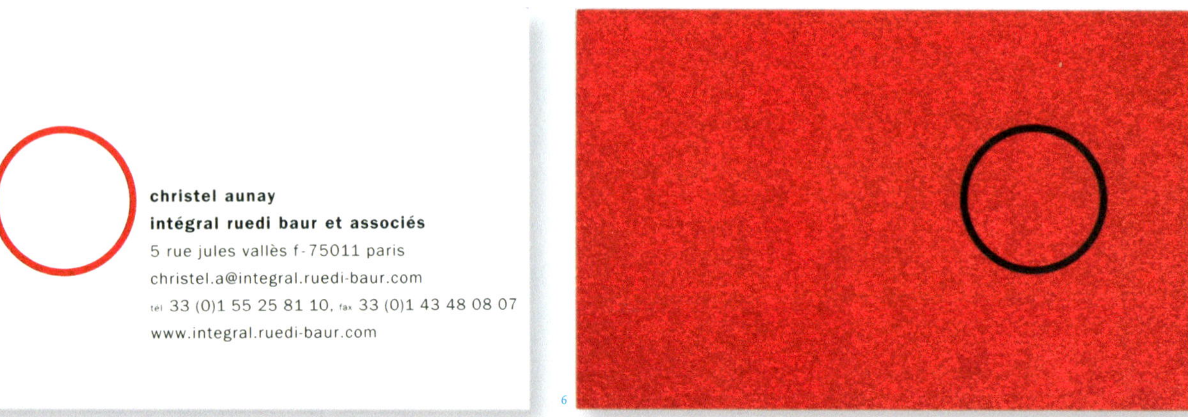

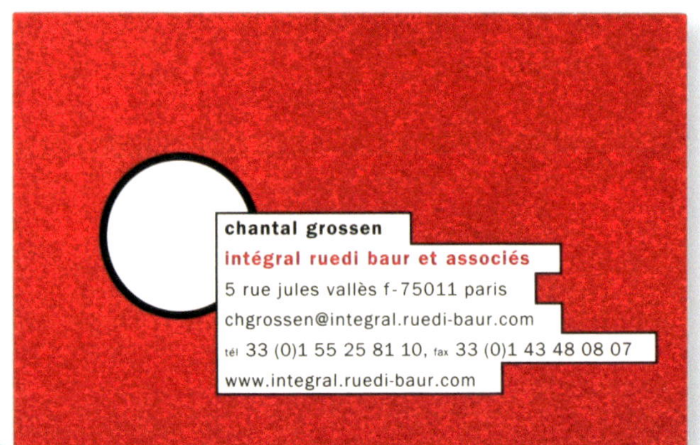

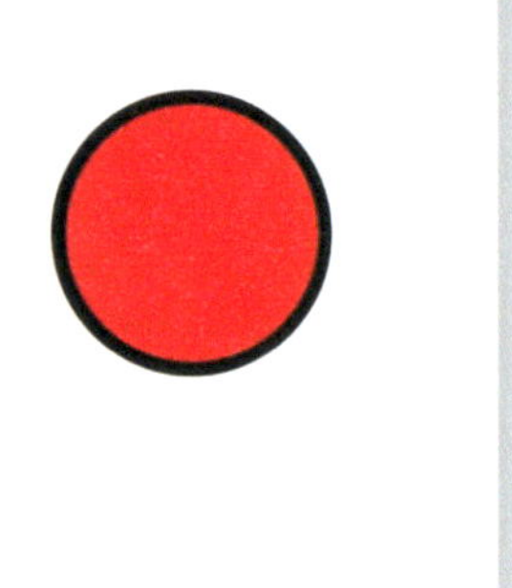

1–4   Rot Designteam / Nicole Elsenbach and Frank Fienbork, Mythos white 280 g, offset printing, 2004
5–8   Intégral / Ruedi Baur et associés, paper, offset printing, 1995

Thomas Gfeller
Typo/Grafik
T⁺F
Murbacherstrasse 34   CH-4056 Basel   gfellergrafik@access.ch
061 322 76 90

Thomas Gfeller
Typo/Grafik
T⁺F
Murbacherstrasse 34   CH-4056 Basel   gfellergrafik@access.ch
061 322 76 90

Read naked

Underware Bas Jacobs
bas@underware.nl
Schouwburgstraat 2, 2511 VA
Den Haag, the Netherlands
tel +31 (0) 70 42 78 115
www.underware.nl

private address LIJNBAANSGRACHT 270-B, 1017 RL AMSTERDAM, 020 622 43 66

Frost Design°
The Gymnasium. 56 Kingsway Place. Sans Walk.
London EC1R OLU. Tel 020 7490 7994. Fax 020 7490 7995
vince@frostdesign.co.uk www.frostdesign.co.uk

Vince Frost

Frost

unit
creative management
amsterdam   **martine nieuwenhuis**

egelantiersstraat 143
1015 ra   amsterdam
postbus   11687
1001 gr   amsterdam
the netherlands
tel   +3120 530 6000
fax   +3120 530 6001
e   martine@unit.nl
www.unit.nl

photographers
illustrators
(art) directors
stylists

Isabel Herzbach
Dipl. Designerin
FON 0049 (0)178 4598950
E-MAIL isi_going@web.de
1   ¶

gülizar çepoğlu

gülizar çepoğlu design e-mail.gulizar@appleonline.net
tel.020 7 371 86 26 mobile.07949 409674
40 ewald road sw6 3nd london

1–2   Thomas Gfeller, orange and blue transparent paper, offset printing, 2003
3–4   Underware, paper, Neobond, offset printing, 2002
5   Frost Design / Vince Frost, Saxton Brilliant White Vellum 300 g, offset printing, 2005
6   Unit / Goodwill (Will Holder), pantone colour print and embossing, 1999
7   Isabel Herzbach, fluorescent paper, digital print 4c, 2003
8   Gulizar Cepoglu, uncoated paper 100 g, ink jet printing, 1996
9   Chaika, polypropilen colour natur 0,3 mm, silk-screen printing, 2004

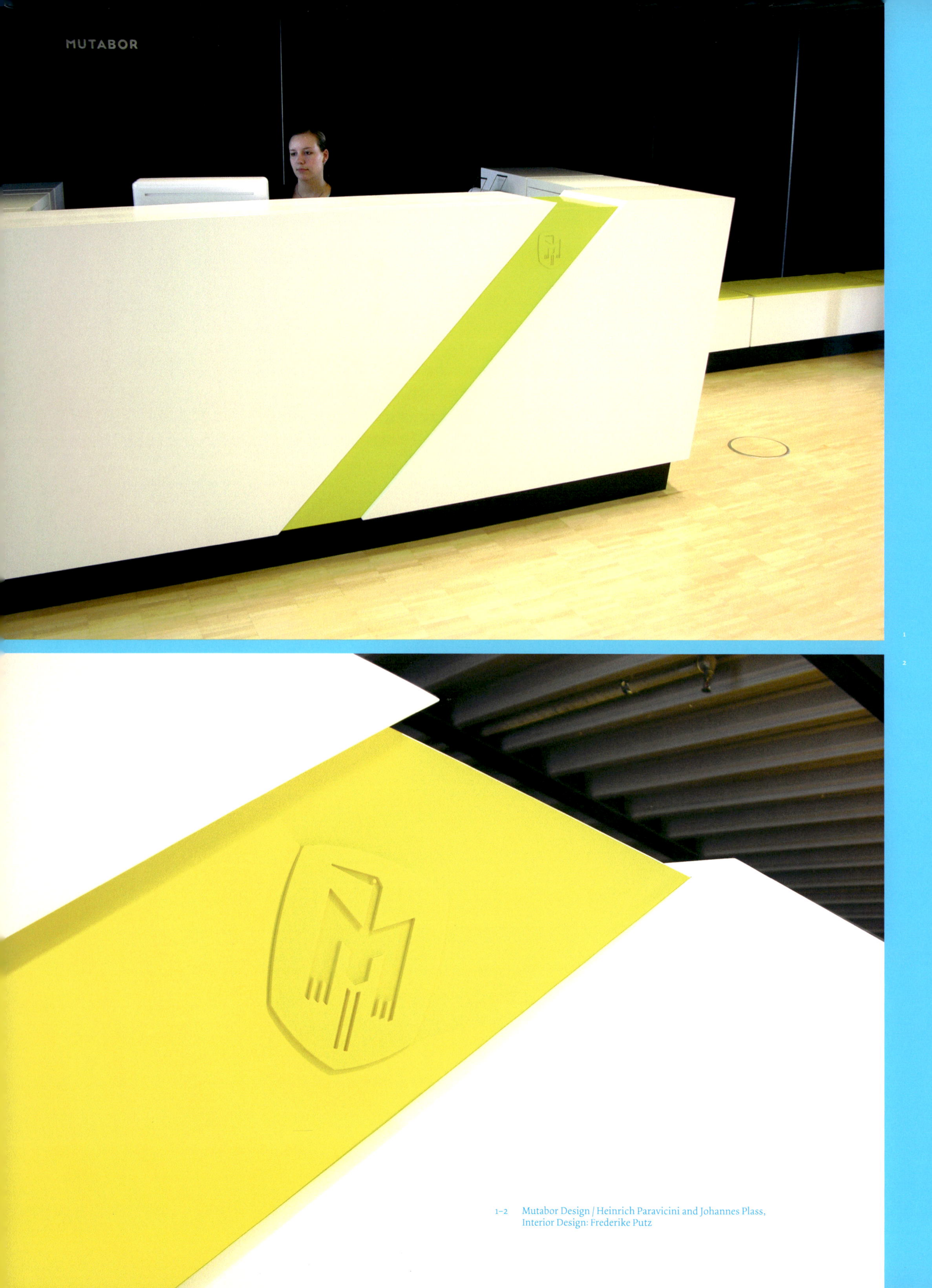

1–2 Mutabor Design / Heinrich Paravicini and Johannes Plass,
Interior Design: Frederike Putz

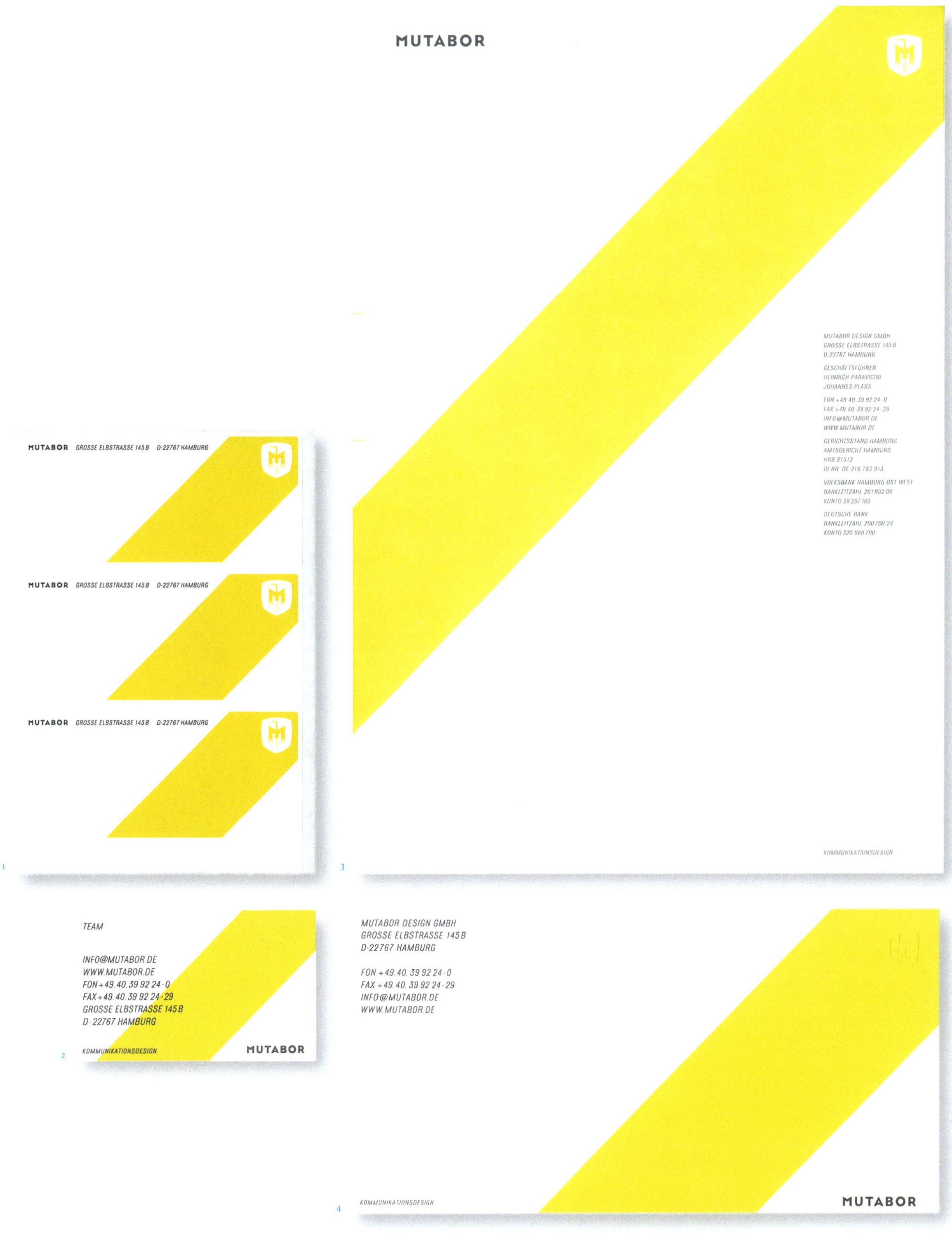

1–4 Mutabor Design / Heinrich Paravicini and Johannes Plass with Christian Tönsmann,
Illustration: Carsten Raffel, embossing

KEEP
—THIS—
COUPON
http://www.i-d.de
<i-D>
0364377524

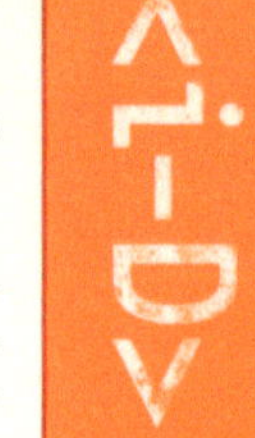
WER
—SIND—
WIR?
http://www.i-d.de
<i-D>
0364377524

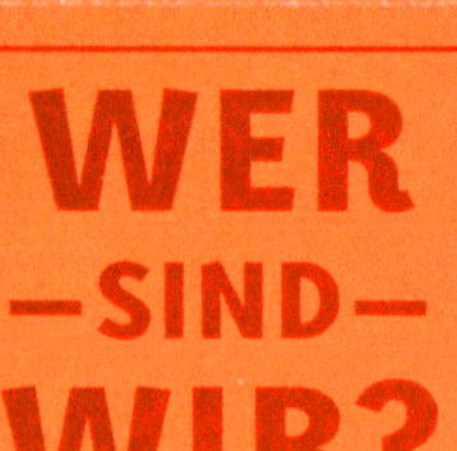
WAS
—MACHEN—
WIR?
http://www.i-d.de
<i-D>
0364377524

WAS
—WOLLEN—
WIR?
http://www.i-d.de
<i-D>
0364377524

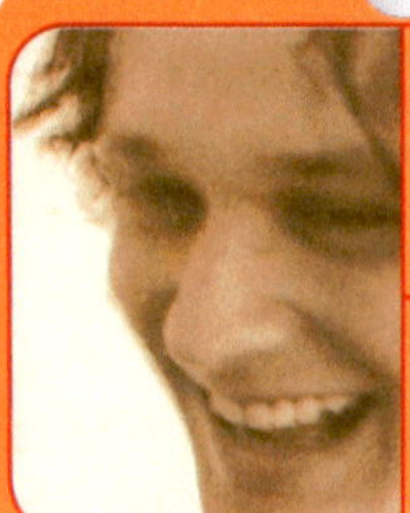
dipl.-mediengestalter
—dirk hildebrandt—
geschäftsführender
gesellschafter,
bereich internet
<i-D> internet + Design
GmbH & Co. KG
erfurter straße 35 · d-99423 weimar
+49
0
36 43 · 77 85
21 fon
29 fax
mobil 0 170 . 3 27 64 61
hille@i-d.de

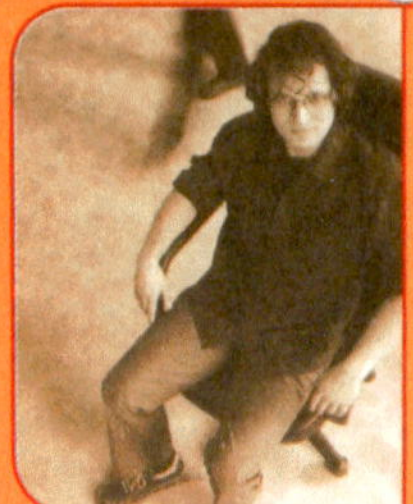
<i-D> internet + Design ist
Kommunikationsdesign an der
Schnittstelle von neuen und
klassischen Medien.

Ich bin Ihr Ansprechpartner für die
Bereiche Internet, Consulting
und Webapplikationsentwicklung.

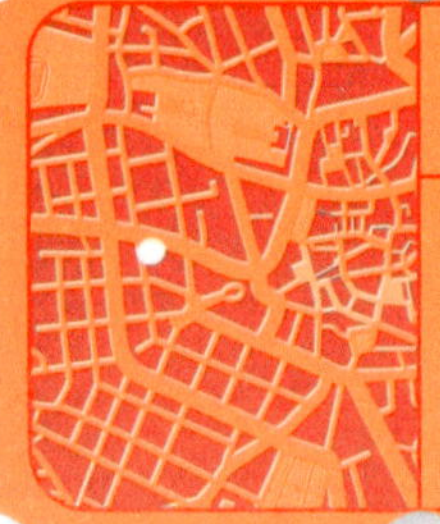
Wir planen, gestalten und realisieren
Screen- und Printmedien, von
Corporate Design bis zur datenbank-
gestützten Internetapplikation, von
Konzeptberatung und Ideenfindung
über die Gestaltung bis zu vielfältigen
Aufgaben innerhalb der Realisierung.

Wir entwickeln individuell auf unsere
Kunden zugeschnittene Lösungen.

Unsere Produkte sind Kommunikation.
Das bedeutet, nicht nur technische
Herausforderungen anzunehmen,
sondern menschliche Kommunikations-
muster zu erkennen und umzusetzen.

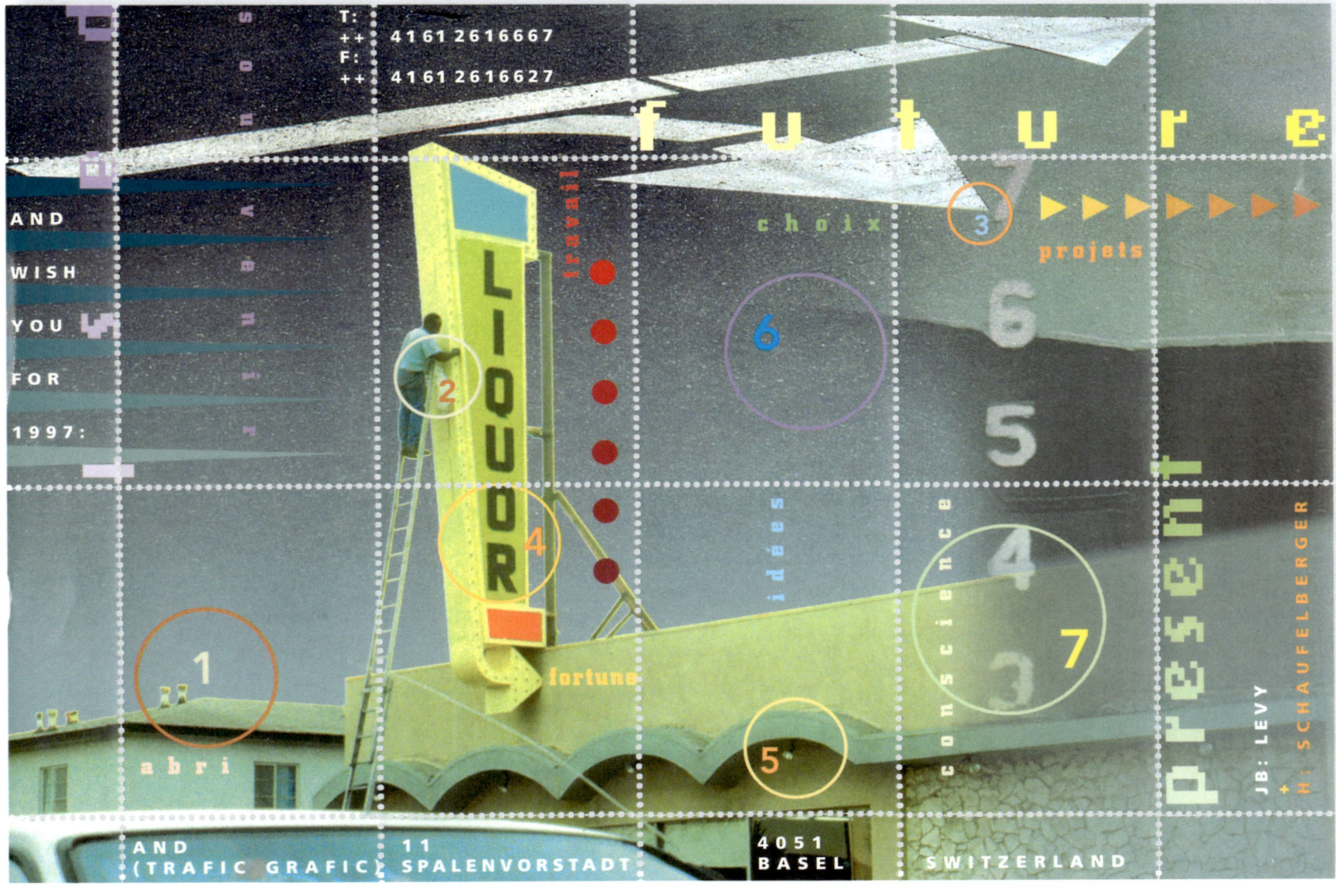

AND (Trafic Grafic) / Jean-Benoit Lévy, New Year's card in form of a stamp sheet, 148,5 x 210 mm, paper, offset printing, 1997

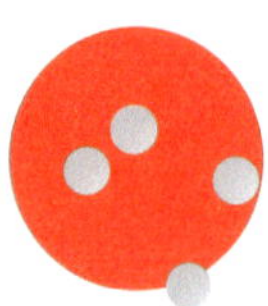

1–2   Great Guns, paper, offset printing, perforation
3   Sandra Hoffmann, paper, offset printing, perforation, 2001

HEINE/LENZ/ZIZKA

HEINE/LENZ/ZIZKA

Heine/Lenz/Zizka Projekte GmbH, Frankfurt/Berlin, Fritzlarer Straße 28–30, 60487 Frankfurt

1

HEINE/LENZ/ZIZKA

Heine/Lenz/Zizka Projekte GmbH, Frankfurt/Berlin, Fritzlarer Straße 28–30, 60487 Frankfurt

2

3

5

HEINE/LENZ/ZIZKA

Peter Zizka

Heine/Lenz/Zizka Projekte GmbH, Frankfurt/Berlin
Fritzlarer Straße 28–30, 60487 Frankfurt
Telefon 069-24 24 24-0, Telefax 069-24 24 24-99
p.zizka@heine-lenz-zizka.com

4

HEINE/LENZ/ZIZKA

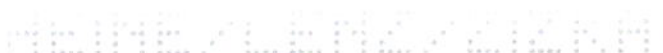

6

According to one of the most frequently quoted truisms, life is not all black and white – Heine/Lenz/Zizka, on the other hand, true lovers of understatement and the different shades of grey, prefer to cite author Bertolt Brecht ('any colour is fine – as long as it's grey') to convey the purity and subtlety of their own approach.

Brecht, who claimed that the only thing more important than a human being is his passport, also inspired their liberal and flexible use of passport-style perforation to transform any paper source into a three-dimensional object – an apposite reflection of the significance of surface structure and materials in Heine/Lenz/Zizka's overall work.

1–2   Heine/Lenz/Zizka, Vellux white, 80 g, offset printing 1/1c and hole punch, 2001
3–4   Heine/Lenz/Zizka, Medley Pure white, 360 g, offset printing 1/1c and hole punch, 2001
5   Heine/Lenz/Zizka, Medley Pure white, 90 g, offset printing 1c and hole punch, 2001
6   Heine/Lenz/Zizka, Medley Pure white, hole punch, 2001

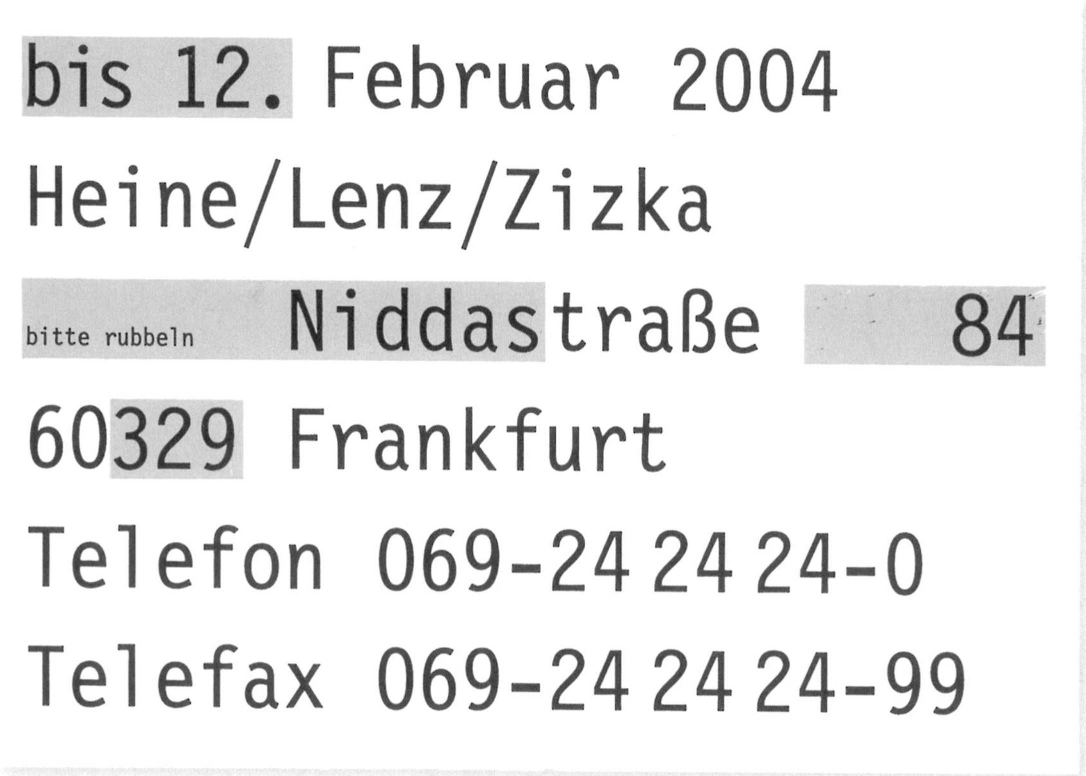

bis **12.** Februar 2004
Heine/Lenz/Zizka
bitte rubbeln **Niddas**traße 84
60329 Frankfurt
Telefon 069-24 24 24-0
Telefax 069-24 24 24-99

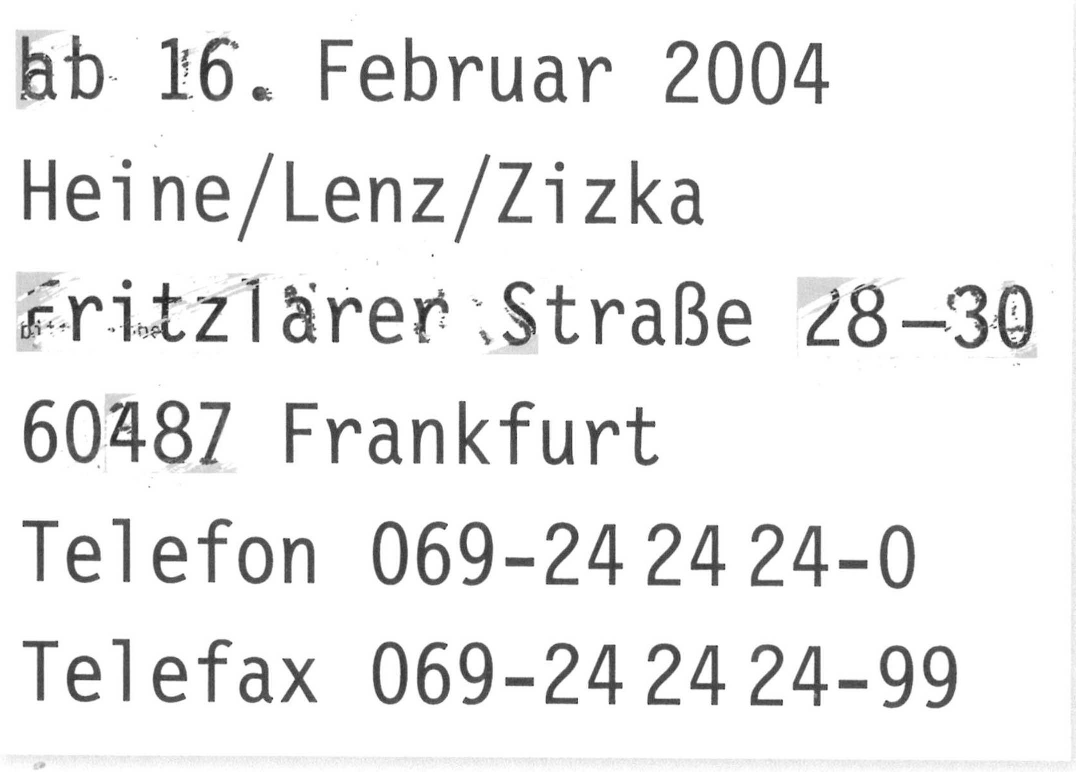

ab 16. Februar 2004
Heine/Lenz/Zizka
Fritzlärer Straße 28–30
60487 Frankfurt
Telefon 069-24 24 24-0
Telefax 069-24 24 24-99

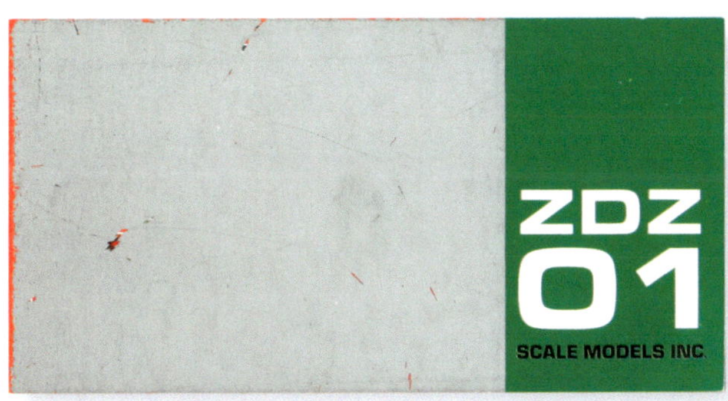

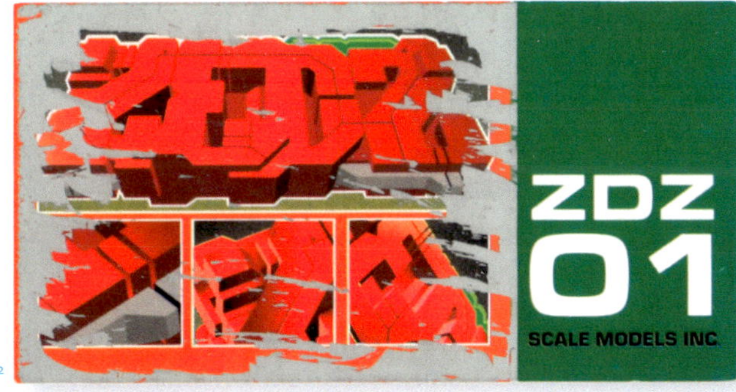

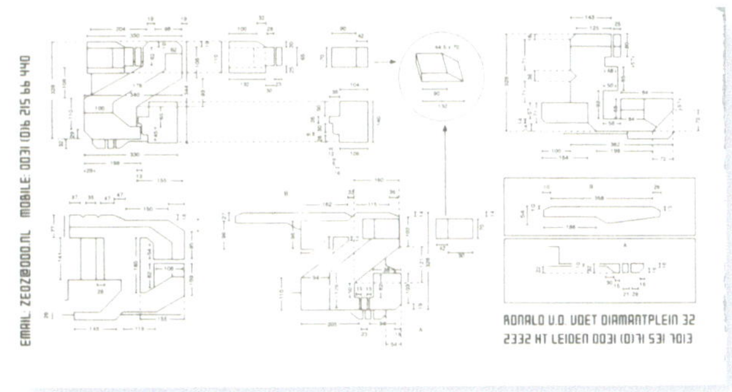

SENSUS DESIGN FACTORY

SENSUS DESIGN FACTORY

Dobrinjska 25 : Zagreb HR-10000 : Croatia
t+f 385 1 3049010 : m 385 98 1874643
kristina.spoljar@post.hinet.hr

WE LOVE YOUR MONEY

1–3   Zedz
4–6   Sensus Design Factory Zagreb / Nedjeljko Spoljar, Sappi Magno, mat paper 300 g,
offset printing 1c and silk-screen printing, 2001–2004

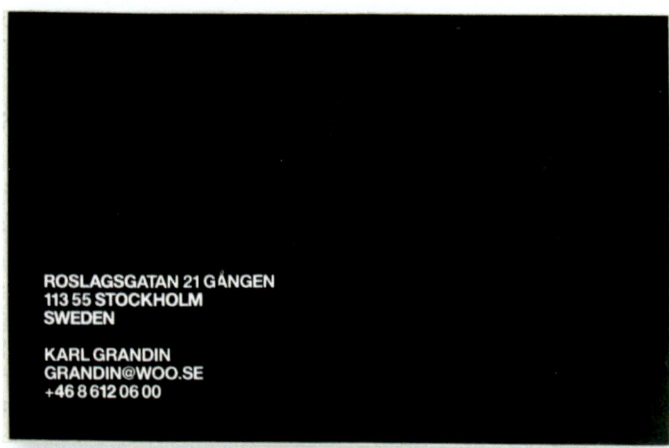

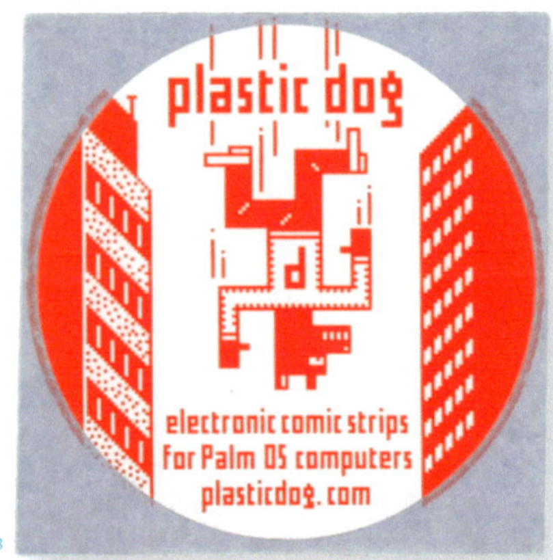

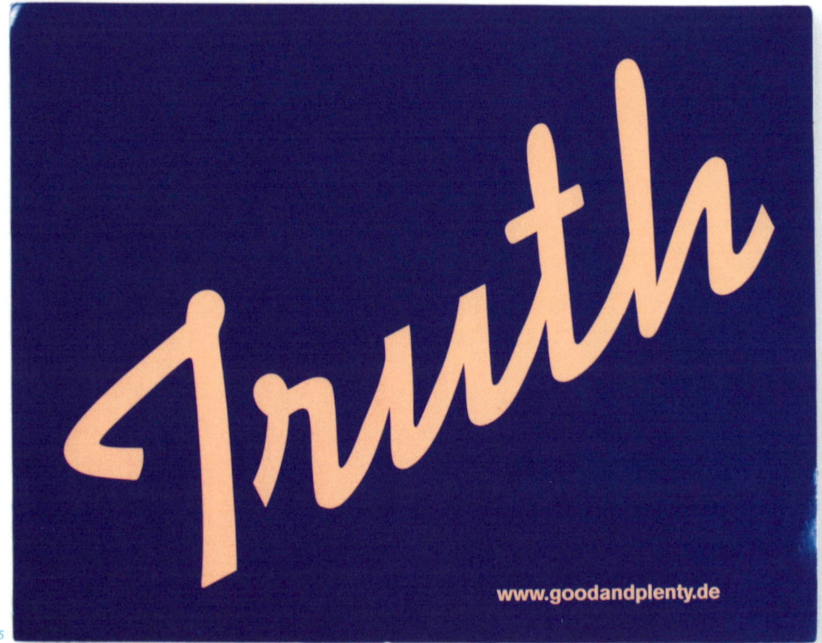

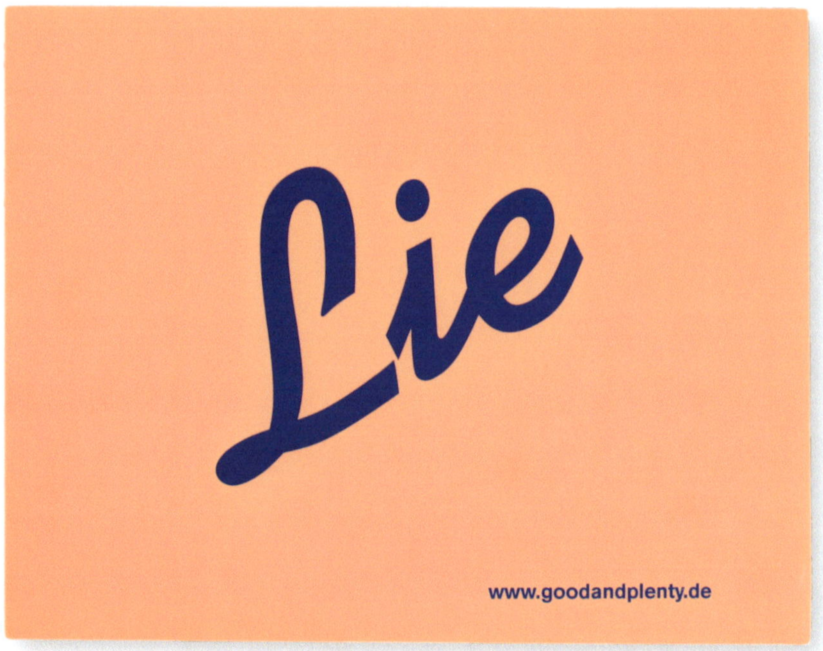

1   Vår / Karl Grandin and Bjorn Atldax, vinyl sticker, silk-screen printing and embossing, 2004
2   Caroline de Vries, fluorescent sticker, silk-screen printing, 2001
3–4   Henning Wagenbreth, sticker, offset printing 1c, 2001
5–6   Bank / Sebastian Bissinger, Goodandplenty is a project by Sebastian Bissinger and Ian Warner,
      sticker, offset printing, 2003
7   Alexander Meyer and Sabina Albanese, adhesive label, laser print, 2002

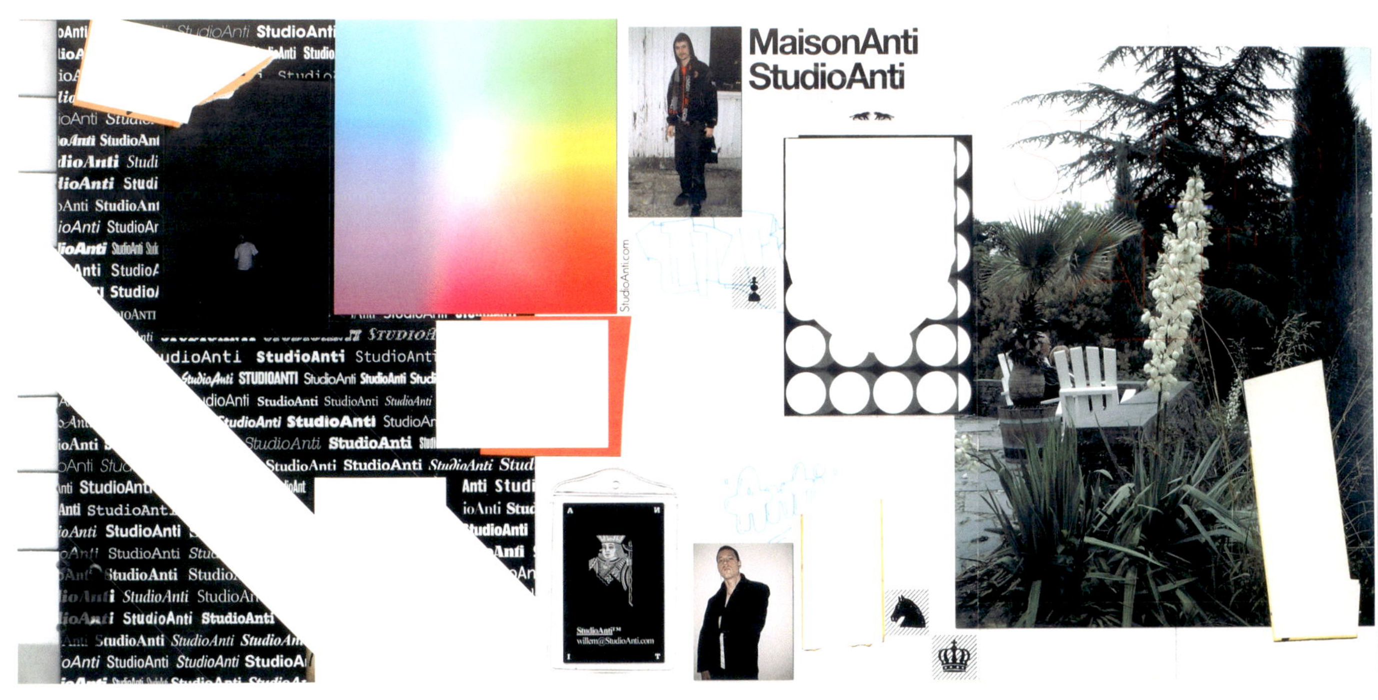

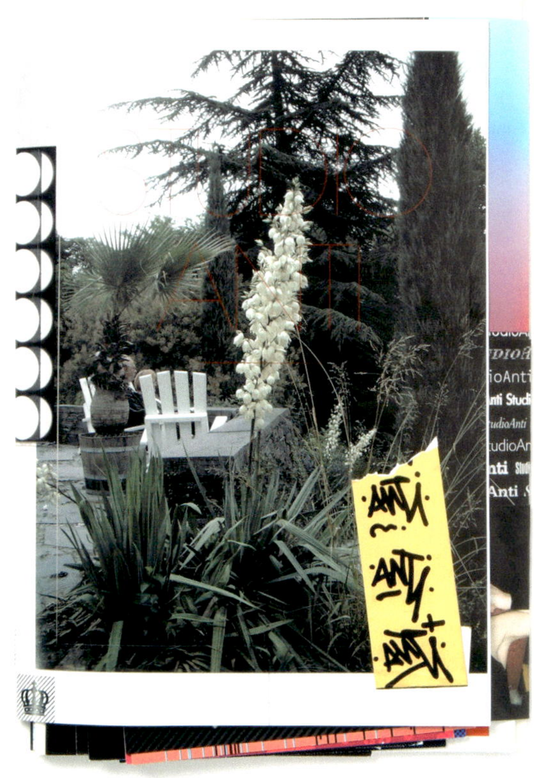

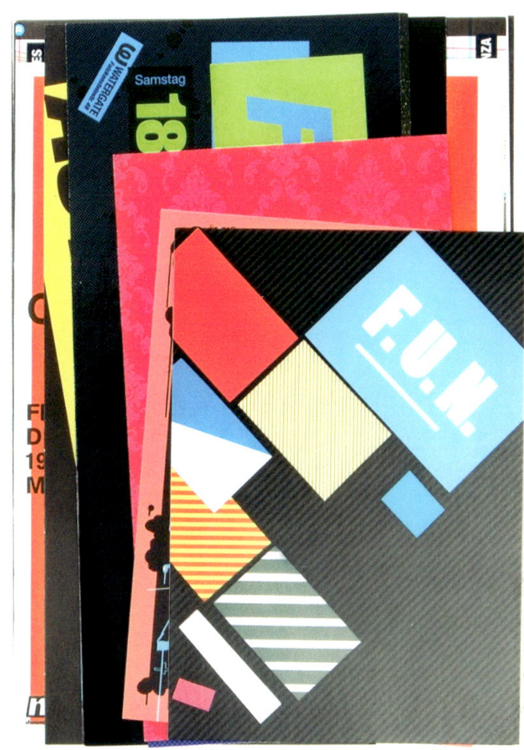

1–3 Studio Anti / Willem Stratmann,
210 x 450 mm, folded 210 x 150, McWhite H 80 g, offset printing, 2003

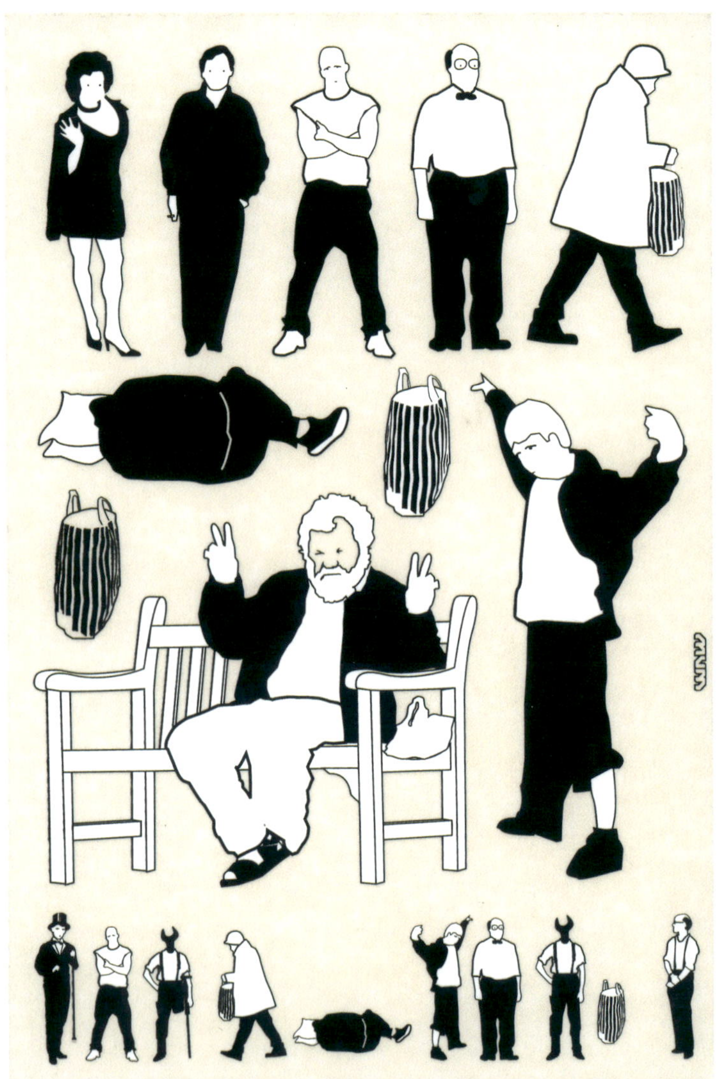

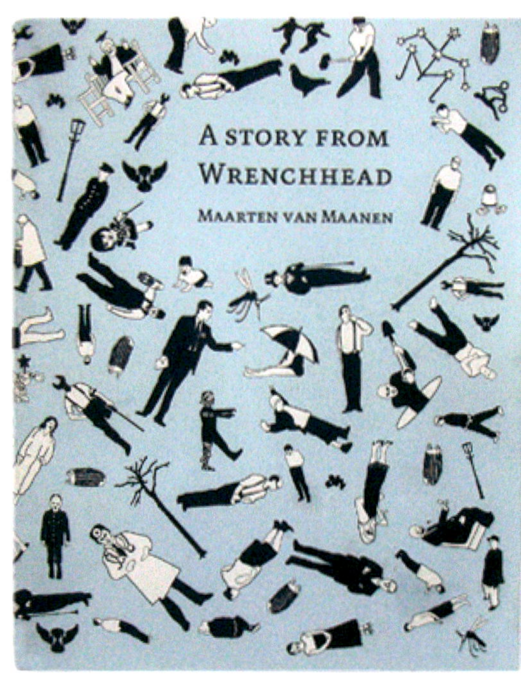

1   MvM / Maarten van Maanen, 160 x 235 mm, sticker, silk-screen printing, 2004
2   MvM / Maarten van Maanen, 160 x 210 mm, paper, offset printing, 2005

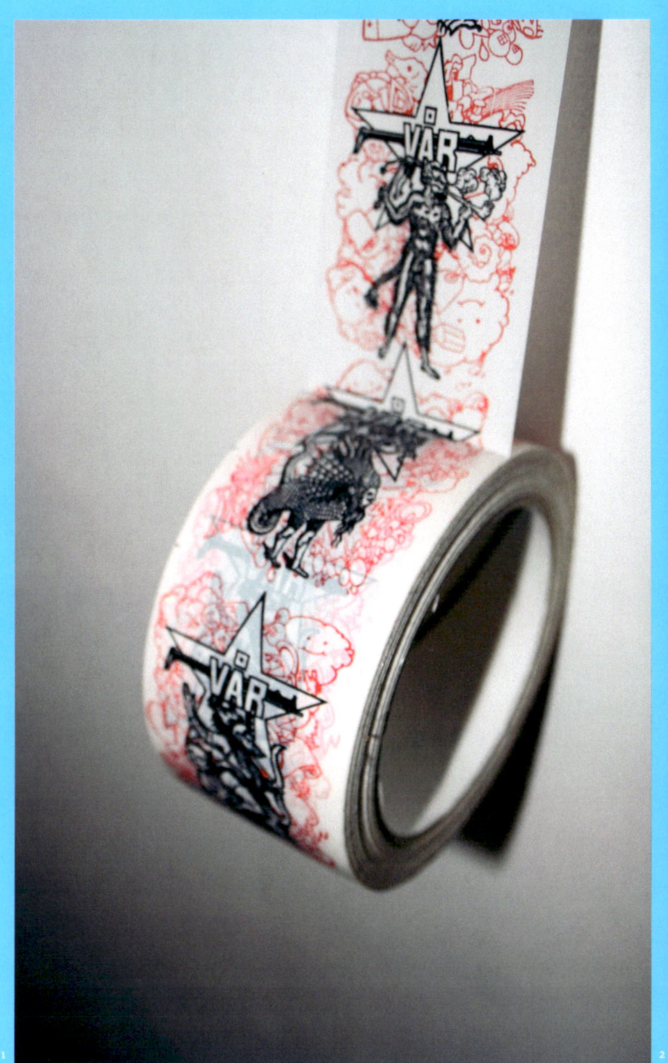

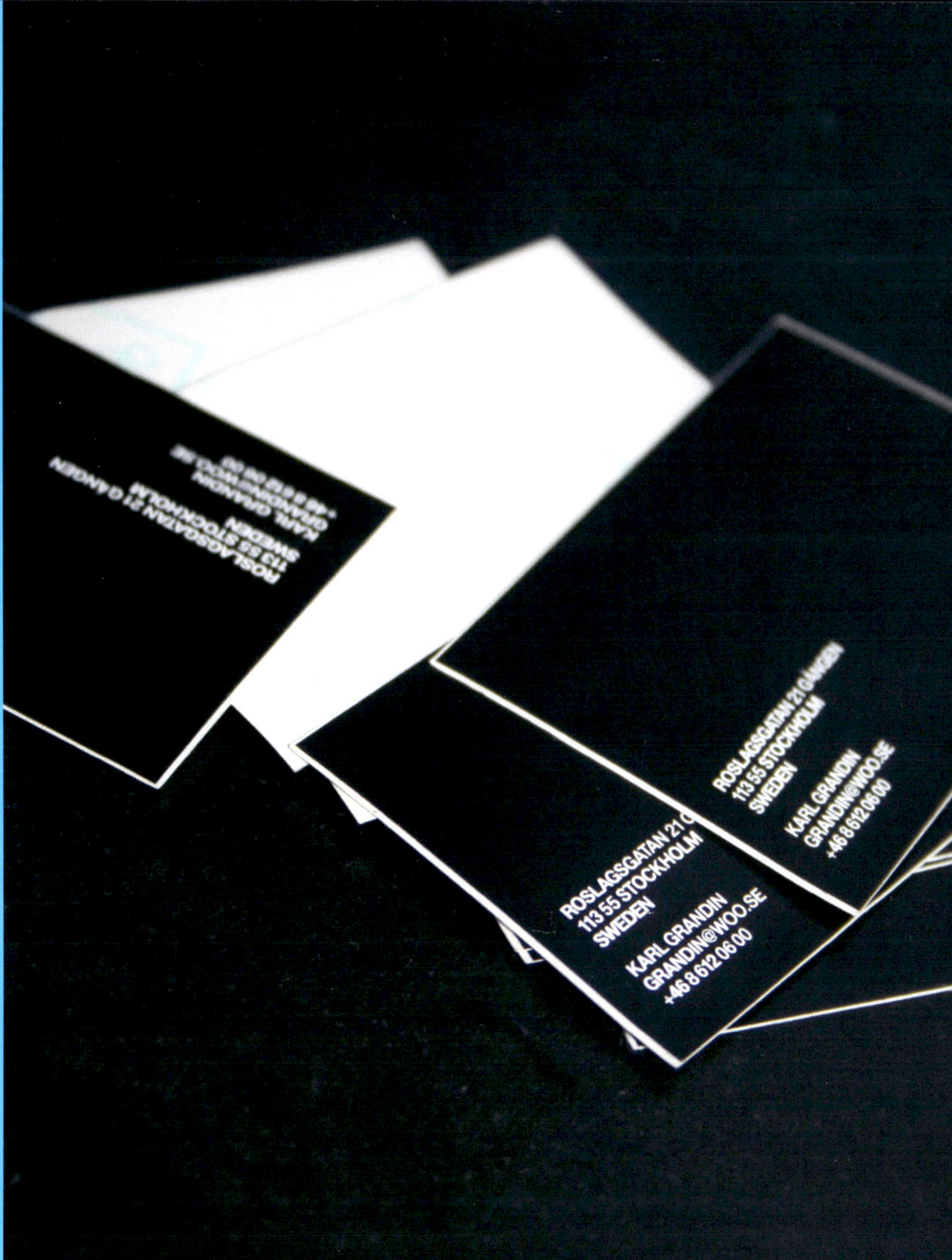

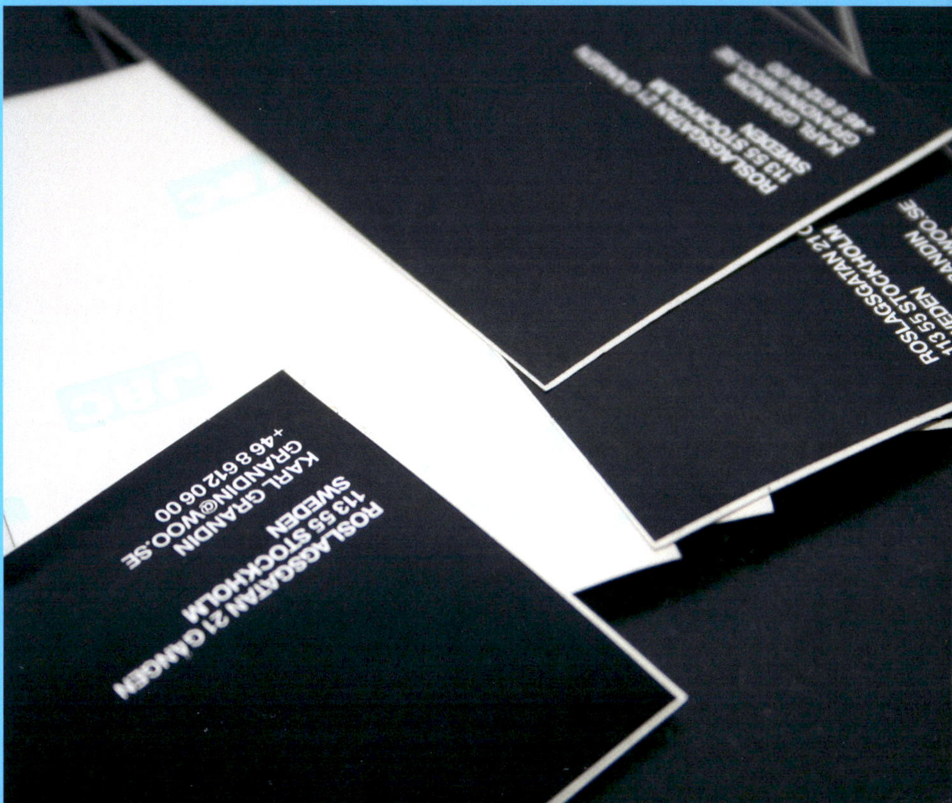

1   Vår / Karl Grandin and Bjorn Atldax, adhesive tape
2–3 Vår / Karl Grandin and Bjorn Atldax, vinyl sticker,
      silk-screen printing and embossing, 2004

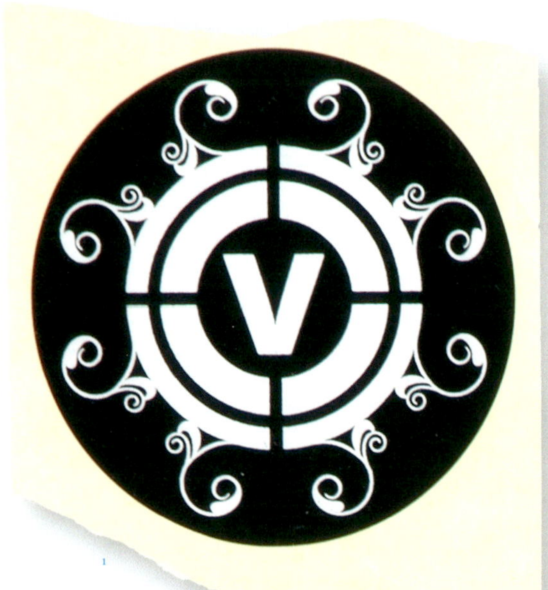
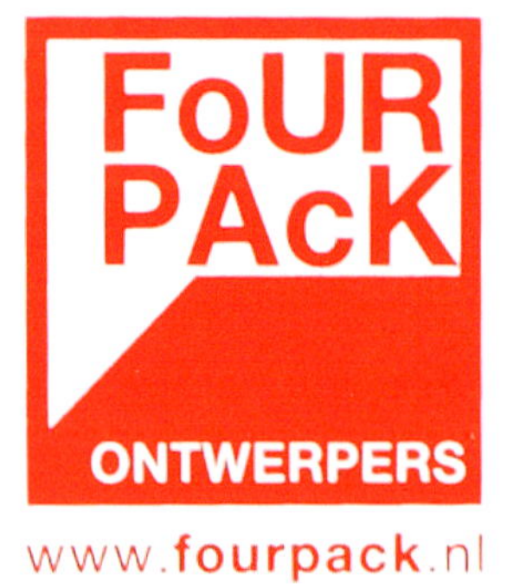

FoUR PAcK
ONTWERPERS
www.fourpack.nl

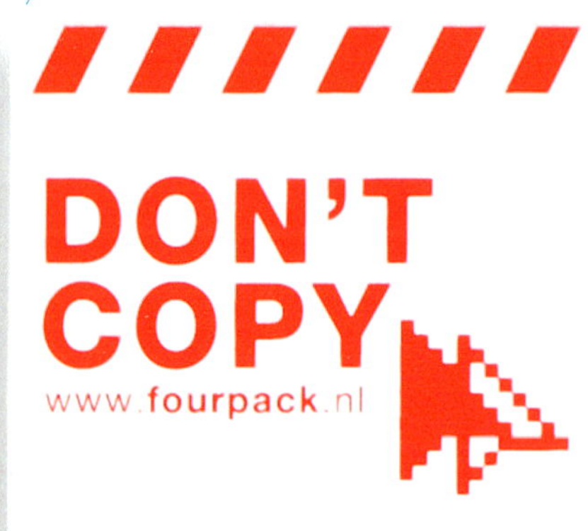

DON'T
COPY
www.fourpack.nl

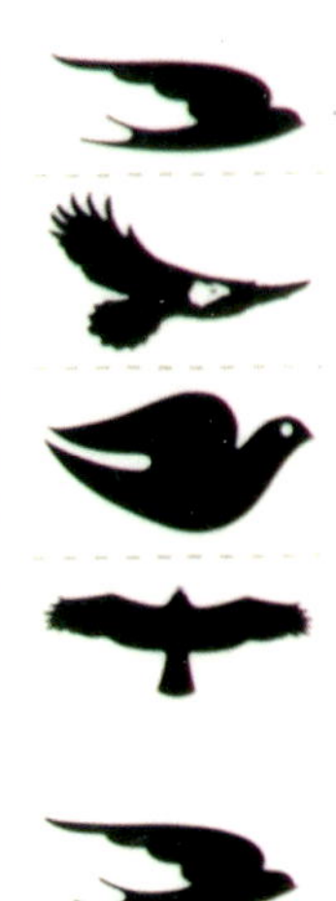
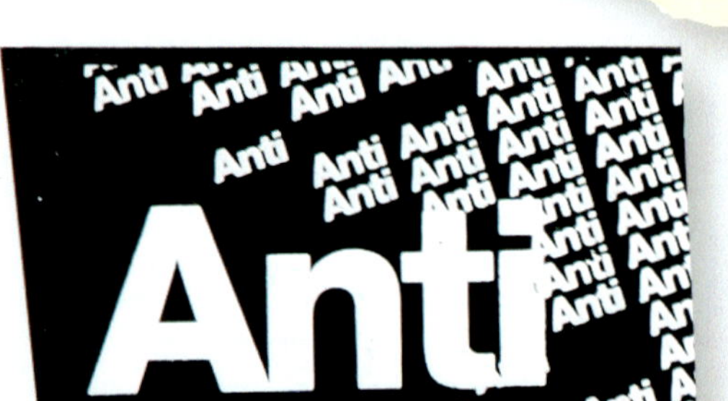

4
www.fourpack.nl/projecten

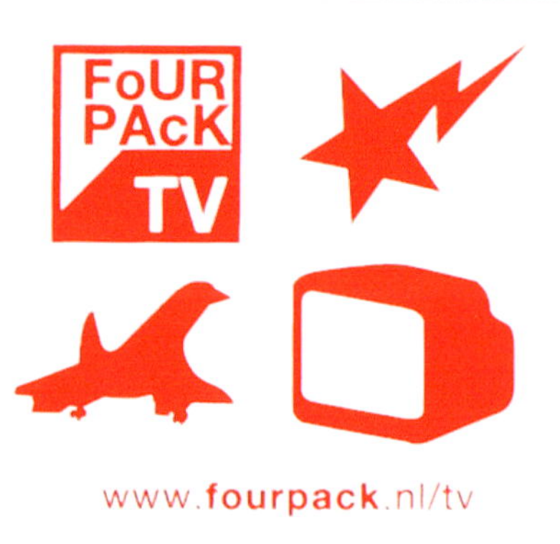

FoUR PAcK
TV
www.fourpack.nl/tv

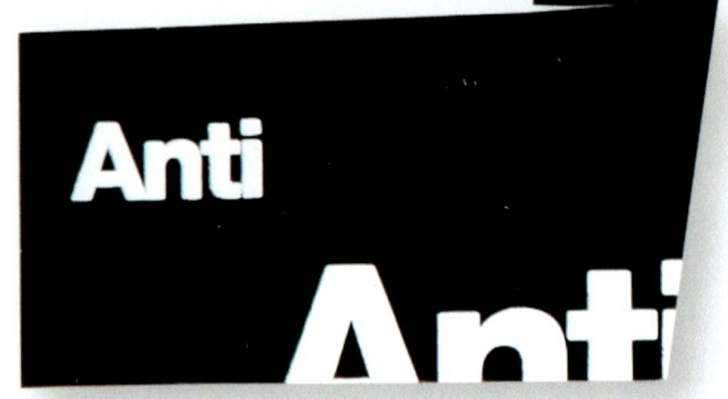
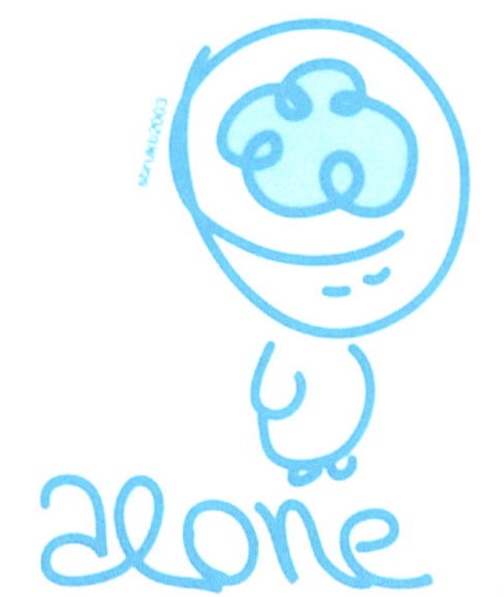

alone

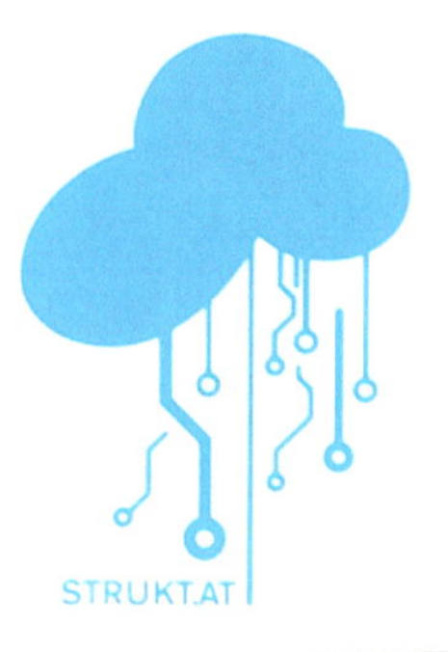

STRUKT.AT

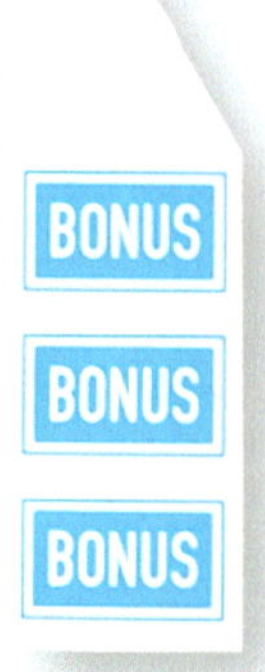

BONUS
BONUS
BONUS

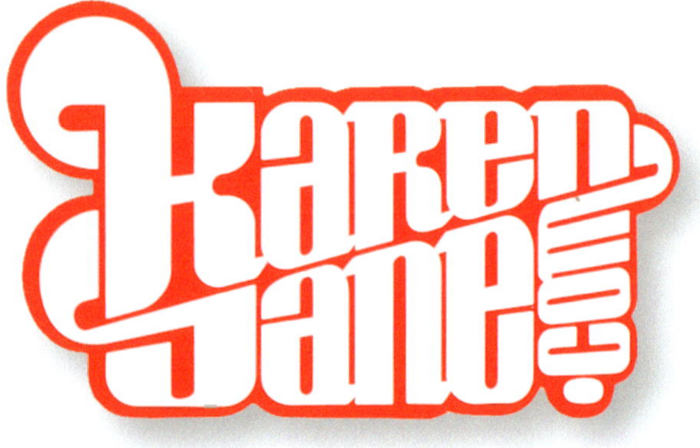
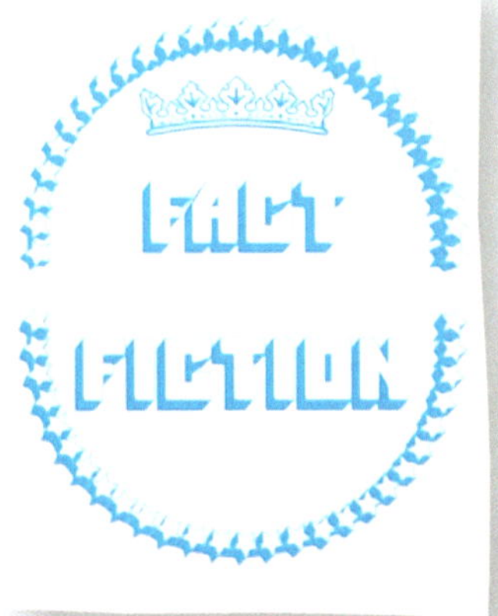
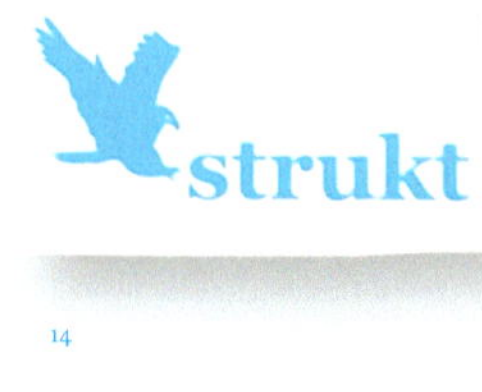

strukt

1

2

3

TM
®
©

cut you® label

cut you® label

6

PRINGLES
IRON MAIDEN
DEF LEPPARD
Deep Purple
Nazareth
BLACK SABBATH
EUROPE
MANOWAR
AC/DC

8

www.zipdesign.co.uk
ZIP

9

7

HAPPYPETS PRODUCTS
TYPE-SHIRT COLLECTION
© 2005 www.happypets.ch

HAPPYPETS PRODUCTS
TYPE-SHIRT COLLECTION
© 2005 www.happypets.ch

MADE IN
NASAEL | UN

MADE IN
NASAEL | UN

MADE IN
NASAEL | UN

4

5

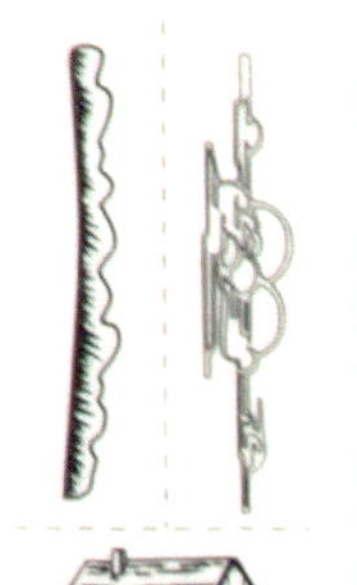

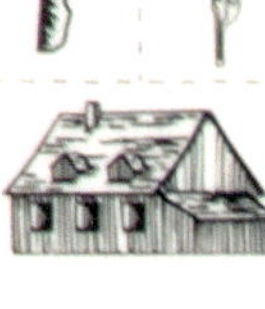

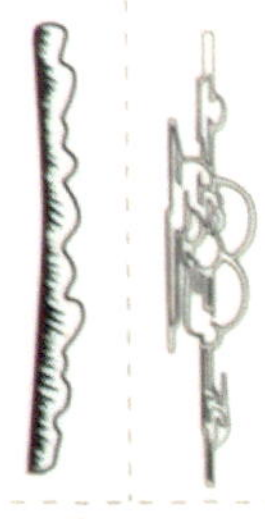

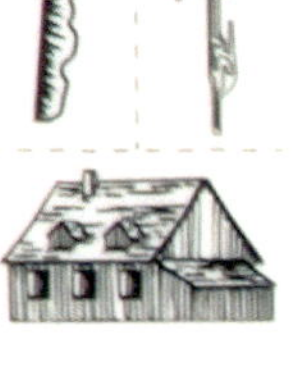

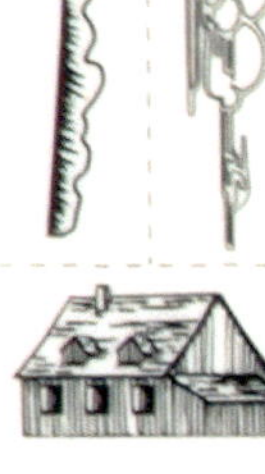

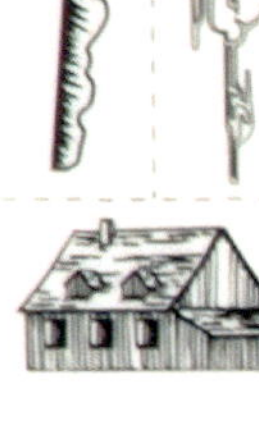

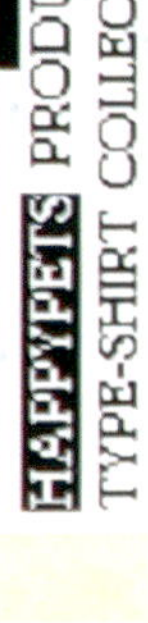

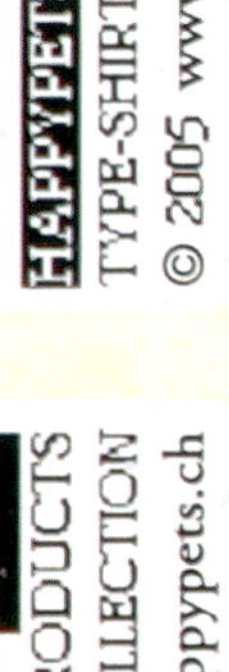

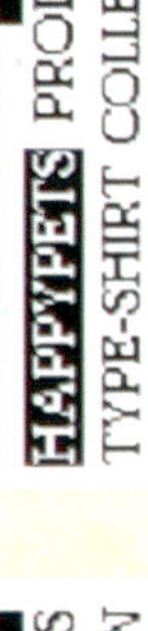

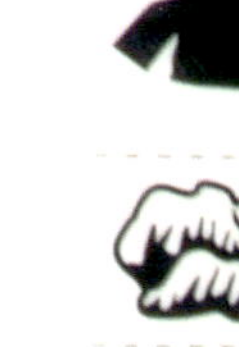

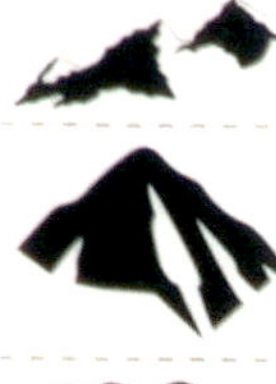

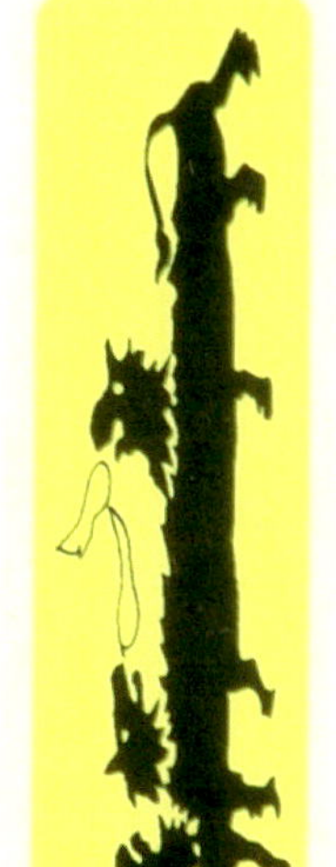

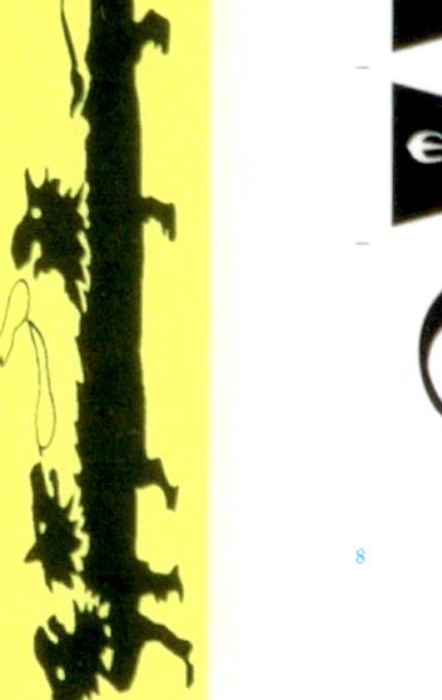

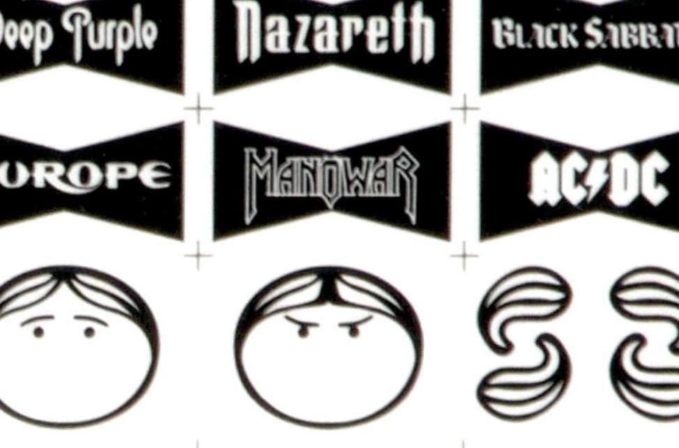

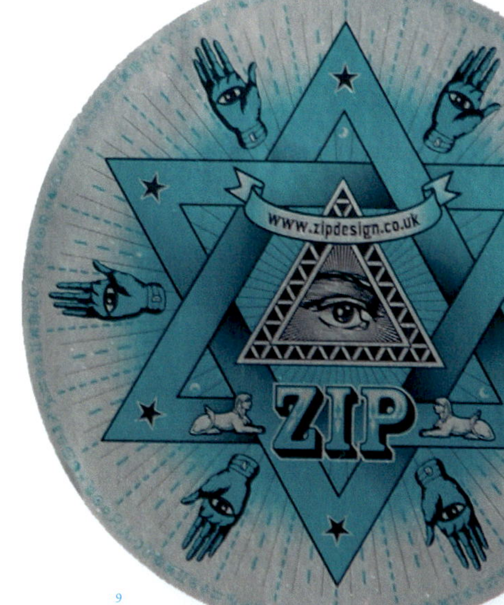

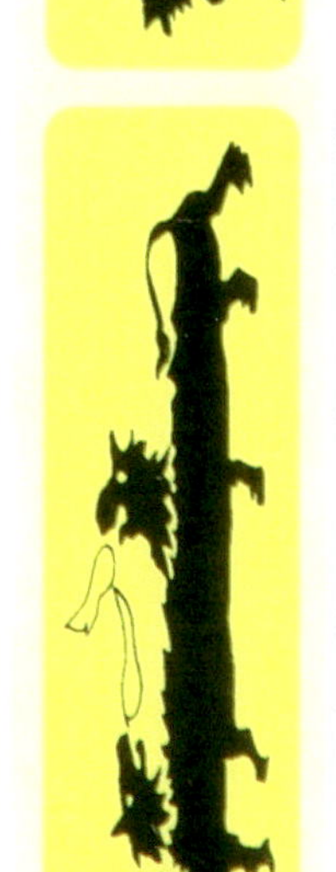

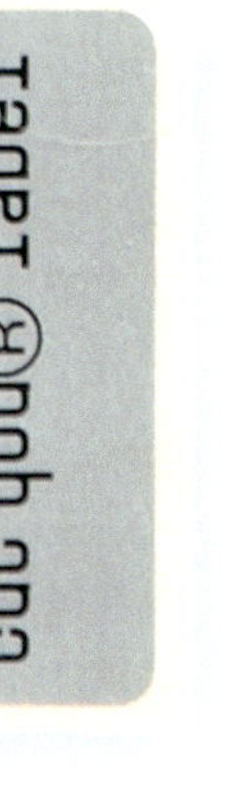

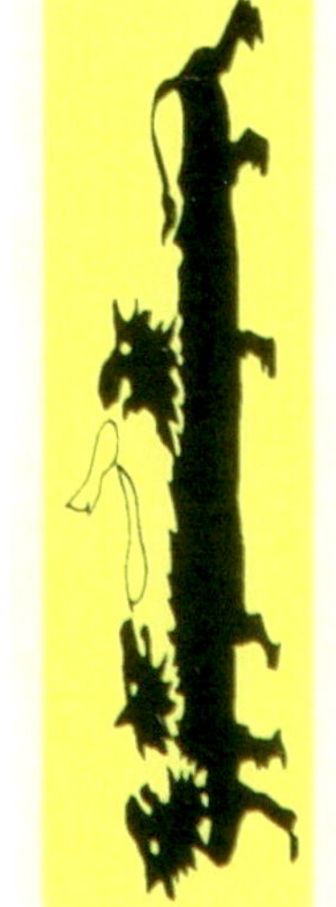

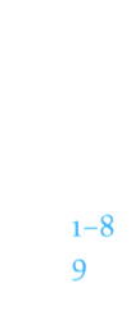

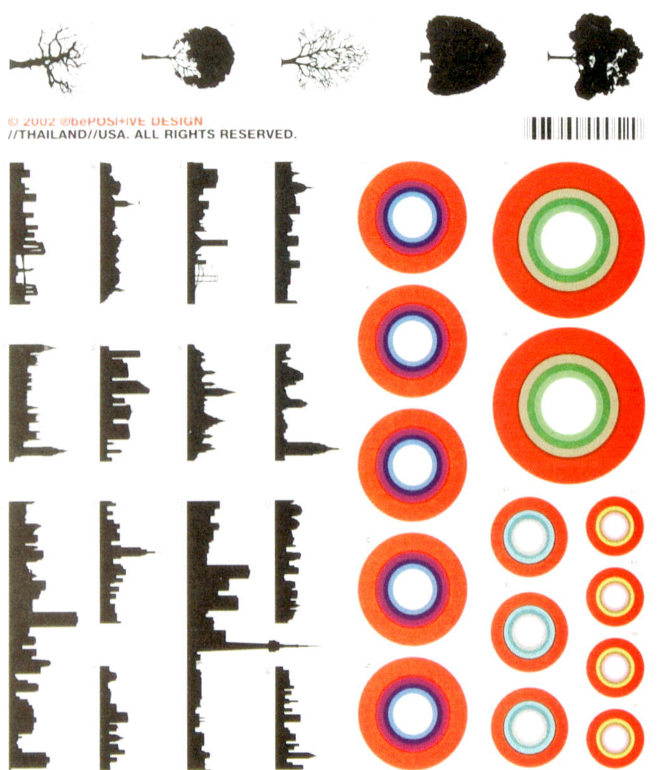

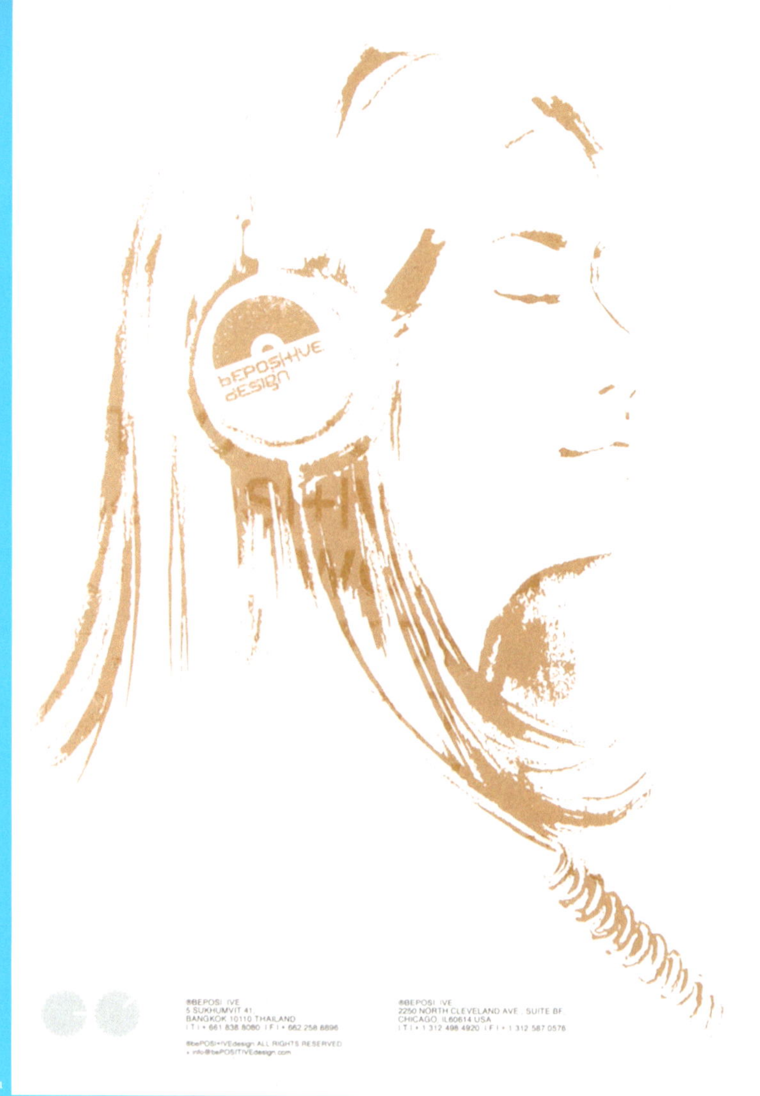

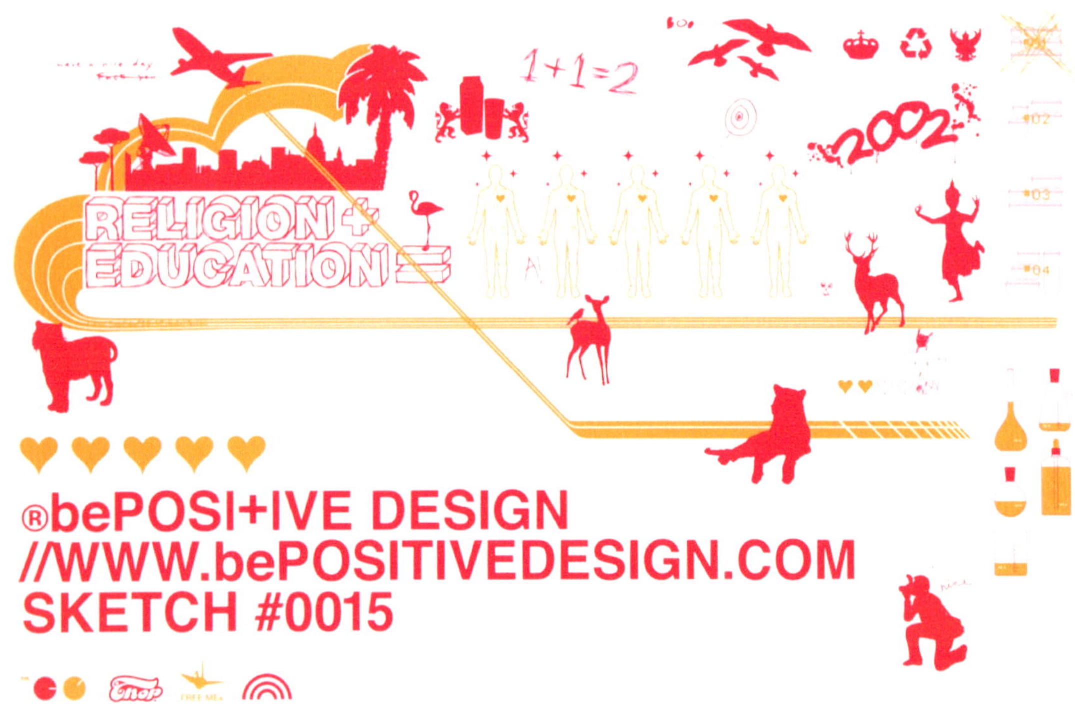

1   Bepositive / Tnop Wangsillapakun, 210 x 148 mm, paper,
    offset printing, 2002
2   Bepositive / Tnop Wangsillapakun, 210 x 148 mm, paper,
    3 spot colours plus Liquid Laminate, 2001
3   Bepositive / Tnop Wangsillapakun, 210 x 148 mm, textured
    paper, 2 spot colours front and 1 spot colour back, 2003

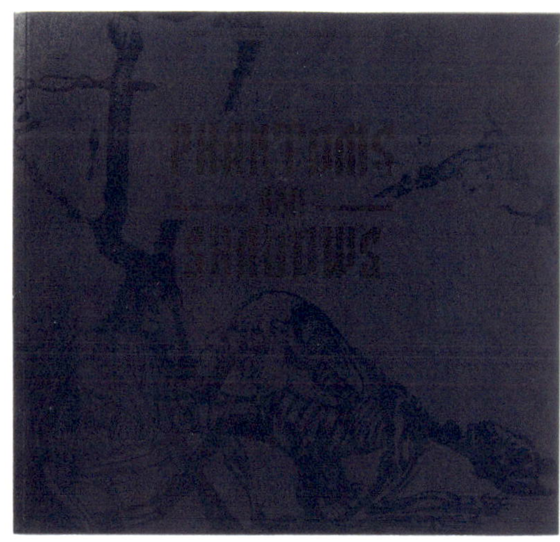

1   Strukt Visual Network / Andreas Koller, 210 x 200 mm, offset printing and
    print varnish, 2003
2   Strukt Visual Network / Johannes Löberbauer,
    210 x 200 mm, offset printing and print varnish, 2004
3   Marc Atlan, 305 x 230 mm, mat black offset paper, Glossy Thermo, 2005

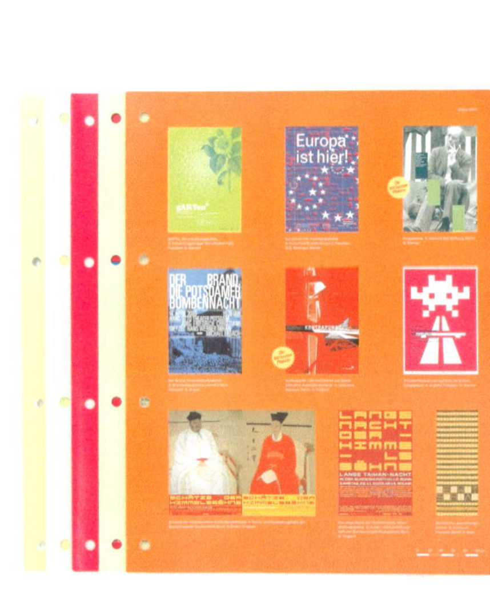

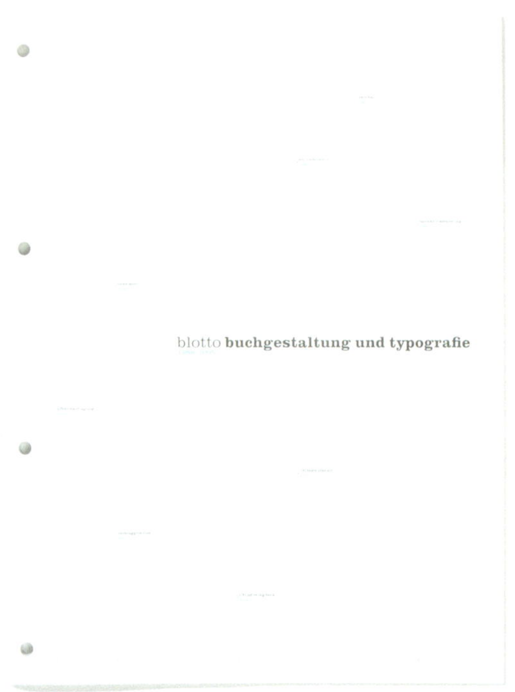

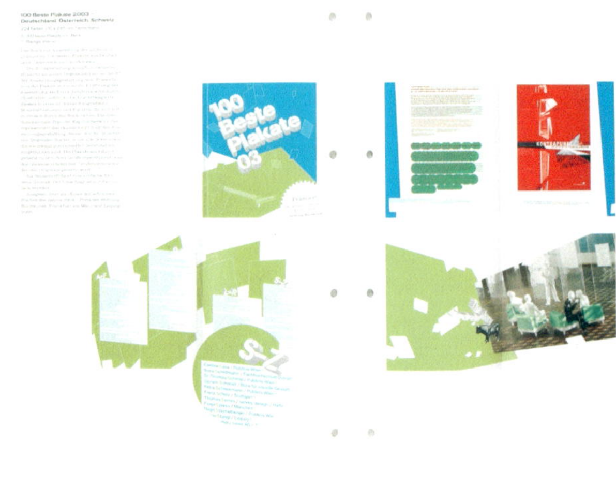

Every year, Berlin-based design team blotto publish a handy four-page A4 leaflet to showcase their most important projects. In this modular set-up, the first page always summarises essential poster designs, followed by a selection of print and interface work and a page covering exhibition projects. This simple, yet effective leaflet is always accompanied by a separate data sheet with information on the company.

To supplement this basic set-up, blotto also release a string of specialised booklets on varying topics, from exhibition graphics and architecture to book design, featuring comprehensive descriptions and a more flexible design approach.

1–2 Blotto / Elvira Barriga, Heike Grebin, Andreas Trogisch, Ian Warner, 210 x 270 mm, offset printing, 1998–2005
3–4 Blotto / Elvira Barriga, Dirk Duijster, Heike Grebin, Andreas Trogisch, Ian Warner, 210 x 270 mm, Samat 180 g, offset printing, 2005

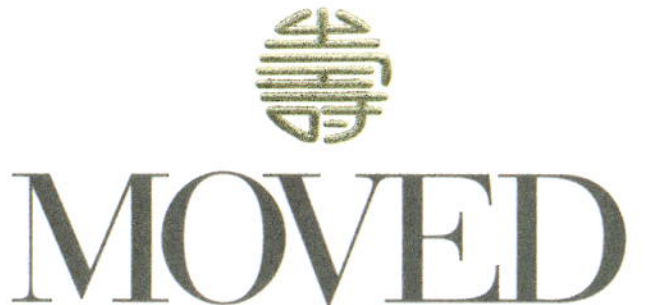

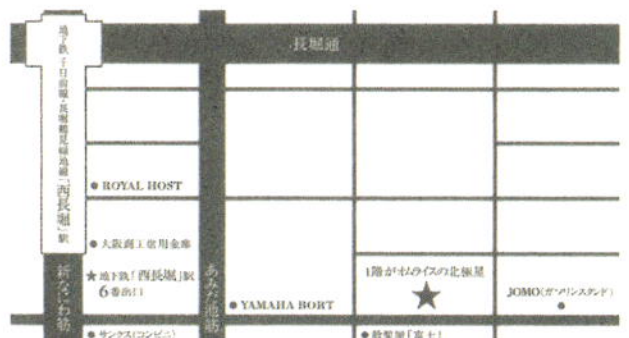

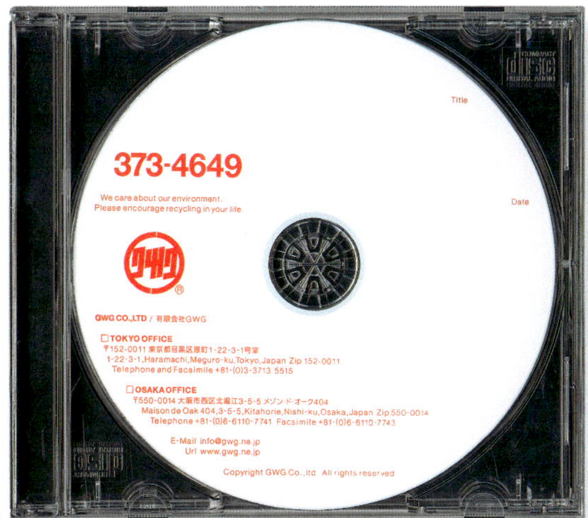

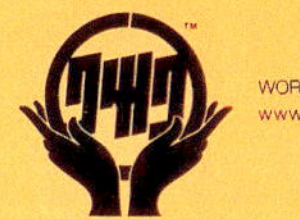

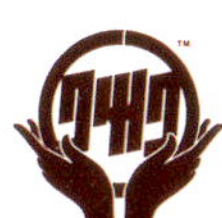

1 GWG Co. Ltd, hot foil and coloured edge
2–4 GWG Co. Ltd, different papers, hot foil
5 GWG Co. Ltd, silk-screen printing 2c

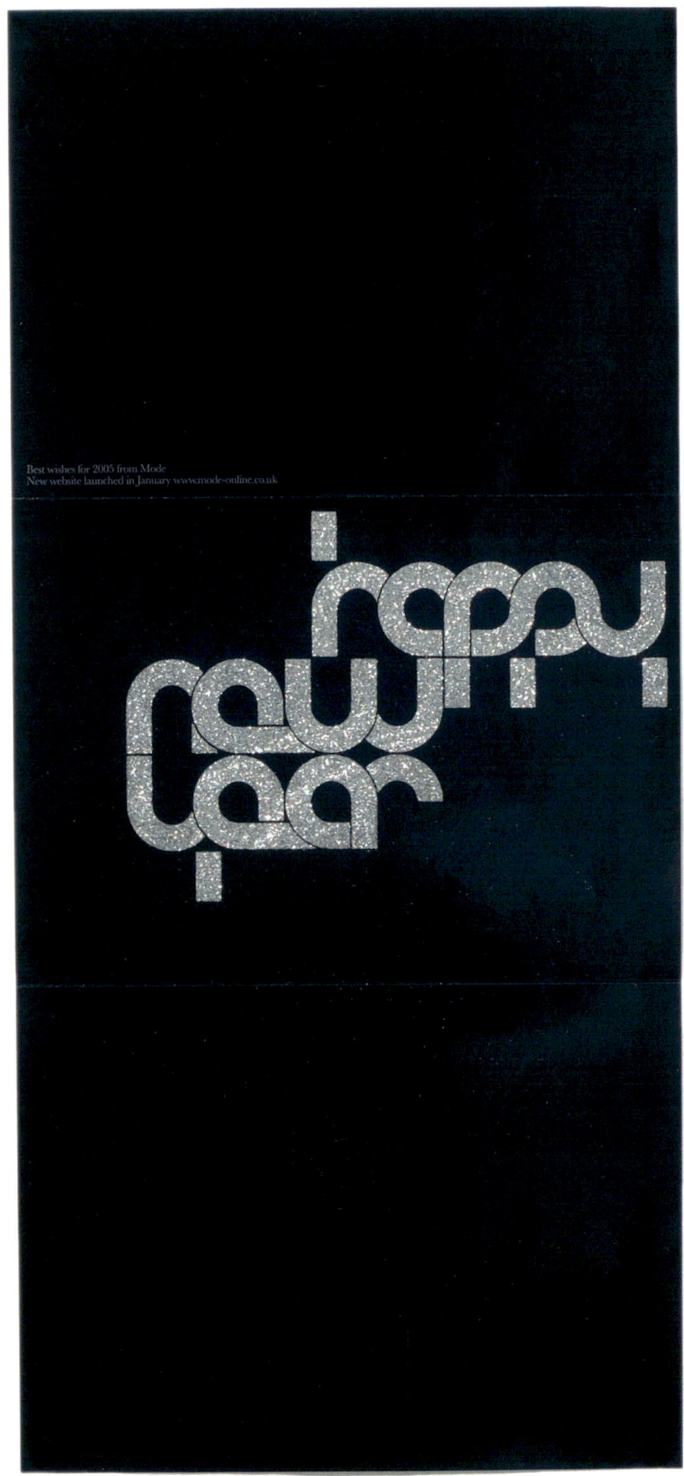

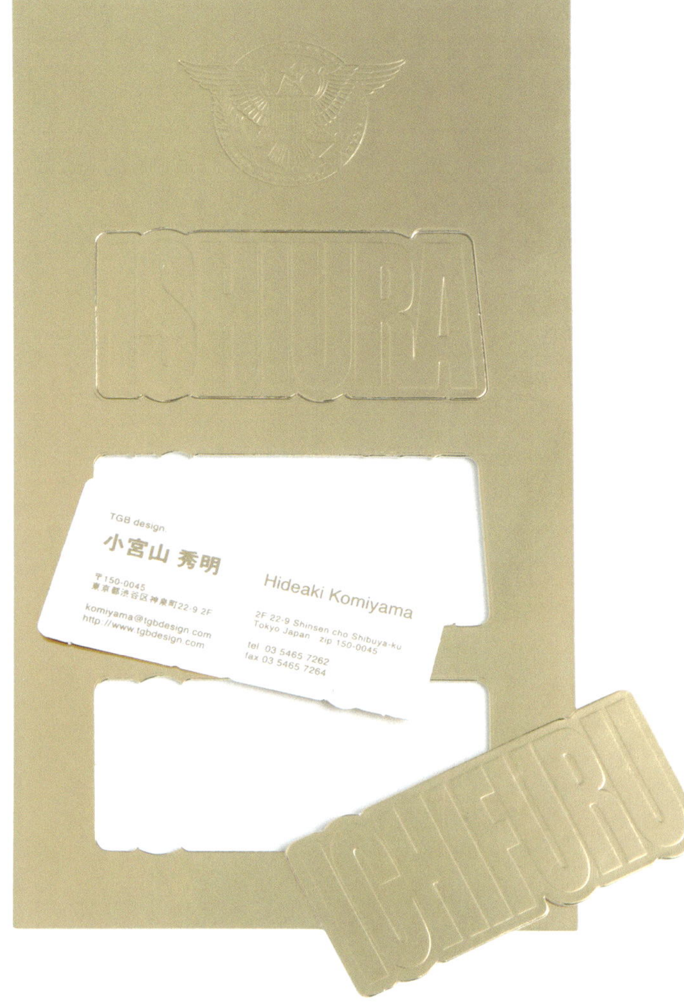

1   Mode / Phil Costin, Ian Styles, Olly Knight, 445 x 148,5 mm folding to A5,
    Splendorlux light weight Nero, offset printing and silk-screen printing with glue
    and silver glitter, 2005
2   TGB Design / Masaru Ishiura, Hideaki Komiyama, Masashi Ichifuru,
    foiled gold paper with embossing, 1995

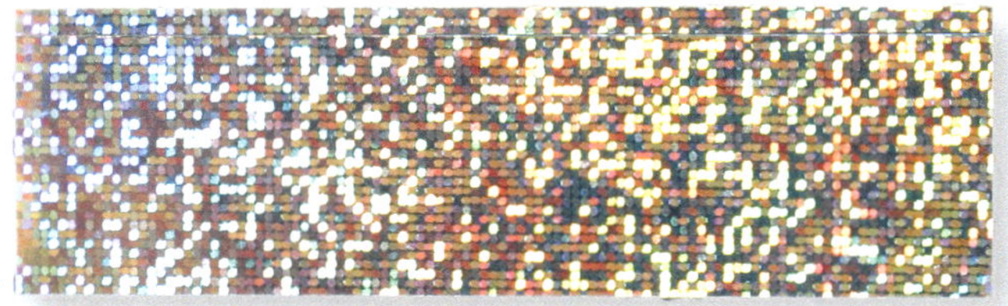

ANDRES@PIXELSTORM.CH
andres wanner
078 824 22 17

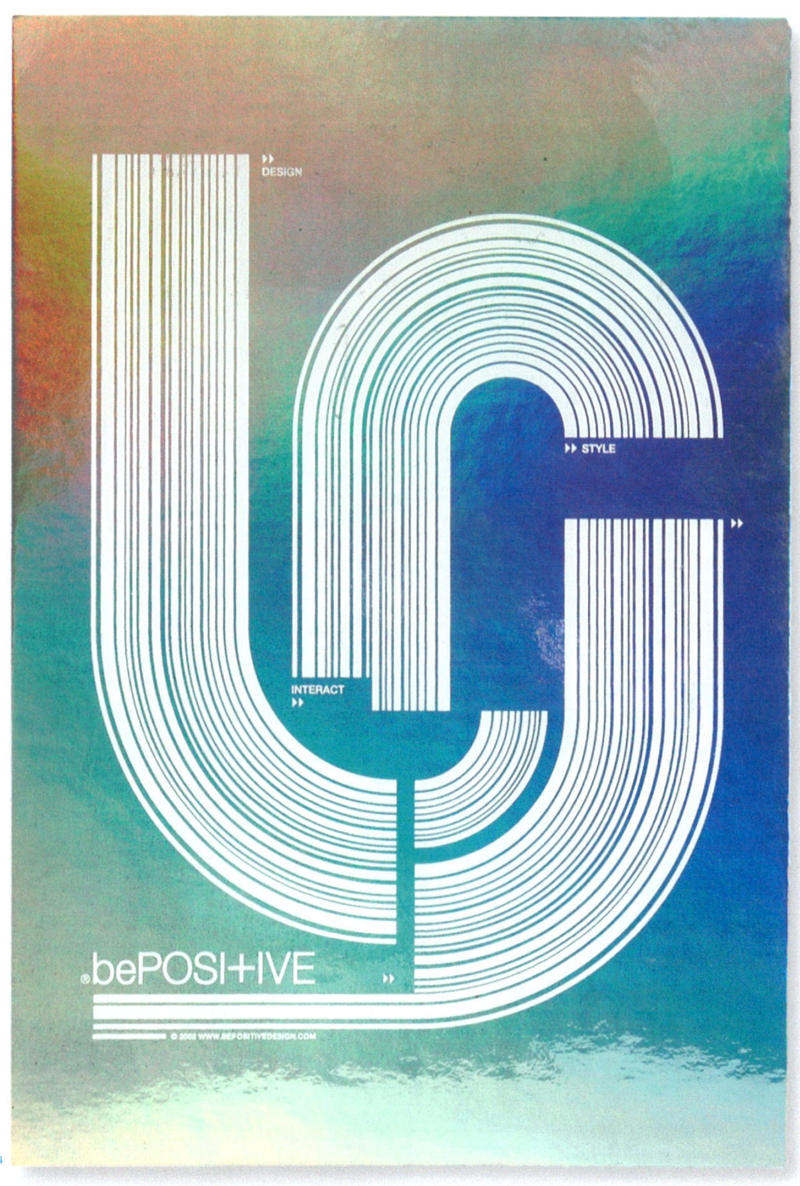

1   Arthur Marek, chromolux, silk-screen printing, 2002
2–3   Pixelstorm / Andres Wanner, 2004
4   Bepositive / Tnop Wangsillapakun, chrome paper, silk-screen printing 1/1 c, 2002
5–6   Studio Anti / Willem Stratmann, 62 x 87 mm, Invercote G 350 g, offset printing, 2004

NEESER UND MUELLER / GRAFIK
GUETERSTR. 143, 4053 BASEL
TELEFON 061 363 24 82
THOMAS NEESER

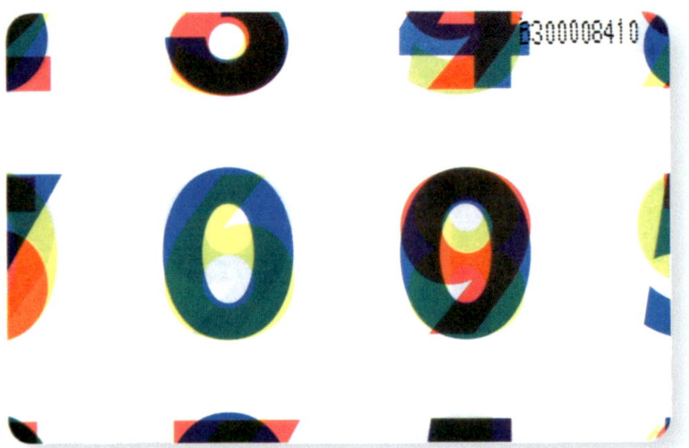

B300008410

Deze telefoonkaart kunt u bij weigering ongefrankeerd, met vermelding van uw naam
en adres, retourneren aan: PTT Telecom / Antwoordnummer 2018 / 8000 VB Zwolle.
Deze kaart is ook in Duitsland (insteekrichting ◀———) te gebruiken. Verbruikte kaarten
kunt u kwijt in de afvalbak in de telefooncel. Deze kaarten worden gerecycled.

1 G

Karel Martens
Monumentenweg 21A
6997 AG Hoog-Keppel
0314 / T: 381389

ptt telecom

ALEXANDER NAGEL

TELEFON
030
88 22 100
88 26 035
NAGEL
FOTOTYPE
SCHLÜTERSTRASSE 39
D-1000 BERLIN 12

| w | http://bepositivedesign.com
| e | info@bepositivedesign.com

bePOSI+IVE

662   001   ___

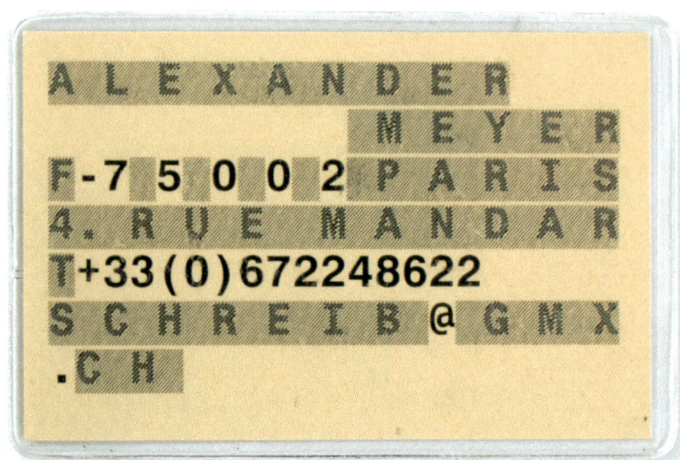

1–2   Neeser & Müller, plastic, embossing, 1997
3–4   Karel Martens, pvc, offset printing, stamp, 1994
5   Bepositive / Tnop Wangsillapakun,
       white matt finish plastic and black sticker on back, silk-screen printing, 2000
6   Nagel Fototype / Ott+Stein, transparent plastic, silk-screen printing, 1982
7   Alexander Meyer, paper, Xerox, 2004

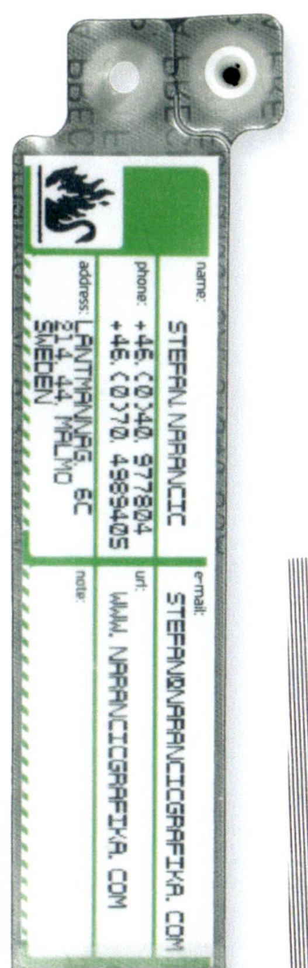

name: STEFAN NARANCIC
phone: +46.(0)40. 977804
+46.(0)70. 4989405
address: LANTMANNAG. 6C
214. 44 MALMÖ
SWEDEN
email: STEFAN@NARANCICGRAFIKA.COM
url: WWW. NARANCICGRAFIKA. COM

S

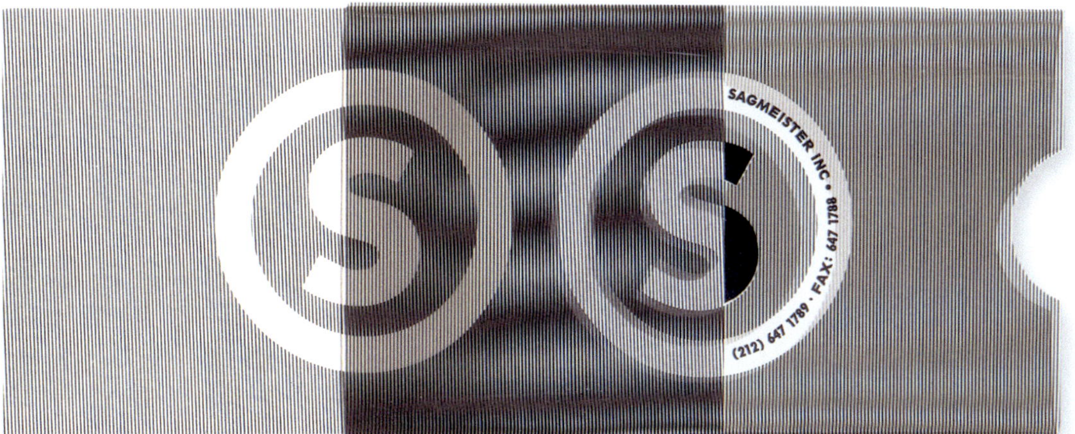

S S
SAGMEISTER INC.
(212) 647 1789 · FAX: 647 1788

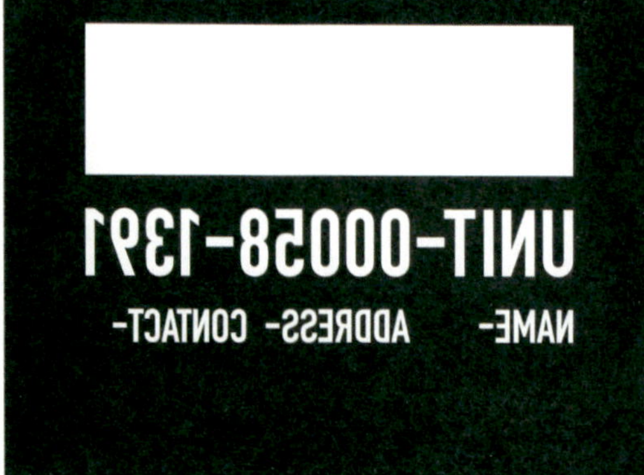

1–4 Unit-1391 / Satoru Inoue, Jacob Wildschiødtz, Troels Faber,
offset paper 60 g, cover 300 g, offset printing, cover with U.V. varnish, 2002

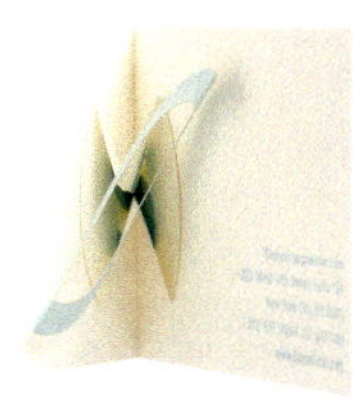

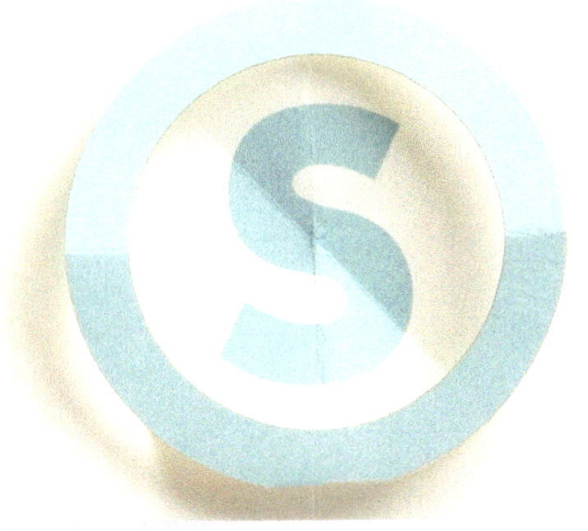

Although Stefan Sagmeister's parents were too thrifty to splurge on the magical beauty of pop-up books, the designer has always had a soft spot for this enchanting technique and even made it part of his design school thesis.

At $1.00 apiece, his new set of pop-up business cards might seem a slight indulgence, yet Sagmeister emphasises the importance of suitable representation: "There were times when we actually got jobs from our business card, so I still consider it money well spent." While the first print run suffered from a few unexpected teething problems, switching to a lighter colour, matt varnishing and a longer drying time quickly solved the conundrum. "And when the outcome looks fine, all process problems are immediately forgotten."

1–3   Sagmeister Inc. / Stefan Sagmeister, Matthias Ernstberger, Sarah Noellenheidt,
       180 x 50 mm, paper 200 g, folded, offset printing, pop-up, 2004

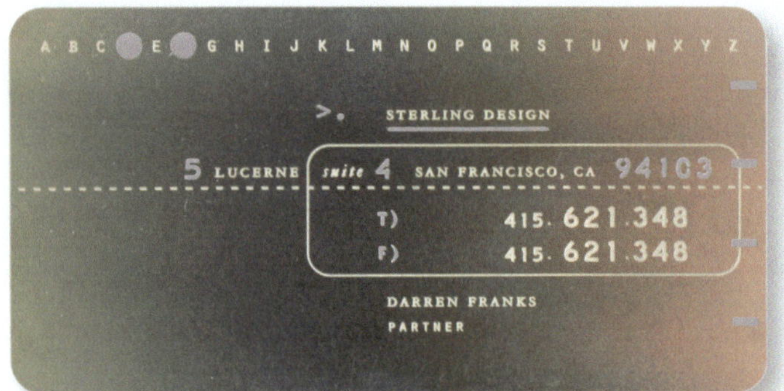

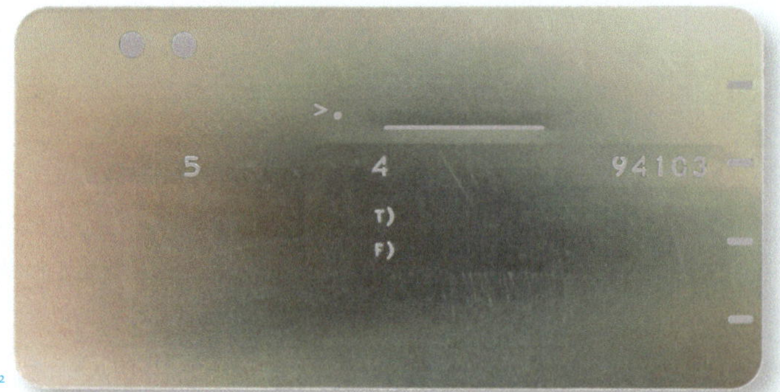

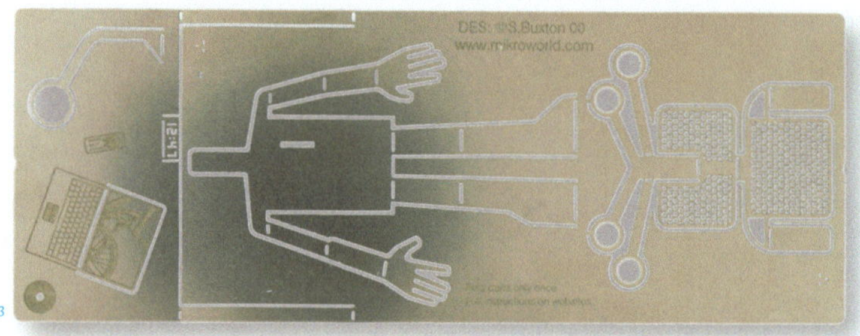

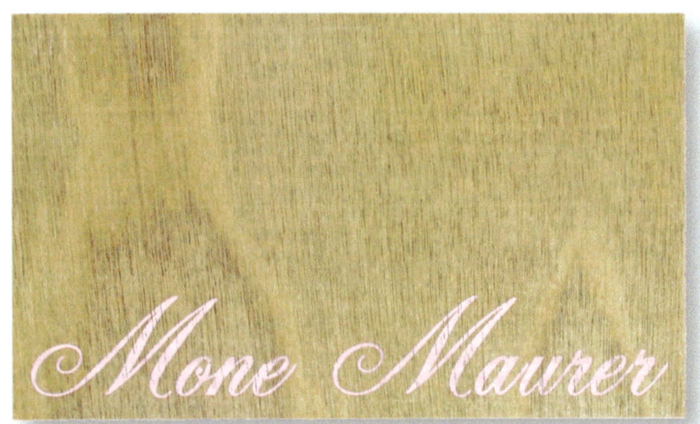

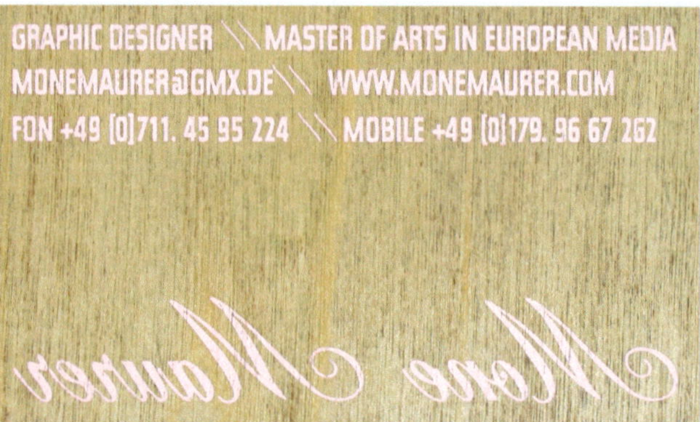

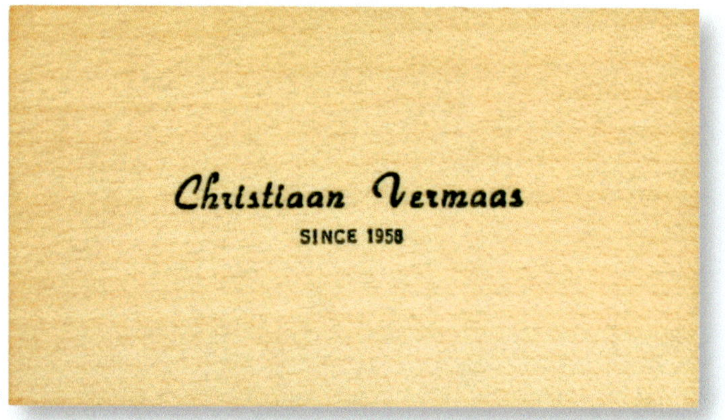

1–2 Jennifer Sterling Design, chrome steel, acid etching and punched
3 Sam Buxton, flat then folded out, 150 micron stainless steel, acid etching, 2000–2002
4–5 Mone Maurer, wood, silk-screen printing, 2004
6 Christiaan Vermaas, wood, engraved typography

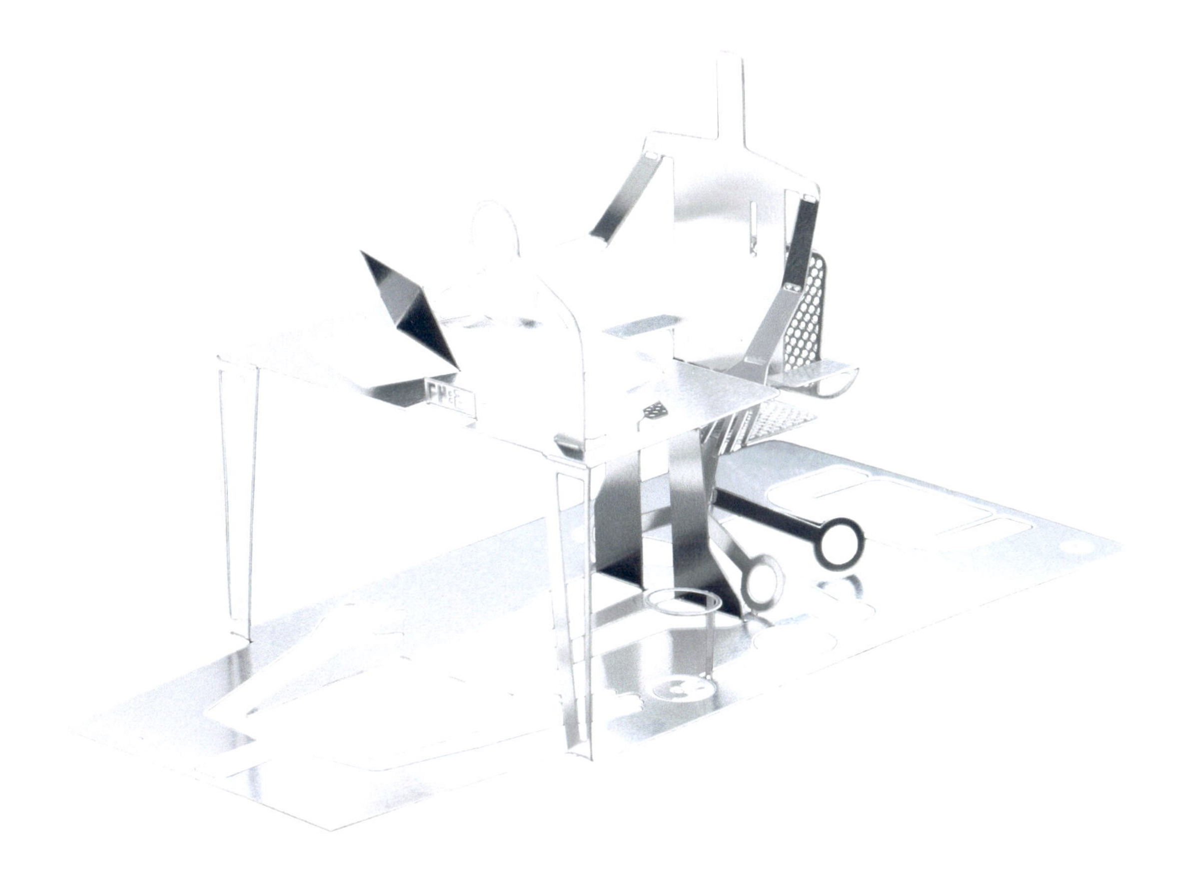

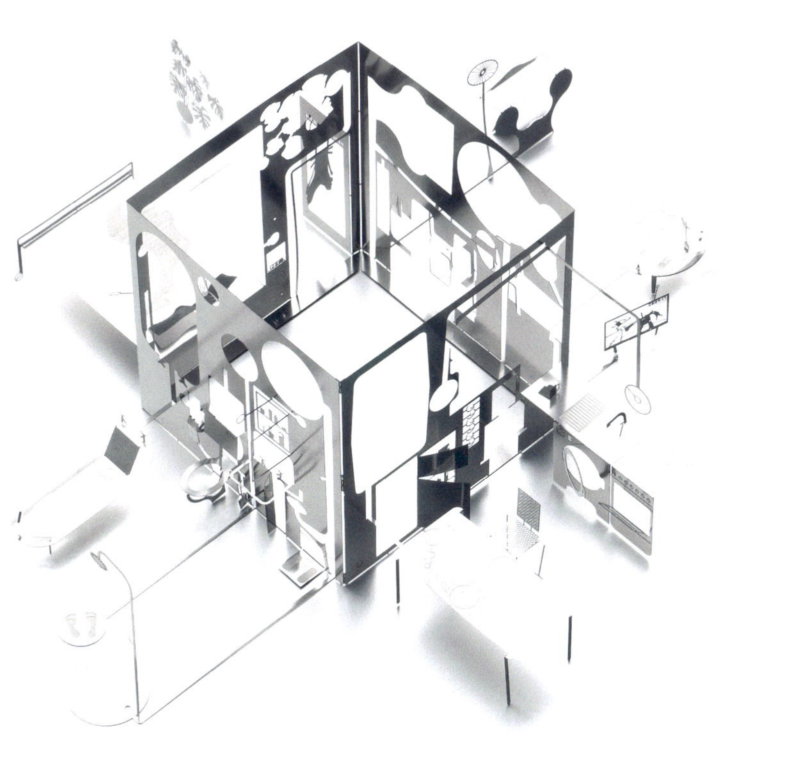

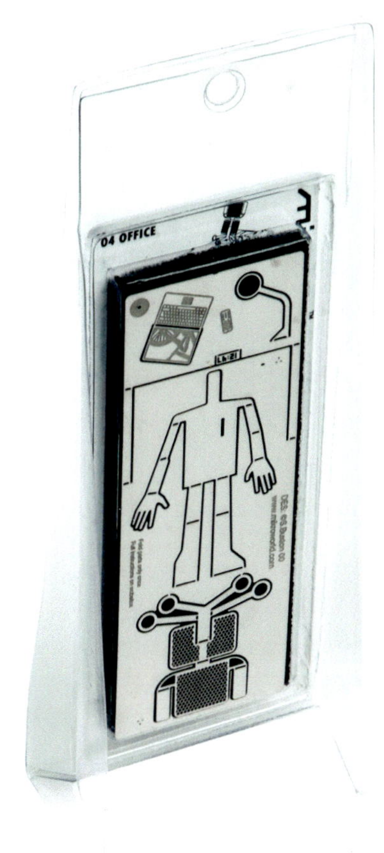

1–2   Sam Buxton, photography: Eugenio Franchi, package: Worldwide Co. London,
printed paper instruction leaflet, Vac formed styrene, 2002
3   Sam Buxton, photography: Eugenio Franchi, flat then folded out,
150 micron stainless steel, acid etching, 2003

Interview:
Lollek und Bollek

Belying their adopted heritage, would-be Poles Lollek and Bollek set up their "Combine for Design Questions and Solutions" right in the German heartland. In their pursuit of conception, art direction and illustration, the winners of many national and international design awards are guided by the principles of "courteousness, charm, honesty – and beauty".

What is your general take on self-representational measures?

Any means of self-portrayal should tell others who you are, what you do and how you can be reached. But also: what a client can expect from you. In addition, they give you the chance to pursue new ideas.
If we had to rate the different means available, we would say:

Gold: personal contact
Silver: the material shown here
Bronze: web page

What was the original reason for inventing your Polish alter egos Lollek and Bollek?

If the earth truly is flat, then Poland is on the sunny side and everything stupid on the other.
Lollek and Bollek met at university and started out in the park by designing record sleeves for Bollek's band, followed by a few jobs for other bands and smallish clients. So really, we were looking for a company name we could also use privately – and that eliminated variants like "Polski – New Media" straight away. We did not want our image to impress, but to convince.

Your current CI is based on a modular set of stickers featuring streams of text and icons, leaving it up to you to highlight the relevant passages

… and all elements can be combined. We have

– chequered labels for handwritten notes and labelling
– rating labels for the Polskistyle factor
– three image labels with typographic animals for situations that can do without words
– short messages with flowery phrases and nonsense
– Lollek and Bollek letterhead on continuous paper
– a "Polskipost" stamp
– Lollek and Bollek business cards

All materials are personalised and become legible at the moment of highlighting.

Among many other, delightful items, there are also some tiny giveaway bags with rather startling content…

These are unique samples from our Polski-style research institute.
We are currently working on some additional versions, e. g. to support the German-Polish friendship.

And how does this "Polskistyle" fit in with your regular design?

We take a Polish view of the world. Sometimes it is easier to look at things from the outside.
In addition, it helps to breaks the ice - and since Poland joined the EU, our customers even pay on time.

How did your CI develop with time?

Our old logo was based on the letters of an old Russian stamping game – above and beyond, we had no further, fixed CI parameters. With their new CI Lollek and Bollek have left the aesthetic Diaspora to explore the new Europe.

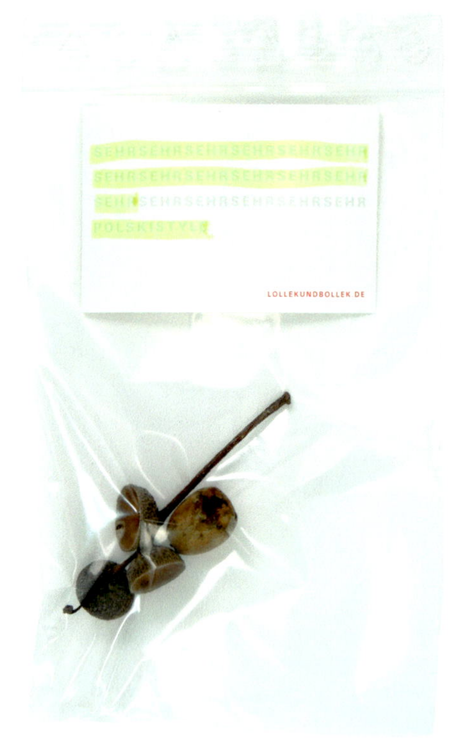
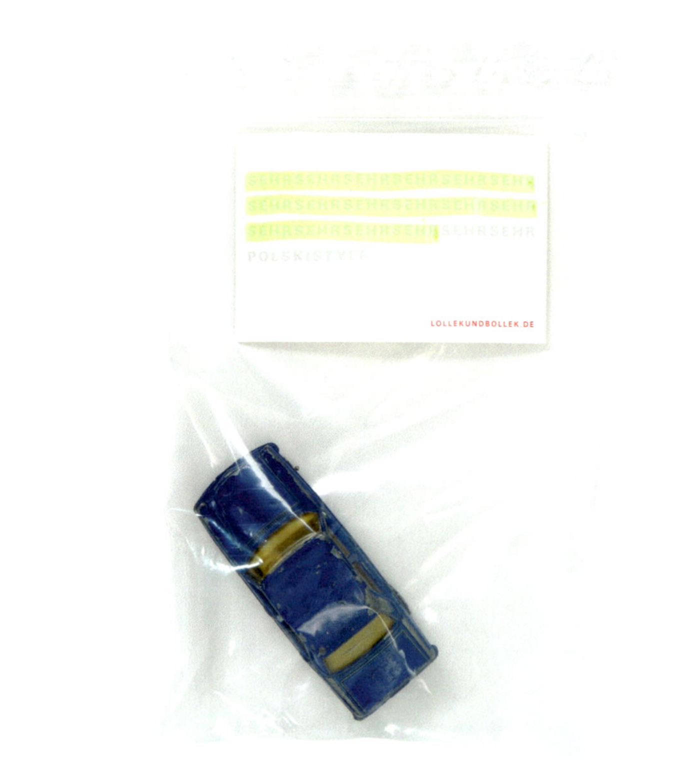
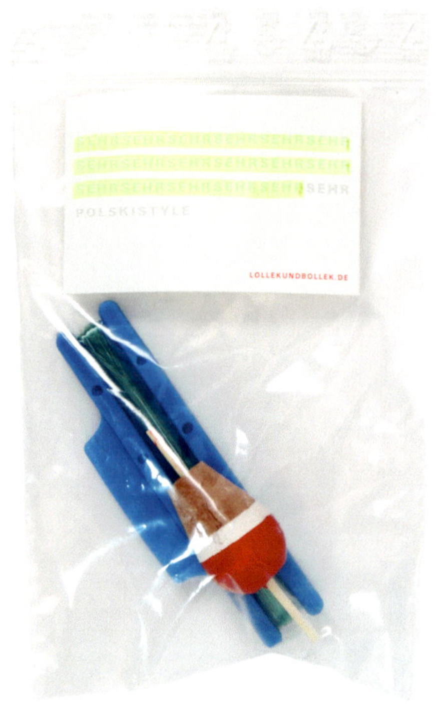
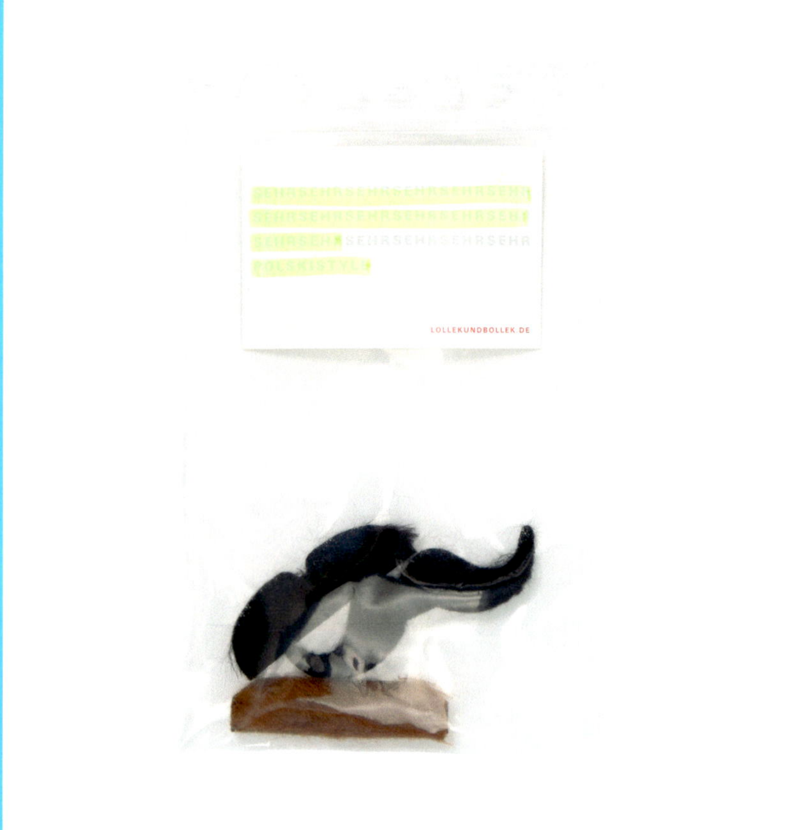

1–4   Lollek und Bollek / Lollek und C. Wiehl, 55 x 85 mm, offset printing, 2003

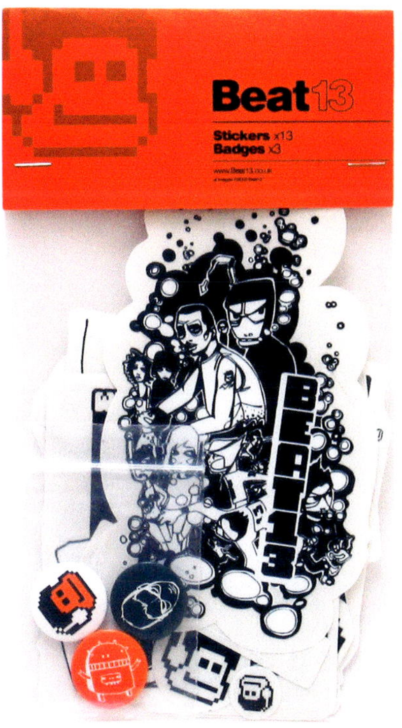

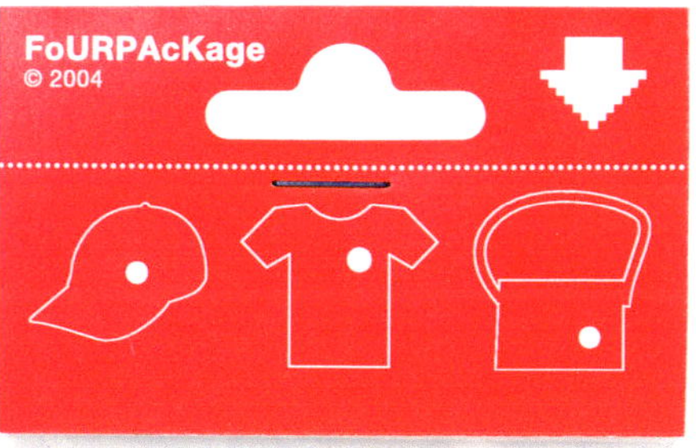

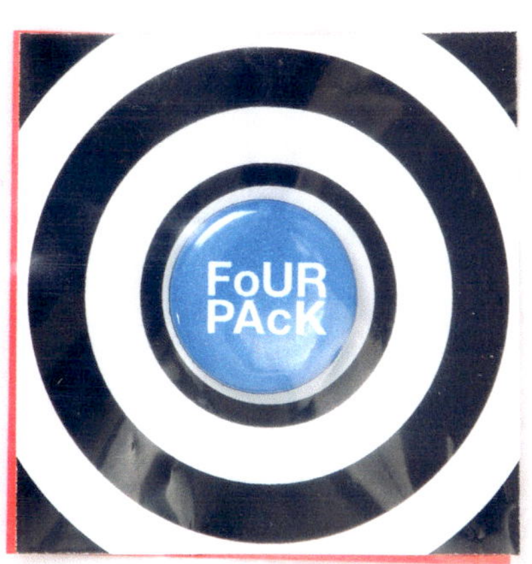

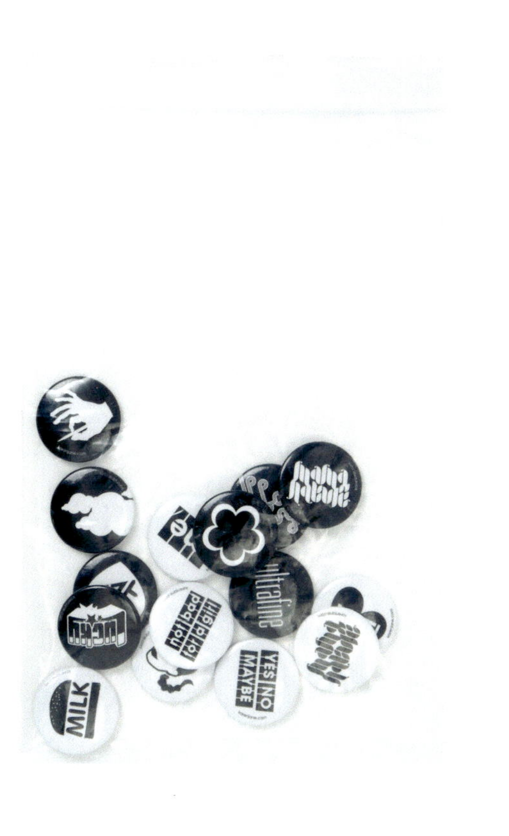

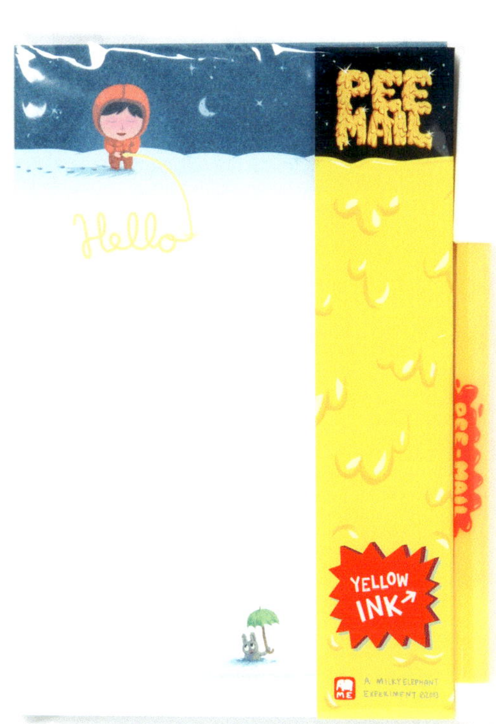

1   Beat 13 / Matt Watkins, illustration: Lucy Mclauchlan, vinyl stickers in card and plastic packing, silk-screen printing, 2002
2   Four Pack Ontwerpers, 70 x 120 mm, button 25 mm ø, plastic bag, card, paper and button, colour copy, 2004
3   Karen Jane, 25 mm pin badge, ink paper plastic metal, 2005
4   Milky Elephant, illustraton: Karl Ackermann, Mumbleboy and Eun-Ha Paek, laser print, 2005

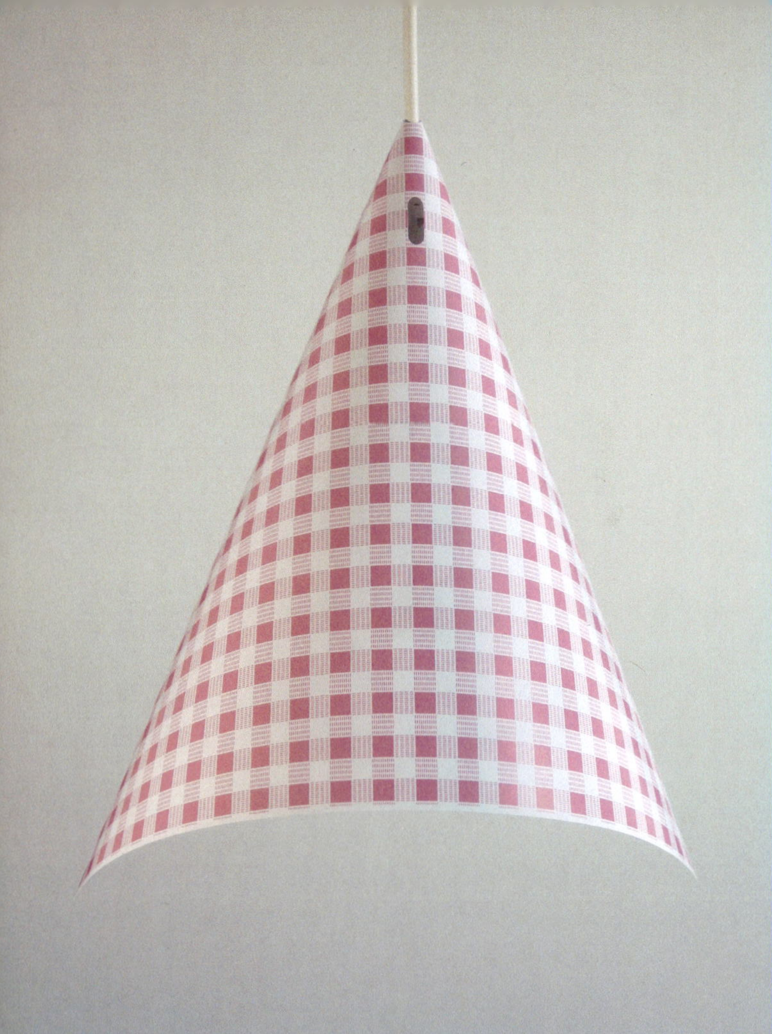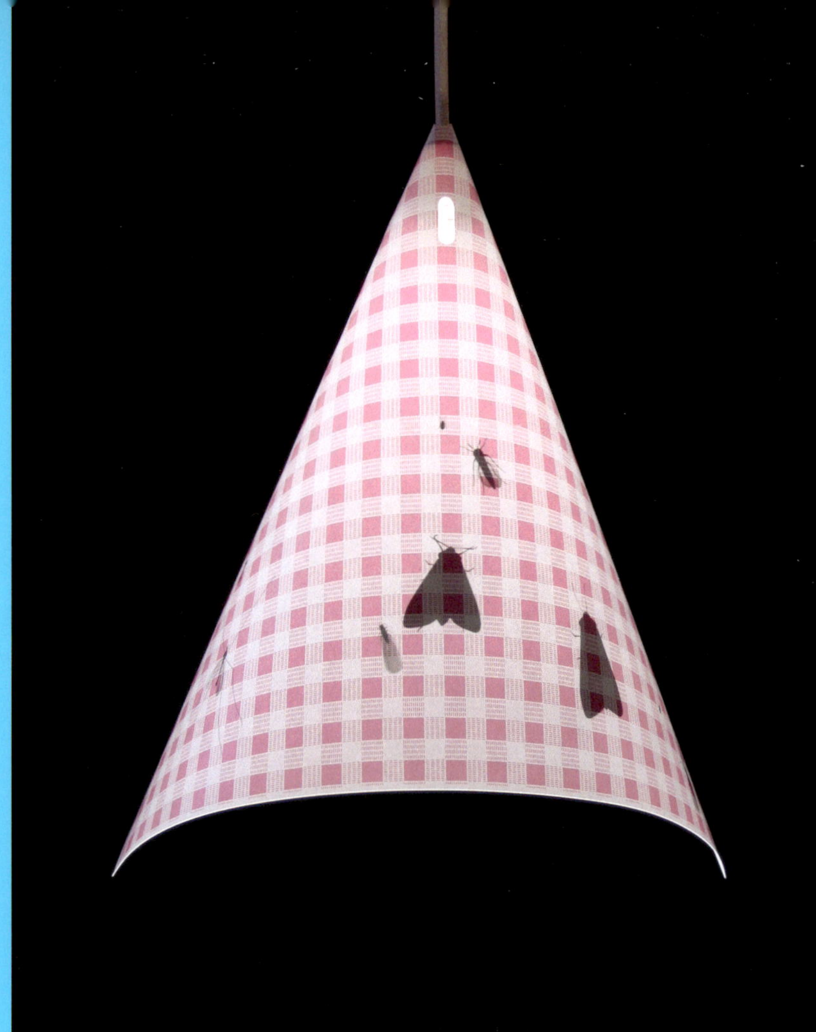

208   1–2   1Kilo, A4, paper, offset printing, 2004

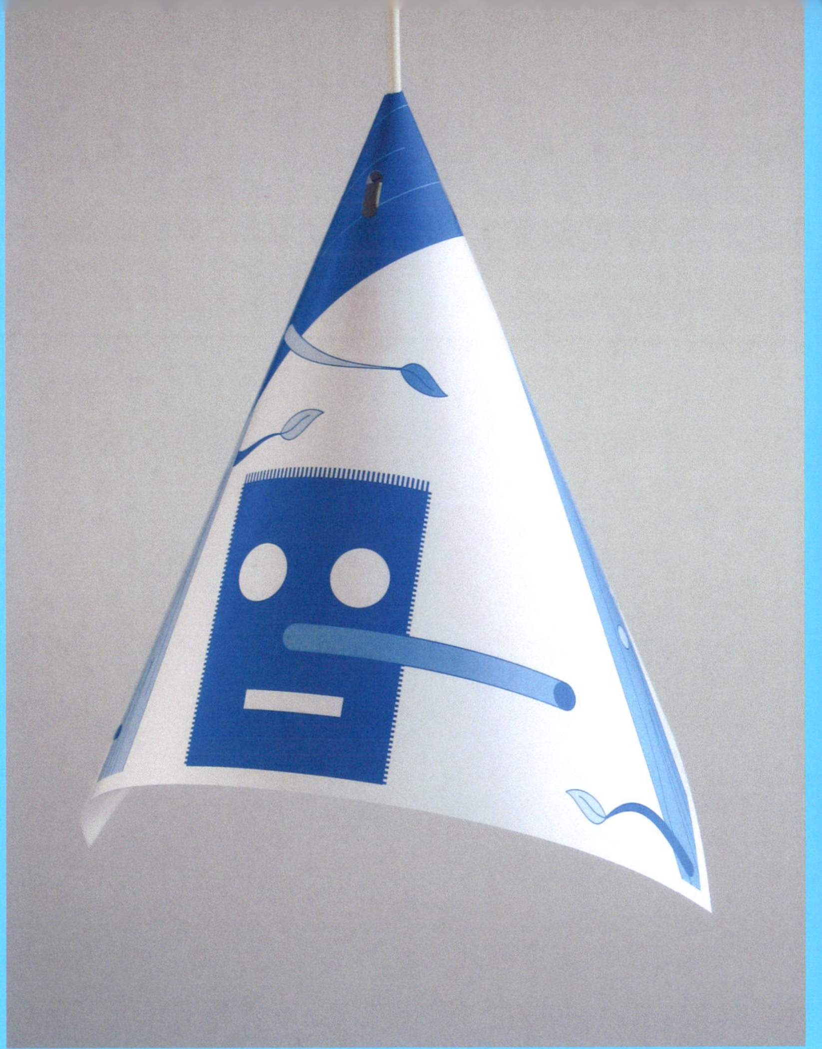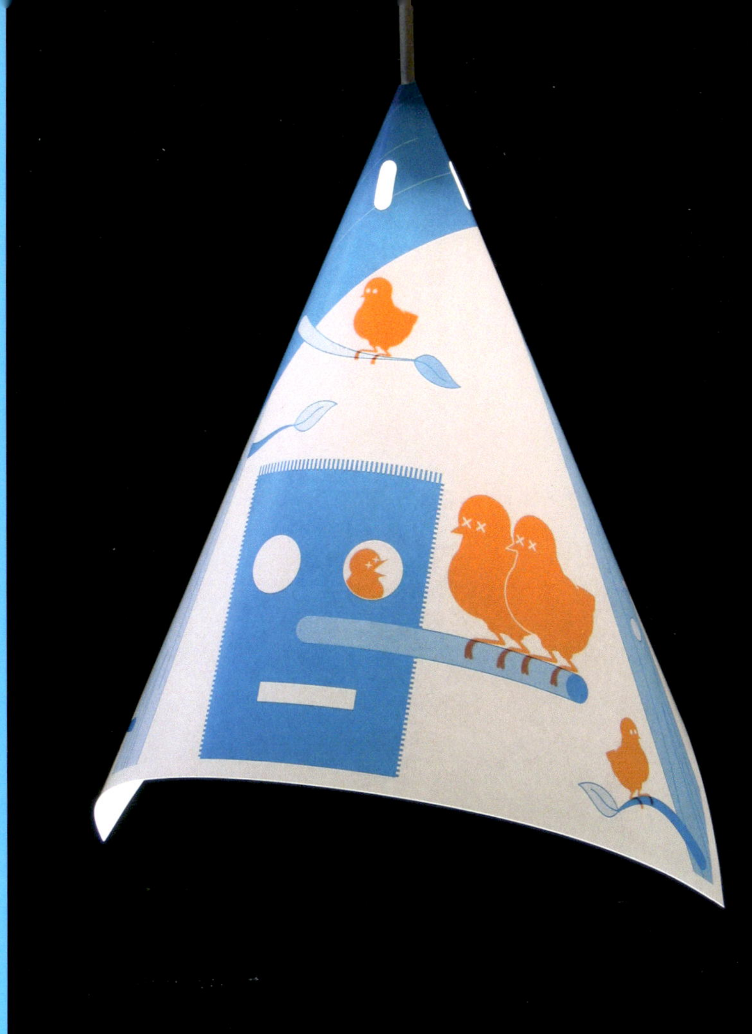

1kilo's Dorothee Wettstein and Hansjakob Fehr "love the idea of things designing themselves – you find a coherent approach, a good basic idea and the solution appears as if from nowhere".
Ardent fans of the on/off theme, a move to Berlin inspired their ingeniously simple range of DIY-lampshades. "On arrival, we wrapped a depressingly naked light bulb in double-sided sketch paper and were surprised by the sudden, see-through animation effect." One shade, double vision. Taking this switched-on design a step further, a small proportion of the pre-cut shades was not perforated, but laser-printed with the duo's contact information for a unique set of calling cards.
Both sales item and clever, low-cost giveaway, the lampshade is supplemented by a range of cutely grotesque nightlight operating on the same premise – again, they will only reveal their true nature when fed with a little energy.

1–2   1Kilo, A4, paper, offset printing, 2004

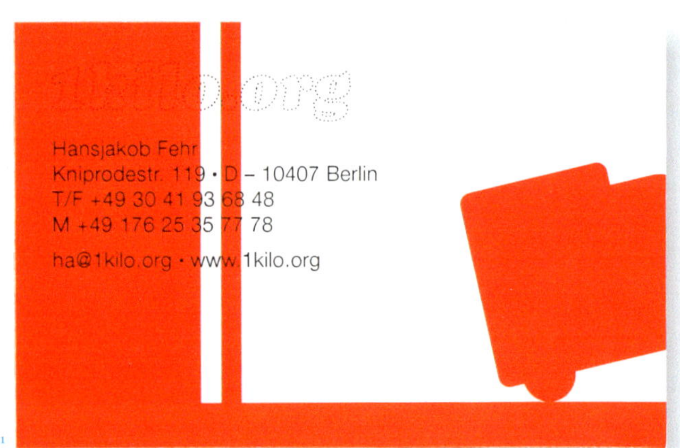

Hansjakob Fehr
Kniprodestr. 119 • D – 10407 Berlin
T/F +49 30 41 93 68 48
M +49 176 25 35 77 78

ha@1kilo.org • www.1kilo.org

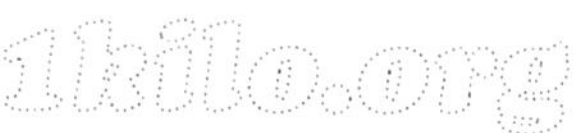

Dorothee Wettstein
Kniprodestr. 119 • D – 10407 Berlin
T/F +49 30 41 93 68 48
M +49 176 290 299 16

do@1kilo.org • www.1kilo.org

Dorothee Wettstein
Kniprodestr. 119 • D – 10407 Berlin
T/F +49 30 41 93 68 48
M +49 176 290 299 16

do@1kilo.org • www.1kilo.org

Dorothee Wettstein
Kniprodestr. 119 • D – 10407 Berlin
T/F +49 30 41 93 68 48
M +49 176 290 299 16

do@1kilo.org • www.1kilo.org

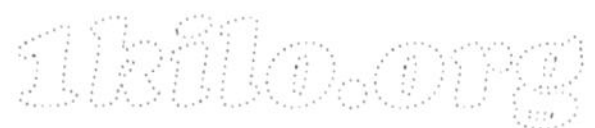

Dorothee Wettstein
Kniprodestr. 119 • D – 10407 Berlin
T/F +49 30 41 93 68 48
M +49 176 290 299 16

do@1kilo.org • www.1kilo.org

Hansjakob Fehr
Kniprodestr. 119 • D – 10407 Berlin
T/F +49 30 41 93 68 48
M +49 176 25 35 77 78

ha@1kilo.org • www.1kilo.org

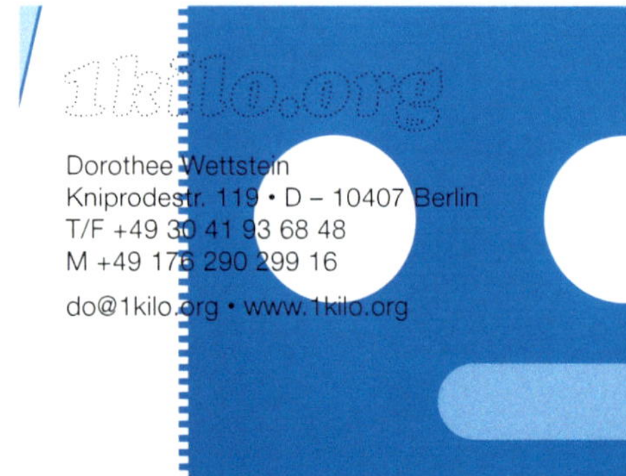

Dorothee Wettstein
Kniprodestr. 119 • D – 10407 Berlin
T/F +49 30 41 93 68 48
M +49 176 290 299 16

do@1kilo.org • www.1kilo.org

Dorothee Wettstein
Kniprodestr. 119 • D – 10407 Berlin
T/F +49 30 41 93 68 48
M +49 176 290 299 16

do@1kilo.org • www.1kilo.org

1–8   1Kilo, paper, offset and laser printing, 2005

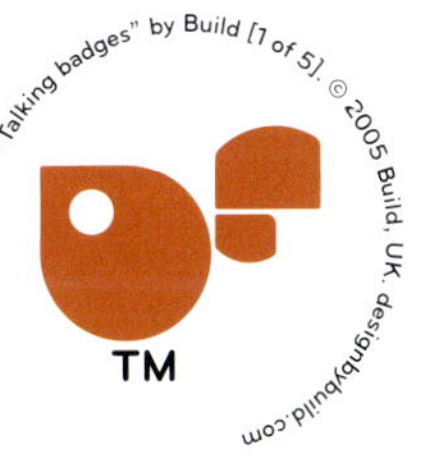

TALKING BIRD[TM] BADGE

ARTWORK

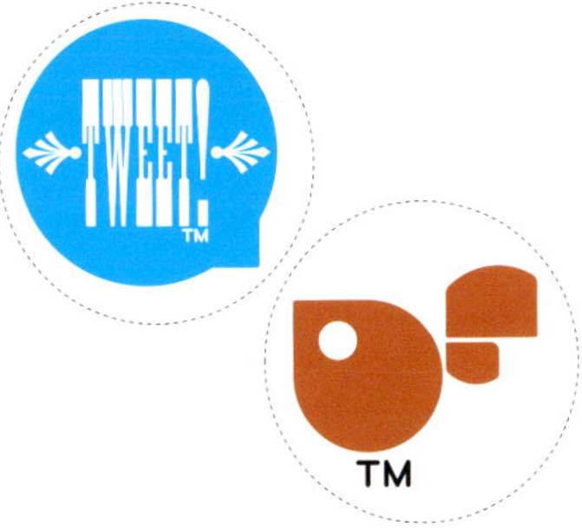

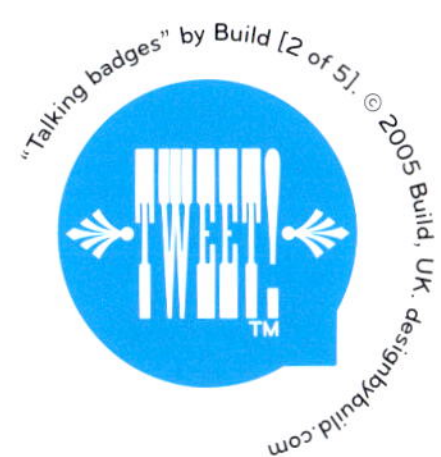

COMBINATION - 01

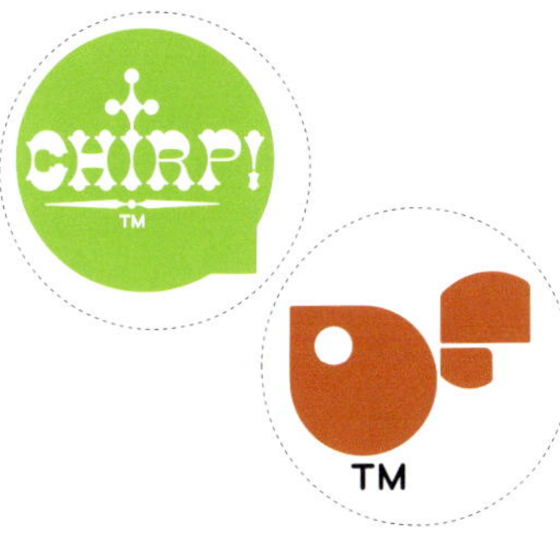

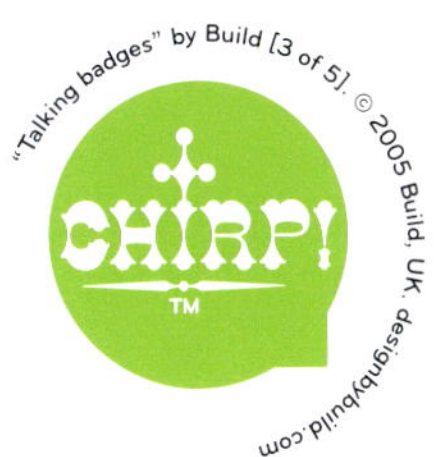

02

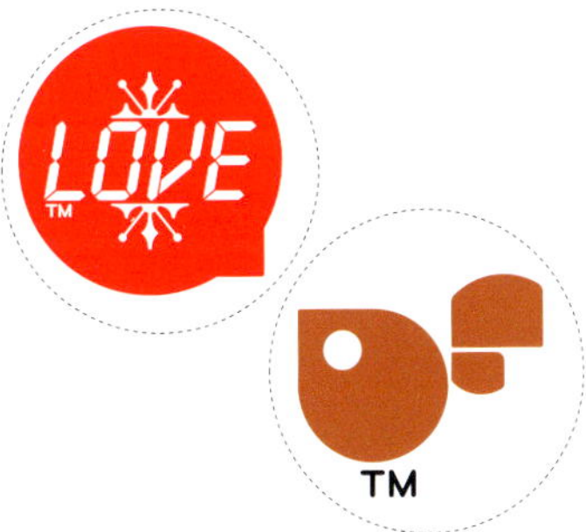

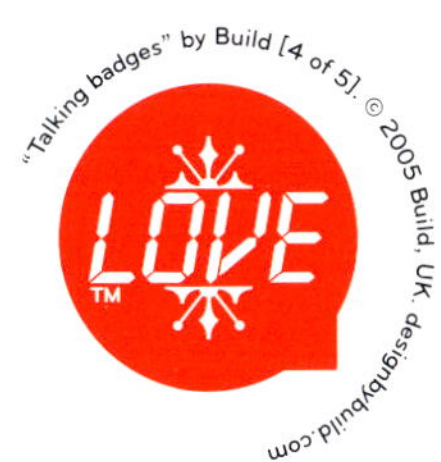

03

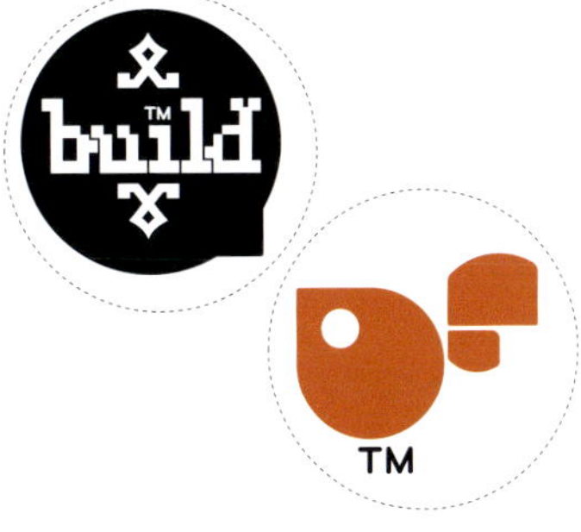

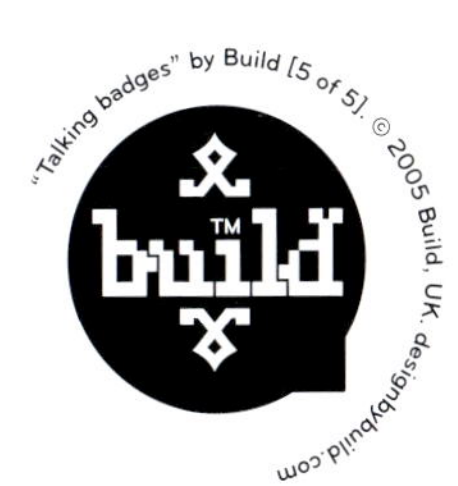

04

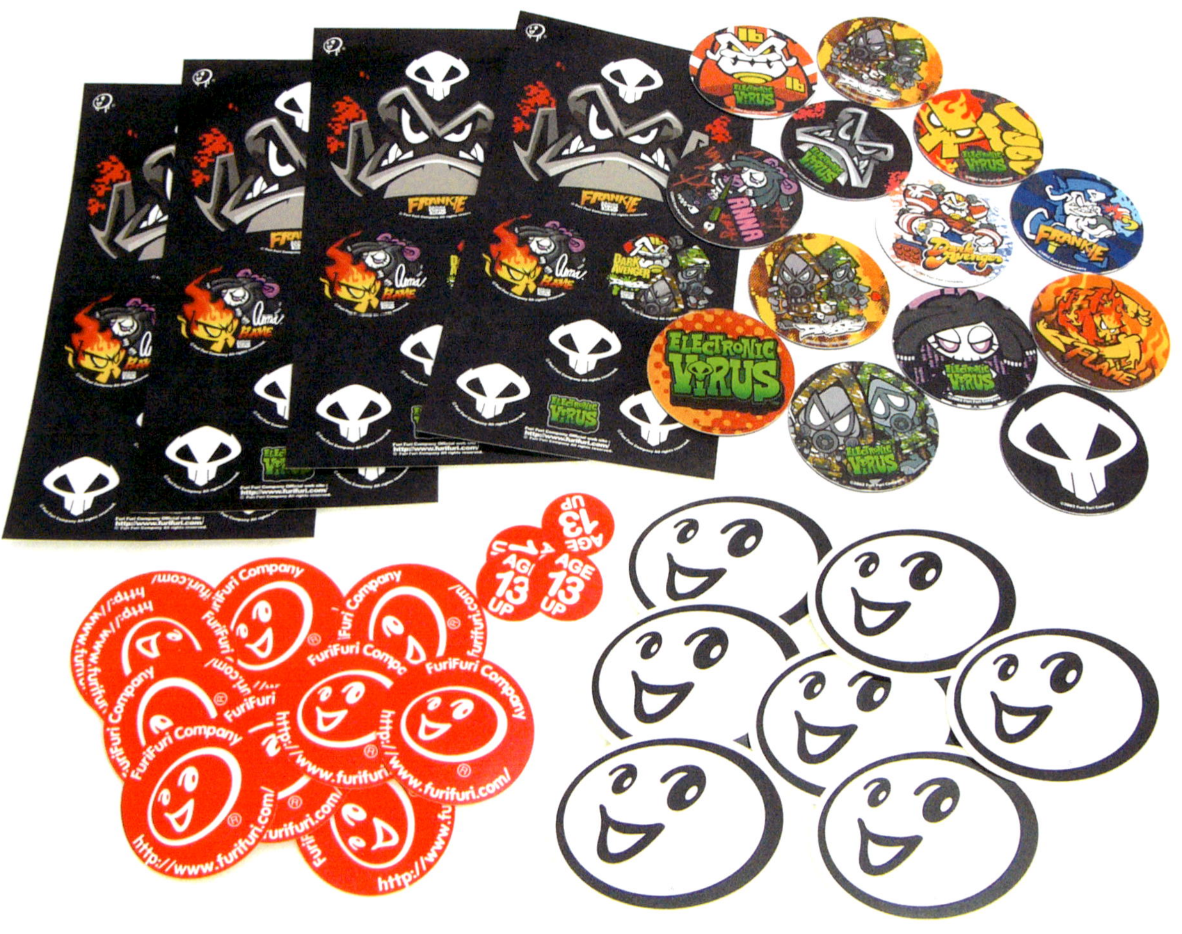

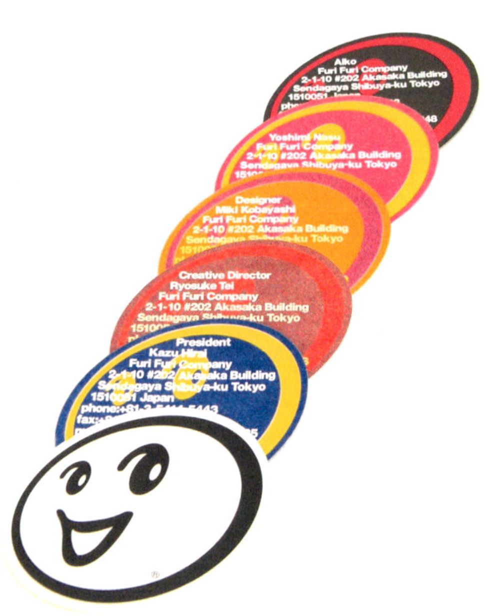

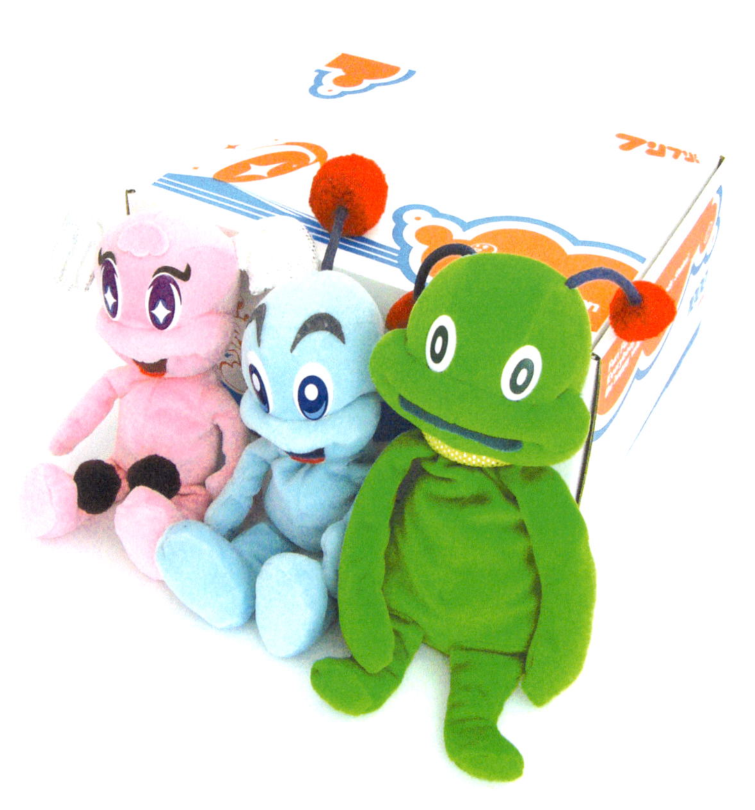

1–2   Furi Furi Company / Ryosuke Tei, 25 x 75 mm, stickers, 2001–2003
212   3   Furi Furi Company / Ryosuke Tei, about 200 mm tall, fabrics, 2001

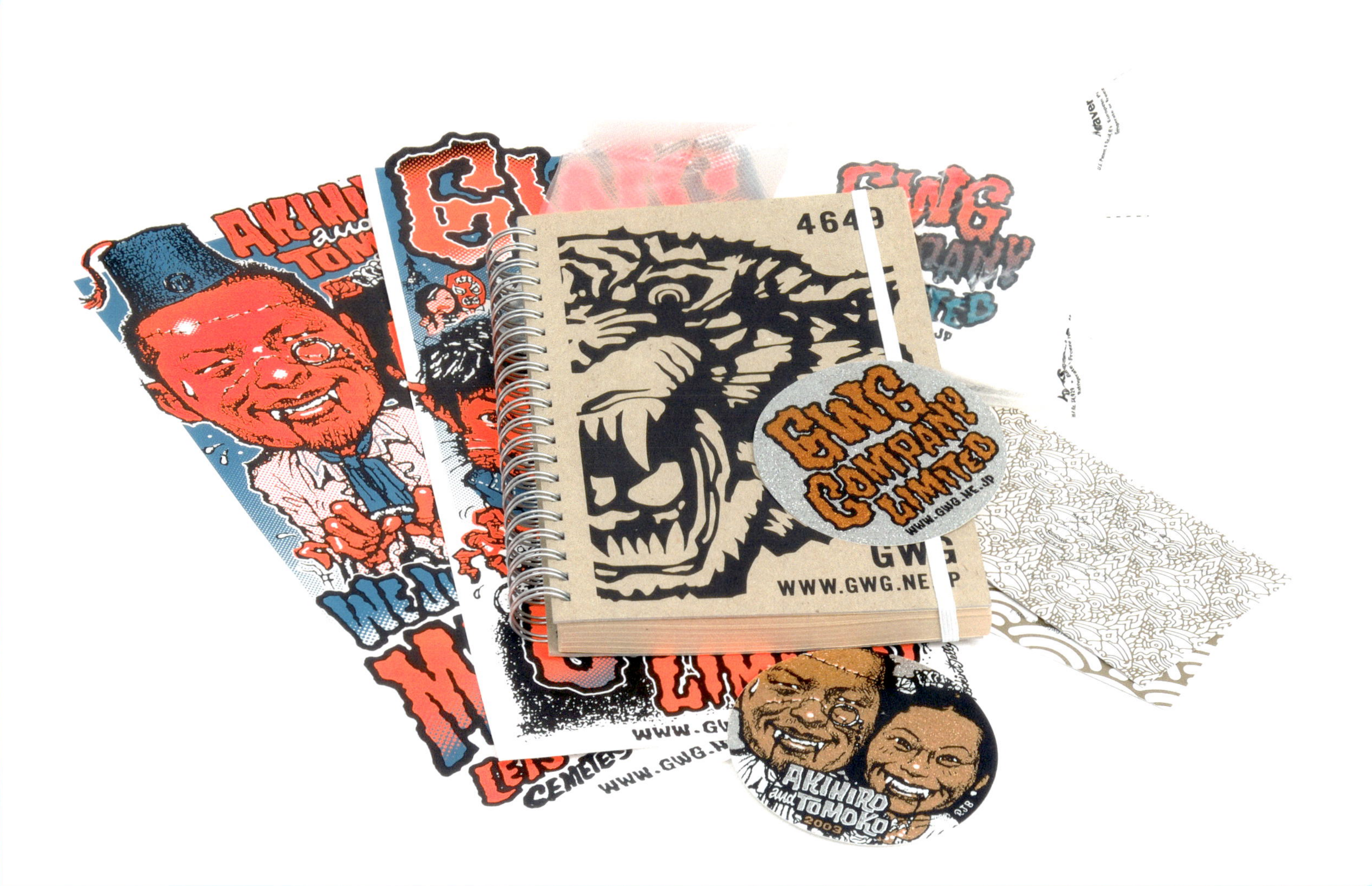

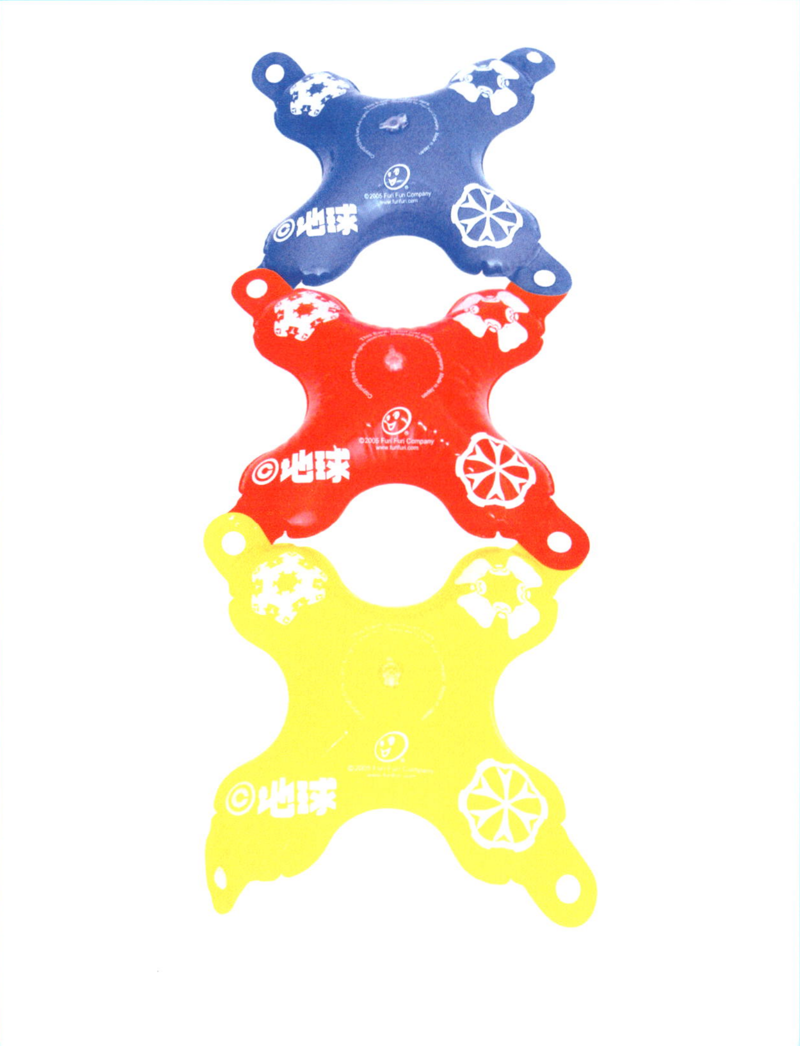

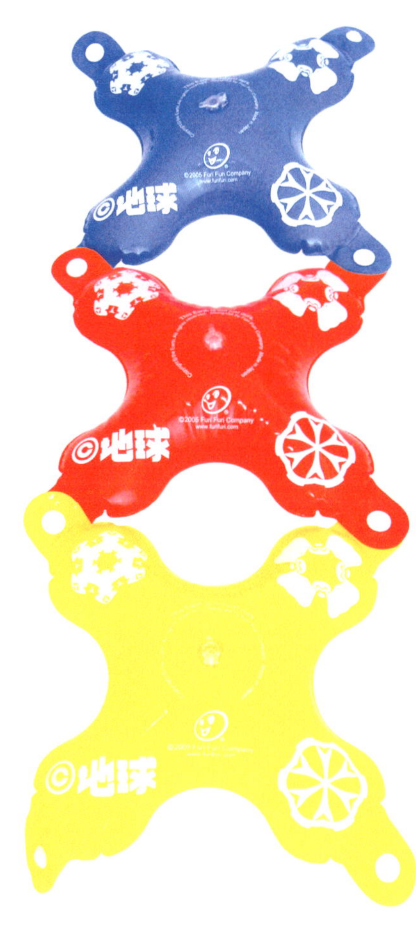

1 GWG Co. Ltd.
2 Furi Furi / Ryosuke Tei, 600 x 400 x 300 mm, pvc, 2005

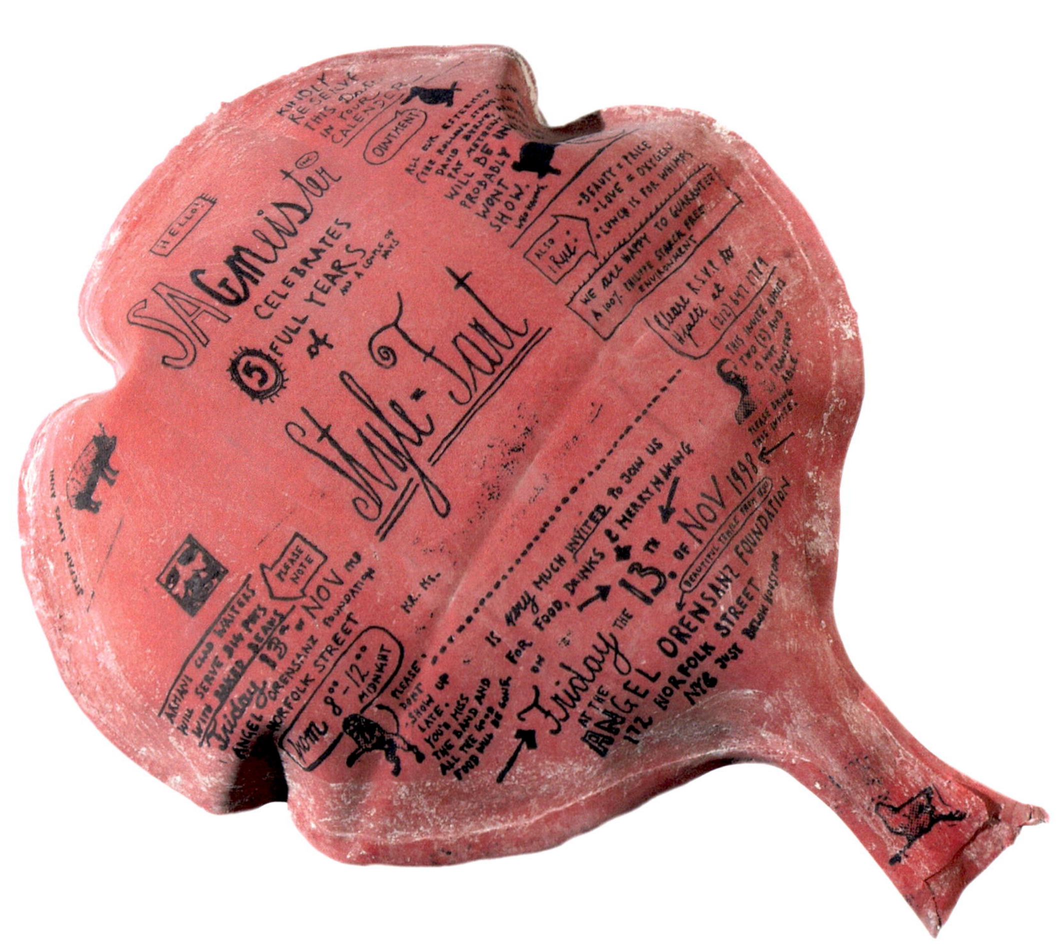

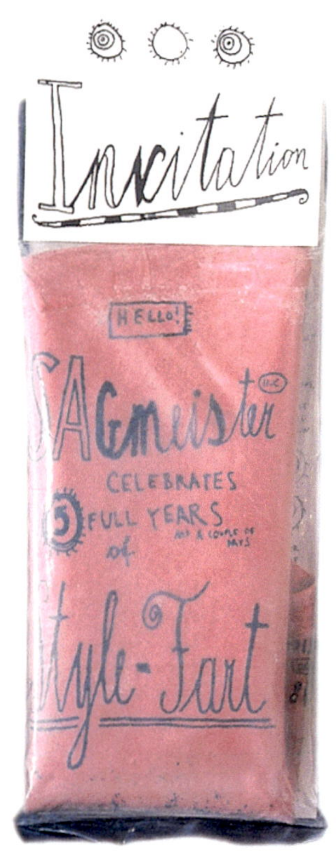

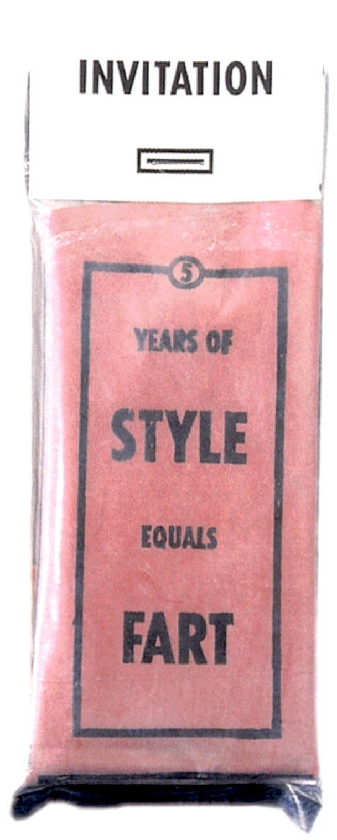

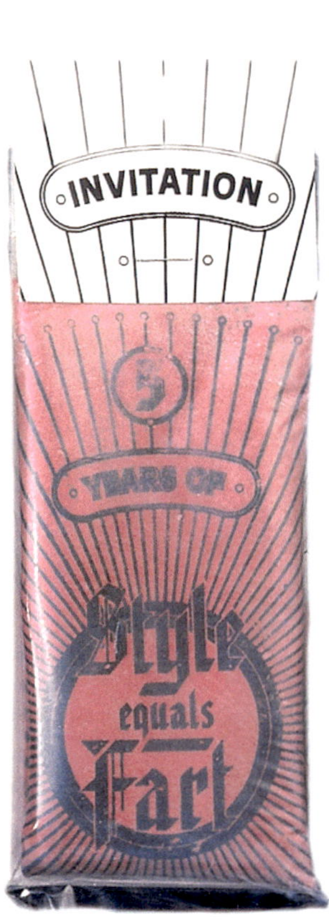

1–2   Sagmeister Inc. / Stefan Sagmeister, 1998

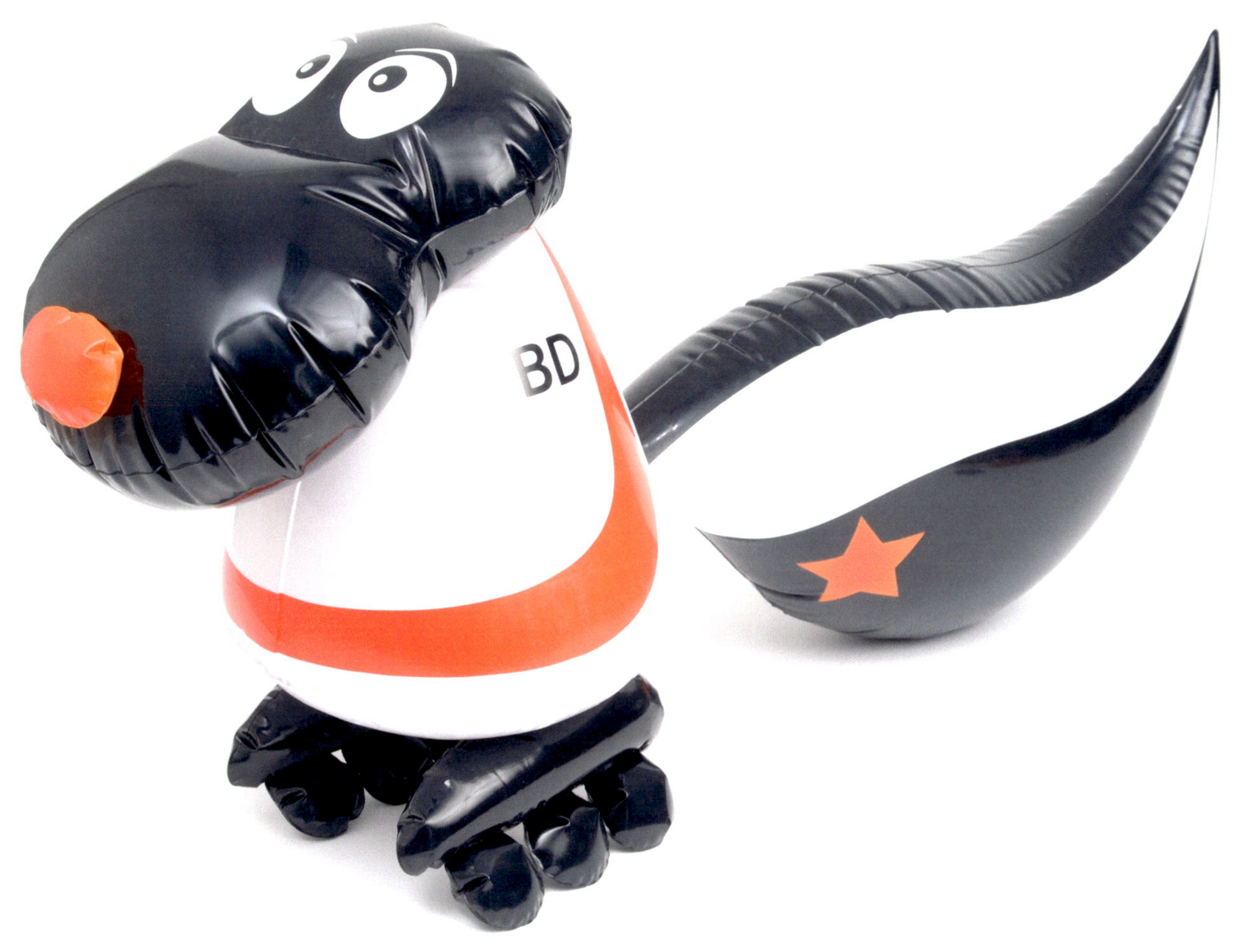

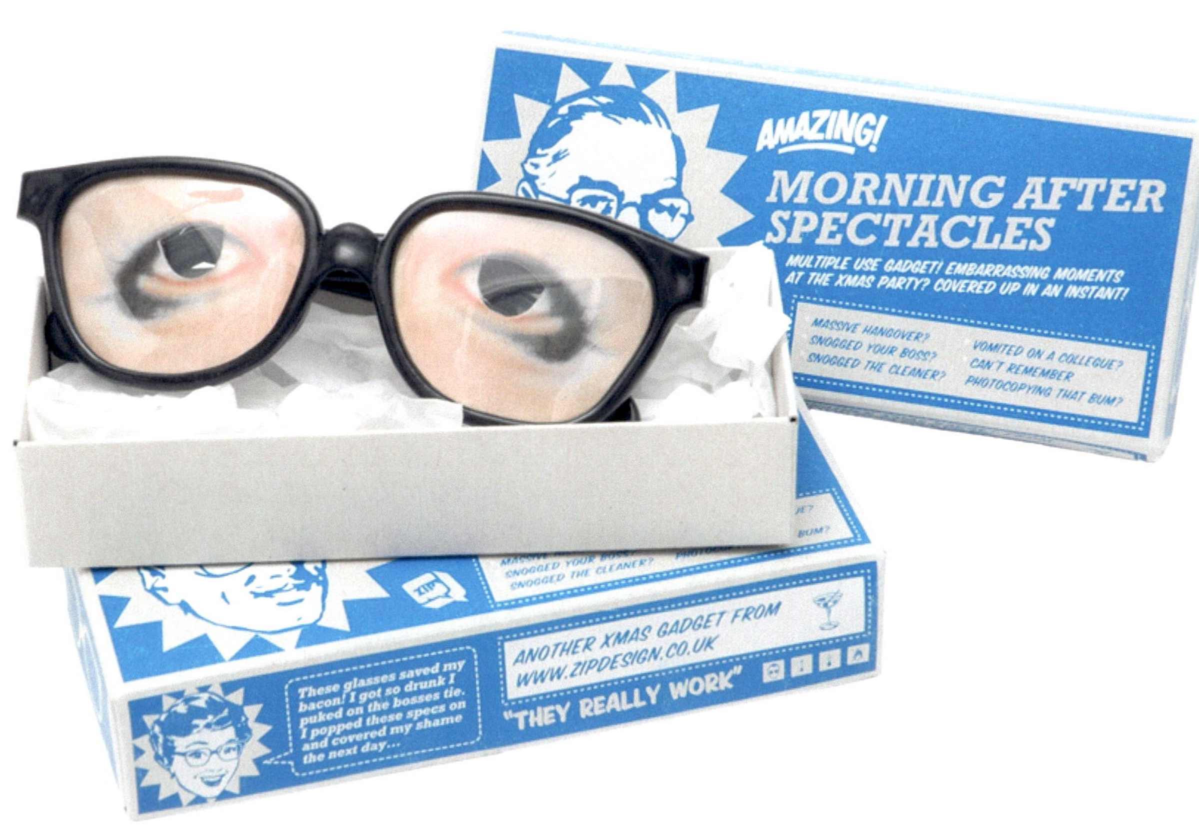

1   Büro Destruct / Lopetz, 600 x 400 x 300 mm, plastic, silk-screen printing, 2003
2   ZIP Design / Neil Bowen, spectacles with case, micron grey board 400 g and fun specs, silk-screen printing 2c, 2003

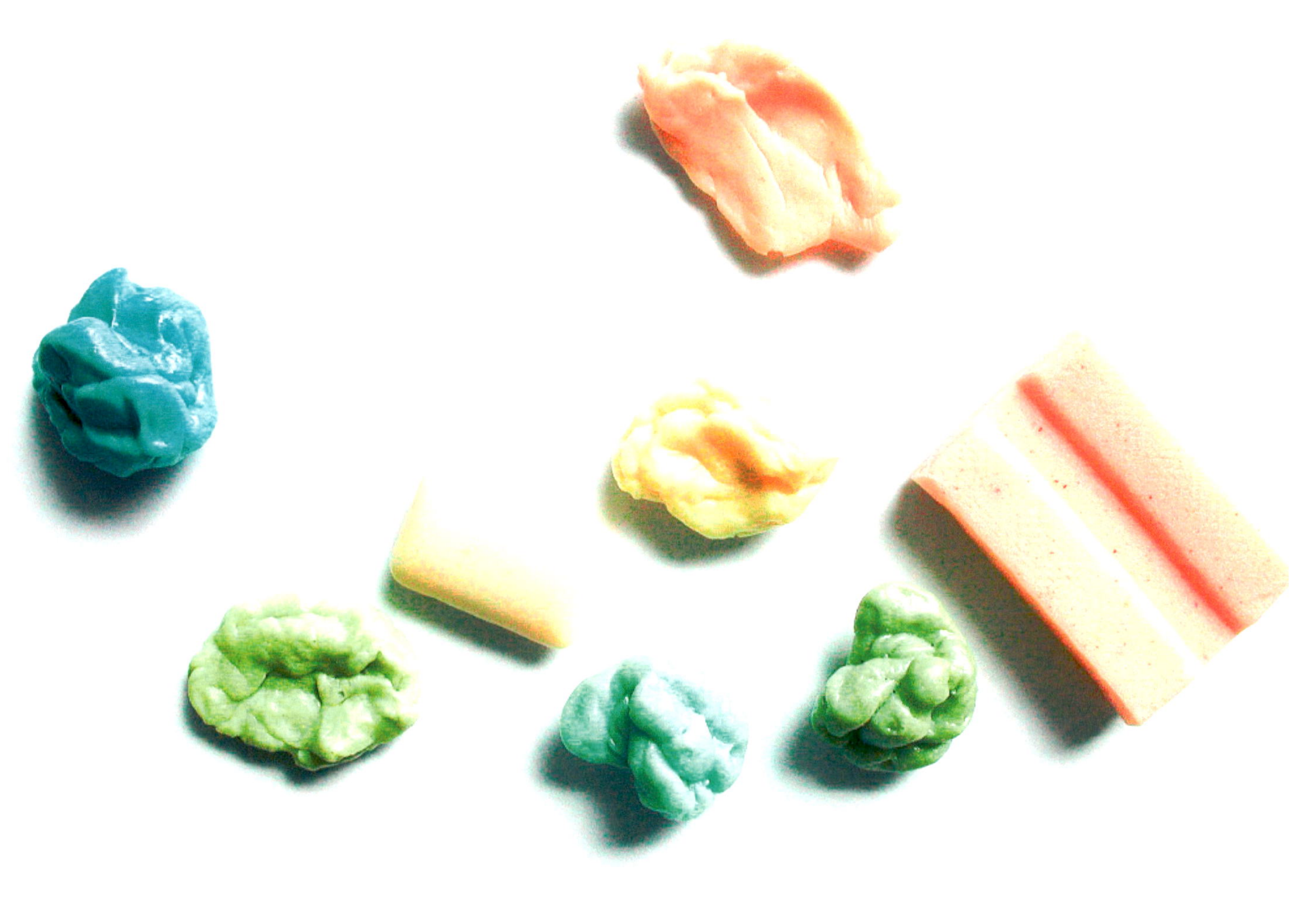

Initially conceived as a slightly unusual Christmas gift, David Clavadetscher's series of irreverent fridge magnets perfectly reflects his general design approach – "always include an element of surprise". A small, practical and most of all startling giveaway, the deceptively realistic, yet strictly non-sticky gum is available in more than ten different shapes and states of disintegration ("rare, medium, well done" according to Clavadetscher) and four icecream-coloured, sugar-free "flavours".

A collaborative effort, all "master" gums were lovingly pre-chewed by Clavadetscher's friends, then turned into highly accurate silicone moulds and cast manually with coloured acrylic resin and a tiny, extra-strong magnet to allow the finished "gum" to adhere to any magnetic surface.

216 David Clavadetscher and Andres Portmann,
used chewing-gum magnet, acrylic resin, magnet, 2004

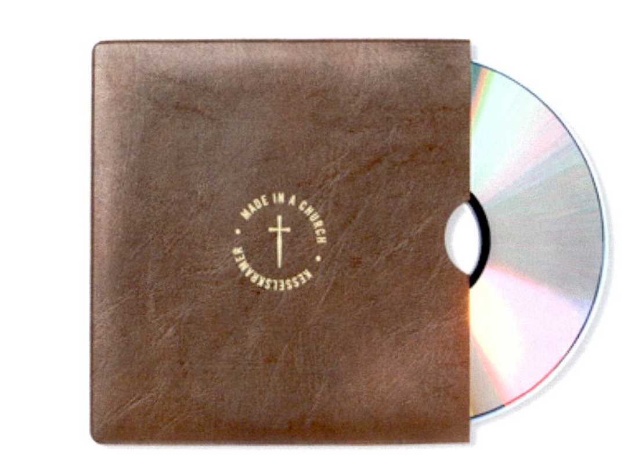

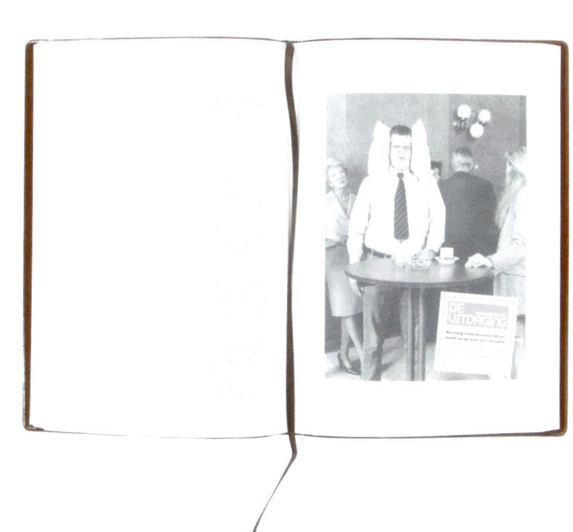

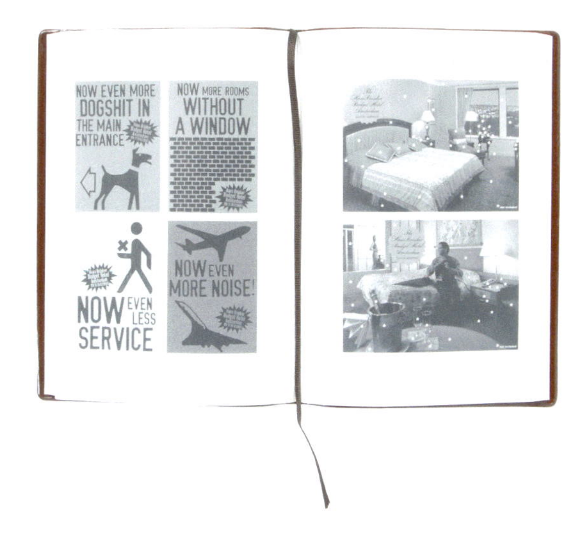

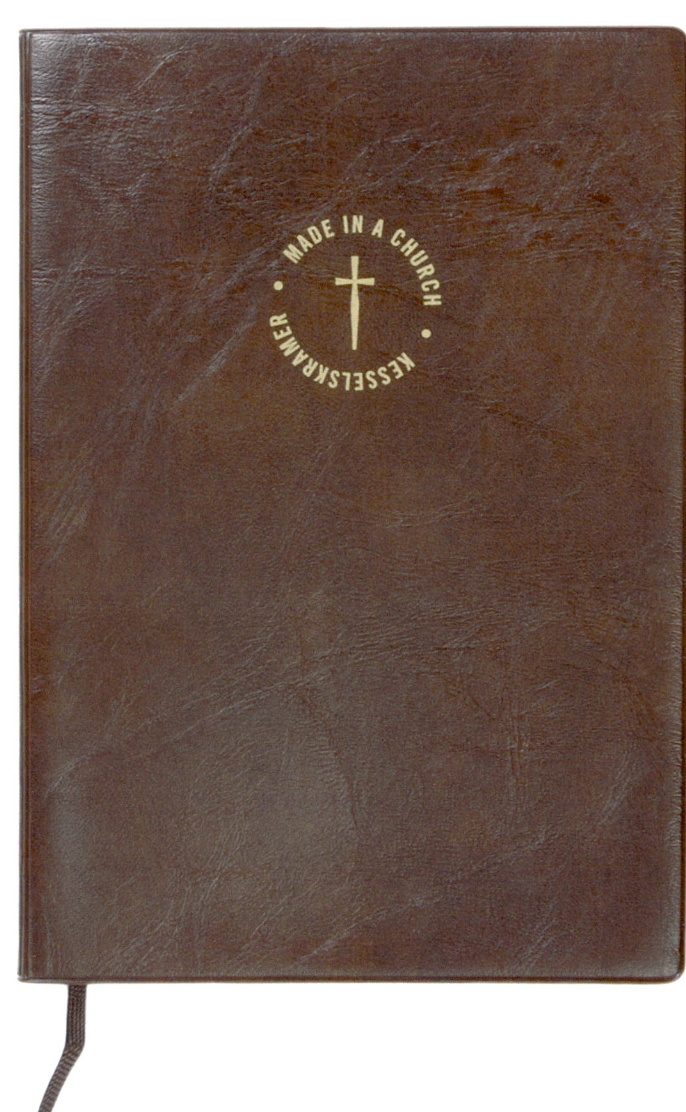

1–4 KesselsKramer, artificial leather and bookmark ribbon, offset printing

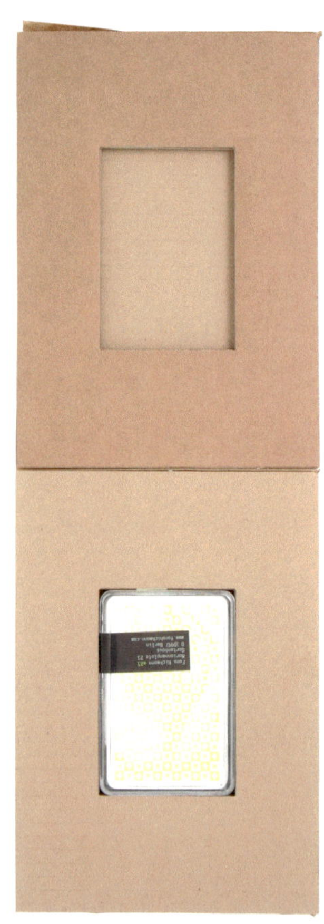

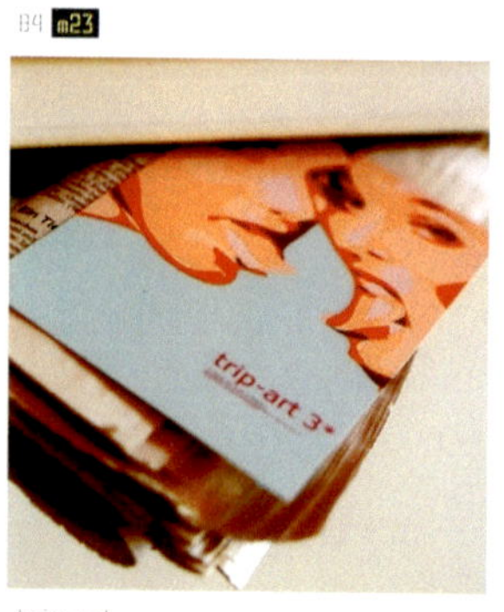

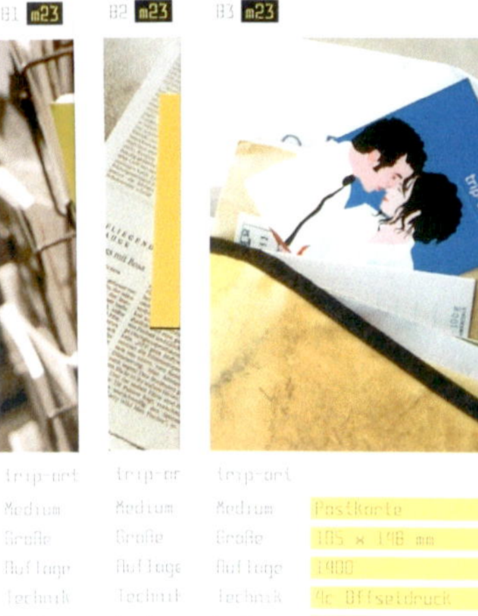

1 Fons Hickmann m23 / Simon Gallus, Barbara Bättig, Fons Hickmann,
   card game, 210 x 150 x 40 mm, cardboard, sticker and cards, punched, 2003–2004
2 Fons Hickmann m23 / Simon Gallus, Barbara Bättig, Fons Hickmann,
   card game, 95 x 65 x 25 mm, plastic cards, offset printing, 2003–2004

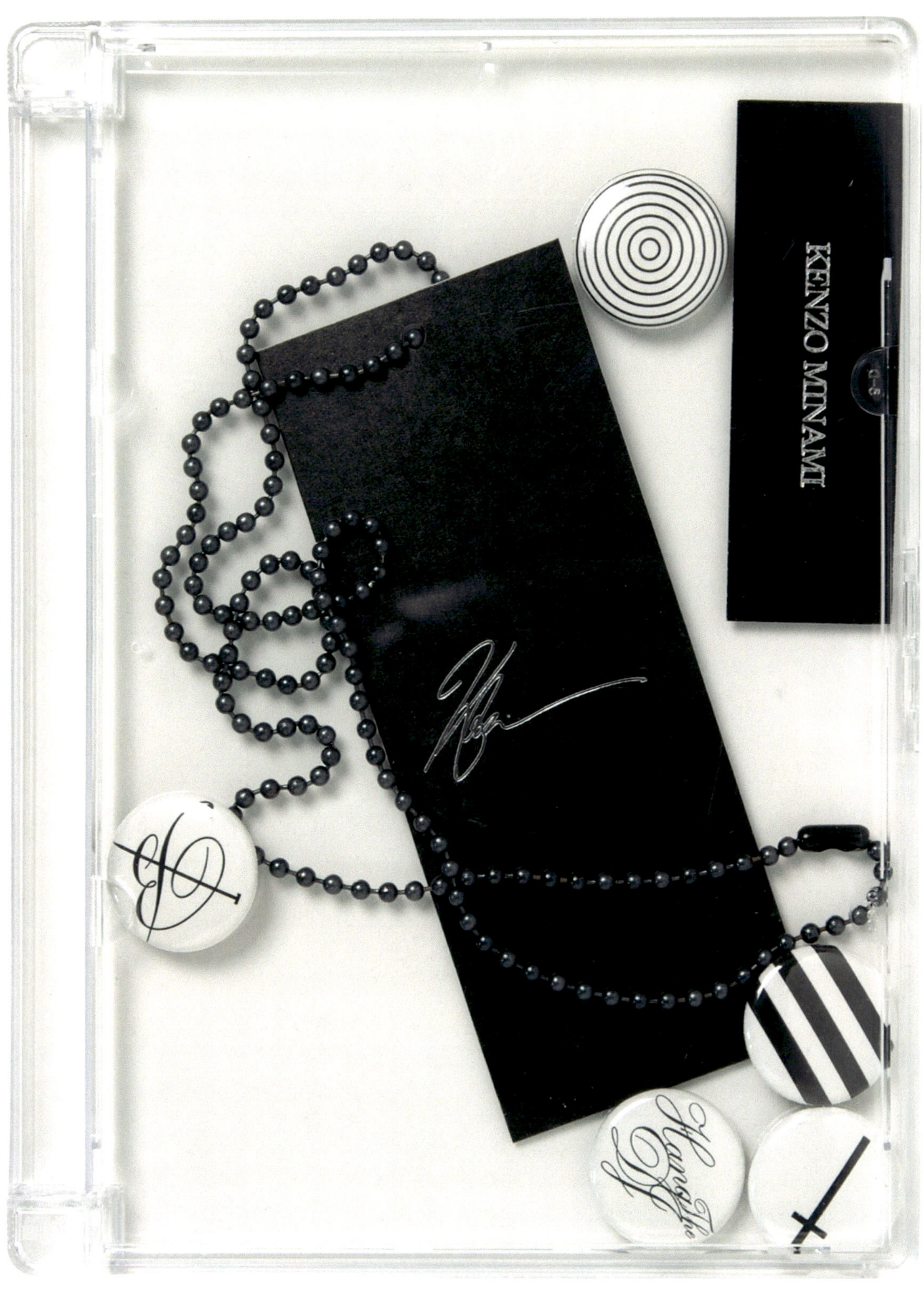

Kenzo Minami, metal pinschain paper, foil printing, 2000

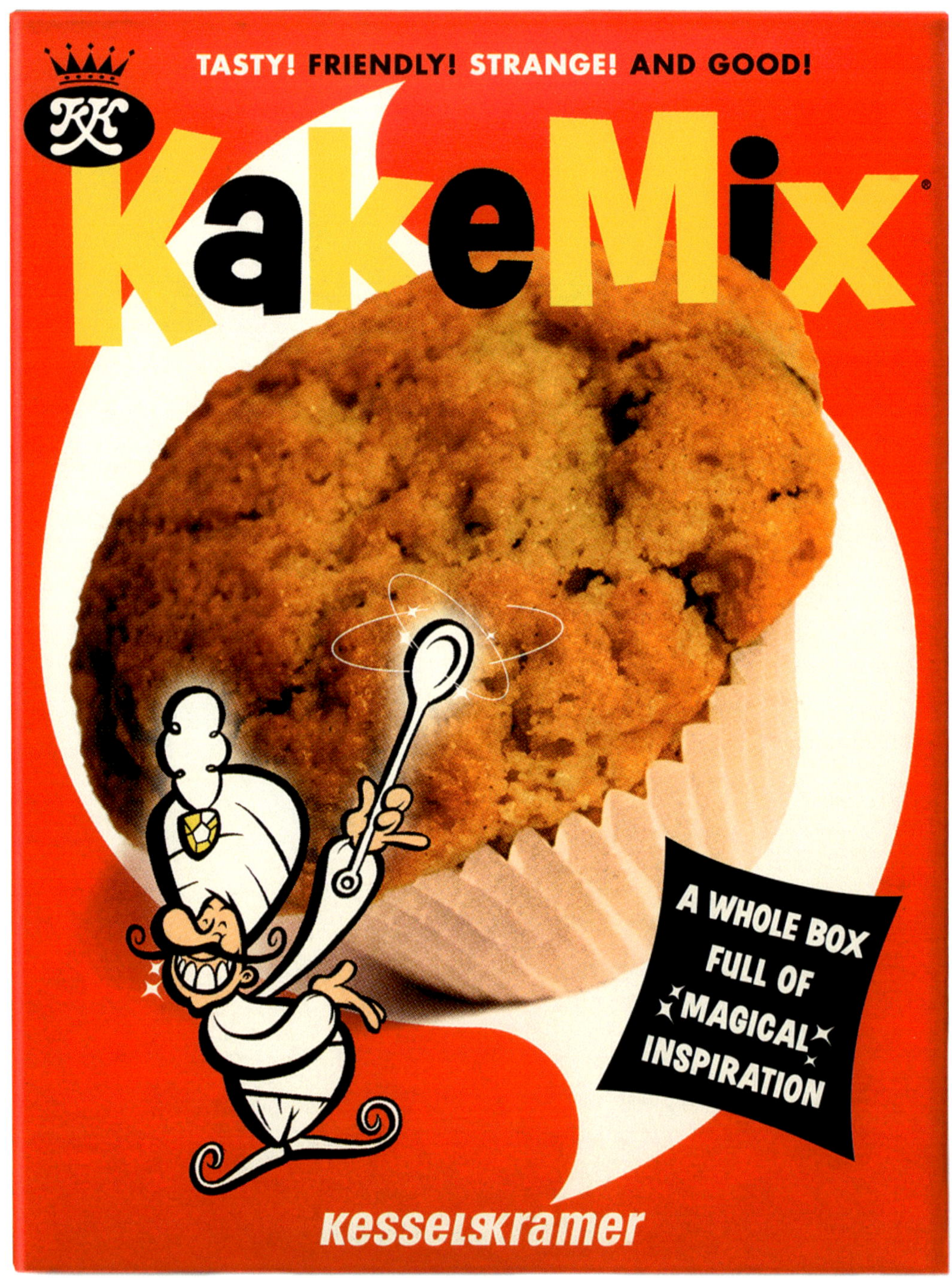

Amsterdam-based creative communications company Kessels Kramer loves to show potential clients that communication can work powerfully in unexpected ways. Worth including for their crazy website alone (which manages to incorporate fake bird sanctuaries, advice on successful farming, private holiday pics – you name it), their challenging style finds a continuation in this delectable 50s style shake'n'bake pack filled with magical inspiration.

A smaller and more intimate way to provide people with a taste of KesselsKramer's philosophy, ideas and personality, this Kake Mix changes the archetypal business gift into something that is creative, passionate – and ultimately tasty.

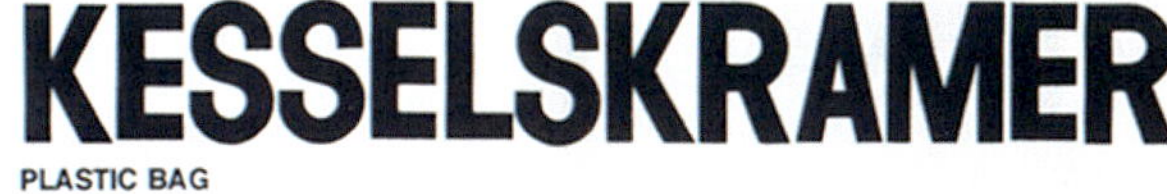

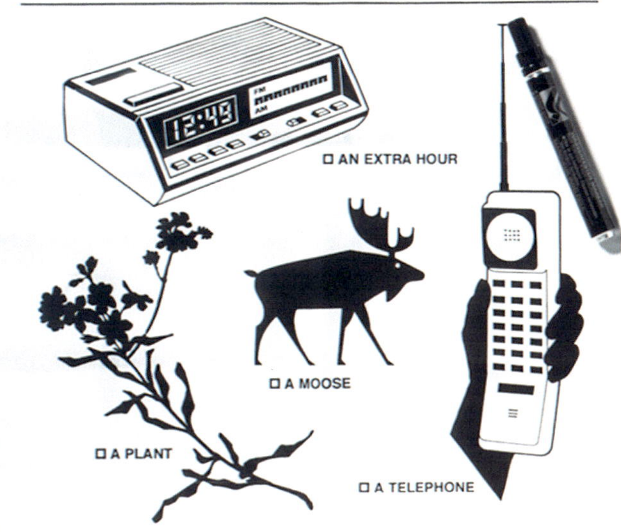

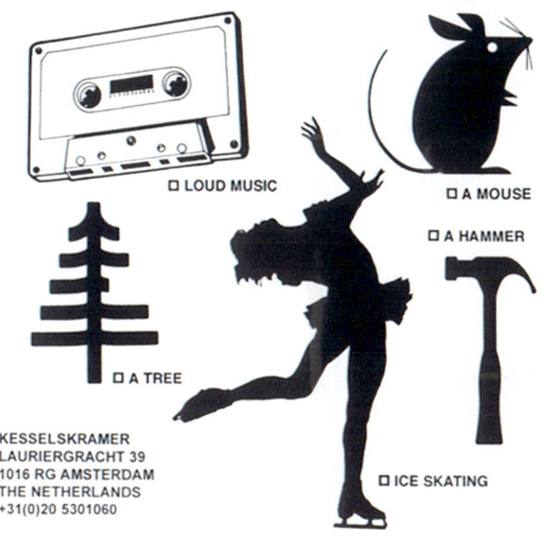

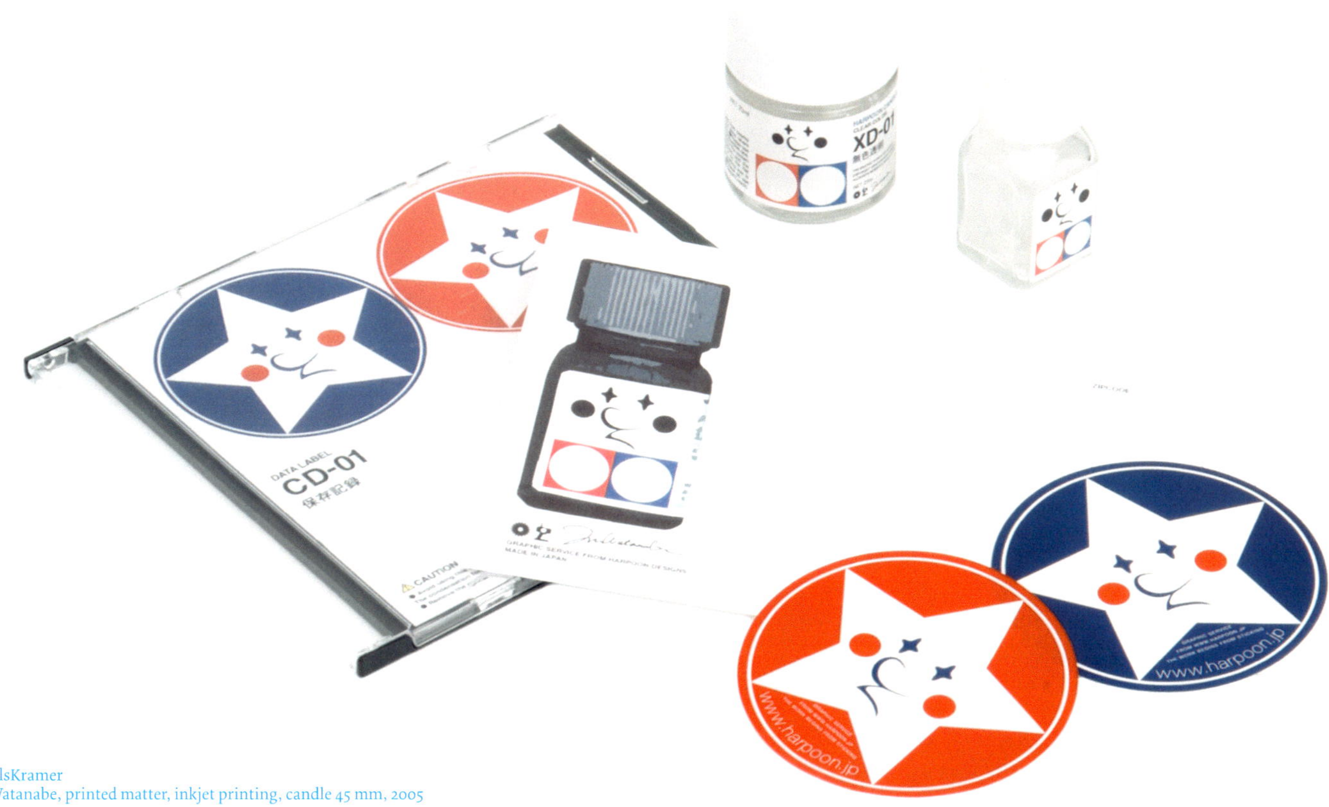

1   KesselsKramer
2   Jun Watanabe, printed matter, inkjet printing, candle 45 mm, 2005

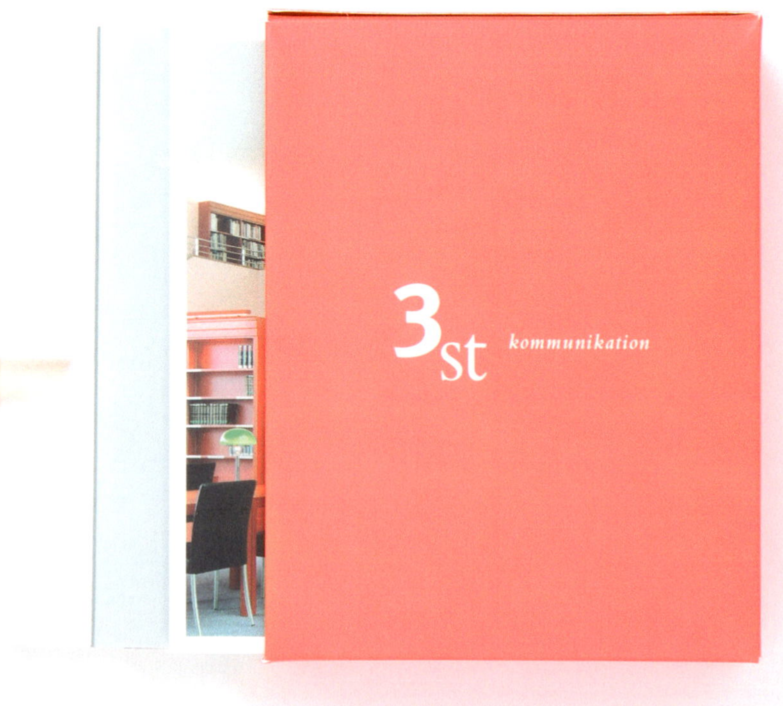

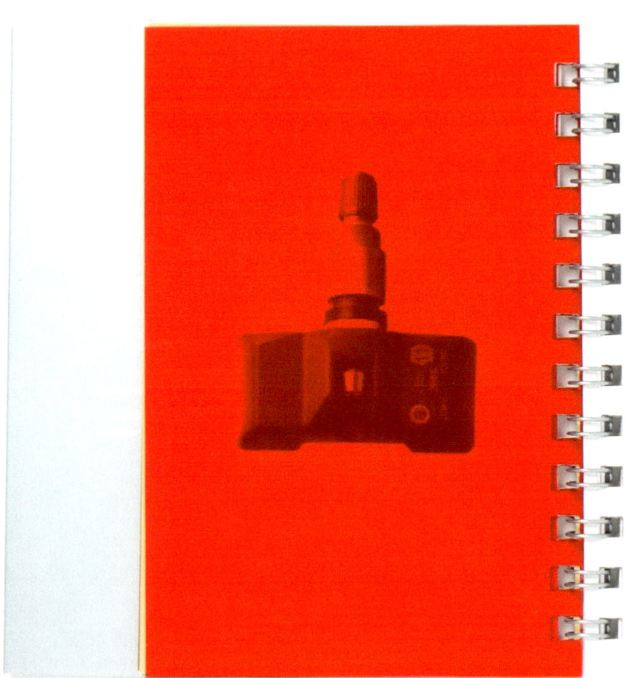

1–2   3st Kommunikation / Florian Heine, 110 x 90 x 30 mm, Nopa Coat Prestige 300 g and 175 g,
offset printing 6/6 c, mat foil laminating, ring binding, 2004

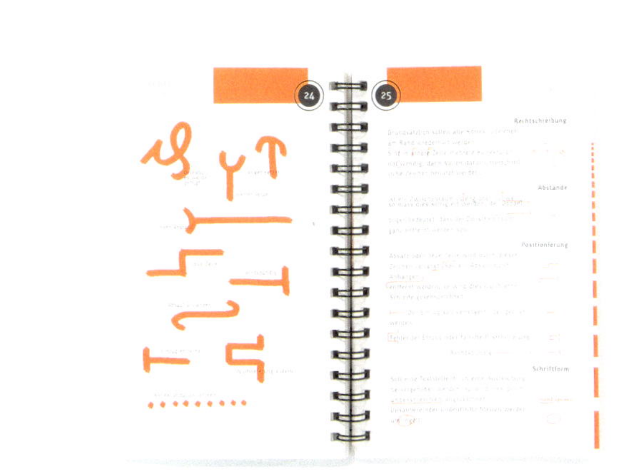

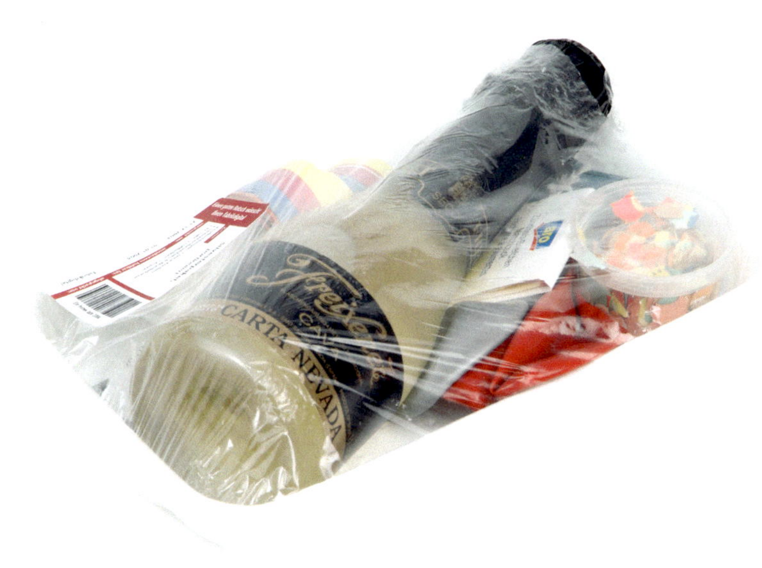

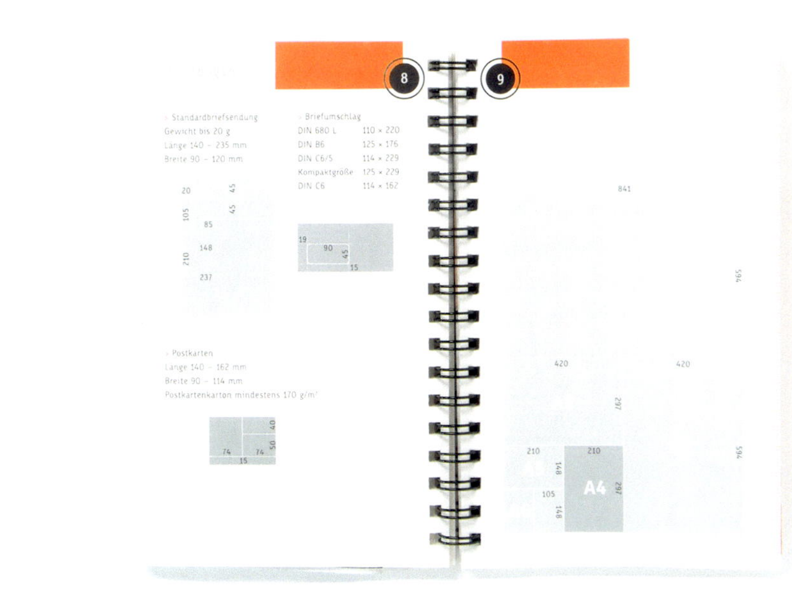

1–3   i-D internet + Design / ja.na Rogge,
PolyArt (PE) from Schneidersöhne, water proofed, offset printing, japan binding, 2002
4   Fabrikdigital / Maik Waidmann, 2003

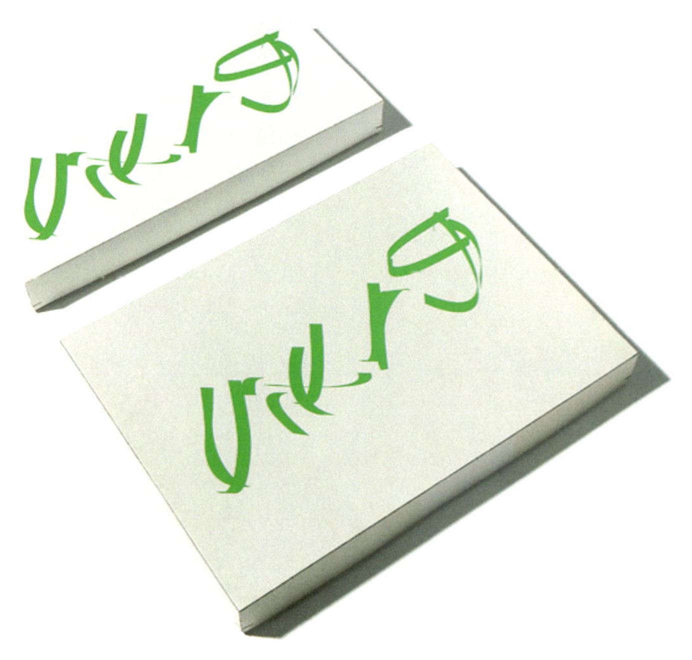

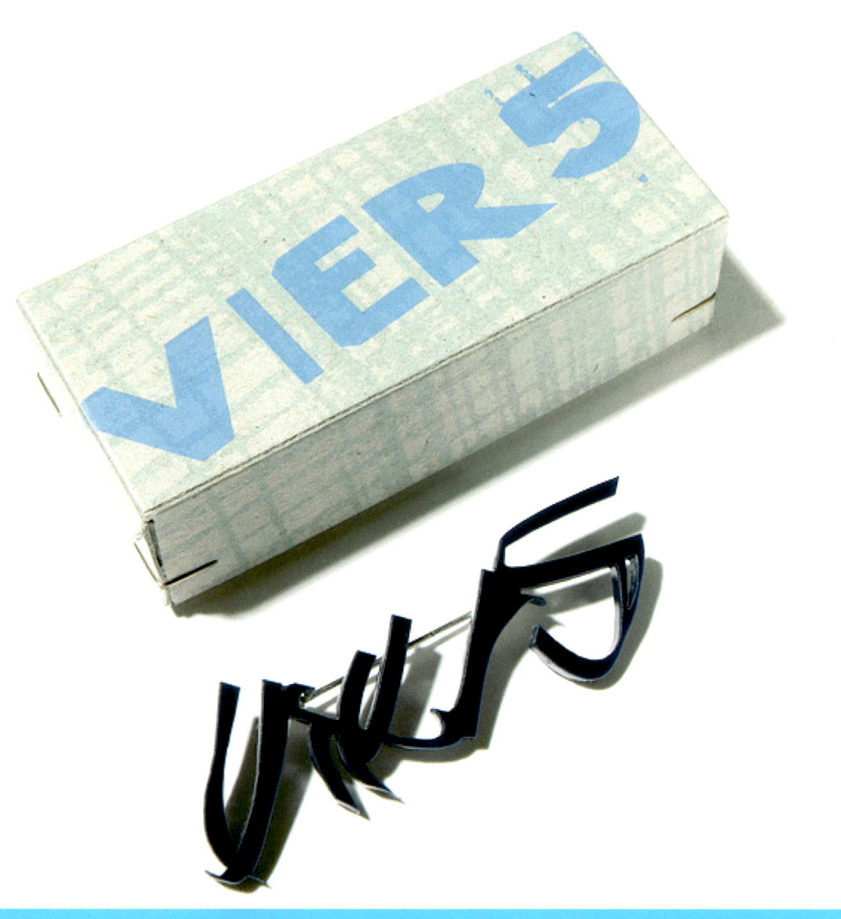

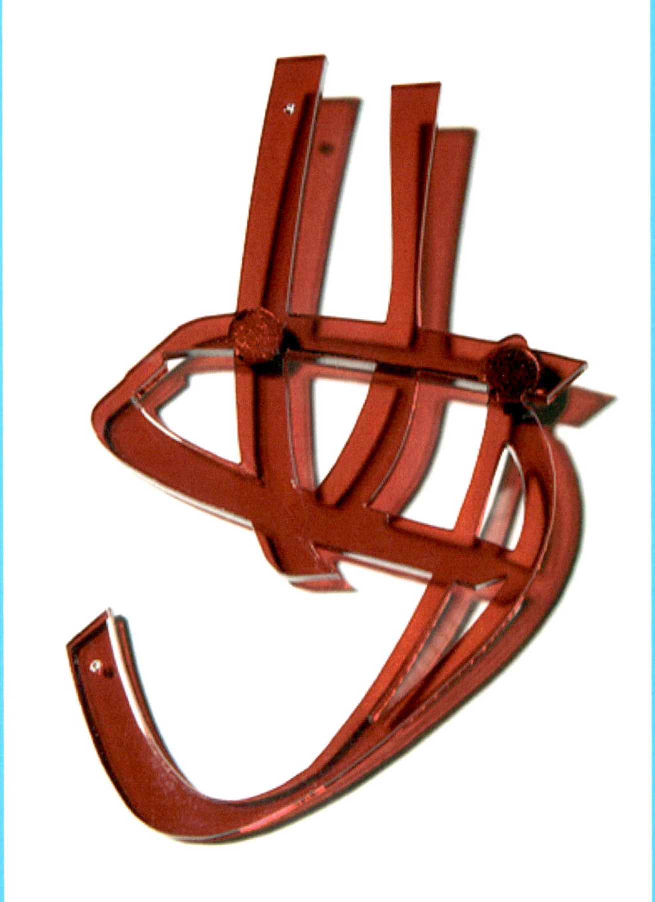

1   Vier5, photography: Michael Habes, 360 x 160 x 40 mm, cardboard,
    silk-screen printing: Renate Vogl, 2002
2   Vier5, photography: Michael Habes, brooch 70 x 25 x 3 mm, plexiglass and silver,
    case 90 x 38 x 25 mm, silk-screen printing, Renate Vogl, 2003
3   Vier5, photography: Michael Habes, brooch 85 x 50 x 3 mm,
    plexiglass, diamonds, silver, production: Susanne Schneider, 2004/2005

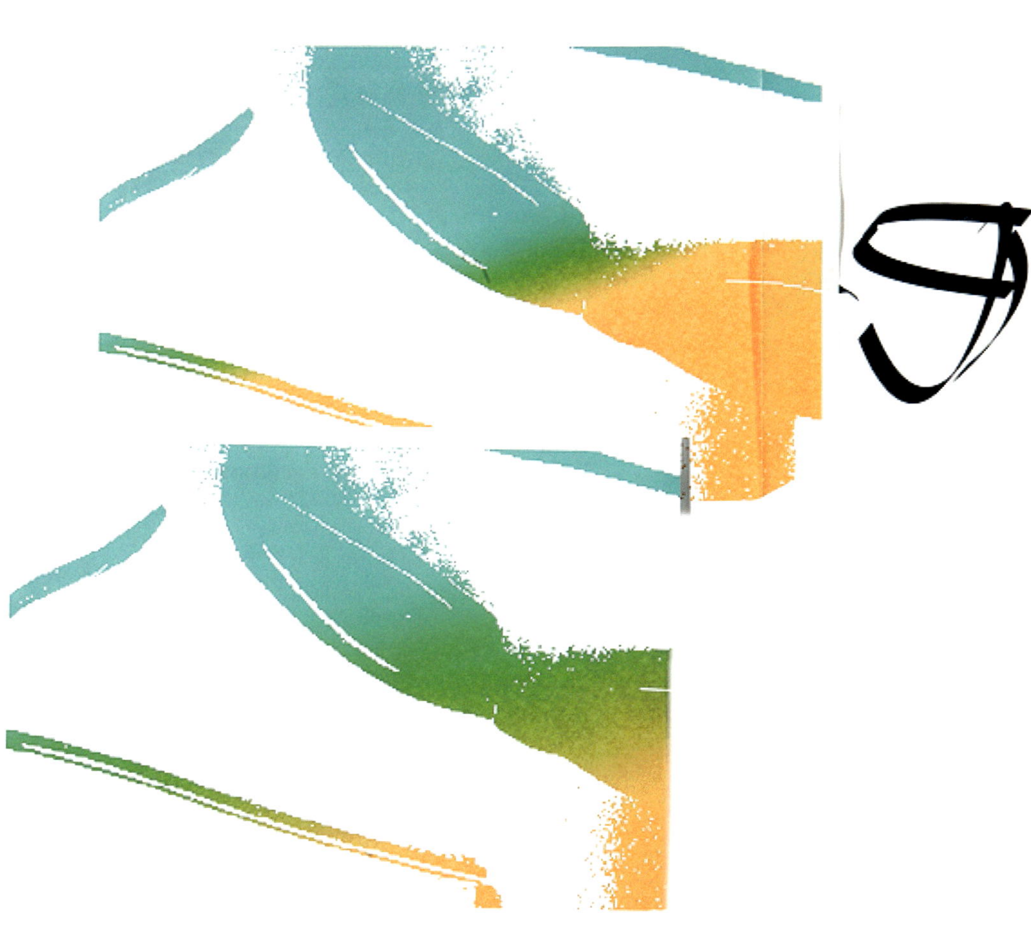

    Vier5, photography: Michael Habes, 325 x 230 mm, silk-screen printing Renate Vogl, 2002

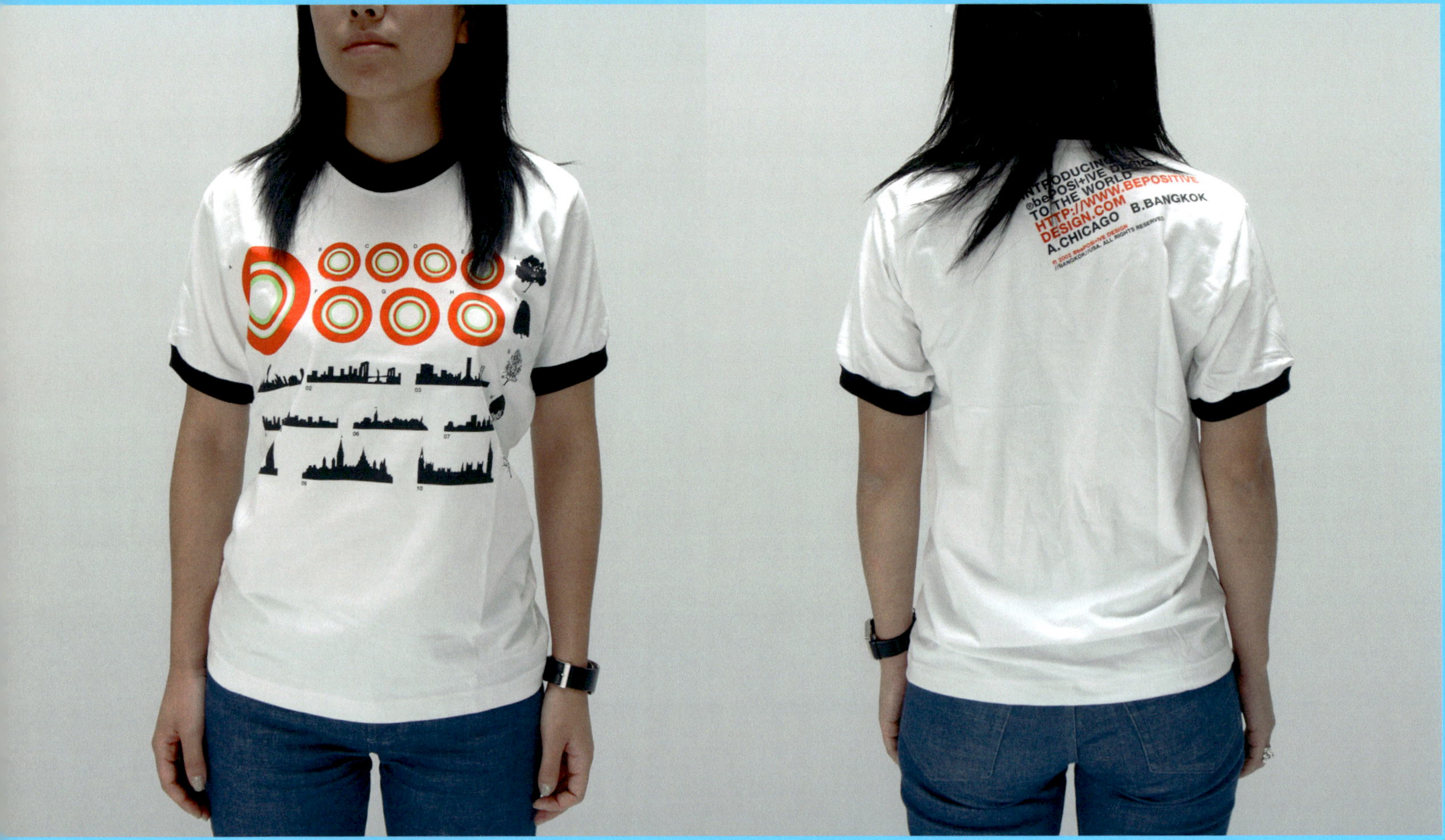

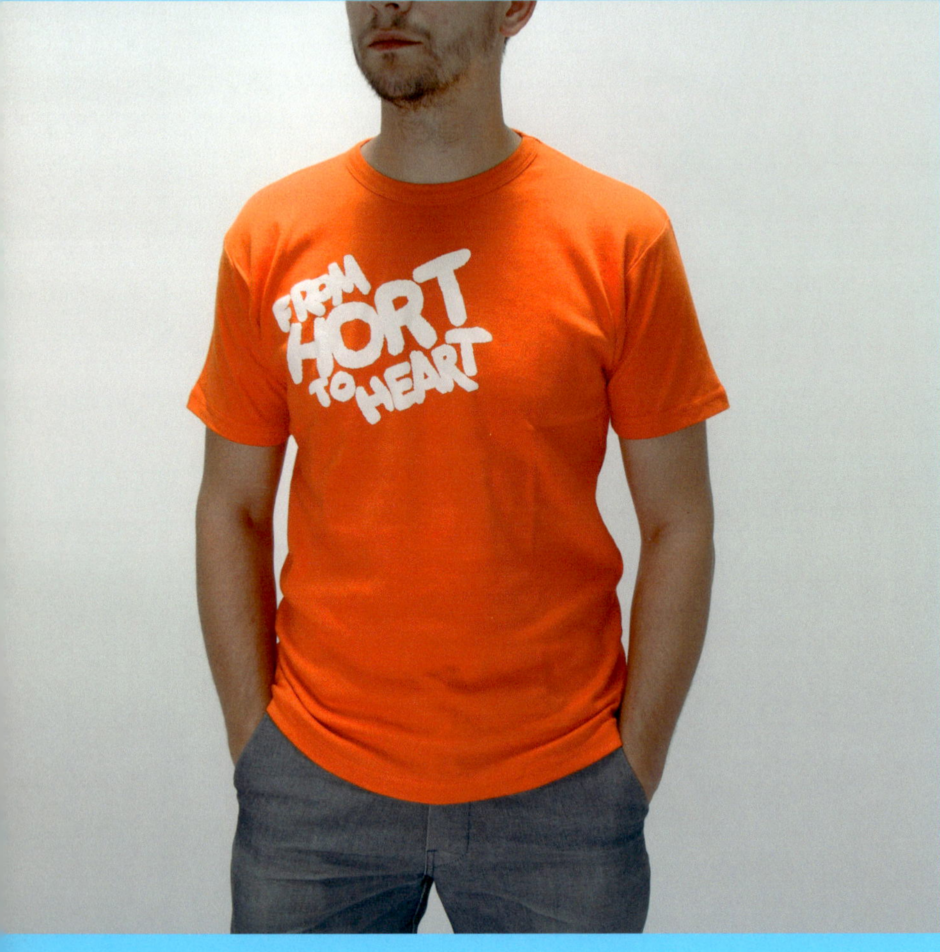

1   Bepositive / Tnop Wangsillapakun, white ring t-shirt, silk-screen printing, 2003
2   Hort, t-shirt, silk-screen printing, 2004

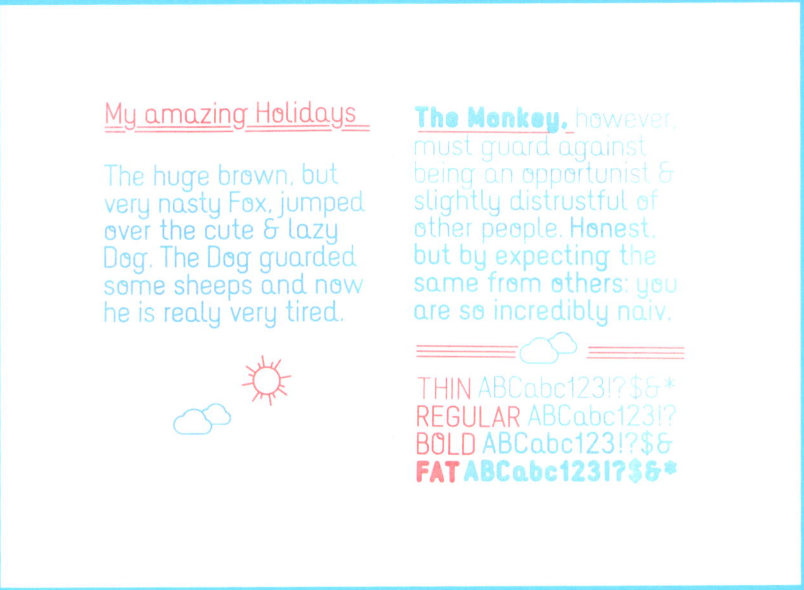

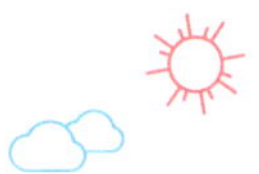

Little more than a year ago, font aficionado Timo Gaessner (123Buero) decided to wear his heart, well typeface, on his sleeve. By now, his sought-after, handcrafted-to-order sweatshirts – bought and worn by hipsters around the world – have become a great example of accidental self-promotion.

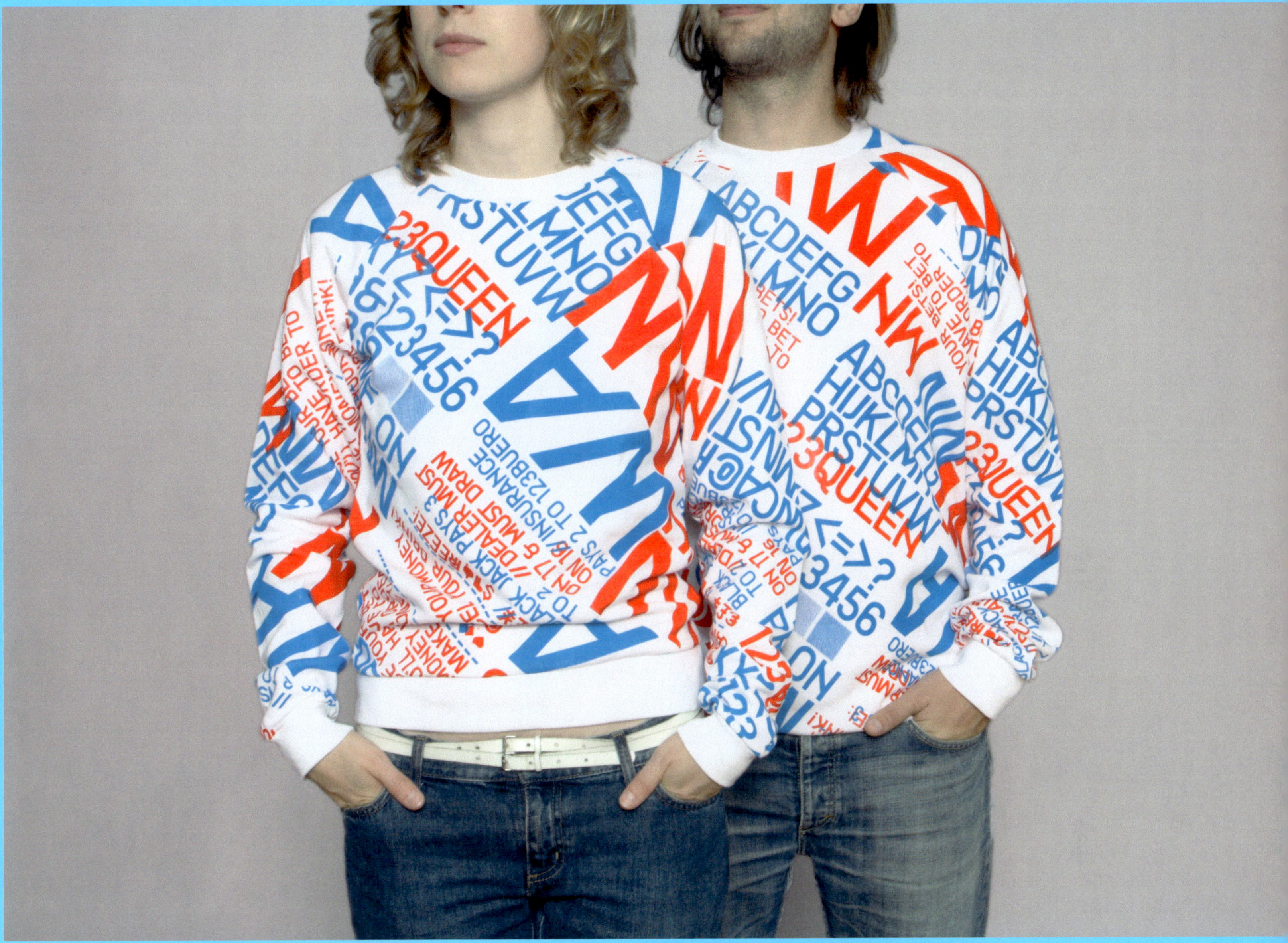

A well-fitting match for any body, each garment is accompanied by its respective typeface, also displayed in Gaessner's charming "Little Font Dictionary" with an apposite dummy text. While 123queen (the more angular sweatshirt variety) conjures up the story of a blackjack Q(ueen), the softer Naiv spins the inane brown dog/lazy fox mantra into a brand new tale. Format, paper type and stapling technique underline the playful exercise character of this primary school-style booklet.

1   123Buero / Timo Gaesser, photography: Maak Roberts, S/M/L/XL, 100% cotton, silk-screen printing, 2005
2   123Buero / Timo Gaesser, paper 60 g, toner Xerox, 2004

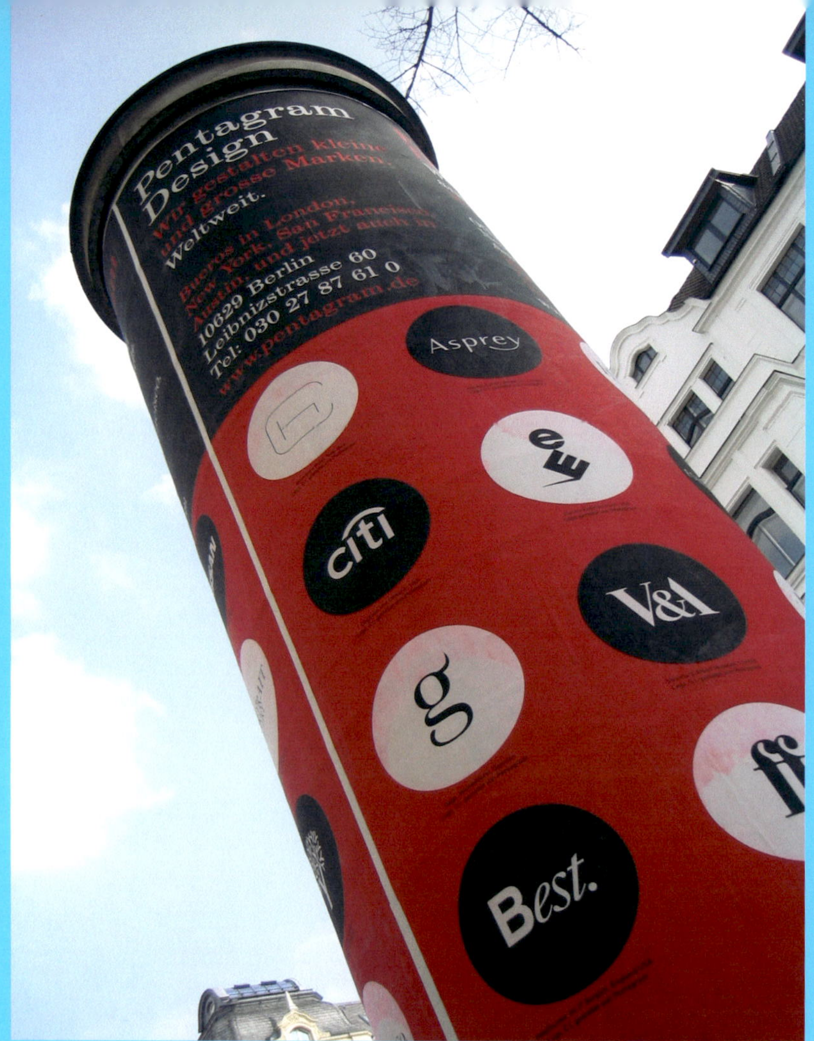

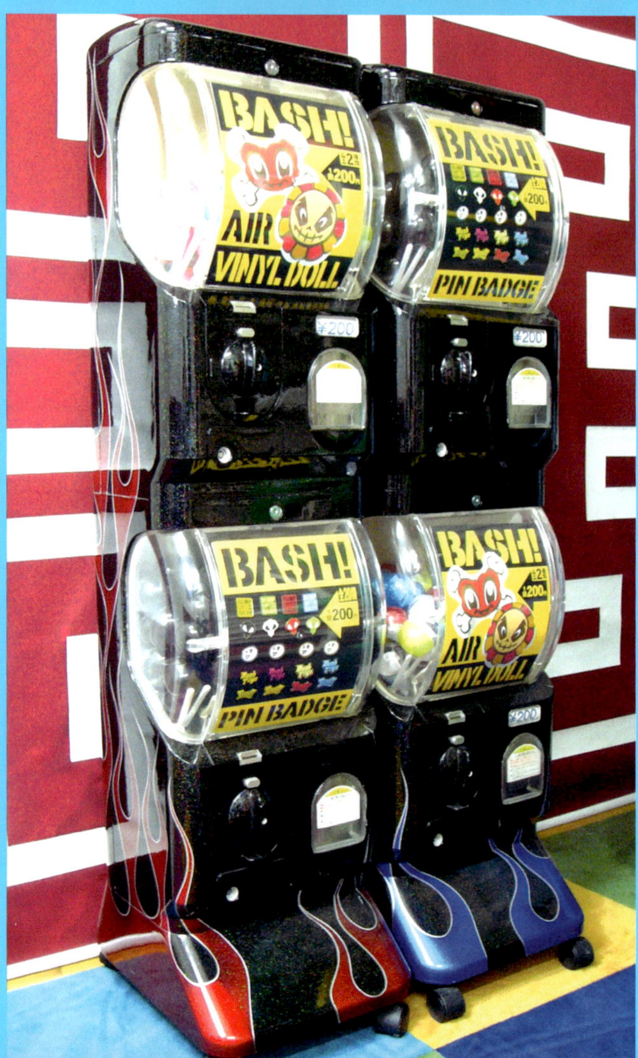

1 Pentagram / Justus Oehler, photography: Justus Oehler, uncoated paper, inkjet, 2005
2 Furi Furi Company, © Yujin, 300 x 1250 mm, 2003

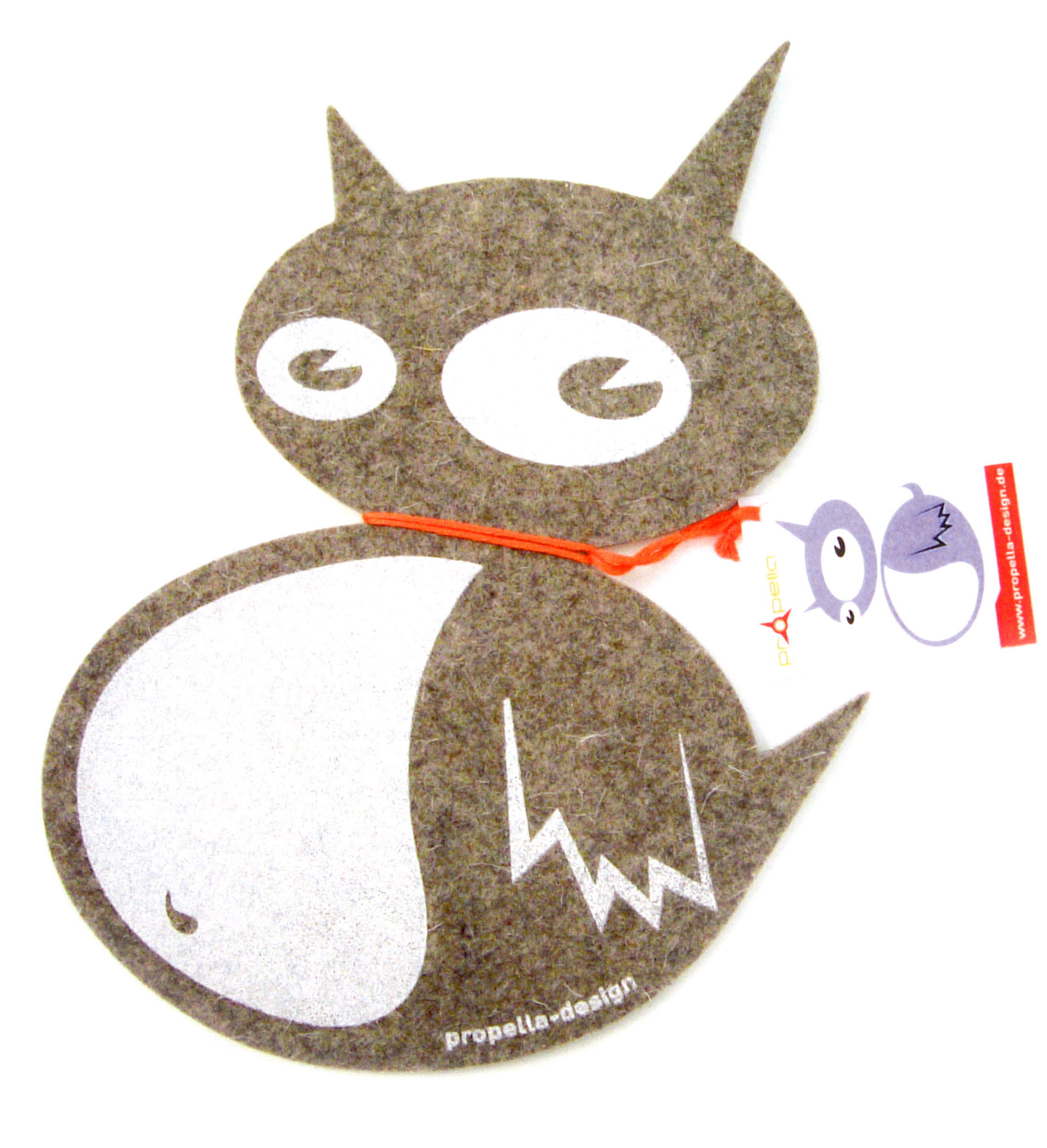

  Propella Konzept + Design / Albanese and Merenda, giveaway, approximately 210 x 297 x 5 mm, felt, silk-screen printing, 2004

Index
by Page

Index
by Page

Index
by Page

Index
by Page

Index
by Page

Index
by Name

Index
by Name

Index
by Name

Imprint

Edited by Robert Klanten, Mika Mischler and Boris Brumnjak
Layout and Design by Mika Mischler and Boris Brumnjak

Foreword by Mika Mischler, Boris Brumnjak and Sonja Commentz
"Introducing" by Justus Oehler
"Pretty in Ink" by Harmen Liemburg
"Biz Cards" by Ina Fliegen
Interviews by Sonja Commentz
Work description Texts by Sonja Commentz

"Introducing" and "Biz Cards" Text translated by Michael Robinson
"Pretty in Ink" Text translated by Annabel Howland

Production Management by Martin Bretschneider and Janni Milstrey

Photography by Andreas Schlegel
Image Processing by Anja Decker

Proof-reading by Michael Robinson

Editorial support Japan by Junko Hanzawa

Published by Die Gestalten Verlag, Berlin
Printed by Offsetdruckerei Grammlich, Pliezhausen
Made in Germany

Bibliographic information published by Die Deutsche Bibliothek
Die Deutsche Bibliothek lists this publication in the Deutsche
Nationalbibliografie; detailed bibliographic data is available on the
Internet at http://dnb.ddb.de.

ISBN 3-89955-087-0

For your local dgv distributor please check out:
www.die-gestalten.de